About this Dictionary

Developments in science and technology today have narrowed down distances between countries, and have made the world a small place. A person living thousands of miles away can learn and understand the culture and lifestyle of another country with ease and without travelling to that country. Languages play an important role as facilitators of communocation in this respect.

To promote such an understanding, **STAR Foreign Language BOOKS** has planned to bring out a series of bilingual dictionaries in which important English words have been translated into other languages, with Roman transliteration in case of languages that have different scripts. This is a humble attempt to bring people of the word closer through the medium of language, thus making communication easy and convenient.

Under this series of *one-to-one dictionaries*, we have published over 40 languages, the list of which has been given in the opening pages. These have all been compiled and edited by teachers and scholars of the relative languages.

Publishers.

Bilingual Dictionaries in this Series

English-Afrikaans / Afrikaans-English	Abraham Venter
English-Albanian / Albanian-English	Theodhora Blushi
English-Amharic / Amharic-English	Girun Asanke
English-Arabic / Arabic-English	Rania-al-Qass
English-Bengali / Bengali-English	Amit Majumdar
English-Bosnian / Bosnian-English	Boris Kazanegra
English-Bulgarian / Bulgarian-English	Vladka Kocheshkova
English-Cantonese / Cantonese-English	Nisa Yang
English-Chinese (Mandarin) / Chinese (Mandarin)-Eng	Y. Shang & R. Yao
English-Croatian / Croatin-English	Vesna Kazanegra
English-Czech / Czech-English	Jindriska Poulova
English-Dari / Dari-English	Amir Khan
English-Estonian / Estonian-English	Lana Haleta
English-Farsi / Farsi-English	Maryam Zaman Khani
English-Gujarati / Gujarati-English	Sujata Basaria
English-Greek / Greek-English	Lina Stergiou
English-Hindi / Hindi-English	Sudhakar Chaturvedi
English-Hungarian / Hungarian-English	Lucy Mallows
English-Korean / Korean-English	Mihee Song
English-Latvian / Latvian-English	Julija Baranovska
English-Lithuanian / Lithuanian-English	Regina Kazakeviciute
English-Marathi / Marathi-English	Sahard Thackerey
English-Nepali / Nepali-English	Anil Mandal
English-Pashto / Pashto-English	Amir Khan
English-Polish / Polish-English	Magdalena Herok
English-Punjabi / Punjabi-English	Teja Singh Chatwal
English-Romanian / Romanian-English	Georgeta Laura Dutulescu
English-Russian / Russian-English	Katerina Volobuyeva
English-Serbian / Serbian-English	Vesna Kazanegra
English-Sinhalese / Sinhalese-English	Naseer Salahudeen
English-Slovak / Slovak-English	Zozana Horvathova
English-Somali / Somali-English	Ali Mohamud Omer
English-Tagalog / Tagalog-English	Jefferson Bantayan
English-Tamil / Tamil-English	Sandhya Mahadevan
English-Thai / Thai-English	Suwan Kaewkongpan
English-Turkish / Turkish-English	Nagme Yazgin
English-Ukrainian / Ukrainian-English	Katerina Volobuyeva
English-Urdu / Urdu-English	S. A. Rahman
English-Vietnamese / Vietnamese-English	Hoa Hoang
English-Yoruba / Yoruba-English	O. A. Temitope

More languages in print

STAR Foreign Language BOOKS

ONE TO ONE
Bilingual Dictionary

English-Romanian
Romanian-English
Dictionary

Compiled by
Georgeta Laura Dutulescu

STAR Foreign Language BOOKS

© Publishers

ISBN : 978 1 905863-96-9

First Edition: 2011
Second Edition: 2013

Published by
STAR Foreign Language BOOKS
a unit of
ibs BOOKS (UK)
Suite 4b, Floor 15, Wembley Point,
1 Harrow Road, Wembley HA9 6DE (U.K.)
E-mail : info@starbooksuk.com
www.foreignlanguagebooks.co.uk

Printed in India at
Star Print-O-Bind, New Delhi-110 020

ENGLISH-ROMANIAN

A

abolish *v.t* a anula
abominable *a* respingator
abound *v.i.* a abunda
about *adv* despre
about *prep* cam
above *adv* deasupra
above *prep.* peste
abreast *adv* alături
abridge *v.t* a prescurta
abridgement *n* prescurtare
abroad *adv* peste graniță
abscond *v.i* a se sustrage
absence *n* absența
absent *a* absent
absent *v.t* a se eschiva (de la)
absolute *a* absolut
absolutely *adv* (în mod) absolut
absolve *v.t* a absolvi
absorb *v.t* a absorbi
abstract *a* abstract
abstract *n* abstracție
abstract *v.t* a sustrage
abstraction *n.* extragere
absurd *a* absurd
absurdity *n* absurditate
abundance *n* abundenta
abundant *a* abundenta
abuse *n* abuz
abuse *v.t.* a abuza
abusive *a* abuziv
academic *a* academic
academy *n* academie
accede *v.t.* a consimți
accelerate *v.t* a accelera
acceleration *n* accelerație
aback *adv.* înapoi
abandon *v.t.* a abandona
abase *v.t.* a înjosi

abasement *n* degradare
abash *v.t.* a face de rușine
abate *v.t.* a reduce
abatement *n.* atenuare
abbey *n.* mânăstire
abbreviate *v.t.* a prescurta
abbreviation *n* prescurtare
abdicate *v.t*, a abdica
abdication *n* abdicare
abdomen *n* abdomen
abdominal *a.* abdominal
abduct *v.t.* a răpi
abduction *n* rapire
abed *adv.* culcat
aberrance *n.* aberatie
abet *v.t.* a ațîța
abetment *n.* instigare
abeyance *n.* suspendare
abhor *v.t.* a detesta
abhorrence *n.* repulsie
abide *v.i* a rabda
abiding *a* statornic
ability *n* îndemânare
abject *a.* nenorocit
ablactate *v. t* a înțărca
ablactation *n* înțărcare
ablaze *adv.* aprins
able *a* capabil
ablush *adv* îmbujorat
ablution *n* curațare
abnegate *v. t* a renega
abnegation *n* renunțare
abnormal *a* anormal
aboard *adv* la bord
abode *n* domiciliu
abolition *v* desființare
aboriginal *a* baștinaș
aborigines *n. pl* baștinași
abort *v.i* a avorta
abortion *n* avort
abortive *adv* prematur
abrogate *v. t.* a abroga

abrupt *a* abrupt
abruption *n* întrerupere
abscess *n* abces
abstain *v.i.* a se abține
abyss *n* abis
accent *n* accent
accent *v.t* a accentua
accept *v.t* a accepta
acceptable *a* acceptabil
acceptance *n* acceptare
access *n* acces
accession *n* sporire
accessory *n* accesoriu
accident *n* accident
accidental *a* întâplător
accipitral *adj* prădalnic
acclaim *n* aplauze
acclaim *v.t* a aplauda
acclamation *n* aclamație
accommodate *v.t* a adapta (la)
accommodation *n.* acomodare
accompany *v.t.* a acompania
accomplice *n* complice
accomplish *v.t.* a realiza
accomplished *a* realizat
accomplishment *n.* îndeplinire
accord *n.* consimțământ
accord *v.t.* a pune de acord
accordingly *adv.* corespunzător
account *n.* cont
account *v.t.* a considera (ca)
accountable *a* răspunzător (de)
accountancy *n.* contabilitate
accountant *n.* contabil
accredit *v.t.* a împuternici
accrete *v.t.* a strânge (laolaltă)
accrue *v.i.* a proveni (din)
accumulate *v.t.* a acumula
accumulation *n* acumulare
accuracy *n.* precizie
accurate *a.* precis
accursed *a.* blestemat

accusation *n* acuzare
accuse *v.t.* a acuza
accused *n.* acuzat
accustom *v.t.* a obișnui cu
accustomed *a.* obișnuit cu
ace *n* as
acephalous *adj.* acefal
acetify *v.* a oțeți
ache *n.* durere
ache *v.i.* a durea
achieve *v.t.* a obține
achievement *n.* dobândire
achromatic *adj* acromatic
acid *a* acid
acid *n* acid
acidity *n.* aciditate
acknowledge *v.* a admite (ca)
acknowledgement *n.* admitere
acne *n* acnee
aconsiderable *a* considerabil
acorn *n.* ghindă
acoustic *a* acustic
acoustics *n.* acustică
acquaint *v.t.* a încunoștința
acquaintance *n.* cunoștința
acquest *n* achiziționare
acquiesce *v.i.* a consimți (la)
acquiescence *n.* consimțământ
acquire *v.t.* a procura
acquirement *n.* procurare
acquit *v.t.* a achita
acquittal *n.* achitare(a unei datorii)
acre *n.* pogon
acreage *n.* suprafața de pogon
acrimony *n* dușmănie
acrobat *n.* acrobat
across *adv.* dincolo
across *prep.* peste
act *n.* act
act *v.i.* a acționa
acting *n.* prefăcătorie

action *n.* faptă
activate *v.t.* a activa
active *a.* activ
activity *n.* activitate
actor *n.* actor
actress *n.* actriţă
actual *a.* actual
actually *adv.* de fapt
acumen *n.* perspicacitate
acute *a.* perspicace
adage *n.* proverb
adamant *a.* tare
adamant *n.* adamant
adapt *v.t.* a adapta (la)
adaptation *n.* adaptare
add *v.t.* a adăuga (la)
addict *n.* persoana cu nărav
addict *v.t.* a se dedica
addiction *n.* înclinaţie
addition *n.* adaos
additional *a.* suplimentar
addle *adj.* încâlcit
address *n.* adresa
address *v.t.* a se adresa
addressee *n.* destinatar
adduce *v.t.* a aduce (dovezi)
adept *a.* alchimist
adept *n.* specialist
adequacy *n.* potrivire
adequate *a.* adecvat
adhere *v.i.* a adera (la)
adherence *n.* aderare
adhesion *n.* adeziune
adhesive *a.* aderent
adhesive *n.* leucoplast
adhibit *v.t.* a aplica (o etichetă
etc.)
adieu *interj.* adio
adieu *n.* rămas bun
adjacent *a.* alăturat
adjective *n.* adjectiv
adjoin *v.t.* a (se) alătura

adjourn *v.t.* a amâna
adjournment *n.* amânare
adjudge *v.t.* a adjudeca
adjunct *n.* adjunct
adjuration *n* implorare
adjust *v.t.* a ajusta
adjustment *n.* ajustare
administer *v.t.* a administra
administration *n.* administrare
administrative *a.* administrativ
administrator *n.* administrator
admirable *a.* admirabil
admiral *n.* amiral
admiration *n.* admiraţie
admire *v.t.* a admira
admissible *a.* admisibil
admission *n.* recunoaştere
admit *v.t.* a recunoaşte
admittance *n.* acces
admonish *v.t.* a mustra
admonition *n.* mustrare
ado *n.* agitaţie
adobe *n.* chirpici
adolescence *n.* adolescenţă
adolescent *a.* tânăr
adopt *v.t.* a adopta
adoption *n* adopţie
adorable *a.* adorabil
adoration *n.* adorare
adore *v.t.* a adora
adorn *v.t.* a înfrumuseţa
adscititious *adj* suplimentar
adulation *n* linguşire
adult *a* adult
adult *n.* adult
adulterate *v.t.* a falsifica
adulteration *n.* falsificare
adultery *n.* adulter
advance *n.* avans
advance *v.t.* a avansa
advancement *n.* avansare
advantage *n.* avantaj

advantage *v.t.* a avantaja
advantageous *a.* avantajos
advent *n.* venire
adventure *n* aventura
adventurous *a.* aventuros
adverb *n.* adverb
adverbial *a.* adverbial
adversary *n.* adversar
adverse *a* advers
adversity *n.* adversitate
advert *v.* a se referi (la)
advertise *v.t.* a face reclamă
advertisement *n* publicitate
advice *n* sfat
advisability *n* sfatuire
advisable *a.* recomandabil
advise *v.t.* a sfătui
advocacy *n.* avocatură
advocate *n* avocat
advocate *v.t.* a pleda (pentru)
aerial *a.* aerian
aerial *n.* antenă
aeriform *adj.* gazos
aerify *v.t.* a vaporiza
aerodrome *n* aerodrom
aeronautics *n.pl.* aeronautică
aeroplane *n.* avion
aesthetic *a.* estetic
aesthetics *n.pl.* estetică
aestival *adj* estival
afar *adv.* departe
affable *a.* amabil
affair *n.* aventură amoroasă
affect *v.t.* a afecta
affectation *n* afectare
affection *n.* afecțiune
affectionate *a.* afectuos
affidavit *n* declarație sub
jurământ
affiliation *n.* afiliere
affinity *n* înrudire
affirm *v.t.* a afirma

affirmation *n* afirmație
affirmative *a* afirmativ
affix *v.t.* a fixa
afflict *v.t.* a mâhni
affliction *n.* mâhnire
affluence *n.* belşug
affluent *a.* îmbelşugat
afford *v.t.* a-şi permite
afforest *v.t.* a împăduri
affray *n* scandal
affront *n* insultă
affront *v.t.* a insulta
afield *adv.* razna
aflame *adv.* aprins
afloat *adv.* plutind
afoot *adv.* pe jos
afore *adv.* înainte
afraid *a.* speriat
afresh *adv.* din nou
after *a* ulterior
after *adv* după aceea
after *conj.* după ce
after *prep.* după
afterwards *adv.* pe urmă
again *adv.* din nou
against *prep.* împotriva
agape *adv.*, cu gura căscată
agaze *adv* cu ochii holbați
age *n.* vârsta
aged *a.* în vârstă de
agency *n.* agenție
agenda *n.* agendă
agent *n* agent
aggravate *v.t.* a agrava
aggravation *n.* agravare
aggregate *v.t.* a strânge într-un tot
aggression *n* agresiune
aggressive *a.* agresiv
aggressor *n.* agresor
aggrieve *v.t.* a îndurera
aghast *a.* înspăimântat
agile *a.* agil

agility *n.* agilitate
agitate *v.t.* a agita
agitation *n* agitare
aglow *adj.* în flăcări
ago *adv.* înainte cu
agog *adj.* în aşteptare
agonize *v.t.* a chinui
agony *n.* agonie
agoraphobia *n.* agorafobie
agrarian *a.* agrar
agree *v.i.* a fi de acord
agreeable *a.* agreabil
agreement *n.* acord
agricultural *a* agricol
agriculture *n* agricultură
agriculturist *n.* agricultor
agronomy *n.* agrònomie
ague *n* malarie
ahead *adv.* înainte
aheap *adv* grămadă
aid *n* ajutor
aid *v.t* a ajuta
aigrette *n* egretă
ail *v.t.* a pricinui durere
ailment *n.* boală
aim *n.* ţintă
aim *v.i.* a ţinti
air *n* aer
aircraft *n.* aeronavă
airy *a.* aerat
ajar *adj.* întredeschis
akin *a.* înrudit
alacrious *adj* ager
alacrity *n.* agerime
alarm *n* alarmă
alarm *v.t* a alarma
alas *interj.* vai!
albeit *conj.* deşi
albion *n* Albion
album *n.* album
albumen *n* albumină
alchemy *n.* alchimie

alcohol *n* alcol
ale *n* bere englezească
alegar *n* oţet din bere
alert *a.* vigilent
alertness *n.* vigilenţă
algebra *n.* algebră
alias *adv.* zis şi
alias *n.* poreclă
alibi *n.* alibi
alien *a.* înstrăinat
alienate *v.t.* a înstrăina
alight *v.i.* a coborî
align *v.t.* a (se) alinia
alignment *n.* aliniere
alike *a.* asemănător
alike *adv* la fel
aliment *n.* aliment
alimony *n.* pensie alimentară
aliquot *n.* alicot
alive *a* viu
alkali *n* bază
all *a.* tot
all *adv* cu totul
all *n* totul
all *pron* toţi
allay *v.t.* a alina
allegation *n.* alegaţie
allege *v.t.* a susţine
allegiance *n.* supunere
allegorical *a.* alegoric
allegory *n.* alegorie
allergy *n.* alergie
alleviate *v.t.* a uşura
alleviation *n.* uşurare
alley *n.* alee
alliance *n.* alianţă
alligator *n* aligator
alliterate *v.* a alitera
alliteration *n.* aliteraţie
allocate *v.t.* a aloca
allocation *n.* alocaţie
allot *v.t.* a distribui

allotment *n.* repartizare
allow *v.t.* a permite
allowance *n.* permisiune
alloy *n.* aliaj
allude *v.i.* a face aluzie (la)
allure *v.t.* a ademeni
allurement *n* ademenire
allusion *n* aluzie
ally *n.* aliat
ally *v.t.* a alia
almanac *n.* almanah
almighty *a.* atotputernic
almond *n.* migdală
almost *adv.* aproape
alms *n.* pomană
aloft *adv.* în sus
alone *a.* singur
along *adv.* înainte
along *prep.* de-a lungul
aloof *adv.* la distanță
aloud *adv.* tare
alpha *n* alfa
alphabet *n.* alfabet
alphabetical *a.* alfabetic
alpinist *n* alpinist
already *adv.* deja
also *adv.* de asemenea
altar *n.* altar
alter *v.t.* a transforma
alteration *n* trasformare
altercation *n.* altercație
alternate *a.* alternant
alternate *v.t.* a alterna
alternative *a.* alternativ
alternative *n.* alternativă
although *conj.* cu toate că
altimeter *n* altimetru
altitude *n.* altitudine
alto *n* alto
altogether *adv.* cu totul
aluminium *n.* aluminiu
always *adv* întotdeauna

am *v* sunt
amalgam *n* amalgam
amalgamate *v.t.* a (se) amalgama
amalgamation *n* amalgamare
amass *v.t.* a aduna
amateur *n.* amator
amaze *v.t.* a uimi
amazement *n.* uimire
ambassador *n.* ambasador
ambient *adj.* ambiant
ambiguity *n.* ambiguitate
ambiguous *a.* ambiguu
ambition *n.* ambiție
ambitious *a.* ambiţios
ambulance *n.* ambulanţă
ambulant *adj* ambulant
ambulate *v.* a se deplasa
ambush *n.* ambuscadă
ameliorate *v.t.* a ameliora
amelioration *n.* ameliorare
amen *interj.* amin
amenable *a* ascultător
amend *v.t.* a amenda
amendment *n.* amendament
amends *n.pl.* despăgubire
amiability *n.* amiabilitate
amiable *a.* amiabil
amicable *adj.* prietenos
amid *prep.* în mijlocul
amiss *adv.* nelalocul lui
amity *n.* prietenie
ammunition *n.* muniţie
amnesia *n* amnezie
amnesty *n.* amnistie
among *prep.* printre
amongst *prep.* între
amoral *a.* amoral
amorous *a.* amoros
amount *n* sumă
amount *v.* a totaliza
amount *v.i* a se ridica (la)
amour *n* amor

ampere n amper
amphibious adj amfibiu
amphitheatre n amfiteatru
ample a. amplu
amplification n amplificare
amplifier n amplificator
amplify v.t. a amplifica
amuck adv. amoc
amulet n. amuletă
amuse v.t. a amuza
amusement n amuzament
an art un
anabaptism n anabaptism
anachronism n anacronism
anaemia n anemie
anaesthesia n anestezie
anaesthetic n. anestezic
anal adj. anal
analogous a. analog (cu)
analogy n. analogie
analyse v.t. a analiza
analysis n. analiză
analyst n laborant
analytical a analitic
anamnesis n anamneză
anarchism n. anarhism
anarchist n anarhist
anarchy n anarhie
anatomy n. anatomie
ancestor n. strămoş
ancestral a. ancestral
ancestry n. neam
anchor n. ancoră
anchorage n ancorare
ancient a. antic
and conj. şi
anecdote n. anecdotă
anemometer n anemometru
anew adv. iarăşi
angel n înger
anger n. furie
angina n anghină

angle n undiţă
angle n. unghi
angry a. supărat
anguish n. chin
angular a. unghiular
anigh adv. aproape
animal n. animal
animate a. animat
animate v.t. a anima
animation n animaţie
animosity n animozitate
animus n duşmănie
ankle n. gleznă
anklet n brăţară pentru gleznă
annalist n. cronicar
annals n.pl. anale
annex v.t. a anexa (la
annexation n anexiune
annihilate v.t. a nimici
annihilation n nimicire
anniversary n. aniversare
announce v.t. a anunţa
announcement n. anunţ
annoy v.t. a enerva
annoyance n. enervare
annual a. anual
annuitant n rentier
annuity n. anuitate
annul v.t. a anula
annulet n ineluş
anoint v.t. a unge
anomalous a anormal
anomaly n anomalie
anon adv. imediat
anonymity n. anonimat
anonymous a. anonim
another a alt
answer n răspuns
answer v.t a răspunde
answerable a. răspunzător (de)
ant n furnică
antagonism n antagonism

antagonist *n.* adversar
antagonize *v.t.* a se opune
antarctic *a.* antarctic
antecedent *a.* antecedent
antecedent *n.* antecedent
antedate *v.t* a anticipa
antelope *n.* antilopă
antenatal *adj.* prenatal
antennae *n.* antenă
anthem *n* imn
anthology *n.* antologie
anthropoid *adj.* antropoid
anti *pref.* anti
anti-aircraft *a.* antiaerian
antic *n* bufonerie
anticipate *v.t.* a anticipa
anticipation *n.* anticipare
antidote *n.* antidor
antinomy *n.* paradox
antipathy *n.* antipatie
antipodes *n.* antipozi
antiquarian *a.* de anticar
antiquarian *n* colecționar de antichități
antiquated *a.* demodat
antique *a.* antic
antiquity *n.* antichitate
antiseptic *a.* antiseptic
antiseptic *n.* antiseptic
antitheist *n* ateu
antithesis *n.* antiteză
antler *n.* corn de cerb
antonym *n.* antonim
anus *n.* anus
anvil *n.* nicovală
anxiety *n* neliniște
anxious *a.* neliniștit
any *a.* orice
any *adv.* întrucâtva
anyhow *adv.* oricum
apace *adv.* repede
apart *adv.* separat

apartment *n.* apartament
apathy *n.* apatie
ape *n* maimuță
ape *v.t.* a maimuțări
aperture *n.* orificiu
apex *n.* culme
aphorism *n* pildă
apiary *n.* stupină
apiculture *n.* apicultură
apish *a.* de maimuță
apologize *v.i.* a-și cere scuze
apology *n.* scuză
apostle *n.* apostol
apostrophe *n.* apostrof
apotheosis *n.* apoteoză
apparatus *n.* aparat
apparel *n.* veșmânt
apparel *v.t.* a înveșmânta
apparent *a.* aparent
appeal *n.* atracție
appeal *v.t.* a apela
appear *v.i.* a apărea
appearance *n* apariție
appease *v.t.* a liniști
append *v.t.* a anexa (la)
appendage *n.* adaos
appendicitis *n.* apendicită
appendix *n.* adaos (la o carte)
appendix *n.* apendice
appetence *n.* poftă (de)
appetite *n.* dorință de
appetite *n.* poftă de mâncare
appetizer *n* aperitiv
applaud *v.t.* a aplauda
applause *n.* aplauze
apple *n.* măr
appliance *n.* dispozitiv
applicable *a.* aplicabil
applicant *n.* aplicant
application *n.* aplicație
apply *v.t.* a aplica
appoint *v.t.* a numi

appointment *n.* programare
apportion *v.t.* a repartiza
apposite *adj* potrivit (pentru)
appraise *v.t.* a evalua
appreciable *a.* apreciabil
appreciate *v.t.* a aprecia
appreciation *n.* apreciere
apprehend *v.t.* a percepe
apprehension *n.* sesizare
apprehensive *a.* inteligent
apprentice *n.* ucenic
apprise *v.t.* a preveni
approach *n.* apropiere
approach *v.t.* a se apropia (de)
approbate *v.t* a aproba
approbation *n.* aprobare
appropriate *a.* adecvat
appropriate *v.t.* a-şi însuşi
appropriation *n.* însuşire
approval *n.* aprobare
approve *v.t.* a aproba
approximate *a.* aproximativ
appurtenance *n* apartenenţă
apricot *n.* caisă
apron *n.* şorţ
apt *a.* în stare (să)
aptitude *n.* aptitudine
aquarium *n.* acvariu
aqueduct *n* apeduct
arable *adj* arabil
arbiter *n.* arbitru
arbitrary *a.* arbitrar
arbitrate *v.t.* a arbitra
arbitration *n.* arbitrare
arbitrator *n.* arbitru
arc *n.* arc
arcade *n* arcadă
arch *a* poznaş
arch *n.* arc
arch *v.t.* a (se) arcui
archaic *a.* arhaic
archangel *n* arhanghel

archbishop *n.* arhiepiscop
archer *n* arcaş
architect *n.* arhitect
architecture *n.* arhitectură
archives *n.pl.* arhive
Arctic *n* arctic
ardent *a.* arzător
ardour *n.* ardoare
arduous *a.* dificil
area *n* zonă
arena *n* arenă
argil *n* argilă
argue *v.t.* a se certa
argument *n.* controversă
argute *adj* iscusit
arid *adj.* sterp
aright *adv* bine
aright *adv.* corect
arise *v.i.* a se ivi
aristocracy *n.* aristocraţie
aristocrat *n.* aristocrat
arithmetic *n.* aritmetică
arithmetical *a.* aritmetic
ark *n* arcă
arm *n.* braţ
arm *v.t.* a înarma
armada *n.* flotă de război
armament *n.* armament
armature *n.* armură
armistice *n.* armistiţiu
armlet *n* braţ de râu
armour *n.* blindaj (de vas, de tanc)
armoury *n.* arsenal
army *n.* armată
around *adv* în apropiere
around *prep.* în jurul
arouse *v.t.* a stârni
arraign *v.* a pune la îndoială
arrange *v.t.* a aranja
arrangement *n.* aranjament
arrant *adj* notoriu

array *n.* etalare
array *v.t.* a rândui
arrest *n.* arestare
arrest *v.t.* a aresta
arrival *n.* sosire
arrive *v.i.* a sosi
arrogance *n.* aroganţă
arrogant *a.* arogant
arrow *n* săgeată
arsenal *n.* arsenal
arsenic *n* arsenic
arson *n* incendiere
art *n.* artă
artery *n.* arteră
artful *a.* dibaci
arthritis *n* artrită
artichoke *n.* anghinare
article *n* articol
articulate *a.* articulat
artifice *n.* artificiu
artificial *a.* artificial
artillery *n.* artilerie
artisan *n.* meşteşugar
artist *n.* artist
artistic *a.* artistic
artless *a.* lipsit de artă
as *adv.* pe când
as *conj.* ca şi
as *pron.* care
asbestos *n.* azbest
ascend *v.t.* a urca
ascent *n.* ascensiune
ascertain *v.t.* a descoperi
ascetic *a.* ascentic
ascribe *v.t.* a atribui
ash *n.* cenuşă
ashamed *a.* ruşinat
ashore *adv.* la mal
aside *adv.* deoparte
aside *n.* aparte
ask *v.t.* a întreba
asleep *adj* adormit

aspect *n.* aspect
asperse *v.* a presăra
aspirant *n.* aspirant
aspiration *n.* aspiraţie
aspire *v.t.* a aspira
ass *n.* măgar
assail *v.* a asalta
assassin *n.* asasin
assassinate *v.t.* a asasina
assassination *n* asasinare
assault *n.* asalt
assault *v.t.* a asalta
assemble *v.t.* a ansambla
assembly *n.* ansamblare
assent *n.* consimţământ
assent *v.i.* a consimţi la
assert *v.t.* a afirma
assess *v.t.* a evalua
assessment *n.* evaluare
asset *n.* bun
assign *v.t.* a repartiza
assignee *n.* mandatar
assimilate *v.* a asimila
assimilation *n* asimilare
assist *v.t.* a asista
assistance *n.* asistenţă
assistant *n.* asistent
associate *a.* asociat
associate *n.* asociat
associate *v.t.* a asocia
association *n.* asociaţie
assort *v.t.* a grupa
assuage *v.t.* a potoli
assume *v.t.* a-şi asuma
assumption *n.* asumare
assurance *n.* asigurare
assure *v.t.* a asigura
asterisk *n.* asterisc
asteroid *n* asteroid
asthma *n.* astmă
astir *adv.* în mişcare
astonish *v.t.* a ului

astonishment *n.* uluire
astound *v.t* a ului
astray *v* a rătăci
astrologer *n.* astrolog
astrology *n.* astrologie
astronaut *n.* astronaut
astronomer *n.* astronom
astronomy *n.* astronomie
asunder *adv.* separat
asylum *n* azil
at *prep.* la
atheism *n* ateism
atheist *n* ateu
athirst *adj.* însetat
athlete *n.* atlet
athletic *a.* atletic
athletics *n.* atletism
athwart *prep.* cruciş
atlas *n.* atlas
atmosphere *n.* atmosferă
atoll *n.* atol
atom *n.* atom
atomic *a.* atomis
atone *v.i.* a ispăşi
atonement *n.* ispăşire
atrocious *a.* atroce
atrocity *n* atrocitate
attach *v.t.* a ataşa
attache *n.* ataşat
attachment *n.* ataşament
attack *n.* atac
attack *v.t.* a ataca
attain *v.t.* a atinge
attainment *n.* realizare
attaint *v.t.* a pune în afara legii
attempt *n.* încercare
attempt *v.t.* a încerca
attend *v.t.* a asista
attendance *n.* asistare
attendant *n.* slujitor
attention *n.* atenţie
attentive *a.* atent

attest *v.t.* a dovedi
attire *n.* îmbrăcăminte
attire *v.t.* a îmbrăca
attitude *n.* atitudine
attorney *n.* procuror
attract *v.t.* a atrage
attraction *n.* atracţie
attractive *a.* atrăgător
attribute *n.* atribut
attribute *v.t.* a atribui
auction *n* licitaţie
audible *a* audibil
audience *n.* audienţă
audit *n.* examinare
audit *v.t.* a examina
auditive *adj.* auditiv
auditor *n.* ascultător
auditorium *n.* auditoriu
auger *n.* burghiu
aught *adv* într-o privinţă oarecare
augment *v.t.* a mări
augmentation *n.* mărire
august *adj* măreţ
August *n.* august
aunt *n.* mătuşă
aurora *n* auroră
auspicate *v.t.* a inaugura
auspice *n.* prevestire
auspicious *a.* favorabil
austere *a.* sever
authentic *a.* autentic
author *n.* autor
authoritative *a.* autoritar
authority *n.* autoritate
authorize *v.t.* a autoriza
autobiography *n.* autobiografie
autocracy *n* autocraţie
autocrat *n* autocrat
autocratic *a* autocrat
autograph *n.* autograf
automatic *a.* automat
automobile *n.* automobil

autonomous *a* autonom
autumn *n.* toamnă
auxiliary *a.* auxiliar
auxiliary *n.* auxiliar
avail *v.t.* a folosi
available *a* disponibil
avarice *n.* avariţie
avenge *v.t.* a răzbuna
avenue *n.* bulevard
average *a.* mediu
average *n.* medie
average *v.t.* a atinge în medie
averse *a.* potrivnic
aversion *n.* aversiune
avert *v.t.* a abate
aviary *n.* crescătorie de păsări
aviation *n.* aviaţie
aviator *n.* aviator
avid *adj.* lacom
avidity *n* aviditate
avoid *v.t.* a evita
avoidance *n.* evitare
avow *v.t.* a admite
avulsion *n.* smulgere
await *v.t.* a aştepta
awake *a* treaz
awake *v.t.* a se trezi
award *n.* premiu
award *v.t.* a acorda
aware *a.* conştient
away *adv.* departe
awe *n.* teamă
awful *a.* teribil
awhile *adv.* pentru un timp
awkward *a.* penibil
axe *n.* topor
axis *n.* axă
axle *n.* osie

B

babble *n.* gângurit
babble *v.i.* a gânguri
babe *n.* prunc
babel *n* hărmălaie
baby *n.* copilaş
bachelor *n.* celibatar
back *adv.* înapoi
back *n.* spate
backbite *v.t.* a calomnia
backbone *n.* coloana vertebrală
background *n.* fundal
backhand *n.* dos al palmei
backslide *v.i.* a da din nou
backward *a.* înapoiat
backward *adv.* în urmă
bacon *n.* slănină
bacteria *n.* bacterie
bad *a.* rău
badge *n.* insignă
badger *n.* bursuc
badly *adv.* grav
baffle *v. t.* a deruta
bag *n.* geanta
bag *v. i.* a vârî în sac
baggage *n.* bagaj
bagpipe *n.* cimpoi
bail *n.* toartă
bail *v. t.* a scoate
bailiff *n.* uşier
bait *n* momeală
bait *v.t.* a pune momeală
bake *v.t.* a coace
baker *n.* brutar
bakery *n* brutărie
balance *n.* echilibru
balance *v.t.* a echilibra
balcony *n.* balcon
bald *a.* chel

bale *n.* balot
baleen *n.* os de balenă
baleful *a.* nenorocit
ball *n.* minge
ballad *n.* baladă
ballet *sn.* balet
balloon *n.* balon
ballot *n* buletin de vot
balm *n.* balsam
balsam *n.* balsam
bamboo *n.* bambus
ban *n.* interdicţie
ban *v.t* a interzice
banal *a.* banal
banana *n.* banană
band *n.* formatie
bandage *~n.* bandaj
bandage *v.t* a bandaja
bandit *n.* bandit
bang *n.* lovitură
bang *v.t.* a lovi
bangle *n.* brăţară
banish *v.t.* a izgoni
banishment *n.* exilare
banjo *n.* banjo
bank *n.* bancă
bank *v.t.* a depune în bancă
banker *n.* bancher
bankrupt *n.* falit
bankruptcy *n.* faliment
banner *n.* steag
banquet *n.* banchet
banquet *v.t.* a oferi un banchet
bantam *n.* cocoş din Bantam
banter *n.* bătaie de joc
banter *v.t.* a ridiculiza
bantling *n.* copil
baptism *n.* botez
baptize *+v.t.* a boteza
bar *n.* bar
bar *v.t* a bara
barb *n.* înţepătură

barbarian *a.* barbar
barbarian *n.* barbar
barbarism *n.* barbarie
barbarity *n* barbaritate
barbarous *a.* barbar
barbed *a.* ghimpat
barber *n.* bărbier
bard *n.* poet
bare *a.* gol
bare *v.t.* a suporta
barely *adv.* abia
bargain *n.* tocmeală
bargain *v.t.* a se tocmi
barge *n.* şalupă
bark *n.* lătrat
bark *v.t.* a lătra
barley *n.* orz
barn *n.* hambar
barometer *n* barometru
barrack *n.* cazarmă
barrage *n.* baraj
barrel *n.* butoi
barren *n* pământ sterp
barricade *n.* baricadă
barrier *n.* barieră
barrister *n.* avocat (pledant)
barter1 *v.t.* a vinde (pe)
barter2 *n.* schimb
base *a.* inferior
base *n.* bază
base *v.t.* a pune bazele
baseless *a.* neântemeiat
basement *n.* subsol
bashful *a.* timid
basic *a.* fundamental
basil *n.* busuioc
basin *n.* bazin
basis *n.* bază
bask *v.i.* a sta la soare
basket *n.* coş
bass *n.* bas
bastard *n.* bastard

bastard *a* nelegitim
bat *n* bâtă
bat *n* liliac
bat *v. i* a lovi cu bâta
batch *n* grup
bath *n* baie
bathe *v. t* a se spăla
baton *n* baston
batsman *n.* jucător de basebal
battalion *n* batalion
battery *n* baterie
battle *n* bătălie
battle *v. i.* a lupta (cu)
bawd *n.* codoaşă
bawl *n.i.* strigăt
bay *n* golf
bayonet *n* baionetă
be *v.t.* a fi
beach *n* plajă
beacon *n* far
bead *n* mărgea
beadle *n.* pedel (la universitate)
beak *n* cioc de pasăre
beaker *n* cupă
beam *n* grindă
beam *v. i* a radia
bean *n.* fasole
bear *n* urs
bear *v.t* a duce
beard *n* barbă
bearing *n* suportare
beast *n* bestie
beastly *a* animalic
beat *n* lovitură
beat *v. t.* a bate
beautiful *a* frumos
beautify *v. t* a înfrumuseţa
beauty *n* frumuseţe
beaver *n* castor
because *conj.* pentru că
beck *n.* pârîu de munte
beckon *v.t.* a chema

beckon *v. i* a face semn
become *v. i* a deveni
becoming *a* potrivit
bed *n* pat
bedding *n.* aşternut
bedevil *v. t* a maltrata
bee *n.* albină
beech *n.* fag
beef *n* carne de vacă
beehive *n.* stup
beer *n* bere
beet *n* sfeclă
beetle *n* gândac
befall *v. t* a se întâmpla (cuiva)
before *adv.* înainte
before *conj* mai curând
before *prep* în faţa
beforehand *adv.* în avans
befriend *v. t.* a favoriza
beg *v. t.* a cerşi
beget *v. t* a genera
beggar *n* cerşetor
begin *v.t* a începe
beginning *n.* început
beguile *v. t* a păcăli
behalf *n* în numele cuiva
behave *v. i.* a se purta bine
behaviour *n* comportament
behead *v. t.* a decapita
behind *adv* în spatele
behind *prep* după
behold *v. t* a zări
being *n* fiinţă
belabour *v. t* a bate zdravăn
belated *adj.* întârziat
belch *v. t* a râgâi
belch *n* erupţie a unui vulcan
belief *n* credinţă
believe *v. t* a crede
bell *n* clopot
belle *n* fată frumoasă
bellicose *a* belicos

belligerency *n* beligeranţă
belligerent *a* beligerant
belligerent *n* beligerant
bellow *v. i* a zbiera
bellows *n.* zbieret
belly *n* burtă
belong *v. i* a aparţine
belongings *n.* bunuri
beloved *a* iubit
below *adv* dedesubt
below *prep* mai jos
belt *n* curea
bemuse *v. t* a năuci
bench *n* bancă
bend *n* aplecare
bend *v. t* a îndoi
beneath *adv* mai jos
beneath *prep* dedesubtul
benefaction *n.* binefacere
beneficial *a* folositor
benefit *n* beneficiu
benefit *v. t.* a beneficia
benevolence *n* bunăvoinţă
benevolent *a* binevoitor
benign *adj* blând
bent *n* înclinare
bequeath *v. t.* a lăsa moştenire
bereave *v. t.* a răpi
bereavement *n* nenorocire
berth *n* cuşetă
beside *prep.* alături
besides *prep* pe lângă
besides *adv* pe lângă aceasta
besiege *v. t* a asedia
beslaver *v. t* a acoperi cu bale
bestow *v. t* a pune la păstrare
bestrew *v. t* a împrăştia
bet *n* pariu
bet *v.i* a paria
betray *v.t.* a trăda
betrayal *n* trădare
betroth *v. t* a logodi

betrothal *n.* logodnă
better *a* mai bun
better *adv.* mai bine
better *v. t* a îmbunătăţi
betterment *n* îmbunătăţire
between *prep* între
beverage *n* băutură
bewail *v. t* a deplânge
beware *v.i.* a se păzi (de)
bewilder *v. t* a zăpăci
bewitch *v.t* a vrăji
beyond *adv.* fără pereche
beyond *prep.* mai presus de
bias *n* înclinaţie
bias *v. t* a înclina
bibber *n* beţiv
bible *n* biblie
bibliographer *n* bibliograf
bibliography +*n* bibliografie
bicentenary *adj* bicentenar
biceps *n* biceps
bicker *v. t* a susura
bicycle *n.* bicicletă
bid *v.t* a licita
bid *n* licitare
bidder *n* licitant
bide *v. t* a aştepta
biennial *adj* bienial
bier *n* catafalc
big *a* mare
bigamy *n* bigamie
bight *n* golf
bigot *n* bigot
bigotry *n* bigotism
bile *n* fiere
bilingual *a* bilingv
bilk *v. t.* a trage pe sfoară
bill *n* notă de plată
billion *n* miliard
billow *n* talaz
billow *v.i* a se umfla
bimonthly *adj.* bilunar

binary *adj* binar
bind *v.t* a fixa
binding *a* care leagă
binocular *n.* binoclu
biographer *n* biograf
biography *n* biografie
biologist *n* biolog
biology *n* biologie
birch *n.* mesteacăn
bird *n* pasăre
birth *n.* naştere
biscuit *n* biscuit
bisect *v. t* a împărţi
bisexual *adj.* bisexual
bishop *n* episcop
bison *n* bizon
bit *n* fărâmă
bitch *n* căţea
bite *n* muşcătură
bite *v. t.* a muşca
bitter *a* amar
bizarre *adj* bizar
blab *v. t. & i* a flecări
black *a* negru
blacken *v. t.* a înnegri
blackmail *n* şantaj
blackmail *v.t* a şantaja
blacksmith *n* fierar
bladder *n* vezică urinară
blade *n.* lamă
blame *n* vină
blame *v. t* a învinovăţi
blanch *v. t. & i* a înălbi
bland *adj.* amabil
blank *a* gol
blank *n* foaie goală
blanket *n* pătură
blare *v. t* a trâmbiţa
blast *n* rafală
blast *v.i* a prăpădi
blaze *n* vâlvătaie
blaze *v.i* a arde cu flăcări

bleach *v. t* a înălbi
blear *adj* tulbure
bleat *n* behăit
bleat *v. i* a behăi
bleb *n* băşică
bleed *v. i* a sângera
blemish *n* pată
blend *n* amestec
blend *v. t* a amesteca
bless *v. t* a binecuvânta
blether *v. i* a flecări
blight *n* pacoste
blind *a* orb
blindage *n* blindaj
blindfold *v. t* a lega la ochi
blindness *n* orbire
blink *v. t. & i* a clipi
bliss *n* fericire
blister *n* băşică (de piele)
blizzard *n* viscol
block *n* butuc
block *v.t* a bloca
blockade *n* blocadă
blockhead *n* nătâng
blood *n* sânge
bloodshed *n* măcel
bloody *a* sângeros
bloom *n* floare
bloom *v.i.* a înflori
blossom *n* floare
blossom *v.i* a înflori
blot *n.* pată
blot *v. t* a păta
blouse *n* bluză
blow *n* suflu
blow *v.i.* a sufla
blue *a* albastru
blue *n* albastru
bluff *n* înşelăciune
bluff *v. t* a trage o cacealma
blunder *n* gafă
blunder *v.i* a comite o gafă

blunt *a* tocit
blur *n* trăsături confuze
blurt *v. t* a divulga fără să vrea
blush *n* roşeaţa
blush *v.i* a roşi
boar *n* porc mistreţ
board *v. t.* a se îmbarca
board *n* tablă
boast *n* laudă
boast *v.i* a se lăuda cu
boat *v.i* a face canotaj
boat *n* barcă
bodice *n* corsaj
bodily *adv.* fizic
bodily *a* trupesc
body *n* corp
bodyguard *n.* pază de corp
bog *n* mlaştină
bogle *n* sperietoare
bogus *a* închipuit
boil *n* fierbere
boil *v.i.* a fierbe
boiler *n* boiler
bold *a.* îndrăzneţ
boldness *n* îndrăzneală
bolt *n* zăvor
bolt *v. t* a zăvorî
bomb *n* bombă
bomb *v. t* a bombarda
bombard *v. t* a bombarda
bomber *n* bombardier
bond *n* legătură
bondage *n* sclavie
bone *n.* os
bonfire *n* rug
bonnet *n* bonetă
bonus *n* bonus
book *n* carte
book *v. t.* a rezerva
bookish *adj* pedant
book-keeper *n* contabil
booklet *n* broşură

book-mark *n.* semn de carte
book-seller *n* librar
boon *n* avantaj
boor *n* persoană necioplită
boost *n* sporire
boost *v. t* a sprijini
boot *n* gheată
booth *n* gheretă
booty *n* pradă
booze *v. i* a bea într-una
border *n* frontieră
border *v.t* a mărgini
bore *n* plictiseală
bore *v. t* a plictisi
born *v.* a naşte
borrow *v. t* a împrumuta
bosom *n* sân
boss *n* şef
botany *n* botanică
botch *v. t* a rasoli
both *a* amândoi
both *pron* ambii
bother *v. t* a deranja
botheration *n* plictiseală
bottle *n* sticlă
bottom *n* fund
bough *n* ramură
boulder *n* bolovan
bouncer *n* lăudăros
bound *n.* legat
boundary *n* graniţă
bountiful *a* darnic
bounty *n* mărinimie
bouquet *n* buchet
bout *n* beţie
bow *v. t* a se supune cuiva
bow *n* arc
bow *n* reverenţă
bowel *n.* intestin
bowl *n* castron
bowl *v.i* a se rostogoli
box *n* cutie

boxing *n* box
boy *n* băiat
boycott *n* boicot
boycott *v. t.* a boicota
boyhood *n* adolescenţă
brace *n* clamă
bracelet *n* brăţară
brag *n* lăudăroşenie
brag *v. i* a se lăuda
brain *n* creier
brake *n* frână
brake *v. t* a frâna
branch *n* sector (de activitate)
brand *n* marcă
brandy *n* coniac
brass *n.* neruşinare
brave *a* curajos
bravery *n* vitejie
brawl *v. i. & n* scandal
bray *n* zbieret de măgar
bray *v. i* a zbiera
breach *n* abuz
bread *n* pâine
breadth *n* amploare
break *n* ruptură
break *v. t* a rupe
breakage *n* rupere
breakdown *n* stricăciune
breakfast *n* mic dejun
breakneck *adj* primejdios
breast *n* sân
breath *n* respiraţie
breathe *v. i.* a respira
breeches *n.* pantaloni bufanţi
breed *n* rasă
breed *v.t* a făta
breeze *n* briză
brevity *n* concizie
brew *v. t.* a fermenta
brewery *n* fabrică de bere
bribe *n* mită
bribe *v. t.* a mitui

brick *n* cărămidă
bride *n* mireasă
bridegroom *n.* mire
bridge *n* pod
bridle *n* căpăstru
brief *a.* scurt
brigade *n.* brigadă
brigadier *n* comandant de brigadă
bright *a* strălucitor
brighten *v. t* a lustrui
brilliance *n* strălucire
brilliant *a* strălucitor
brim *n* margine
brine *n* saramură
bring *v. t* a aduce
brink *n.* margine
brisk *adj* ager
bristle *n* ţepi (din barbă)
british *adj* englezesc
brittle *a.* fragil
broad *a* lat
broadcast *n* transmisiune
broadcast *v. t* a transmite
brocade *n* brocart
brochure *n* broşură
broker *n* agent de schimb
bronze *n. & adj* bronz
brood *n* droaie
brook *n.* pârîu
broom *n* mătură
broth *n* bulion
brothel *n* bordel
brother *n* frate
brotherhood *n* frăţie
brow *n* sprânceană
brown *a* brun
brown *n* maron
browse *n* a răsfoi
bruise *n* vânătaie
bruit *n* zvon
brush *n* perie

brutal *a* brutal
brute *n* brut
bubble *n* balon (de săpun)
bucket *n* găleată
buckle *n* cataramă
bud *n* mugur
budge *v. i. & n* a se clinti
budget *n* buget
buff *n* piele de bivol
buffalo *n.* bivol
buffoon *n* bufon
bug *n.* gândac
bugle *n* goarnă
build *n* construcție
build *v. t* a clădi
building *n* clădire
bulb *n.* bec
bulk *n* volum
bulky *a* voluminos
bull *n* bulă
bulldog *n* buldog
bullet *n* glonț
bulletin *n* buletin
bullock *n* bou
bully *n* huligan
bully *v. t.* a intimida
bulwark *n* baston
bumper *n.* bară de protecție
bumpy *adj* râpos
bunch *n* mănunchi
bundle *n* snop
bungalow *n* vilă
bungle *n* lucru de mântuială
bungle *v. t* a strica
bunk *n* cabină de dormit
bunker *n* magazie
buoy *n* geamandură
buoyancy *n* stare de plutire
burden *n* povară
burden *v. t* a împovăra
burdensome *a* împovărător
Bureacuracy *n.* birocrație

bureau *n.* birou
bureaucrat *n* birocrat
burglar *n* spărgător
burglary *n* spargere
burial *n* înmormântare
burk *v. t* a arde
burn *n* arsură
burn *v. t* a frige
burrow *n* vizuină
burst *n* izbucnire
burst *v. i.* a izbucni
bury *v. t.* a îngropa
bus *n* autobuz
bush *n* tufiș
business *n* afacere
businessman *n* afacerist
bustle *v. t* a zori
busy *a* ocupat
but *conj.* totuși
but *prep* dar
butcher *n* măcelar
butcher *v. t* a măcelări
butter *n* unt
butter *v. t* a unge cu unt
butterfly *n* fluture
buttermilk *n* zer
button *n* nasture
button *v. t.* a încheia cu nasturi
buy *v. t.* a cumpăra
buyer *n.* cumpărător
buzz *v. i* a bâzâi
buzz *n.* bâzâit
by *adv* alături
by *prep* lângă
bye-bye *interj.* la revedere
by-election *n* alegeri
   suplimentare
bylaw, bye-law *n* decizie pe loc
bypass *n* ocol
by-product *n* produs secundar
byword *n* proverb

C

cab *n.* taxi
cabaret *n.* cabaret
cabbage *n.* varză
cabin *n.* cabină
cabinet *n.* dulap
cable *n.* cablu
cable *v. t.* a fixa un cablu
cache *n* magazie secretă
cachet *n* semn distinctiv
cackle *v. i* a cotcodăci
cactus *n.* cactus
cad *n* ticălos
cadet *n.* mezin
cadge *v. i* a cerşi
cage *n.* cuşcă
cake *n.* prăjitură
calamity *n.* calamitate
calcium *n* calciu
calculate *v. t.* a calcula
calculation *n.* calcul
calculator *n* calculator
calendar *n.* calendar
calf *n.* viţel
call *v. t.* a chema
call *n.* apel
caller *n* vizitator
calligraphy *n* caligrafie
calling *n.* chemare
callous *a.* îngroşat
callow *adj* novice
calm *n.* calm
calm *v. t.* a calma
calm *n.* linişte
calmative *adj* calmant
calorie *n.* calorie
calumniate *v. t.* a calomnia
camel *n.* cămilă
camera *n.* aparat de fotografiat

camlet *n* stofă din păr de cămilă
camp *n.* tabără
camp *v. i.* a campa
campaign *n.* campanie
camphor *n.* camfor
can *v.* a conserva
can *v. t.* a putea
can *n.* conservă
canal *n.* canal
canard *n* ştire falsă
cancel *v. t.* a anula
cancellation *n* anulare
cancer *n.* cancer
candid *a.* sincer
candidate *n.* candidat
candle *n.* lumânare
candour *n.* candoare
candy *n.* bomboane
candy *v. t.* a fierbe zahăr
cane *v. t.* a împleti din trestie
cane *n.* trestie
canister *n.* canistră
cannon *n.* tun
cannonade *n. v. & t* canonadă
canon *n* canon
canopy *n.* boltă
canteen *n.* cantină
canter *n* galop mic
cantonment *n.* cantonament
canvas *n.* pânză
canvass *v. t.* a dezbate o problemă
cap *v. t.* a pune un capac
cap *n.* şapcă
capability *n.* capabilitate
capable *a.* capabil
capacious *a.* încăpător
capacity *n.* capacitate
cape *n.* capă
capital *a.* fundamental
capital *n.* capitală
capitalist *n.* capitalist
capitulate *v. t* a capitula

caprice *n.* capriciu
capricious *a.* capricios
capsize *v. i.* a (se) răsturna
capsular *adj* în formă de capsulă
captain *n.* căpitan
captaincy *n.* funcția de căpitan
caption *n.* arestare
captivate *v. t.* a captiva
captive *a.* captiv
captive *n.* captiv
captivity *n.* captivitate
capture *n.* captură
capture *v. t.* a captura
car *n.* automobil
carat *n.* carat
caravan *n.* caravană
carbide *n.* carbid
carbon *n.* carbon
card *n.* carte (de joc)
cardboard *n.* carton
cardinal *n.* cardinal
cardinal *a.* principal
care *v. i.* a avea grijă
care *n.* grijă
career *n.* carieră
careful *a* grijuliu
careless *a.* neglijent
caress *v. t.* a mângâia
cargo *n.* încarcătură
caricature *n.* caricatură
carious *adj* cariat
carnage *n* carnagiu
carnival *n* carnaval
carol *n* colindă
carpenter *n.* tâmplar
carpentry *n.* tâmplărie
carpet *n.* covor
carriage *n.* trăsură
carrier *n.* cărăuş
carrot *n.* morcov
carry *v. t.* a căra
cart *n.* cărucior

cartage *n.* cărăuşie
carton *n* cutie de carton
cartoon *n.* desen animat
cartridge *n.* cartuş
carve *v. t.* a ciopli
cascade *n.* cascadă
case *n.* caz
cash *v. t.* a încasa
cash *n.* bani gheață
cashier *n.* casier
casing *n.* învelitoare
cask *n* butoi
casket *n* sicriu
cassette *n.* casetă
cast *n.* a face socoteli
cast *v. t.* a lepăda
caste *n* castă
castigate *v. t.* a critica aspru
casting *n* turnare
cast-iron *n* fontă
castle *n.* castel
castor oil *n.* ulei de ricină
casual *a.* degajat
casualty *n.* victimă
cat *n.* pisică
catalogue *n.* catalog
cataract *n.* cataractă
catch *n.* pradă
catch *v. t.* a prinde
categorical *a.* categoric
category *n.* categorie
cater *v. i* a se ocupa (de)
caterpillar *n* omidă
cathedral *n.* catedrală
catholic *a.* catolic
cattle *n.* vite
cauliflower *n.* conopidă
causal *adj.* cauzal
cause *v.t* a cauza
cause *n.* cauză
caustic *a.* caustic
caution *v. t.* a avertiza

caution *n.* precauţie
cautious *a.* precaut
cavalry *n.* cavalerie
cave *n.* peşteră
cavern *n.* cavernă
cavil *v. t* a face şicane
cavity *n.* cavitate
caw *v. i.* a croncăni
caw *n.* croncănit
cease *v. i.* a înceta
ceaseless ~*a.* neâncetat
cedar *n.* cedru
ceiling *n.* tavan
celebrate *v. t. & i.* a celebra
celebration *n.* sărbătorire
celebrity *n* celebritate
celestial *adj* ceresc
celibacy *n.* celibat
cell *n.* celulă
cellar *n* pivniţă
cellular *adj* celular
cement *v. t.* a (se) cimenta
cement *n.* ciment
cemetery *n.* cimitir
cense *v. t* a tămâia
censer *n* cădelniţă
censor *v. t.* a cenzura
censor *n.* cenzor
censorious *adj* cusurgiu
censorship *n.* cenzură
censure *n.* blamare
censure *v. t.* a cenzura
census *n.* recensământ
cent *n* cent
centenarian *n* centenar
centenary *n.* centenar
centennial *adj.* centenar
center *n* centru
centigrade *a.* centigrad
centipede *n.* miriapod
central *a.* central
centre *n* centru

centrifugal *adj.* centrifugal
centuple *n. & adj* însutit
century *n.* secol
ceramics *n* ceramică
cereal *a* cerealier
cereal *n.* cereală
cerebral *adj* cerebral
ceremonial *a.* de ceremonie
ceremonious *a.* ceremonios
ceremony *n.* ceremonie
certain *a* sigur
certainly *adv.* cu siguranţă
certificate *n.* certificat
certify *v. t.* a certifica
cesspool *n.* hazna
chain *n* lanţ
chair *n.* scaun
chairman *n* preşedinte
challenge *v. t.* a provoca
challenge *n.* provocare
chamber *n.* sală
chamberlain *n* şambelan
champion *n.* campion
champion *v. t.* a susţine (o cauză)
chance *n.* şansă
chancellor *n.* cancelar
chancery *n* curtea de justiţie
change *n.* schimbare
change *v. t.* a schimba
channel *n* canal tv
chant *n* psalmodiere
chaos *n.* haos
chaotic *adv.* haotic
chapel *n.* capelă
chapter *n.* capitol
character *n.* caracter
charge *n.* încărcare
charge *v. t.* a încărca
chariot *n* car de război
charitable *a.* caritabil
charity *n.* caritate
charm1 *n.* farmec

charm2 *v. t.* a fermeca
chart *n.* hartă
charter *n* privilegiu
chase1 *v. t.* a urmări
chase2 *n.* urmărire
chaste *a.* cast
chastity *n.* castitate
chat1 *n.* taifas
chat2 *v. i.* a sta la taifas
chatter *v. t.* a ciripi
chauffeur *n.* şofer
cheap *a* ieftin
cheapen *v. t.* a ieftini
cheat *n.* înşelăciune
cheat *v. t.* a înşela
check *n* cec
check *v. t.* a controla
checkmate *n* mat (şah)
cheek *n* obraz
cheep *v. i* a piui
cheer *n.* înveselire
cheer *v. t.* a înveseli
cheerful *a.* voios
cheerless *a* posomorât
cheese *n.* brânză
chemical *n.* chimicale
chemical *a.* chimic
chemist *n.* chimist
chemistry *n.* chimie
cheque *n.* cec
cherish *v. t.* a păstra în suflet
chess *n.* şah
chest *n* piept
chestnut *n.* castană
chew *v. t* a mesteca
chicken *n.* pui (de găină)
chide *v. t.* a dojeni
chief *a.* şef
chieftain *n.* şef de trib
child *n* copil
childhood *n.* copilărie
childish *a.* copilăresc

chiliad *n.* o mie
chill *n.* răceală
chilly *a* friguros
chimney *n.* şemineu
chimpanzee *n.* cimpanzeu
chin *n.* bărbie
china *n.* porţelan
chirp *n* ciripit
chirp *v.i.* a ciripi
chisel *v. t.* a sculpta
chisel *n* daltă
chit *n.* puşti
chivalrous *a.* cavaleresc
chivalry *n.* cavalerism
chlorine *n* clor
chloroform *n* cloroform
chocolate *n* ciocolată
choice *n.* alegere
choir *n* cor
choke *v. t.* a se îneca
cholera *n.* holeră
choose *v. t.* a alege
chop *v. t* a ciopli
chord *n.* coardă
chorus *n.* cor
Christ *n.* Hristos
Christendom *n.* creştinătate
Christian *a.* creştinesc
Christian *n* creştin
Christianity *n.* creştinism
Christmas *n* Crăciun
chronic *a.* cronic
chronicle *n.* cronică
chronology *n.* cronologie
chuckle *v. i* a chicoti
chum *n* tovarăş
church *n.* biserică
churchyard *n.* curtea bisericii
churl *n* bădăran
churn *n.* putinei
churn *v. t. & i.* a frământa
cigar *n.* ţigară de foi

cigarette *n.* țigară
cinema *n.* cinema
cinnabar *n* cinabru
cinnamon *n* scorțișoară
cipher, cipher *n.* cifru
circle *n.* cerc
circuit *n.* circuit
circular *a* circular
circular *n.* circular
circulate *v. i.* a circula
circulation *n* circulație
circumference *n.* circumferință
circumspect *adj.* circumspect
circumstance *n* circumstanță
circus *n.* circ
citadel *n.* citadelă
cite *v. t* a cita
citizen *n* cetățean
citizenship *n* cetățenie
citric *adj.* citric
city *n* oraș
civic *a* civic
civil *a* cetățenesc
civilian *n* civil
civilization *n.* civilizație
civilize *v. t* a civiliza
clack *n. & v. i* trăncăneală
claim *v. t* a pretinde
claim *n* pretenție
claimant *n* reclamant
clamber *v. i* a se cățăra
clamour *v. i.* a face gălăgie
clamour *n* gălăgie
clamp *n* clemă
clandestine *adj.* clandestin
clap *n* aplaudare
clap *v. i.* a pocni
clarification *n* clarificare
clarify *v. t* a clarifica
clarion *n.* goarnă
clarity *n* claritate
clash *v. t.* a ciocni

clash *n.* ciocnire
clasp *n* agrafă
class *n* clasă
classic *n* clasic
classic *a* clasic
classical *a* clasic
classification *n* clasificare
classify *v. t* a clasifica
clause *n* clauză
claw *n* a zgâria
clay *n* lut
clean *v. t* a curăța
clean *n* curat
cleanliness *n* curățenie
cleanse *v. t* a face curățenie
clear *a* clar
clear *v. t* a clarifica
clearance *n* clarificare
clearly *adv* limpede
cleft *n* crăpătură
clergy *n* cler
clerical *a* clerical
clerk *n* funcționar
clever *a.* deștept
clew *n.* ghem
click *n.* pocnitură
client *n..* client
cliff *n.* râpă
climate *n.* climă
climax *n.* punct culminant
climb *v.t* a se cățăra
climb1 *n.* cățărare
cling *v. i.* a se agăța
clinic *n.* clinică
clink *n.* clinchet
cloak *n.* mantie
clock *n.* ceas
clod *n.* bulgăre
cloister *n.* mănăstire
close *a.* apropiat
close *v. t* a închide
close *n.* închidere

closet *n.* dulap
closure *n.* încheiere
clot *n.* cheag
clot *v. t* a închega
cloth *n* cârpă
clothe *v. t* a îmbrăca
clothes *n.* haine
clothing *n* îmbrăcăminte
cloud *n.* nor
cloudy *a* înnorat
clove *n* cuişor
clown *n* clavn
club *n* club
clue *n* indiciu
clumsy *a* stângaci
cluster *n* ciorchine
cluster *v. i.* a se aduna
clutch *n* ambreiaj
clutter *v. t* a învălmăşi
coach *n* antrenor
coachman *n* vizitiu
coal *n* cărbune
coalition *n* coaliţie
coarse *a* grosolan
coast *n* coastă
coat *n* haină
coating *n* strat
coax *v. t* a îndupleca
cobalt *n* cobalt
cobbler *n* cârpaci
cobra *n* cobra
cobweb *n* pânză de păianjen
cocaine *n* cocaină
cock *n* cocoş
cocker *v. t* a cocoloşi
cockle *v. i* a se încreţi
cock-pit *n.* carlingă
cockroach *n* gândac de bucătărie
coconut *n* nucă de cocos
code *n* cod
coefficient *n.* coeficient
co-exist *v. i* a coexista

co-existence *n* coexistenţă
coffee *n* cafea
coffin *n* sicriu
cog *n* zimţ
cogent *adj.* convingător
cognate *adj* înrudit
cognizance *n* semn distinctiv
cohabit *v. t* a convieţui
coherent *a* coerent
coin *n* monedă
coinage *n* sistem monetar
coincide *v. i* a coincide
coir *n* fibră de nucă de cocos
coke *v. t* cocs
cold *a* rece
cold *n* frig
collaborate *v. i* a colabora
collaboration *n* colaborare
collapse *v. i* a se prăbuşi
collar *n* guler
colleague *n* coleg
collect *v. t* a colecta
collection *n* colecţie
collective *a* colectiv
collector *n* colector
college *n* colegiu
collide *v. i.* a se ciocni
collision *n* tamponare
collusion *n* complotare
colon *n* colon
colon *n* două puncte
colonel *n.* colonel
colonial *a* colonial
colony *n* colonie
colour *v. t* a vopsi
colour *n* culoare
column *n* coloană
coma *n.* comă
comb *n* pieptene
combat *v. t.* a combate
combat1 *n* luptă
combatant1 *n* combatant

combination *n* combinaţie
combine *v. t* a combina
come *v. i.* a veni
comedian *n.* comediant
comedy *n.* comedie
comet *n* cometă
comfit *n.* bomboană
comfort *v. t* a consola
comfort1 *n.* confort
comfortable *a* confortabil
comic *n* comic
comic *a* comic
comical *a* comic
comma *n* virgulă
command *n* comandă
command *v. t* a comanda
commandant *n* comandant
commander *n* căpitan de vas
commemorate *v. t.* a comemora
commemoration *n.* comemorare
commence *v. t* a începe
commencement *n* început
commend *v. t* a interesa
commendable *a.* recomandabil
commendation *n* recomandare
comment *n* comentariu
comment *v. i* a comenta
commentary *n* comentariu
commentator *n* comentator
commerce *n* comerţ
commercial *a* comercial
commiserate *v. t* a compătimi
commission *n.* comision
commissioner *n.* comisionar
commit *v. t.* a comite
committee *n* comitet
commodity *n.* comoditate
common *a.* comun
commoner *n.* om de rând
commonplace *a.* banal
commonwealth *n.* comunitate
commotion *n* tulburare

communal *a* comunal
commune *v. t* a se consfătui (cu)
communicate *v. t* a comunica
communication *n.* comunicare
communiqué *n.* comunicat
communism *n* comunism
community *n.* comunitate
commute *v. t* a comuta
compact *a.* compact
compact *n.* pudră sau fard presat
companion *n.* companion
company *n.* companie
comparative *a* comparativ
compare *v. t* a compara
comparison *n* comparaţie
compartment *n.* compartiment
compass *n* busolă
compassion *n* compasiune
compel *v. t* a constrânge
compensate *v.t* a compensa
compensation *n* compensaţie
compete *v. i* a concura
competence *n* competenţă
competent *a.* competent
competition *n.* competiţie
competitive *a* competitiv
compile *v. t* a alcătui
complacent *adj.* mulţumit de sine
complain *v. i* a se plânge
complaint *n* plângere
complaisance *n.* politeţe
complaisant *adj.* politicos
complement *n* complement
complementary *a* complementar
complete *a* complet
complete *v. t* a termina
completion *n* completare
complex *a* complicat
complex *n* complex
complexion *n* culoare a pielii
compliance *n.* bunăvoinţă

compliant *adj.* binevoitor
complicate *v. t* a complica
complication *n.* complicaţie
compliment *n.* compliment
compliment *v. t* a complimenta
comply *v. i* a se supune
component *adj.* component
compose *v. t* a compune
composition *n* compunere
compositor *n* culegător
compost *n* bălegar
composure *n.* calm
compound *a* compus
compound *n* amestec
compound *n* compus
compound *v. i* a ajunge la un acord
comprehend *v. t* a înţelege
comprehension *n* înţelegere
comprehensive *a* cuprinzător
compress *v. t.* a comprima
compromise *v. t* a compromite
compromise *n* compromis
compulsion *n* constrângere
compulsory *a* obligatoriu
compunction *n.* remuşc re
computation *n.* evaluare
compute *v.t.* a calcula
comrade *n.* tovarăş
concave *adj.* concav
conceal *v. t.* a ţine secret
concede *v.t.* a recunoaşte
conceive *v. t* a concepe
concentrate *v. t* a concentra
concentration *n.* concentrare
concept *n* concept
conception *n* concepţie
concern *n* preocupare
concern *v. t* a interesa
concert *n.* concert
concert2 *v. t* a aranja
concession *n* concesie

conch *n.* scoică
conciliate *v.t.* a împăca
concise *a* concis
conclude *v. t* a încheia
conclusion *n.* concluzie
conclusive *a* final
concoct *v. t* a pregăti
concoction *n.* născocire
concord *n.* armonie
concrete *n* beton
concrete *a* concret
concrete *v. t* a solidifica
concubinage *n.* concubinaj
concubine *n* concubină
condemn *v. t.* a condamna
condemnation *n* condamnare
condense *v. t* a condensa
condition *n* condiţie
conditional *a* condiţional
condole *v. i.* a exprima condoleanţe
condolence *n* condoleanţă
condonation *n.* iertare
conduct *n* conduită
conduct *v. t* a dirija
conductor *n* dirijor
cone *n.* cor
confectioner *n* cofetar
confectionerv *n* cofetărie
confer *v. i* a conferi
conference *n* conferinţă
confess *v. t.* a mărturisi
confession *n* mărturisire
confidant *n* confident
confide *v. T* a destăinui
confidence *n* credinţă
confident *a.* încrezător
confidential *a.* confidenţial
confine *v. t* a îngrădi
confinement *n.* caṛ vitate
confirm *v. t* a confirma
confirmation *n* confirmare

confiscate *v. t* a confisca
confiscation *n* confiscare
conflict *n.* conflict
conflict *v. i* a fi în conflict
confluence *n* îmbulzeală
confluent *adj.* confluent
conformity *n.* conformitate
confraternity *n.* confrerie
confrontation *n.* confruntare
confuse *v. t* a încurca
confusion *n* confuzie
confute *v.t.* a combate (cu dovezi)
congenial *a* plăcut
congratulate *v. t* a felicita
(pentru)
congratulation *n* felicitare
congress *n* congres
conjecture *n* presupunere
conjecture *v. t* a presupune
conjugal *a* conjugal
conjugate *v.t. & i.* a conjuga
conjunct *adj.* combinat
conjunctiva *n.* conjunctiv/
conjuncture *n.* conjunctură
conjure *v.i.* a conjura
conjure *v.t.* a invoca (spiritele)
connect *v. t.* a conecta
connection *n* conexiune
connivance *n.* încuviințare
conquer *v. t* a cuceri
conquest *n* cucerire
conscience *n* conştiinţă
conscious *a* conştient
consecrate *v.t.* a consacra
consecutive *adj.* consecutiv
consecutively *adv* consecutiv
consensus *n.* consens
consent *v. i* a fi de acord
consent *n.* consimţământ
consequence *n* consecinţă
consequent *a* ulterior
conservative *n* conservare

conservative *a* conservator
conserve *v. t* a conserva
consider *v. t* a considera
considerate *a.* moderat
consideration *n* consideraţie
considering *prep.* ţinând seama
(de)
consign *v. t.* a încredinţa (cuiva)
consign *v.t.* a consemna
consignment *n.* consemnare
consist *v. i* a consta în
consistence,-cy *n.* consecvenţă
consistent *a* consistent
consolation *n* consolare
console *v. t* a consola
consolidate *v. t.* a consolida
consolidation *n* consolidare
consonance *n.* consonanţă
consonant *n.* consoană
consort *n.* vas de escortă
conspectus *n.* conspect
conspicuous *a.* evident
conspiracy *n.* conspiraţie
conspirator *n.* complotist
conspire *v. i.* a conspira
constable *n* poliţist
constant *a* constant
constellation *n.* constelaţie
constipation *n.* constipaţie
constituency *n* corp electoral
constituent *n.* element
constitutiv
constituent *adj.* constitutiv
constitute *v. t* a constitui
constitution *n* constituţie
constrict *v.t.* a contracta
construct *v. t.* a construi
construction *n* construcţie
consult *v. t* a consulta
consultation *n* consultaţie
consume *v. t* a consuma
consumption *n* consumaţie

consumption *n* tuberculoză
contact *n.* contact
contact *v. t* a contacta
contagious *a* contagios
contain *v.t.* a conţine
contaminate *v.t.* a contamina
contemplate *v. t* a contempla
contemplation *n* contemplare
contemporary *a* contemporar
contempt *n* sfidare
contemptuous *a* obraznic
contend *v. i* a susţine
content *a.* mulţumit
content *n* conţinut
content *n.* mulţumire
content *v. t* a mulţumi
contention *n* dispută
contentment *n* satisfacţie
contest *n.* concurs
contest *v. t* a concura (cu)
context *n* context
continent *n* continent
continental *a* continental
contingency *n.* eventualitate
continual *adj.* continuu
continuation *n.* continuare
continue *v. i.* a continua
continuity *n* continuitate
continuous *a* neâncetat
contour *n* contur
contra *pref.* contra
contraception *n.* contracepţie
contract *n* contract
contract *v. t* a contracta
contractor *n* furnizor
contradict *v. t* a contrazice
contradiction *n* contradicţie
contrary *a* contrar
contrast *n* contrast
contrast *v. t* a contrasta
contribute *v. t* a contribui
contribution *n* contribuţie

control *n* control
control *v. t* a controla
controller *n.* regulator
controversy *n* controversă
contuse *v.t.* a contuziona
conundrum *n.* ghicitoare
convene *v. t* a convoca
convenience *n.* convenienţă
convenient *a* convenabil
convent *n* mănăstire
convention *n.* convenţie
conversant *adj.* competent (în)
conversant *a* familiarizat (cu)
conversation *n* conversaţie
converse *v.t.* a conversa
conversion *n* schimbare
convert *v. t* a converti
convert *n* convertit
convey *v. t.* a transmite
conveyance *n* transmitere
convict *n* condamnat
convict *v. t.* a condamna
conviction *n* convingere
convince *v. t* a convinge
convivial *adj.* jovial
convocation *n.* convocare
convoke *v.t.* a convova
convolve *v.t.* a (se) înfăşura
coo *n* gângurit
coo *v. i* a gânguri
cook *v. t* a găti
cook *n* bucătar
cooker *n* maşină de gătit
cool *a* răcoros
cool *v. i.* a răci
cooler *n* frigorifer
co-operate *v. i* a coopera
co-operation *n* cooperare
co-operative *a* cooperatist
co-ordinate *v.t* a coordona
co-ordinate *adj* coordonat
co-ordination *n* coordonare

coot *n.* lişiţă
co-partner *n* părtaş
cope *v. i* a face faţă
coper *n.* geambaş
copper *n* aramă
coppice *n.* crâng
copulate *v.i.* a se împerechea
copy *n* copie
copy *v. t* a copia
coral *n* coral
cord *n* funie
cordate *adj.* în formă de inimă
cordial *a* cordial
core *n.* miez
coriander *n.* coriandru
cork *n.* dop
cormorant *n.* cormoran
corn *n* porumb
cornea *n* cornee
corner *n* colţ
cornet *n.* cornet
coronation *n* încoronare
coronet *n.* diademă
corporal *a* corporal
corporate *adj.* corporativ
corporation *n* corporaţie
corps *n* corp (de armată)
corpse *n* cadavru
correct *a* corect
correct *v. t* a corecta
correction *n* corecţie
correlate *v.t.* a pune in corelaţie
correlation *n.* corelaţie
correspond *v. i* a corespunde
correspondence *n.*
    corespondenţă
correspondent *n.* corespondent
corridor *n.* coridor
corroborate *v.t.* a confirma
corrosive *adj.* corosiv
corrupt *v. t.* a corupe
corrupt *a.* corupt

corruption *n.* corupţie
cosmetic *a.* cosmetic
cosmetic *n.* (preparat) cosmetic
cosmic *adj.* cosmic
cost *n.* cost
cost *v.t.* a costa
costal *adj.* costal
costly *a.* costisitor
costume *n.* costum
cosy *a.* confortabil
cot *n.* colibă
cote *n.* şopron
cottage *n* căsuţă
cotton *n.* bumbac
couch *n.* canapea
cough *n.* tuse
cough *v. i.* a tuşi
council *n.* consiliu
councillor *n.* consilier
counsel *n.* sfat
counsel *v. t.* a se sfătui
counsellor *n.* sfătuitor
count *n.* socoteală
count *v. t.* a număra
countenance *n.* expresie
counter *n.* tejghea
counter *v. t* a se opune
counteract *v.t.* a contracara
countercharge *n.* contraacuzare
counterfeit *a.* falsificat
counterfeiter *n.* falsificator
countermand *v.t.* a contramanda
counterpart *n.* omolog
countersign *v. t.* a contrasemna
countess *n.* contesă
countless *a.* nenumărat
country *n.* ţară
county *n.* judeţ
coup *n.* lovitură de stat
couple *n* cuplu
couple *v. t* a (se) cupla
couplet *n.* cuplet

coupon *n.* cupon
courage *n.* curaj
courageous *a.* curajos
courier *n.* curier
course *n.* curs
court *n.* tribunal
court *v. t.* a curta
courteous *a.* curtenitor
courtesan *n.* curtezană
courtesy *n.* curtoazie
courtier *n.* curtean
courtship *n.* petiţie
courtyard *n.* curtea casei
cousin *n.* văr
covenant *n.* pact
cover *n.* copertă
cover *v. t.* a acoperi
coverlet *n.* cuvertură
covet *v.t.* a râvni
cow *n.* vacă
cow *v. t.* a intimida
coward *n.* laş
cowardice *n.* laşitate
cower *v.i.* a se ghemui
cozy *adj* comfortabil
crab *n* crab
crack *n* crăpatură
crack *v. i* a crăpa
cracker *n* plesnitoare
crackle *v.t.* a sfărâma
cradle *n* sanie de lansare
craft *n* meşteşug
craftsman *n* meşteşugar
crafty *a* viclean
cram *v. t* a îndopa
crane *n* cocor
crash *n* accident
crash *v. i* a zdrobi
crass *adj.* cras
crate *n.* coş mare
crave *v.t.* a tânji
craw *n.* guşă

crawl *n* târîre
crawl *v. t* a se târî
craze *n* ţicneală
crazy *a* nebun
creak *v. i* a scârţâi
creak *n* scârţâit
cream *n* frişcă
crease *n* dungă
create *v. t* a crea
creation *n* creaţie
creative *adj.* creativ
creator *n* creator
creature *n* creatură
credible *a* credibil
credit *n* credit
creditable *a* demn de laudă
creditor *n* creditor
credulity *adj.* credulitate
creed *n.* crez
creek *n.* pârâu
creep *v. i* a-i da fiori
creeper *n* căţărătoare
cremate *v. t* a incinera
cremation *n* incinerare
crest *n* creastă
crew *n.* echipaj
crib *n.* pat de copil
cricket *n* greiere
crime *n* crimă
criminal *a* criminal
criminal *n* criminal
crimp *n* recrutor
crimple *v.t.* a (se) încreţi
crimson *n* carmin
cringe *v. i.* a se ploconi
cripple *n* infirm
crisis *n* criză
crisp *a* crocant
criterion *n* criteriu
critic *n* critic
critical *a* primejdios
criticism *n* critică

2. 2p= 1K

criticize v. t a critica
croak n. orăcăit
crockery n. olărit
crocodile n crocodil
crook n cârjă
crop n recoltă
cross a irascibil
cross n cruce
cross v. t a traversa
crossing n. traversare
crotchet n. cârlig
crouch v. i. a se ghemui
crow n cioară
crow v. i a cânta cucurigu
crowd n mulțime
crown n coroană
crown v. t a încorona
crucial adj. decisiv
crude a crud
cruel a nemilos
cruelty n cruzime
cruise v.i. a face o croazieră
cruiser n crucișător
crumb n firimitură
crumble v. t a fărâmița
crusade n cruciadă
crush v. t a zdrobi
crust n. crustă
crutch n cârjă
cry n plânset
cry v. i a plânge
cryptography n. criptografie
crystal n cristal
cub n pui (de animal sălbatic)
cube n cub
cuckold n. soț înșelat
cuckoo n cuc
cucumber n castravete
cudgel n ciomag
cue n tac (de biliard)
cuff n manșetă
cuff v. t a lovi cu pumnul

cuisine n. bucătarie
culminate v.i. a culmina
culpable a vinovat
culprit n acuzat
cult n cult
cultivate v. t a cultiva
cultural a cultural
culture n cultură
culvert n. canal de scurgere
cunning a viclean
cunning n șiretenie
cup n. ceașcă
cupboard n dulap
cupidity n lăcomie
curable a vindecabil
curative a curativ
curb n frâu
curb v. t a frâna
curcuma n. turmeric
curd n lapte prins
cure n vindecare
cure v. t. a vindeca
curfew n tocsin
curiosity n curiozitate
curious a curios
curl n. buclă
currency n circulație monetară
current n curent
current a curent
curriculum n plan de studii
curse n blestem
curse v. t a blestema
cursory a pripit
curt a concis
curtail v. t a tăia din
curtain n perdea
curve n curbă
curve v. t a (se) curba
cushion n pernă (de divan)
cushion v. t a așeza pe pernă
custard n cremă de ouă
custodian n tutore

custody *v* a da în grija
custom *n.* obicei
customary *a* obișnuit
customer *n* client
cut *n* tăietură
cut *v. t* a tăia
cutis *n.* dermă
cycle *n* ciclu
cyclic *a* ciclic
cyclist *n* ciclist
cyclone *n.* ciclon
cylinder *n* cilindru
cynic *n* cinic
cypher cypress *n* chiparos

dabble *v. i.* a umezi
dad, daddy *n* tăticu
daffodil *n.* narcisă galbenă
daft *adj.* smintit
dagger *n.* pumnal
daily *a* cotidian
daily *n.* (ziar) cotidian
daily *adv.* zilnic
dainty *a.* rafinat
dainty *n.* delicatese
dairy *n* lăptărie
dais *n.* estradă
daisy *n* margaretă
dale *n* vale
dam *n* stăvilar
damage *v. t.* a strica
damage *n.* pagubă
dame *n.* damă
damn *v. t.* a blestema
damnation *n.* blestem
damp *a* umed
damp *v. t.* a umezi

damp *n* umezeală
damsel *n.* domnișoară
da..ce *n* dans
dance *v. t.* a dansa
dandelion *n.* păpădie
dandle *v.t.* a dezmierda
dandruff *n* mătreață
dandy *n* filfizon
danger *n.* pericol
dangerous *a* periculos
dangle *v. t* a legăna
dank *adj.* umed și rece
dap *v.i.* a sări
dare *v. i.* a îndrăzni
daring *a* îndrăzneț
daring *n.* îndrăzneală
dark *a* întunecat
dark *n* întuneric
darkle *v.i.* a (se) întuneca
darling *a* drăguț
darling *n* favorit
dart *n.* săgeată
dash *n* izbitură
dash *v. t.* a azvârli cu putere
date *n* întâlnire
date *v. t* a se întâlni
daub *n.* tencuială
daub *v. t.* a tencui
daughter *n* fiică
daunt *v. t* a speria
dauntless *a* neânfricat
dawdle *v.i.* a trândăvi
dawn *n* zori de zi
dawn *v. i.* a se crăpa de ziuă
day *n* zi
daze *n* uluire
daze *v. t* a ului
dazzle *n* lumină orbitoare
dazzle *v. t.* a străluci orbitor
deacon *n.* diacon
dead *a* mort
deadlock *n* fundătură

deadly *a* mortal
deaf *a* surd
deal *n* afacere
deal *v. i* a trata despre ceva
dealer *n* negustor
dealings *n.* tranzacţii
dean *n.* decan
dear *a* drag
dearth *n* foamete
death *n* moarte
debar *v. t.* a exclude (de la)
debase *v. t.* a înjosi
debate *v. t.* dezbate
debate *n.* dezbatere
debauch *n* desfrâu
debauch *v. t.* a perveti
debauchee *n* destrăbălat
debauchery *n* depravare
debility *n* debilitate
debit *n* debit
debit *v. t* a debita
debris *n* epavă
debt *n* datorie
debtor *n* datornic
decade *n* decadă .
decadent *a* decadent
decamp *v. i* a ridica corturile
decay *v. i* a decădea
decay *n* decădere
decease *n* deces
decease *v. i* a deceda
deceit *n* înşelăciune
deceive *v. t* a înşela
december *n* decembrie
decency *n* decenţă
decent *a* decent
deception *n* decepţie
decide *v. t* a decide
decimal *a* zecimal
decimate *v.t.* a decima
decision *n* decizie
decisive *a* decisiv

deck *n* punte
deck *v. t* a împodobi
declaration *n* declaraţie
declare *v. t.* a declara
decline *n* declin
decline *v. t.* a scădea
declivous *adj.* înclinat
decompose *v. t.* a se descompune
decomposition *n.* descompunere
decontrol *v.t.* a scoate de sub
) control
decorate *v. t* a decora
decoration *n* decoraţie
decorum *n* bunăcuviinţă
decrease *n* descreştere
decrease *v. t* a descreşte
decree *n* decret
decree *v. i* a decreta
dedicate *v. t.* a dedica
dedication *n* dedicaţie
deduct *v.t.* a scădea
deed *n* acţiune
deem *v.i.* a crede
deep *a.* adânc
deer *n* cerb
defamation *n* defăimare
defame *v. t.* a defăima
default *n.* lipsă
defeat *n* înfrângere
defeat *v. t.* a înfrânge
defect *n* defect
defence *n* apărare
defend *v. t* a apăra
defendant *n* acuzat
defensive *adv.* defensiv
deference *n* apărare
defiance *n* sfidare
deficient *adj.* deficient
deficit *n* deficit
defile *n.* a spurca
define *v. t* a defini
definite *a* hotărât

definition *n* definiție
deflation *n.* dezumflare
deflect *v.t. & i.* a face să devieze
deft *adj.* abil
degrade *v. t* a degrada
degree *n* grad
deist *n.* deist
deity *n.* zeitate
deject *v. t* a deprima
dejection *n* deprimare
delay *v.t. & i.* a întârzia
delegate *v. t* a delega
delegation *n* delegare
delete *v. t* a șterge
deliberate *a* intenționat
deliberate *v. i* a delibera
deliberation *n* deliberare
delicate *a* delicat
delicious *a* delicios
delight *n* încântare
delight *v. t.* a încânta
deliver *v. t* a livra
delivery *n* livrare
delta *n* deltă (a unui râu)
delude *v.t.* a înșela
delusion *n.* amăgire
demand *n* pretenție
demand *v. t* a pretinde
demarcation *n.* demarcație
demerit *n* defect
democracy *n* democrație
democratic *a* democratic
demolish *v. t.* a dărâma
demon *n.* demon
demonetize *v.t.* a demonetiza
demonstrate *v. t* a demonstarte
demonstration *n.* demonstrație
demoralize *v. t.* a demonraliza
demur *n* ezitare
demur *v. t* a ezita
den *n* vizuină
denial *n* negare

denote *v. i* a denota
denounce *v. t* a denunța
dense *a* dens
density *n* densitate
dentist *n* dentist
denude *v.t.* a dezgoli
denunciation *n.* denunțare
deny *v. t.* a nega
depart *v. i.* a pleca
department *n* departament
departure *n* plecare
depauperate *v.t.* a degenera
depend *v. i.* a depinde
dependence *n* dependența
dependent *a* dependent (de)
depict *v. t.* a descrie
deplorable *a* deplorabil
deploy *v.t.* a desfășura
deponent *n.* verb deponent
deport *v.t.* a deporta
depose *v. t* a demite
deposit *n.* depozit
deposit *v. t* a depozita
depot *n* depou
depreciate *v.t.i.* a deprecia
depress *v. t* a deprima
depression *n* depresie
deprive *v. t* a priva
depth *n* adâncime
deputation *n* delegație
depute *v. t* a delega
deputy *n* delegat
derail *v. t.* a deraia
derive *v. t.* a proveni
descend *v. i.* a coborî
descendant *n* descendent
descent *n.* coborâre
describe *v. t* a descrie
description *n* descriere
descriptive *a* descriptiv
desert *n* pustietate
desert *v. t.* a dezerta

deserve v. t. a merita
design n. schiţă
design v. t. a face un proiect
desirable a dezirabil
desire n dorinţă
desire v.t a dori
desirous a dornic
desk n birou
despair n disperare
despair v. i a dispera
desperate a disperat
despicable a mârşav
despise v. t a dispreţui
despot n despot
destination n destinaţie
destiny n destin
destroy v. t a distruge
destruction n distrugere
detach v. t a detaşa
detachment n detaşament
detail n detaliu
detail v. t a detalia
detain v. t a reţine
detect v. t a detecta
detective a detectiv
detective n. detectiv
determination n. determinare
determine v. t a determina
dethrone v. t a detrona
develop v. t. a dezvolta
development n. dezvoltare
deviate v. i a devia
deviation n deviere
device n dispozitiv
devil n diavol
devise v. t a născoci
devoid a lipsit de
devote v. t a devota
devotee n adept
devotion n devotament
devour v. t a devora
dew n. rouă

diabetes n diabet
diagnose v. t a diagnostica
diagnosis n diagnostic
diagram n diagramă
dial n. cadran
dialect n dialect
dialogue n dialog
diameter n diametru
diamond n diamant
diarrhoea n diaree
diary n jurnal
dice n. zaruri
dice v. i. a juca zaruri
dictate v. t a dicta
dictation n dictare
dictator n dictator
diction n dicţie
dictionary n dicţionar
dictum n maximă
didactic a didactic
die n zar (de joc)
die v. i a muri
diet n dietă
differ v. i a diferi
difference n diferenţă
different a diferit
difficult a dificil
difficulty n dificultate
dig v.t. a săpa
dig n săpat
digest v. t. a digera
digest n. publicaţie informativă
digestion n digestie
digit n cifră
dignify v.t a onora
dignity n demnitate
dilemma n dilemă
diligence n silinţă
diligent a silitor
dilute a diluat
dilute v. t a dilua
dim a întunecos

dim *v. t* a întuneca
dimension *n* dimensiune
diminish *v. t* a diminua
din *n* zgomot
dine *v. t.* a lua masa
dinner *n* cină
dip *n.* înmuiere (într-un lichid)
dip *v. t* a înmuia
diploma *n* diplomă
diplomacy *n* diplomație
diplomat *n* diplomat
diplomatic *a* diplomatic
dire *a* cumplit
direct *a* direct
direct *v. t* a direcționa
direction *n* direcție
director *n.* director
directory *n* anuar
dirt *n* murdărie
dirty *a* murdar
disability *n* incapacitate
disable *v. t* a schilodi
disabled *a* invalid
disadvantage *n* dezavantaj
disagree *v. i* a nu fi de acord
disagreement *n.* dezacord
disappear *v. i* a dispărea
disappearance *n* dispariție
disappoint *v. t.* a dezamăgi
disapproval *n* dezaprobare
disapprove *v. t* a dezaproba
disarm *v. t* a dezarma
disarmament *n.* dezarmare
disaster *n* dezastru
disastrous *a* dezastruos
disc *n.* disc
discard *v. t* a arunca
discharge *n.* descărcare
discharge *v. t* a descărca
disciple *n* discipol
discipline *n* disciplină
disclose *v. t* a dezvălui

discomfort *n* neliniște
disconnect *v. t* a deconecta
discontent *n* nemulțumire
discontinue *v. t* a întrerupe
discord *n* dezacord
discount *n* reducere
discourage *v. t.* a descuraja
discourse *n* disertație (asupra)
discourteous *a* nepoliticos
discover *v. t* a descoperi
discovery *n.* descoperire
discretion *n* discernământ
discriminate *v. t.* a distinge (din, dintre)
discrimination *n* discriminare
discuss *v. t.* a discuta
disdain *n* dispreț
disdain *v. t.* a dispreț
disease *n* boală
disguise *n* deghizare
disguise *v. t* a deghiza
dish *n* veselă
dishearten *v. t* a descuraja
dishonest *a* necinstit
dishonesty *n.* necinste
dishonour *n* dezonoare
dishonour *v. t* dezonoare
dislike *n* antipatie
dislike *v. t* a-i displăcea
disloyal *a* neloial
dismiss *v. t.* a concedia
dismissal *n* concediere
disobey *v. t* a nu se supune
disorder *n* dezordine
disparity *n* diferență
dispensary *n* dispensar
disperse *v. t* a dispersa
displace *v. t* a deplasa
display *n* expunere
display *v. t* a expune
displease *v. t* a nemulțumi
displeasure *n* nemulțumire

disposal *n* dispunere
dispose *v. t* a dispune
disprove *v. t* a respinge
dispute *n* dispută
dispute *v. i* a se certa
disqualification *n* descalificare
disqualify *v. t.* a descalifica
disquiet *n* neliniște
disregard *n* nesocotire
disregard *v. t* a nesocoti
disrepute *n* dezonoare
disrespect *n* nepolitețe
disrupt *v. t* a sfărâma
dissatisfaction *n* nemulțumire
dissatisfy *v. t.* a nemulțumi
dissect *v. t* a diseca
dissection *n* disecție
dissimilar *a* diferit
dissolve *v.t* a dizolva
dissuade *v. t* a sfătui să nu
distance *n* distanță
distant *a* distant
distil *v. t* a distila
distillery *n* distilerie
distinct *a* distinct
distinction *n* dictincție
distinguish *v. i* a distinge
distort *v. t* a deforma
distress *n* întristare profundă
distress *v. t* a îndurera
distribute *v. t* a distribui
distribution *n* distribuție
district *n* district
distrust *n* neîncredere
distrust *v. t.* a suspecta
disturb *v. t* a tulbura
ditch *n* șanț
ditto *n.* reproducere
dive *v. i* a plonja
dive *n* plonjon
diverse *a* divers
divert *v. t* a distrage

divide *v. t* a despărți
divine *a* divin
divinity *n* divinitate
division *n* diviziune
divorce *n* divorț
divorce *v. t* a divorța
divulge *v. t* a divulga
do *v. t* a face
docile *a* docil
dock *n.* doc
doctor *n* doctor
doctorate *n* doctorat
doctrine *n* doctrină
document *n* document
dodge *n* truc
dodge *v. t* a evita
doe *n* căprioară
dog *n* câine
dog *v. t* a se ține după
dogma *n* dogmă
dogmatic *a* dogmatic
doll *n* păpușă
dollar *n* dolar
domain *n* domeniu
dome *n* dom
domestic *a* domestic
domestic *n* servitor
domicile *n* domiciliu
dominant *a* dominant
dominate *v. t* a domina
domination *n* dominare
dominion *n* dominațtie
donate *v. t* a dona
donation *n.* donație
donkey *n* măgar
donor *n* donator
doom *n* sentință
doom *v. t.* a destina
door *n* ușă
dose *n* doză
dot *n* punct
dot *v. t* a puncta

double *a* dublu
double *n* dublură
double *v. t.* a dubla
doubt *n* îndoială
doubt *v. i* a se îndoi de
dough *n* cocă
dove *n* porumbel
down *v. t* a doborî
down *adj.* care coboară
down *adv* jos
downfall *n* prăbuşire
downpour *n* ploaie torenţială
downright *a* complet
downright *adv* în întregime
downward *a* înclinat
downward *adv* în jos
downwards *adv* la vale
dowry *n* zestre
doze *n.* moţăială
doze *v. i* a moţăi
dozen *n* duzină
draft *n* proiect
draft *v. t* a schiţa
draftsman *n* desenator (tehnic)
drag *n* obstacol
drag *v. t* a târî
dragon *n* balaur
drain *n* canal de scurgere
drain *v. t* a scurge
drainage *n* canalizare
dram *n* duşcă
drama *n* dramă
dramatic *a* dramatic
dramatist *n* dramaturg
draper *n* postăvar
drastic *a* drastic
draught *n* curent (de aer)
draw *n* tiraj
draw *v.t* a trage (o carte de joc)
drawback *n* inconvenient
drawer *n* desenator
drawing *n* extragere

drawing-room *n* salon
dread *n* spaimă
dread *a* înspăimântător
dread *v.t* a-i fi groază de
dream *n* vis
dream *v. i.* a visa
drench *v. t* a înmuia
dress *n* rochie
dress *v. t* a îmbrăca
dressing *n* îmbrăcare
drill *n* sfredel
drill *v. t.* a instrui
drink *n* băutură
drink *v. t* a bea
drip *n* picurare
drip *v. i* a picura
drive *n* avânt
drive *v. t* a conduce
driver *n* şofer
drizzle *n* burniţă
drizzle *v. i* a burniţa
drop *v. i* a scăpa
drop *n* picătură
drought *n* secetă
drown *v.i* a se îneca
drug *n* medicament
druggist *n* farmacist
drum *n* tobă
drum *v.i.* a bate toba
drunkard *n* beţivan
dry *a* uscat
dry *v. i.* a usca
dual *a* dual
duck *n.* raţă
duck *v.i.* a cufunda
due *a* cuvenit
due *adv* precis
due *n* datorie
duel *n* duel
duel *v. i* a (se) duela
duke *n* duce
dull *a* tont

dull *v. t.* a toci
duly *adv* la timp
dumb *a* posac
dunce *n* nătâng
dung *n* bălegar
duplicate *a* dublu
duplicate *n* duplicat
duplicate *v. t* a dubla
duplicity *n* duplicitate
durable *a* durabil
duration *n* durată
during *prep* în timpul
dusk *n* crepuscul
dust *n* praf
dust *v.t.* a şterge praful
duster *n* cârpă de praf
dutiful *a* conştiincios
duty *n* îndatorire
dwarf *n* pitic
dwell *v. i* a trăi
dwelling *n* locuinţă
dwindle *v. t* a se micşora
dye *n* vopsea
dye *v. t* a vopsi
dynamic *a* dinamic
dynamics *n.* dinamică
dynamite *n* dinamită
dynamo *n* dinam
dynasty *n* dinastie
dysentery *n* dizenterie

E

each *pron.* unul pe altul
each *a* fiecare
eager *a* doritor
eagle *n* vultur
ear *n* ureche
early *a* devreme

early *adv* devreme
earn *v. t* a câştiga
earnest *a* zelos
earth *n* pământ
earthen *a* de pământ
earthly *a* pământesc
earthquake *n* cutremur
ease *n* uşurinţă
ease *v. t* a uşura
east *adv* spre est
east *a* răsăritean
east *n* est
easter *n* Paşte
eastern *a* estic
easy *a* uşor
eat *v. t* a mânca
eatable *a* comestibil
eatable *n.* hrană
ebb *n* reflux
ebb *v. i* a decădea
ebony *n* abanos
echo *n* ecou
echo *v. t* a face ecou
eclipse *n* eclipsă
economic *a* economic
economical *a* economic
economics *n.* economie
economy *n* economisire
edge *n* margine
edible *a* comestibil
edifice *n* edificiu
edit *v. t* a edita
edition *n* ediţie
editor *n* editor
editorial *a* editorial
editorial *n* editorial
educate *v. t* a educa
education *n* educaţie
efface *v. t* a şterge
effect *n* efect
effect *v. t* a efectua
effective *a* efectiv

effeminate *a* castrat
efficacy *n* eficacitate
efficiency *n* eficienţă
efficient *a* eficient
effigy *n* figură
effort *n* efort
egg *n* ou
egotism *n* egotism
eight *n* opt
eighteen *a* optsprezece
eighty *n* optzeci
either *a.*, oricare
either *adv.* de asemenea
eject *v. t.* a scoate
elaborate *a* elaborat
elaborate *v. t* a elabora
elapse *v. t* a scurge
elastic *a* elastic
elbow *n* cot
elder *a* mai mare
elder *n* persoană mai în vârstă
elderly *a* vârstnic
elect *v. t* a alege
election *n* alegere
electorate *n* corpul alegătorilor
electric *a* electric
electricity *n* electricitate
electrify *v. t* a electriza
elegance *n* eleganţă
elegant *adj* elegant
elegy *n* elegie
element *n* element
elementary *a* elementar
elephant *n* elefant
elevate *v. t* a ridica
elevation *n* ridicare
eleven *n* unsprezece
elf *n* spiriduş
eligible *a* eligibil
eliminate *v. t* a elimina
elimination *n* eliminare
elope *v. i* a fugi (cu iubitul/a)

eloquence *n* elocvenţă
eloquent *a* elocvent
else *a* altceva
else *adv* în plus
elucidate *v. t* a elucida
elude *v. t* a evita
elusion *n* eludare
elusive *a* derutant
emancipation *n.* emancipare
embalm *v. t* a îmbălmăsa
embankment *n* îndiguire
embark *v. t* a îmbarca
embarrass *v. t* a face de ruşine
embassy *n* amasadă
embitter *v. t* a amărâ
emblem *n* emblemă
embodiment *n* întruchipare
embody *v. t.* a întruchipa
embolden *v. t.* a încuraja
embrace *n* îmbrăţişare
embrace *v. t.* a îmbrăţişa
embroidery *n* broderie
embryo *n* embrion
emerald *n* smarald
emerge *v. i* a ieşi la iveală
emergency *n* urgenţă
eminent *a* eminent
emissary *n* emisar
emit *v. t* a emite
emolument *n* remuneraţie
emotion *n* emoţie
emotional *a* emoţional
emperor *n* împărat
emphasis *n* emfază
emphasize *v. t* a sublinia
emphatic *a* accentuat
empire *n* imperiu
employ *v. t* a angaja
employee *n* angajat
employer *n* patron
employment *n* angajare
empower *v. t* a împuternici

empress *n* împărăteasă
empty *v* a goli
empty *a* gol
emulate *v. t* a încerca să întreacă
enable *v. t* a face posibil
enact *v. t* a decreta
enamel *n* smalţ
enamour *v. t* a încânta
encase *v. t* a pune
enchant *v. t* a încânta
encircle *v. t.* a încercui
enclose *v. t* a alătura
enclosure *n.* anexă
encompass *v. t* a înconjura
encounter *n.* întâlnire
(neprevăzută)
encounter *v. t* a da peste
encourage *v. t* a încuraja
encroach *v. i* a încălca
encumber *v. t.* a împovăra
encyclopaedia *n.* enciclopedie
end *n.* sfârşit
end *v. t* a sfârşi
endanger *v. t.* a primejdui
endear *v.t* a îndrăgi
endearment *n.* mângâiere
endeavour *n* strădanie
endeavour *v.i* a se strădui
endorse *v. t.* a gira
endow *v. t* a dota
endurable *a* suportabil
endurance *n.* rezistenţă
endure *v.t.* a îndura
enemy *n* inamic
energetic *a* energetic
energy *n.* energie
enfeeble *v. t.* a slăbi
enforce *v. t.* a stărui asupra
enfranchise *v.t.* a acorda drept
de vot
engage *v. t* a logodi
engagement *n.* logodnă

engine *n* motor (de maşină)
engineer *n* inginer
English *n* engleză
engrave *v. t* a grava
engross *v.t* a absorbi
engulf *v.t* a înghiţi
enigma *n* enigmă
enjoy *v. t* a se bucura de
enjoyment *n* delectare
enlarge *v. t* a lărgi
enlighten *v. t.* a lumina
enlist *v. t* a înrola
enliven *v. t.* a însufleţi
enmity *n* duşmănie
enormous *a* enorm
enough *a* destul
enough *adv* îndeajuns
enrage *v. t* a înfuria
enrapture *v. t* a fermeca
enrich *v. t* a îmbogăţi
enrol *v. t* a înrola
enshrine *v. t* a păstra cu evlavie
enslave *v.t.* a înrobi
ensue *v.i* a reieşi (din)
ensure *v. t* a asigura
entangle *v. t* a încurca
enter *v. t* a intra
enterprise *n* întreprindere
entertain *v. t* a distra
entertainment *n.* distracţie
enthrone *v. t* a întrona
enthusiasm *n* entuziasm
enthusiastic *a* entuziastic
entice *v. t.* a momi
entire *a* întreg
entirely *adv* în întregime
entitle *v. t.* a intitula
entity *n* entitate
entomology *n.* entomologie
entrails *n.* măruntaie
entrance *n* intrare
entrap *v. t.* a prinde în capcană

entreat *v. t.* a ruga stăruitor
entreaty *n.* rugăminte
entrust *v. t* a încredinţa
entry *n* intrare
enumerate *v. t.* a enumera
envelop *v. t* a învălui
envelope *n* plic
enviable *a* de invidiat
envious *a* invidios
environment *n.* mediu
envy *v. t* a invidia
envy *n* invidie
epidemic *n* epidemie
epigram *n* epigramă
epilepsy *n* epilepsie
epilogue *n* epilog
episode *n* episod
epitaph *n* epitaf
epoch *n* epocă
equal *n* egal
equal *a* egal
equal *v. t* a egala
equality *n* egalitate
equalize *v. t.* a egaliza
equate *v. t* a face egal
equation *n* ecuaţie
equator *n* ecuator
equilateral *a* echilateral
equip *v. t* a echipa
equipment *n* echipament
equitable *a* echitabil
equivalent *a* echivalent
equivocal *a* ambiguu
era *n* eră
eradicate *v. t* a eradica
erase *v. t* a şterge
erect *a* în picioare
erect *v. t* a ridica
erection *n* erecţie
erode *v. t* a eroda
erosion *n* eroziune
erotic *a* erotic

err *v. i* a greşi
errand *n* comision
erroneous *a* greşit
error *n* greşală
erupt *v. i* a erupe
eruption *n* erupţie
escape *n* evadare
escape *v. i* a evada
escort *n* escortă
escort *v. t* a escorta
especial *a* special
essay *n.* eseu
essay *v. t.* a pune la încercare
essayist *n* eseist
essence *n* esenţă
essential *a* esenţial
establish *v. t.* a stabili
establishment *n* aşezământ
estate *n* moşie
esteem *n* estimare
esteem *v. t* a estima
estimate *n.* estimaţie
estimate *v. t* a estima
estimation *n* estimare
eternal *adv* etern
eternity *n* eternitate
ether *n* eter
ethical *a* etic
ethics *n.* etică
etiquette *n* etichetă
etymology *n.* etim<ilogie
eunuch *n* eunuc
evacuate *v. t* a evacua
evacuation *n* evacuare
evade *v. t* a evada
evaluate *v. t* a evalua
evaporate *v. i* a evapora
evasion *n* sustragere
even *a* egal
even *adv* chiar (şi)
even *v. t* a face egal (cu)
evening *n* seară

event *n* eveniment
eventually *adv.* eventual
ever *adv* vreodată
evergreen *a* veşnic verde
evergreen *n* plantă veşnic verde
everlasting *a.* etern
every *a* fiecare
evict *v. t* a izgoni
eviction *n* izgonire
evidence *n* mărturie
evident *a.* evident
evil *a* rău
evil *n* rău
evoke *v. t* a evoca
evolution *n* evoluţie
evolve *v.t* a se dezvolta
ewe *n* oaie
exact *a* exact
exaggerate *v. t.* a exagera
exaggeration *n.* exagerare
exalt *v. t* a înălţa
examination *n.* examen
examine *v. t* a examina
examinee *n* candidat la examen
exam'ner *n* examinator
example *n* exemplu
excavate *v. t.* a escava
excavation *n.* excavare
exceed *v.t* a depăşi (cu)
excel *v.i* a excela
excellence *n.* excelenţă
excellency *n* excelenţă
excellent *a.* excelent
except *prep* afară de
except *v. t* a excepta
exception *n* excepţie
excess *n* exces
exchange *n* lucru schimbat pe altul
exchange *v. t* a schimba (ceva) (pe)
excise *n* impozit indirect

excite *v. t* a impresiona puternic
exclaim *v.i* a exclama
exclamation *n* exclamaţie
exclude *v. t* a exclude
exclusive *a* exclusiv
excommunicate *v. t.* a excomunica
excursion *n.* excursie
excuse *n* scuză
excuse *v.t* a scuza
execute *v. t* a executa
execution *n* execuţie
executioner *n.* călău
exempt *adj* scutit (de)
exempt *v. t.* a scuti (de)
exercise *n.* exerciţiu
exercise *v. t* a exersa
exhaust *v. t.* a epuiza
exhibit *n.* exponat
exhibit *v. t* a expune
exhibition *n.* expoziţie
exile *n.* exil
exile *v. t* a exila
exist *v.i* a exista
existence *n* existenţă
exit *n.* ieşire
expand *v.t.* a desfăşura
expansion *n.* expansiune
expect *v. t* a (se) aştepta
expectation *n.* aşteptare
expedient *a* oportun
expedite *v. t.* a urgenta
expedition *n* expediţie
expel *v. t.* a elimina (din şcoală)
expend *v. t* a cheltui
expenditure *n* cheltuire
expense *n.* cheltuială
expensive *a* scump (la preţ)
experience *n* experienţă
experience *v. t.* a trăi (o întâmplare)

experiment *n* experienţă
  (ştiinţifică)
expert *a* expert
expert *n* expert
expire *v.i.* a expira
expiry *n* expirare
explain *v. t.* a explica
explanation *n* explicaţie
explicit *a.* explicit
explode *v. t.* a exploda
exploit *n* exploatare
exploit *v. t* a exploata
exploration *n* explorare
explore *v.t* a explora
explosion *n.* explozie
explosive *a* exploziv
explosive *n.* exploziv
exponent *n* exponent
export *v. t.* a exporta
export *n* export
expose *v. t* a expune
express *a* expres
express *n* tren expres
express *v. t.* a exprima
expression *n.* expresie
expressive *a.* expresiv
expulsion *n.* expulzare
extend *v. t* a extinde
extent *n.* întindere
external *a* extern
extinct *a* stins
extinguish *v.t* a stinge
extol *v. t.* a ridica în slăvi
extra *a* suplimentar
extra *adv* în plus
extract *n* extras
extract *v. t* a extrage
extraordinary *a.* extraordinar
extravagance *n* extravanţă
extravagant *a* extravagant
extreme *a* extrem
extreme *n* extremă

extremist *n* extremist
exult *v. i* a exulta
eye *n* ochi
eyeball *n* pupilă
eyelash *n* geană
eyelet *n* capsă
eyewash *n* colir

F

fable *n.* fabulă
fabric *n* structură
fabricate *v.t* a născoci
fabrication *n* născocire
fabulous *a* fabulos
facade *n* faţadă
face *n* faţa
face *v.t* a sta cu faţa spre
facet *n* faţetă
facial *a* facial
facile *a* facil
facilitate *v.t* a facilita
facility *n* facilitate
fac-simile *n* facsimil
fact *n* fapt
faction *n* fracţiune
factious *a* fracţionist
factor *n* factor
factory *n* fabrică
faculty *n* facultate
fad *n* capriciu
fade *v.i* a se ofili
faggot *n* legătură
fail *v.i* a eşua
failure *n* eşua
faint *a* leşin
faint *v.i* a leşina
fair *a* cinstit
fair *n.* bâlci

fairly *adv.* destul de
fairy *n* zână
faith *n* credință
faithful *a* fidel
falcon *n* şoim
fall *n* cădere
fall *v.i.* a cădea
fallacy *n* eroare
fallow *n* pământ nelucrat
false *a* fals
falter *v.i* a şovăi
fame *n* faimă
familiar *a* familiar
family *n* familie
famine *n* foamete
famous *a* faimos
fan *n* admirator
fanatic *a* fanatic
fanatic *n* fanatic
fancy *n* imaginație
fancy *v.t* a se simți atras de
fantastic *a* fantastic
far *adv.* departe
far *n* distanță mare
farce *n* farsă
fare *n* tarif
farewell *interj.* adio!
farewell *n* rămas bun
farm *n* fermă
farmer *n* fermier
fascinate *v.t* a fascina
fascination *n.* fascinație
fashion *n* modă
fashionable *a* la modă
fast *a* rapid
fast *adv* repede
fast *n* post
fast *v.i* a posti
fasten *v.t* a fixa
fat *a* gras
fat *n* grăsime
fatal *a* fatal

fate *n* soartă
father *n* tată
fathom *n* pătrundere a minții
fathom *v.t* a sonda
fatigue *n* oboseală
fatigue *v.t* a obosi
fault *n* vină
faulty *a* deficient
fauna *n* faună
favour *v.t* a favoriza
favour1 *n* favoare
favourable *a* favorabil
favourite *a* favorit
favourite *n* favorit
fear *n* frică
fear *v.i* a-i fi frică
fearful *a.* înspăimântător
feasible *a* realizabil
feast *n* ospăț
feast *v.i* a chefui
feat *n* faptă vitejească
feather *n* pană
feature *n* trăsătură
February *n* februarie
federal *a* federal
federation *n* federație
fee *n* taxă
feeble *a* plăpând
feed *n* alimentație
feed *v.t* a hrăni
feel *v.t* a simți
feeling *n* sentiment
feign *v.t* a simula
felicitate *v.t* a felicita
felicity *n* potrivire
fell *v.t* a trânti la pământ
fellow *n* individ
female *a* feminin
female *n* femelă
feminine *a* feminin
fence *n* gard
fence *v.t* a îngrădi (cu)

fend *v.t* a feri
ferment *n* ferment
ferment *v.t* a fermenta
fermentation *n* fermentaţie
ferocious *a* feroce
ferry *n* bac
ferry *v.t* a trece cu bacul
fertile *a* fertil
fertility *n* fertilitate
fertilize *v.t* a fertiliza
fertilizer *n* fertilizator
fervent *a* fierbinte
fervour *n* dogoare
festival *n* festival
festive *a* festiv
festivity *n* festivitate
festoon *n* ghirlandă
fetch *v.t* a se duce după
fetter *n* fiare
fetter *v.t* a pune în fiare
feud *n.* vrajbă
feudal *a* feudal
fever *n* febră
few *a* câţiva
fiasco *n* fiasco
fibre *n* fibră
fickle *a* schimbător
fiction *n* ficţiune
fictitious *a* fictiv
fiddle *v.i* a se fâţâi
fiddle *n* scripcă
fidelity *n* fidelitate
fie *interj* uf!
field *n* câmp
fiend *n* persoană diabolică
fierce *a* violent
fiery *a* arzător
fifteen *n* cinsprezece
fifty *n.* cincizeci
fig *n* smochin
fight *n* luptă
fight *v.t* a se lupta

figment *n* născocire
figurative *a* simbolic
figure *n* siluetă
figure *v.t* a schiţa
file *v.i.* a merge în rând
file *n* dosar
file *n* pilă
file *n* şlefuire
file *v.t* a clasa
file *v.t* a pili
fill *v.t* a umple
film *n* film
film *v.t* a filma
filter *n* filtru
filter *v.t* a filtra
filth *n* murdărie
filthy *a* murdar
fin *n* aripioară înotătoare
final *a* final
finance *n* finanţe
finance *v.t* a finanţa
financial *a* financiar
financier *n* capitalist
find *v.t* a găsi
fine *a* fin
fine *n* timp frumos
fine *v.t* a amenda
finger *n* deget
finger *v.t* a atinge cu degetul
finish *n* sfârşit
finish *v.t* a termina
finite *a* finit
fir *n* pin
fire *n* foc
fire *v.t* a declanşa (o armă)
firm *n.* firmă
firm *a* ferm
first *a* prim(ul)
first *adv* întâi
fiscal *a* fiscal
fish *n* peşte
fish *v.i* a pescui

fisherman *n* pescar
fissure *n* fisură
fist *n* pumn
fit *adj* în formă
fit *n* acces
fit *v.t* a corupe prin mită
fitful *a* capricios
fitter *n* persoană ce probează
five *n* cinci
fix *n* încurcătură
fix *v.t* a repara
flabby *a* fleşcăit
flag *n* steag
flagrant *a* flagrant
flame *n* flacă
flannel *n* flanelă
flare *n* pâlpâire
flare *v.i* a pâlpâi
flash *n* sclipire
flash *v.i* a trece ca fulgerul
flask *n* ploscă
flat *a* turtit
flat *n* apartament
flatter *v.t* a flata
flattery *n* flatare
flavour *n* aromă
flaw *n* spărtură
flea *n.* purice
flee *v.i* a fugi (de)
fleece *n* lână
fleece *v.t* a tunde (o oaie)
fleet *n* flotă
flesh *n* carne
flexible *a* flixibil
flicker *n* licărire
flicker *v.t* a licări
flight *n* zbor
flimsy *a* subţire
fling *v.t* a azvârli
flippancy *n* neseriozitate
flirt *n* flirt
flirt *v.i* a flirta

float *v.i* a lansa pe apă
flock *n* turmă
flock *v.i* a se aduna
flog *v.t* a biciui
flood *n* inundaţie
flood *v.t* a inunda
floor *n* podea
floor *v.t* a pardosi
flora *n* floră
florist *n* florar
flour *n* făină
flourish *v.i* a înflori
flow *n* curgere
flow *v.i* a curge
flower *n* floare
flowery *a* împodobit
fluent *a* fluent
fluid *a* fluid
fluid *n* fluid
flush *n* torent
flush *v.i* a curge şiroaie
flute *n* flaut
flute *v.i* a cânta la flaut
flutter *n* încercare riscantă
flutter *v.t* a flutura
fly *n* muscă
fly *v.i* a zbura
foam *n* spumă
foam *v.t* a face spumă
focal *a* focal
focus *n* focar
focus *v.t* a se concentra
fodder *n* nutreţ
foe *n* duşman
fog *n* ceaţă
foil *v.t* a depăşi
fold *n* cută
fold *v.t* a îndoi
foliage *n* frunziş
follow *v.t* a urma
follower *n* persoană la rând
folly *n* prostie

foment *v.t* a obloji
fond *a* preferat
fondle *v.t* a mângâia
food *n* mâncare
fool *n* prost
foolish *a* caraghios
foot *n* laba piciorului
for *conj.* pentru că
for *prep* pentru
forbid *v.t* a interzice
force *n* forţă
force *v.t* a forţa
forceful *a* puternic
forcible *a* viguros
forearm *n* antebraţ
forearm *v.t* a înarma din vreme
forecast *v.t* a prognoza
forefather *n* strămoş
forefinger *n* deget arătător
forehead *n* frunte
foreign *a* străin
foreigner *n* străin
foreleg *n* picior din faţă
forelock *n* zuluf
foreman *n* maistru
foremost *a* principal
forenoon *n* înainte de masă
forerunner *n* precursor
foresee *v.t* a prevedea
foresight *n* previziune
forest *n* pădure
forestall *v.t* a dejuca
forester *n* pădurar
forestry *n* silvicultură
foretell *v.t* a prezice
forethought *n* anticipare
forever *adv* veşnic
forewarn *v.t* a avertiza
foreword *n* prefaţă
forfeit *n* confiscare
forfeit *v.t* a pierde
forfeiture *n* confiscare

forge *n* forjă
forge *v.t* a forţa
forgery *n* falsificare
forget *v.t* a uita
forgetful *a* uituc
forgive *v.t* a ierta
forlorn *a* părăsit
form *n* formă
form *v.t.* a forma
formal *a* formal
format *n* format
formation *n* formare
former *a* anterior
former *pron* primul
formerly *adv* pe vremuri
formidable *a* formidabil
formula *n* formulă
formulate *v.t* a formula
forsake *v.t.* a părăsi
fort *n.* fort
forte *n.* forte
forth *adv.* mai departe
forthcoming *a.* care vor apărea
fortify *v.t.* a fortifica
fortitude *n.* stăpânire de sine
fort-night *n.* chenzină
fortress *n.* fortăreaţă
fortunate *a.* norocos
fortune *n.* avere
forty *n.* patruzeci
forum *n.* for
forward *a.* din faţă
forward *adv* înainte
forward *v.t* a înainta
fossil *n.* fosilă
foster *v.t.* a creşte
foul *a.* murdar
found *v.t.* a fonda
foundation *n.* fundaţie
founder *n.* întemeietor
foundry *n.* topitorie
fountain *n.* fântână

four *n.* patru
fourteen *n.* paisprezece
fowl *n.* pasăre de curte
fowler *n.* vânător de păsări
fox *n.* vulpe
frachise *n.* franciză
fraction *n.* fracție
fracture *n.* fractură
fracture *v.t* a fractura
fragile *a.* fragil
fragment *n.* fragment
fragrance *n.* parfum
fragrant *a.* parfumat
frail *a.* firav
frame *n* ramă
frame *v.t.* a înrăma
frank *a.* sincer
frantic *a.* nebunesc
fraternal *a.* frățesc
fraternity *n.* fraternitate
fratricide *n.* fratricid
fraud *n.* fraudă
fraudulent *a.* necinstit
fray *n* luptă
free *a.* gratuit
free *v.t* a elibera
freedom *n.* libertate
freeze *v.i.* a îngheța
freight *n.* marfă
French *a.* franțuzesc
French *n* limba franceză
frenzy *n.* frenezie
frequency *n.* frecvență
frequent *n.* frecvent
fresh *a.* prospăt
fret *n.* neliniște
fret *v.t.* a fi neliniștit
friction *n.* fricțiune
Friday *n.* vineri
fridge *n.* frigider
friend *n.* prieten
fright *n.* spaimă

frighten *v.t.* a speria
frigid *a.* frigid
frill *n.* volan
fringe *n.* breton
fringe *v.t* a-i face breton
frivolous *a.* frivol
frock *n.* sutană
frog *n.* broască
frolic *v.i.* a zburda
from *prep.* de la
front *a* frontal
front *n.* față
front *v.t* a fronta
frontier *n.* frontieră
frost *n.* ger
frown *n.* încruntare
frown *v.i* a se încrunta
frugal *a.* frugal
fruit *n.* fruct
fruitful *a.* rodnic
frustrate *v.t.* a frustra
frustration *n.* frustrare
fry *v.t.* a prăji
fuel *n.* combustibil
fugitive *a.* fugar
fugitive *n.* fugitiv
fulfil *v.t.* a împlini
fulfilment *n.* împlinire
full *a.* plin
full *adv.* complet
fullness *n.* deplinătate
fully *adv.* cu desăvârșire
fumble *v.i.* a se scotoci
fun *n.* veselie
function *n.* funcție
functionary *n.* funcționar
fund *n.* fond
fundamental *a.* fundamental
funeral *n.* înmormântare
fungus *n.* ciupercă
funny *n.* nostim
fur *n.* blană

furious *a.* furios
furl *v.t.* a înfăşura
furnace *n.* furnal
furnish *v.t.* a mobila
furniture *n.* mobilă
furrow *n.* brazdă
further *a* mai mult
further *adv.* mai departe
fury *n.* furie
fuse *n* fitil
fuse *v.t.* a (se) topi
fusion *n.* fuziune
fuss *n.* zarvă
fuss *v.i* a face zarvă
futile *a.* inutil
futility *n.* zădărnicie
future *n* viitor

gabble *v.i.* a bolborosi
gadfly *n.* tăun
gag *n.* truc
gag *v.t.* a truca
gaiety *n.* veselie
gain *n* câştig
gain *v.t.* a câştiga
gainsay *v.t.* a contrazice
gait *n.* mers
galaxy *n.* galaxie
gale *n.* vânt puternic
gallant *a.* galant
gallantry *n.* galanterie
gallery *n.* galerie
gallon *n.* galon
gallop *n.* galop
gallop *v.t.* a galopa
gallows *n.* . spânzurătoare
galore *adv.* din belşug

galvanize *v.t.* a galvaniza
gamble *n* joc de noroc
gamble *v.i.* a risca
gambler *n.* jucător
game *n.* joc
game *v.i* a juca pe bani
gander *n.* gâscan
gang *n.* gaşcă
gangster *n.* gangster
gap *n* gaură
gape *v.i.* a căsca
garage *n.* garaj
garb *n.* veşmânt
garb *v.t* a înveşmânta
garbage *n.* gunoi
garden *n.* grădină
gardener *n.* grădinar
gargle *v.i.* a gargarisi
garland *n.* ghirlandă
garlic *n.* usturoi
garment *n.* îmbrăcăminte
garter *n.* jartieră
gas *n.* gaz
gasket *n.* garnitură
gasp *n.* suspin adânc
gasp *v.i* a gâfâi
gastric *a.* gastric
gate *n.* poartă
gather *v.t.* a aduna
gauge *n.* măsură-standard
gauntlet *n.* mănuşă (de armură)
gay *a.* imoral
gaze *n* privire fixă
gaze *v.t.* a contempla
gazette *n.* gazetă
gear *n.* viteză
geld *v.t.* a castra
gem *n* nestemată
gender *n.* gen
general *a.* general
generally *adv.* general
generate *v.t.* a genera

generation *n.* generare
generator *n.* generator
generosity *n.* generozitate
generous *a.* generos
genius *n.* geniu
gentle *a.* genil
gentleman *n.* gentleman
gentry *n.* mică nobilime
genuine *a.* sincer
geographer *n.* geograf
geographical *a.* geografic
geography *n.* geografie
geological *a.* geologic
geologist *n.* geolog
geology *n.* geologie
geometrical *a.* geometric
geometry *n.* geometrie
germ *n.* germen
germicide *n.* bactericid
germinate *v.i.* a germina
germination *n.* germinație
gerund *n.* gerunziu
gesture *n.* faptă
get *v.t.* a ajunge
ghastly *a.* palid
ghost *n.* duh
giant *n.* gigant
gibbon *n.* gibon
gibe *n* glumă răutăcioasă
gibe *v.i.* a glumi răutăcios
giddy *a.* amețitor
gift *n.* cadou
gifted *a.* înzestrat
gigantic *a.* gigantic
giggle *v.i.* a chicoti
gild *v.t.* a auri
gilt *n* aurire
ginger *n.* ghimbir
giraffe *n.* girafă
gird *v.t.* a lega la mijloc,
girder *n.* grindă
girdle *n.* cingătoare

girdle *v.t* a încinge
girl *n.* fată
girlish *a.* de fată
gist *n.* esență
give *v.t.* a da
glacier *n.* ghețar
glad *a.* bucuros
gladden *v.t.* a (se) înveseli
glamour *n.* farmec
glance *n.* aruncătură de privire
glance *v.i.* a arunca o privire (la)
gland *n.* glandă
glare *n.* strălucire orbitoare
glare *v.i* a străluci orbitor
glass *n.* pahar
glaze *n* luciu
glaze *v.t.* a căpăta luciu
glazier *n.* geamgiu
glee *n.* compoziție muzicală
glide *v.t.* a aluneca
glider *n.* planorist
glimpse *n.* viziune rapidă
glitter *n* scânteiere
glitter *v.i.* a scânteia
globe *n.* glob
gloom *n.* întuneric
gloomy *a.* întunecos
glorification *n.* glorificare
glorify *v.t.* a glorifica
glorious *a.* glorios
glory *n.* glorie
gloss *n.* luciu
glossary *n.* glosar
glossy *a.* lucios
glove *n.* mănușă
glow *v.i.* a luci
glow *n* luciu
glucose *n.* glucoză
glue *n.* lipici
glut *n* săturare
glut *v.t.* a ghiftui
glutton *n.* lacom

gluttony *n.* lăcomie
glycerine *n.* glicerină
go *v.i.* a merge
goad *n.* imbold
goad *v.t* a îmboldi vitele
goal *n.* țintă
goat *n.* capră
gobble *v.i* a se îndopa
goblet *n.* cupă
god *n.* zeu
goddess *n.* zeiță
godhead *n.* divinitate
godly *a.* evlavios
godown *n.* antrepozit
godsend *n.* noroc neprevăzut
gold *n.* aur
golden *a.* auriu
goldsmith *n.* aurar
golf *n.* golf
gong *n.* gong
good *a.* bun
good *n* bine
good-bye *interj.* la revedere
goodness *n.* bunătate
goodwill *n.* bunăvoință
goose *n.* gâscă
gooseberry *n.* agriș
gorgeous *a.* splendid
gorilla *n.* gorilă
gospel *n.* evanghelie
gossip *n.* bârfă
gourd *n.* tărtăcuță
gout *n.* gută
govern *v.t.* a guverna
governance *n.* autoritate
governess *n.* guvernantă
government *n.* guvern
governor *n.* guvernator
gown *n.* halat
grab *v.t.* a apuca
grace *n.* grație
grace *v.t.* a înzestra

gracious *a.* grațios
gradation *n.* gradație
grade *n.* categorie
grade *v.t* a clasa
gradual *a.* gradual
graduate *n* recipient gradat
graduate *v.i.* a absolvi
graft *n.* altoi
graft *v.t* a altoi
grain *n.* grână
grammar *n.* gramatică
grammarian *n.* gramatician
gramme *n.* gram
gramophone *n.* gramofon
grand *a.* măreț
grandeur *n.* grandoare
grant *n* alocație
grant *v.t.* a acorda
grape *n.* strugure
graph *n.* grafic
graphic *a.* grafic
grapple *n.* cârlig
grapple *v.i.* a se lupta
grasp *n* strânsoare
grasp *v.t.* a strânge
grass *n* iarbă
grate *n.* vatră
grate *v.t* a rade
grateful *a.* recunoscător
gratification *n.* gratificație
gratis *adv.* gratis
gratitude *n.* recunoștință
gratuity *n.* bacșiș
grave *a.* grav
grave *n.* mormânt
gravitate *v.i.* a gravita
gravitation *n.* gravitație
gravity *n.* gravitate
graze *n* rosătură
graze *v.i.* a roade
grease *n* grăsime
grease *v.t* a unge

greasy *a.* unsuros
great *a* măreţ
greed *n.* lăcomie
greedy *a.* lacom
Greek *n.* grec
Greek *a* grecesc
green *a.* verde
green *n* (culoare) verde
greenery *n.* verdeaţă
greet *v.t.* a întâmpina
grenade *n.* grenadă
grey *a.* gri
greyhound *n.* ogar
grief *n.* necaz
grievance *n.* plângere
grieve *v.t.* a se necăji
grievous *a.* amarnic
grind *v.i.* a trudi
grinder *n.* maşină de pisat
grip *n* apucare
grip *v.t.* a apuca
groan *n* geamăt
groan *v.i.* a geme
grocer *n.* băcan
grocery *n.* băcănie
groom *n.* mire
groom *v.t* a ţesăla (un cal)
groove *n.* făgaş
groove *v.t* a scobi
grope *v.t.* a căuta pe bâjbâite
gross *a* grosolan
gross *n.* masă
grotesque *a.* grotesc
ground *n.* teren
group *n.* grup
group *v.t.* a (se) grupa
grow *v.t.* a creşte
grower *n.* producător
growl *n* mârîială

growl *v.i.* a mârâi
growth *n.* crestere
grudge *n* pică
grudge *v.t.* ciudă
grumble *v.i.* a mormăi
grunt *n.* infanterist
grunt *v.i.* a grohăi
guarantee *n.* garanţie
guarantee *v.t* a garanta
guard *n* gardă
guard *v.i.* a păzi
guardian *n.* gardian
guerilla *n.* gherilă
guess *n.* ghiceală
guess *v.i* a ghici
guest *n.* musafir
guidance *n.* călăuzire
guide *v.t.* a călăuzi
guide *n.* ghid
guild *n.* organizaţie
guile *n.* viclenie
guilt *n.* vină
guilty *a.* vinovat
guise *n.* veşmânt
guitar *n.* chitară
gulf *n.* golf
gull *n* pescăruş
gull *n.* credul
gull *v.t* a înşela
gulp *n.* înghiţitură
gum *n.* gingie
gun *n.* pistol
gust *n.* rafală
gutter *n.* rigolă
guttural *a.* gutural
gymnasium *n.* gimnaziu
gymnast *n.* gimnast
gymnastic *a.* gimnastic
gymnastics *n.* gimnastică

H

habeas corpus *n.* ?
habit *n.* obicei
habitable *a.* locuibil
habitat *n.* loc al unei plante
habitation *n.* habitaţie
habituate *v. t.* a deprinde
hack *v.t.* a ciopârţi
hag *n.* surpătură
haggard *a.* buimăcit
haggle *v.i.* a se tocmi
hail *n.* grindină
hail *v.i* a ploua cu grindină
hail *v.t* a striga,
hair *n* păr
hale *a.* viguros
half *a* pe jumătate
half *n.* jumătate
hall *n.* hol
hallmark *n.* marcaj
hallow *v.t.* a sfinţi
halt *n* haltă
halt *v. t.* a se opri
halve *v.t.* a înjumătăţi
hamlet *n.* cătun
hammer *n.* ciocan
hammer *v.t* a ciocăni
hand *n* mână
hand *v.t* a înmâna
handbill *n.* foaie volantă
handbook *n.* manual
handcuff *n.* cătuşe
handcuff *v.t* a încătuşa
handful *n.* un pumn
handicap *n* handicap
handicap *v.t.* a handicapa
handicraft *n.* meserie
handiwork *n.* muncă manuală
handkerchief *n.* batistă

handle *n.* mâner
handle *v.t* a mânui
handsome *a.* frumos
handy *a.* îndemânatic
hang *v.t.* a atârna
hanker *v.i.* a râvni la
haphazard *a.* întâmplător
happen *v.t.* a se întâmpla
happening *n.* întâmplare
happiness *n.* fericire
happy *a.* fericit
harass *v.t.* a hărţui
harassment *n.* hărţuire
harbour *n.* port
harbour *v.t* a adăposti
hard *a.* greu
harden *v.t.* a întări
hardihood *n.* îndrăzneală
hardly *adv.* cu greu
hardship *n.* dificultate
hardy *adj.* rezistent
hare *n.* iepure de câmp
harm *n.* rău
harm *v.t* a răni
harmonious *a.* armonios
harmonium *n.* armoniu
harmony *n.* armonie
harness *n.* ham
harness *v.t* a înhăma
harp *n.* harpă
harsh *a.* aspru
harvest *n.* recoltă
haste *n.* grabă
hasten *v.i.* a se grăbi
hasty *a.* grăbit
hat *n.* pălărie
hatchet *n.* baltag
hate *n.* ură
hate *v.t.* a urî
haughty *a.* semeţ
haunt *n* loc de întâlnire
haunt *v.t.* a bântui

have *v.t.* a avea
haven *n.* port
havoc *n.* dezastru
hawk *n* şoim
hawker *n* negustor ambulant
hawthorn *n.* măceş
hay *n.* fân
hazard *n.* hazard
hazard *v.t* a (se) hazarda
haze *n.* ceaţă uşoară
hazy *a.* ceţos
he *pron.* el
head *n.* cap
head *v.t* a conduce
headache *n.* durere de cap
heading *n.* titlu
headlong *adv.* pornit
headstrong *a.* încăpăţânat
heal *v.i.* a vindeca
health *n.* sănătate
healthy *a.* sănătos
heap *n.* morman
heap *v.t* a îngrămădi
hear *v.t.* a auzi
hearsay *n.* zvon
heart *n.* inimă
hearth *n.* vatră
heartily *adv.* din toată inima
heat *n.* căldură
heat *v.t* a încălzi
heave *v.i.* a se înălţa
heaven *n.* rai
heavenly *a.* divin
hedge *n.* gard viu
hedge *v.t* a îngrădi
heed *n* băgare de seamă
heed *v.t.* a lua în seamă
heel *n.* călcâi
hefty *a.* robust
height *n.* înălţime
heighten *v.t.* a înălţa
heinous *a.* ticălos

heir *n.* moştenitor
hell *a.* iad
helm *n.* cârmă
helmet *n.* cască
help *n* ajutor
help *v.t.* a ajuta
helpful *a.* de ajutor
helpless *a.* neputincios
helpmate *n.* tovarăş
hemisphere *n.* emisferă
hemp *n.* cânepă
hen *n.* găină
hence *adv.* de aici înainte
henceforth *adv.* de acum încolo
henceforward *adv.* de azi înainte
henchman *n.* agent
her *a* al ei
her *pron.* pe ea
herald *n.* vestitor
herald *v.t* a vesti
herb *n.* iarbă
herd *n.* cireadă
here *adv.* aici
hereabouts *adv.* pe aici
hereafter *adv.* de azi înainte
hereditary *n.* ereditar
heredity *n.* ereditate
heritable *a.* apt de a moşteni
heritage *n.* moştenire
hermit *n.* pustnic
hermitage *n.* pustnicie
hernia *n.* hernie
hero *n.* erou
heroic *a.* eroic
heroine *n.* eroină
heroism *n.* eroism
herring *n.* herig
hesitant *a.* şovăitor
hesitate *v.i.* a ezita
hesitation *n.* ezitare
hew *v.t.* a despica (cu securea)
heyday *n.* floare

hibernation *n.* hirbernare
hiccup *n.* sughiț
hide *n.* piele de animal
hide *v.t* a (se) ascunde
hideous *a.* hidos
hierarchy *n.* ierarhie
high *a.* înalt
highly *adv.* cât se poate de
Highness *n.* Alteța
highway *n.* autostradă
hilarious *a.* vesel
hilarity *n.* veselie
hill *n.* deal
hillock *n.* deluşor
him *pron.* el
hinder *v.t.* a împiedica
hindrance *n.* obstacol
hint *n.* indiciu
hint *v.i* a sugera
hip *n* şold
hire *n.* închiriere
hire *v.t* a închiria
hireling *n.* mercenar
his *pron.* a lui
hiss *n* şuierat (de şarpe)
hiss *v.i* a şuiera
historian *n.* istoric
historic *a* . istoric
historical *a.* istoric
history *n.* istorie
hit *n* lovitură
hit *v.t.* a lovi
hitch *n.* hop
hither *adv.* încoace
hitherto *adv.* până acum
hive *n.* stup
hoarse *a.* răguşit
hoax *n.* păcăleală
hoax *v.t* a păcăli
hobby *n.* pasiune
hobby-horse *n.* cal de lemn
hockey *n.* hochei

hoist *v.t.* a ridica
hold *n.* prindere
hold *v.t* a ține
hole *n* gaură
hole *v.t* a găuri
holiday *n.* sărbătoare
hollow *a.* scobit
hollow *n.* scobitură
hollow *v.t* a se scobi,
holocaust *n.* holocaust
holy *a.* sfânt
homage *n.* omagiu
home *n.* casă
homicide *n.* omucidere
homoeopath *n.* homeopat
homogeneous *a.* omogen
honest *a.* sincer
honesty *n.* sinceritate
honey *n.* miere
honeycomb *n.* turtă de miere
honeymoon *n.* lună de miere
honorarium *n.* onorariu
honorary *a.* de onoare
honour *n.* onoare
honour *v. t* a onora
honourable *a.* onorabil
hood *n.* glugă
hoodwink *v.t.* a lega la ochi
hoof *n.* copită
hook *n.* cârlig
hooligan *n.* huligan
hoot *n.* huiduială
hoot *v.i* a huidui
hop *n* omitere
hop *v. i* a omite
hope *n* speranță
hope *v.t.* a spera
hopeful *a.* încrezător
hopeless *a.* disperat
horde *n.* hoardă
horizon *n.* orizont
horn *n.* corn

hornet *n.* bărzăun
horrible *a.* oribil
horrify *v.t.* a îngrozi
horror *n.* oroare
horse *n.* cal
horticulture *n.* horticultură
hose *n.* furtun
hosiery *n.* magazin de tricotaje
hospitable *a.* ospitalier
hospital *n.* spital
hospitality *n.* ospitalitate
host *n.* gazdă
hostage *n.* ostatec
hostel *n.* cămin
hostile *a.* ostil
hostility *n.* ostilitate
hot *a.* fierbinte
hotchpotch *n.* ghiveci
hotel *n.* hotel
hound *n.* copoi
hour *n.* oră
house *n* casă
house *v.t* a adăposti
how *adv.* cum
however *adv.* oricum
however *conj* totuşi
howl *n* urlet
howl *v.t.* a urla
hub *n.* centru
hubbub *n.* învălmăşeală
huge *a.* imens
hum *n* zumzăit
hum *v. i* a zumzăi
human *a.* uman
humane *a.* uman
humanitarian *a* umanitar
humanity *n.* umanitate
humanize *v.t.* a umaniza
humble *a.* umil
humdrum *a.* monoton
humid *a.* umed
humidity *n.* umiditate

humiliate *v.t.* a umili
humiliation *n.* umilinţă
humility *n.* modestie
humorist *n.* umorist
humorous *a.* comic
humour *n.* umor
hunch *n.* cocoaşă
hundred *n.* sută
hunger *n* foame
hungry *a.* flămând
hunt *n* vânătoare
hunt *v.t.* a vâna
hunter *n.* vânător
huntsman *n.* vânător
hurdle1 *n.* obstacol
hurl *v.t.* a arunca
hurrah *interj.* ura!
hurricane *n.* uragan
hurry *n* grabă
hurry *v.t.* a grăbi
hurt *n* rană
hurt *v.t.* a durea
husband *n* soţ
husbandry *n.* agricultură
hush *n* tăcere
hush *v.i* a face să tacă
husk *n.* teacă
husky *a.* voinic
hut *n.* colibă
hyaena, hyena *n.* hienă
hybrid *a.* corcit
hybrid *n* corcitură
hydrogen *n.* hidrogen
hygiene *n.* igienă
hygienic *a.* igienic
hymn *n.* imn religios
hyperbole *n.* hiperbolă
hypnotism *n.* hipnotism
hypnotize *v.t.* a hipnotiza
hypocrisy *n.* ipocrizie
hypocrite *n.* ipocrit
hypocritical *a.* prefăcut

hypothesis *n.* ipoteză
hypothetical *a.* ipotetic
hysteria *n.* isterie
hysterical *a.* isteric

I *pron.* eu
ice *n.* gheață
iceberg *n.* aisberg
icicle *n.* țurțur
icy *a.* înghețat
idea *n.* idee
ideal *a.* ideal
ideal *n* ideal
idealism *n.* idealism
idealist *n.* idealist
idealistic *a.* idealist
idealize *v.t.* a idealiza
identical *a.* identic
identify *v.t.* a identifica
identity *n.* identitate
idiom *n.* dialect
idiomatic *a.* idiomatical
idiot *n.* idiot
idiotic *a.* prostesc
idle *a.* trândav
idleness *n.* vanitate
idler *n.* leneș
idol *n.* idol
idolater *n.* idolatru
if *conj.* dacă
ignoble *a.* de jos
ignorance *n.* ignoranță
ignorant *a.* ignorant
ignore *v.t.* a ignora
ill *a.* bolnav
ill *adv.* cu greu
ill *n* rău

illegal *a.* ilegal
illegibility *n.* ilizibilitate
illegible *a.* neciteț
illegitimate *a.* nelegitim
illicit *a.* ilicit
illiteracy *n.* analfabetism
illiterate *a.* incult
illness *n.* boală
illogical *a.* ilogic
illuminate *v.t.* a ilumina
illumination *n.* iluminare
illusion *n.* iluzie
illustrate *v.t.* a ilustra
illustration *n.* ilustrare
image *n.* imagine
imagery *n.* plasticitate
imaginary *a.* imaginar
imagination *n.* imaginație
imagine *v.t.* a imagina
imitate *v.t.* a imita
imitation *n.* imitație
imitator *n.* imitator
immaterial *a.* imaterial
immature *a.* imatur
immaturity *n.* imaturitate
immeasurable *a.* nemăsurat
immediate *a* imediat
immemorial *a.* străvechi
immense *a.* imens
immensity *n.* imensitate
immerse *v.t.* a înmuia
immersion *n.* imersiune
immigrant *n.* imigrant
immigrate *v.i.* a imigra
immigration *n.* imigrație
imminent *a.* iminent
immodest *a.* prezumțios
immodesty *n.* lipsă de modestie
immoral *a.* imoral
immorality *n.* imoralitate
immortal *a.* imortal
immortality *n.* imortalitate

immortalize *v.t.* a imortaliza
immovable *a.* (de) nemişcat
immune *a.* imun
immunity *n.* imunitate
immunize *v.t.* a imuniza
impact *n.* impact
impart *v.t.* a împărtăşi
impartial *a.* imparţial
impartiality *n.* imparţialitate
impassable *a.* de netrecut
impasse *n.* impas
impatience *n.* nerăbdare
impatient *a.* nerăbdător
impeach *v.t.* a blama
impeachment *n.* blam
impede *v.t.* a împiedica
impediment *n.* impediment
impenetrable *a.* de nepătruns
imperative *a.* imperativ
imperfect *a.* imperfect
imperfection *n.* imperfecţiune
imperial *a.* imperial
imperialism *n.* imperialism
imperil *v.t.* a primejdui
imperishable *a.* nepieritor
impersonal *a.* impersonal
impersonate *v.t.* a personifica
impersonation *n.* personificare
impertinence *n.* impertinenţă
impertinent *a.* impertinent
impetuosity *n.* impetuozitate
impetuous *a.* impetuos
implement *n.* instrument
implement *v.t.* a executa
implicate *v.t.* a implica
implication *n.* implicaţie
implicit *a.* implicit
implore *v.t.* a implora
imply *v.t.* a implica
impolite *a.* nepoliticos
import *n.* import
import *v.t.* a importa

importance *n.* importanţă
important *a.* important
impose *v.t.* a impune
imposing *a.* impunător
imposition *n.* impunere
impossibility *n.* imposibilitate
impossible *a.* imposibil
impostor *n.* impostor
imposture *n.* impostură
impotence *n.* ipotenţă
impotent *a.* ipotent
impoverish *v.t.* a împovăra
impracticability *n.* impractibilitate
impracticable *a.* impracticabil
impress *v.t.* a impresiona
impression *n.* impresie
impressive *a.* impresionant
imprint *n.* imprimare
imprint *v.t.* a imprima
imprison *v.t.* a întemniţa
improper *a.* nepotrivit
impropriety *n.* necuviinţă
improve *v.t.* a îmbunătăţi
improvement *n.* îmbunătăţire
imprudence *n.* imprudenţă
imprudent *a.* imprudent
impulse *n.* impuls
impulsive *a.* impulsiv
impunity *n.* impunitate
impure *a.* impur
impurity *n.* impuritate
impute *v.t.* a imputa
in *prep.* în
inability *n.* inabilitate
inaccurate *a.* inexact
inaction *n.* nemişcare
inactive *a.* inactiv
inadmissible *a.* inadmisibil
inanimate *a.* monoton
inapplicable *a.* inaplicabil
inattentive *a.* neatent

inaudible a. de neauzit
inaugural a. inaugurat
inauguration n. inaugurare
inauspicious a. neatent
inborn a. înnăscut
incalculable a. incalculabil
incapable a. incapabil
incapacity n. incapacitate
incarnate a. încarnat
incarnate v.t. a încarna
incarnation n. încarnare
incense v.t. a tămâia
incense n. tămâie
incentive n. a tămâia
inception n. început
inch n. incie
incident n. incident
incidental a. incidental
incite v.t. a incita
inclination n. înclinaţie
incline v.i. a înclina
include v.t. a include
inclusion n. includere
inclusive a. inclus
incoherent a. incoerent
income n. venit
incomparable a. incomparabil
incompetent a. incompetent
incomplete a. incomplet
inconsiderate a. nesocotit
inconvenient a. incomod
incorporate a. încorporat
incorporate v.t. a încorpora
incorporation n. incorporare
incorrect a. incorect
incorrigible a. incorigibil
incorruptible a. incoruptibil
increase n sporire
increase v.t. a spori
incredible a. incredibil
increment n. încorporat
incriminate v.t. a incrimina

incubate v.i. a cloci(ouă)
inculcate v.t. a inculca
incumbent a oblibatoriu
incumbent n. beneficiar
incur v.t. a atrage asupra sa
incurable a. incurabil
indebted a. îndatorat
indecency n. indecenţă
indecent a. indecent
indecision n. nehotărâre
indeed adv. în(tr-)adevăr
indefensible a. fără apărare
indefinite a. nedefinit
indemnity n. asigurare
indentification n. identificare
independence n. independenţă
independent a. independent
indescribable a. de nedescris
index n. index
Indian a. indian
indicate v.t. a indica
indication n. inticaţie
indicative a. indicative
indicator n. indicator
indict v.t. a urmări
indictment n. acuzare
indifference n. indiferenţă
indifferent a. indiferent
indigenous a. indigen
indigestible a. indigest
indigestion n. indigestie
indignant a. indignat
indignation n. indignaţie
indigo n. indigo
indirect a. indirect
indiscipline n. indisciplină
indiscreet a. indiscret
indiscretion n. indiscreţie
indiscriminate a. indiscriminat
indispensable a. indispensabil
indisposed a. indispus
indisputable a. indiscutabil

indistinct *a.* indistinct
individual *a.* individual
individualism *n.* individualism
individuality *n.* individualitate
indivisible *a.* indivizibil
indolent *a.* indolent
indomitable *a.* de neâmblânzit
indoor *a.* intern
indoors *adv.* înăuntru
induce *v.t.* a convinge
inducement *n.* convingere
induct *v.t.* a induce
induction *n.* inducere
indulge *v.t.* a face pe plac
indulgence *n.* indulgenţă
indulgent *a.* indulgent
industrial *a.* industrial
industrious *a.* sârguincios
industry *n.* industrie
ineffective *a.* ineficace
inert *a.* inert
inertia *n.* inerţie
inevitable *a.* inevitabil
inexact *a.* inexact
inexorable *a.* inexorabil
inexpensive *a.* ieftin
inexperience *n.* lipsă de
    experienţă
inexplicable *a.* inexplicabil
infallible *a.* infailibil
infamous *a.* infam
infamy *n.* infamie
infancy *n.* minorat
infant *n.* minor
infanticide *n.* pruncucidere
infantile *a.* infantil
infantry *n.* infanterie
infatuate *v.t.* a suci capul (cuiva)
infatuation *n.* a suci capul
    (cuiva)
infect *v.t.* a infecta
infection *n.* infecţie

infectious *a.* infecţios
infer *v.t.* a deduce (din)
inference *n.* raţionament
inferior *a.* inferior
inferiority *n.* inferioritate
infernal *a.* infern
infinite *a.* infinit
infinity *n.* infinitate
infirm *a.* debil
infirmity *n.* infirmitate
inflame *v.t.* a înflăcăra
inflammable *a.* inflamabil
inflammation *n.* inflamaţie
inflammatory *a.* inflamator
inflation *n.* inflaţie
inflexible *a.* inflexibil
inflict *v.t.* a da (o lovitură etc.)
influence *n.* influenţă
influence *v.t.* a influenţa
influential *a.* influent
influenza *n.* val (de entuziasm
    etc.)
influx *n.* afluenţă
inform *v.t.* a informa
informal *a.* fără forme legale
information *n.* informaţie
informative *a.* informativ
informer *n.* informator
infringe *v.t.* a contraveni la
infringement *n.* infracţiune
infuriate *v.t.* a înfuria
infuse *v.t.* a face o infuzie de
infusion *n.* infuzie
ingrained *a.* impregnat
ingratitude *n.* nerecunoştinţă
ingredient *n.* ingredient
inhabit *v.t.* a locui
inhabitable *a.* locuibil
inhabitant *n.* locuitor
inhale *v.i.* a inhala
inherent *a.* inerent
inherit *v.t.* a moşteni

inheritance *n.* moştenire
inhibit *v.t.* a împiedica
inhibition *n.* inhibiţie
inhospitable *a.* neospitalier
inhuman *a.* inuman
inimical *a.* potrivnic
inimitable *a.* inimitabil
initial *a.* iniţial
initial *n.* iniţială
initial *v.t* a scrie cu iniţiale
initiate *v.t.* a iniţia
initiative *n.* iniţiativă
inject *v.t.* a injecta
injection *n.* injecţie
injudicious *a.* nechibzuit
injunction *n.* ordin
injure *v.t.* a răni
injurious *a.* jignitor
injury *n.* rană
injustice *n.* nedreptate
ink *n.* cerneală
inkling *n.* idee vagă
inland *adv.* spre interior
inland *a.* interior
inmate *n.* locatar
inmost *a.* lăuntric
inn *n.* han
innate *a.* înnăscut
inner *a.* cerc (al ţintei)
innermost *a.* cel mai intim
innings *n.* mandat
innocence *n.* inocenţă
innocent *a.* inocent
innovate *v.t.* a inova
innovation *n.* inovaţie
innovator *n.* inovator
innumerable *a.* nenumărat
inoculate *v.t.* a inocula
inoculation *n.* inoculare
inoperative *a.* inoperant
inopportune *a.* inoportun
input *n.* (mărime de) intrare

inquest *n.* anchetă
inquire *v.t.* a se informa (despre)
inquiry *n.* cercetare
insane *a.* nebun
insanity *n.* demenţă
insatiable *a.* nesătul
inscribe *v.t.* a înscrie
inscription *n.* inscripţie
insect *n.* insectă
insecticide *n.* insecticid
insecure *a.* nesigur
insecurity *n.* nesiguranţă
insensibility *n.* insensibilitate
insensible *a.* insensibil
inseparable *a.* inseparabil
insert *v.t.* a introduce
insertion *n.* inserţie
inside *a* intern
inside *adv.* înăuntru
inside *prep.* înăuntrul
inside *n.* interior
insight *n.* pătrundere
insignificance *n.* lipsă de
  importanţă
insignificant *a.* nesemnificativ
insincere *a.* nesincer
insincerity *n.* nesinceritate
insinuate *v.t.* a insinua
insinuation *n.* insinuare
insipid *a.* insipid
insipidity *n.* insipiditate
insist *v.t.* a insista
insistence *n.* insistenţă
insistent *a.* insistent
insolence *n.* insolenţă
insolent *a.* insoloent
insoluble *n.* insolubil
insolvency *n.* insolvenţă
insolvent *a.* insolvent
inspect *v.t.* a inspecta
inspection *n.* inspecţie
inspector *n.* inspector

inspiration *n.* inspirație
inspire *v.t.* a inspira
instability *n.* instabilitate
install *v.t.* a instala
installation *n.* instalație
instalment *n.* rată
instance *n.* exemplu
instant *a.* instant
instant *n.* instant
instantaneous *a.* instantaneu
instantly *adv.* instantaneu
instigate *v.t.* a instiga
instigation *n.* instigare
instinct *n.* instinct
instinctive *a.* instinctiv
institute *n.* institut
institution *n.* instituție
instruct *v.t.* a instructa
instruction *n.* instrucție
instructor *n.* instructor
instrument *n.* instrument
instrumental *a.* instrumental
insubordinate *a.* nedisciplinat
insubordination *n.* indisciplina
insufficient *a.* insuficient
insular *a.* insular
insularity *n.* caracter de insulă
insulate *v.t.* a izola
insulation *n.* izolare
insulator *n.* izolator
insult *n.* insultă
insult *v.t.* a insulta
insupportable *a.* insuportabil
insurance *n.* asigurare
insure *v.t.* a asigura
insurgent *n.* răsculat
insurgent *a.* răsculat
insurmountable *a.* de neânvins
insurrection *n.* insurecție
intact *a.* intact
intangible *a.* intangibil
integral *a.* integral

integrity *n.* integritate
intellect *n.* intelect
intellectual *a.* intelectual
intellectual *n.* intelectual
intelligence *n.* inteligență
intelligent *a.* inteligent
intelligentsia *n.* intelectualitate
intelligible *a.* inteligibil
intend *v.t.* a intenționa
intense *a.* intens
intensify *v.t.* a intensifica
intensity *n.* intensitate
intensive *a.* intensiv
intent *a.* hotărât
intent *n.* intenție
intention *n.* intenție
intentional *a.* intenționat
intercept *v.t.* a intercepta
interception *n.* interceptare
interchange *n.* alternanță
interchange *v.* a schimba (idei)
intercourse *n.* relații sexuale
interdependence *n.*
   interdependență
interdependent *a.*
   interdependent
interest *n.* interes
interested *a.* interesat
interesting *a.* interesant
interfere *v.i.* a interveni
interference *n.* interferență
interim *n.* provizorat
interior *a.* interior
interior *n.* interior
interjection *n.* interjecție
interlock *v.t.* a încleşta
interlude *n.* interludiu
intermediary *n.* intermediar
intermediate *a.* intermediar
interminable *a.* interminabil
intermingle *v.t.* a (se) amesteca
intern *v.t.* a interna

internal *a.* intern
international *a.* internaţional
interplay *n.* joc combinat
interpret *v.t.* a interpreta
interpreter *n.* interpret
interrogate *v.t.* a interoga
interrogation *n.* interogaţie
interrogative *a.* interogativ
interrogative *n* interogativ
interrupt *v.t.* a întrerupe
interruption *n.* întrerupere
intersect *v.t.* a intersecta
intersection *n.* intersecţie
interval *n.* interval
intervene *v.i.* a interveni
intervention *n.* intervenţie
interview *n.* interviu
interview *v.t.* a intervieva
intestinal *a.* intestinal
intestine *n.* intestin
intimacy *n.* intimitate
intimate *a.* intim
intimate *v.t.* a sugera
intimation *n.* sugestie
intimidate *v.t.* a intimida
intimidation *n.* intimidare
into *prep.* în
intolerable *a.* intolerabil
intolerance *n.* intoleranţă
intolerant *a.* intolerant
intoxicant *n.* băutură alcoolică
intoxicate *v.t.* a intoxica
intoxication *n.* intoxicaţie
intransitive *a. (verb)* intranzitiv
intricate *a.* încurcat
intrigue *n* intrigă
intrigue *v.t.* a intriga
intrinsic *a.* intim
introduce *v.t.* a prezenta
introduction *n.* introducere
introductory *a.* introductiv
introspect *v.i.* a se cerceta pe sine

introspection *n.* introspecţie
intrude *v.t.* a băga cu forţa (în)
intrusion *n.* prezenţă nepotrivită
intuition *n.* intuiţie
intuitive *a.* intuitiv
invade *v.t.* a invada
invalid *a.* infirm
invalid *a.* care n-are putere legală
invalid *n* invalid
invalidate *v.t.* a invalida
invaluable *a.* inestimabil
invasion *n.* invazie
invective *n.* invectivă
invent *v.t.* a inventa
invention *n.* invenţie
inventive *a.* inventiv
inventor *n.* inventator
invert *v.t.* a inversa
invest *v.t.* a investi
investigate *v.t.* a investiga
investigation *n.* investigaţie
investment *n.* investiţie
invigilate *v.t.* a supraveghea
invincible *a.* de neânvins
inviolable *a.* inviolabil
invisible *a.* invizibil
invitation *n* invitaţie
invite *v.t.* a invita
invocation *n.* invocare
invoice *n.* factură
invoke *v.t.* a invoca
involve *v.t.* a implica
inward *a.* intern
inwards *adv.* în interior
irate *a.* mâniat
ire *n.* furie
Irish *a.* irlandez
Irish *n.* Irlandeză
irksome *a.* supărător
iron *n.* fier de călcat
iron *v.t.* a călca

ironical *a.* ironic
irony *n.* ironie
irradiate *v.i.* a iradia
irrational *a.* irațional
irreconcilable *a.* incompatibil
irrecoverable *a.* incomparabil
irregular *a.* neregulat
irregularity *n.* neregularitate
irrelevant *a.* irelevant
irrespective *a.* independent (de)
irresponsible *a.* iresponsabil
irrigate *v.t.* a iriga
irrigation *n.* irigare
irritable *a.* iritabil
irritant *a.* iritant
irritant *n.* iritant
irritate *v.t.* a irita
irritation *n.* iritare
irruption *n.* erupție
island *n.* insulă
isle *n.* insulă
isolate *v.t.* a izola
isolation *n.* izolare
issue *n.* problemă
issue *v.i.* a rezulta (din)
it *pron.* acesta, aceasta
Italian *a.* italian
Italian *n.* Italiană
italic *a.* italic
itch *n.* mâncărime
itch *v.i.* a-l mânca pielea
item *n.* articol
ivory *n.* fildeş
ivy *n* iederă

J

răsuflate

jack *n.* individ
jack *v.t.* a renunța la
jackal *n.* şacal
jacket *n.* jachetă
jade *n.* învelitoare
jail *n.* jad
jailer *n.* temnicer
jam *n.* dulceață
jam *v.t.* a strivi
jar *n.* borcan
jargon *n.* jargon
jasmine, jessamine *n.* iasomie
jaundice *n.* prejudecăți
jaundice *v.t.* a stârni invidia
javelin *n.* lance
jaw *n.* maxilar
jay *n.* gaiță
jealous *a.* gelos
jealousy *n.* gelozie
jean *n.* doc
jeer *v.i.* a-şi bate joc (de)
jelly *n.* jeleu
jeopardize *v.t.* a primejdui
jeopardy *n.* primejdie
jerk *n.* nenoricit
jerky *a.* zdruncinător
jersey *n.* jerseu
jest *n.* farsă
jest *v.i.* a face glume
jet *n.* țâşnitură
Jew *n.* evreu
jewel *n.* bijuterie
jewel *v.t.* a împodobi cu bijuterii
jeweller *n.* bijutier
jewellery *n.* bijuterii
jingle *n.* clinchet
jingle *v.i.* a zăngăni
job *n.* serviciu
jobber *n.* intermediar
jobbery *n.* speculă (la bursă)
jocular *a.* poznaş
jog *v.t.* a zdruncina

join *v.t.* a se ataşa (unui grup)
joiner *n.* tâmplar
joint *n.* articulaţie
jointly *adv.* impreună
joke *n.* glumă
joke *v.i.* a glumi
joker *n.* glumeţ
jolly *a.* jovial
jolt *n.* zguduitură
jolt *v.t.* a zdruncina
jostle *n.* ciocnire
jostle *v.t.* a îmbrânci
jot *n.* iotă
jot *v.t.* a mâzgăli
journal *n.* cotidian
journalism *n.* jurnalism
journalist *n.* jurnalist
journey *n.* călătorie
journey *v.i.* a călători
jovial *a.* jovial
joviality *n.* jovialitate
joy *n.* bucurie
joyful, joyous *a* bucuros
judge *n.* judecată
judge *v.i.* a judeca
judgement *n.* judecată
judicial *a.* judiciar
judicious *a.* chibzuit
jug *n.* urcior
juggle *v.t.* a jongla
juggler *n.* jongler
juice *n* suc
juicy *a.* zemos
jumble *n.* talmeş-balmeş
jumble *v.t.* a (se) amesteca
jump *n.* săritură
jump *v.i* a sări
junction *n.* intersecţie
juncture *n.* încheietură
jungle *n.* junglă
junior *a.* junior
junior *n.* junior

junk *n.* resturi
jurisdiction *n.* jurisdicţie
jurisprudence *n.* jurisprudenţă
jurist *n.* jurist
juror *n.* jurat
jury *n.* juraţi
juryman *n.* jurat
just *a.* drept
just *adv.* numai
justice *n.* justiţie
justifiable *a.* justificabil
justification *n.* justificare
justify *v.t.* a justifica
jute *n.* iută
juvenile *a.* juvenil

keen *a.* înfocat
keep *v.t.* a păstra
keeper *n.* îngrijitor
keepsake *n.* amintire
kennel *n.* coteţ
kerchief *n.* broboadă
kernel *n.* boabă
kerosene *n.* gaz lampant
ketchup *n.* sos picant de roşii
kettle *n.* ibric
key *n.* cheie
key *v.t* a închide cu cheie
kick *n.* lovitură cu piciorul
kick *v.t.* a lovi cu piciorul
kid *n.* puşti
kidnap *v.t.* a răpi
kidney *n.* rinichi
kill *v.t.* a ucide
kiln *n.* cuptor
kin *n.* neam
kind *a* amabil

kind *n.* gen
kindergarten ; *n.* grădiniţă
kindle *v.t.* a incedia
kindly *adv.* cu gentileţe
king *n.* rege
kingdom *n.* regat
kinship *n.* înrudire
kiss *n.* sărut
kiss *v.t.* a săruta
kit *n.* vas mic (de lemn)
kitchen *n.* bucătărie
kite *n.* uliu
kith *n.* prieteni
kitten *n.* pisicuţă
knave *n.* escroc
knavery *n.* escrocherie
knee *n.* genunchi
kneel *v.i.* a îngenunchea
knife *n.* cuţit
knight *n.* cavaler
knight *v.t.* a face cavaler
knit *v.t.* a împleti
knock *v.t.* a ciocăni (în)
knot *n.* nod
knot *v.t.* a înnoda
know *v.t.* a şti
knowledge *n.* ştiinţă

label *n.* etichetă
label *v.t.* a eticheta
labial *a.* labial
laboratory *n.* laborator
labour *v.i.* a (se) trudi
labour *n.* trudă
labourer *n.* salahor
labyrinth *n.* labirint
lace *v.t.* a lega în şnururi

lace *n.* panglică
lachrymose *a.* plângăreţ
lack *n.* lipsă
lack *v.t.* a fi lipsit de
lackey *n.* lacheu
lacklustre *a.* lipsit de culoare
laconic *a.* laconic
lactometer *n.* lactometru
lactose *n.* lactoză
lacuna *n.* lacună
lacy *a.* de dantela turna
lad *n.* flăcău
ladder *n.* scară
lade *v.t.* a încărca
ladle *n.* polonic
ladle *v.t.* a turna
lady *n.* doamnă
lag *v.i.* a zăbovi
laggard *n.* molâu
lagoon *n.* lagună
lair *n.* vizuină
lake *n.* lac
lama *n.* lada
lamb *n.* miel
lambkin *n.* mieluşel
lame *a.* schilod
lame *v.t.* a schilodi
lament *n* lament
lament *v.i.* a se lamenta
lamentable *a.* lamentabil
lamentation *n.* lamentare
laminate *v.t.* a lamina
lamp *n.* lanternă
lampoon *n.* pamflet
lampoon *v.t.* a scrie pamflete
lance *n.* suliţă
lance *v.t.* a străpunge cu suliţa
lancer *n.* lăncier
lancet *a.* lanţetă
land *n.* pământ
land *v.i.* a ateriza
landing *n.* aterizare

landscape *n.* peisaj
lane *n.* trecătoare
language *n.* limbaj
languish *v.i.* a lâncezi
lank *a.* leşcăit
lantern *n.* felinar
lap *n.* poală
lapse *n* răstimp
lapse *v.i.* a decădea
lard *n.* osânză topită
large *a.* larg
largesse *n.* largheţe
lark *n.* ciocârlie
lascivious *a.* lasciv
lash *n* geană
lash *n* lovitură cu biciul
lass *n.* fetişcană
last *adv.* ultima dată
last *n* ultima clipă
last *v.i.* a dura
last1 *a.* ultimul
lasting *a.* durabil
lastly *adv.* în sfârşit
latch *n.* zăvor
late *a.* târziu
late *adv.* cu întârziere
lately *adv.* în ultimul timp
latent *a.* latent
lath *n.* şipcă
lathe *n.* strung
lather *n.* spumă (de săpun
latitude *n.* latitudine
latrine *n.* latrină
latter *a.* mai târziu
lattice *n.* zăbrele
laud *n* imn de laudă
laud *v.t.* a elogia
laudable *a.* lăudabil
laugh *n.* râs
laugh *v.i* a râde
laughable *a.* de râs
laughter *n.* râs

launch *n.* lansare a unei nave
launch *v.t.* a lansa (o navă) la apă
launder *v.t.* a spăla (şi a călca)
laundress *n.* spălătoreasă
laundry *n.* lengerie de spălat
laureate *a.* laureat
laurel *n.* dafin
lava *n.* lavă
lavatory *n.* toaletă
lavender *n.* levănţică
lavish *a.* risipitor (cu)
lavish *v.t.* a risipi
law *n.* lege
lawful *a.* conform legii
lawless *a.* fără de lege
lawn *n.* pajişte
lawyer *n.* avocat
lax *a.* destins
laxative *n.* laxativ
laxative *a* laxativ
laxity *n.* destindere
lay *n* întindere
lay *a.* laic
lay *v.t.* a culca
layer *n.* persoană care aşază
layman *n.* laic
laze *v.i.* a trândăvi
laziness *n.* lene
lazy *n.* leneş
lea *n.* păşune
leach *v.t.* a filtra
lead *n.* conducere
lead *n.* prioritate
lead *v.t.* a conduce
leaden *a.* de plumb
leader *n.* lider
leadership *n.* direcţie
leaf *n.* frunză
leaflet *n.* foaie volantă
leafy *a.* frunzos
league *n.* ligă
leak *n.* scurgere (a unui lichid)

leak *v.i.* a curge
leakage *n.* scurgere de gaz
lean *n.* înclinare
lean *v.i.* a de înclina
leap *n* salt
leap *v.i.* a sări peste
learn *v.i.* a învăţa
learned *a.* învăţat
learner *n.* şcolar
learning *n.* învăţătură
lease *n.* închiriere
lease *v.t.* a închiria
least *a.* cel mai puţin
least *adv.* cel mai puţin
leather *n.* piele
leave *n.* rămas bun
leave *v.t.* a pleca
lecture *n.* lectură
lecture *v* a face morală
lecturer *n.* conferenţiar
ledger *n.* registru
lee *n.* adăpost
leech *n.* lipitoare
leek *n.* praz
left *a.* stâng
left *n.* stânga
leftist *n* membru din stânga
leg *n.* picior
legacy *n.* succesiune
legal *a.* legal
legality *n.* legalitate
legalize *v.t.* a legaliza
legend *n.* legendă
legendary *a.* legendar
legible *a.* lizibil
legion *n.* legiune
legionary *n.* legionar
legislate *v.i.* a face legi
legislation *n.* legislaţie
legislative *a.* legislativ
legislator *n.* legislator
legislature *n.* legislatură

legitimacy *n.* legitimitate
legitimate *a.* legitim
leisure *n.* răgaz
leisurely *a.* care nu e grăbit
leisurely *adv.* cu încetul
lemon *n.* lămâie
lemonade *n.* limonadă
lend *v.t.* a împrumuta
length *n.* lungime
lengthen *v.t.* a lungi
lengthy *a.* lung
lenience, leniency *n.* indulgenţă
lenient *a.* indulgent
lens *n.* lentilă
lentil *n.* linte
Leo *n.* zodia Leu
leonine *a* leonin
leopard *n.* leopard
leper *n.* lepros
leprosy *n.* lepră
leprous *a.* lepros
less *a.* mai puţin
less *adv.* mai puţin
less *n* cantitate mai mică
less *prep.* fără
lessen *v.t* a (se) micşora
lesser *adv.* mai mic
lesson *n.* lecţie
lest *conj.* numai să nu
let *v.t.* a lăsa
lethal *a.* letal
lethargic *a.* letargic
lethargy *n.* letargie
letter *n* scrisoare
level *a* nivelat
level *n.* nivel
level *v.t.* a nivela
lever *n.* pârghie
leverage *n.* pârghie
levity *n.* uşurinţă
levy *n.* percepere
levy *v.t.* a percepe

lewd *a.* neruşinat
lexicography *n.* lexicografie
lexicon *n.* vocabular
liability *n.* răspundere
liable *a.* răspunzător
liaison *n.* legătură
liar *n.* mincinos
libel *v.t.* a calomnia
libel *n.* calomnie
liberal *a.* liberal
liberalism *n.* liberalism
liberality *n.* liberalitate
liberate *v.t.* a elibera
liberation *n.* eliberare
liberator *n.* eliberator
libertine *n.* libertin
liberty *n.* libertate
librarian *n.* bibliotecar
library *n.* librărie
licence *n.* licenţă
license *v.t.* a autoriza
licensee *n.* deţinător al autorizaţiei
licentious *a.* libertin
lick *v.t.* a linge
lick *n* calomnie
lid *n.* capac
lie *n* minciună
lie *v.i* a fi întins,
lie *v.i.* a minţi
lien *n.* privilegiu
lieu *n.* loc
lieutenant *n.* locotenent
life *n* viaţă
lifeless *a.* fără viaţă
lifelong *a.* pentru toată viaţa
lift *n.* ridicare
lift *v.t.* a se ridica
light *a* uşor
light *n.* lumină
light *v.t.* a aprinde (un foc)
lighten *v.i.* a lumina

lighter *n.* brichetă
lignite *n.* lignit
like *v.t.* a-i plăcea
like *a.* asemănător cu
like *conj.* ca
like *n.* seamăn
likelihood *n.* verosimilitate
likely *a.* probabil
liken *v.t.* a face asemănător (cu)
likeness *n.* asemănare
likewise *adv.* de asemenea
liking *n.* plac
lilac *n.* culoarea liliacului
lily *n.* liliac
limb *n.* cracă
limber *n* mlădios
limber *v.t.* a ataşa chesonul
lime *n.* clei de prins păsări
lime *n.* lămâie mică
lime *v.t* a încleia
limelight *n.* lumină oxihidrică
limit *n.* limită
limit *v.t.* a limita
limitation *n.* limitare
limited *a.* limitat
limitless *a.* fără limită
line *n.* linie
line *v.t.* a alinia
line *v.t.* a linia
lineage *n.* număr de rânduri
linen *n.* pânză (de in)
lingo *n.* dialect
linguist *n.* lingual
linguistic *a.* lingvistic
linguistics *n.* lingvistică
lining *n* dublură
link *n.* verigă (de lanţ)
link *v.t* a împreuna
linseed *n.* sămânţă de in
lion *n* leu
lioness *n.* leoaică
lip *n.* buză

liquefy *v.t.* a (se) lichefia
liquid *a.* lichid
liquid *n* lichid
liquidate *v.t.* a lichida
liquidation *n.* lichidare
liquor *n.* băutură (alcoolică)
lisp *n* freamăt (de frunze)
lisp *v.t.* a (se) bâlbâi
list *n.* listă
list *v.t.* a lista
listen *v.i.* a asculta
listener *n.* ascultător
listless *a.* apatic
lists *n.* liste
literacy *n.* cultură generală
literal *a.* de tipar
literate *a.* ştiutor de carte
literature *n.* literatură
litigant *n.* litigiu
litigate *v.t.* a da în litigiu
litigation *n.* litigiu
litre *n.* litru
litter *v.t.* a făta
litter *n.* targă
little *n.* distanţă mică
little *a.* mic
little *adv.* puţin
littoral *a.* de litoral
liturgical *a.* liturgic
live *a.* în viaţă
live *v.i.* a trăi
lively *a.* plin de viaţă
liver *n.* ficat
livery *n.* livrea
living *a.* viu
living *n* trai
lizard *n.* şopârlă
load *n.* încărcătură
load *v.t.* a încărca
loadstar *n.* steaua polară
loadstone *n.* magnet natural
loaf *n.* pâine întreagă

loaf *v.i.* a hoinări
loafer *n.* hoinar
loan *n.* împrumut
loan *v.t.* a da cu împrumut
loath *a.* greţos
loathe *v.t.* a-i fi silă
loathsome *a.* respingător
lobby *n.* culoar
lobe *n.* lob (de frunză)
lobster *n.* homar
local *a.* local
locale *n.* loc al unei acţiuni
locality *n.* aşezare
localize *v.t.* a localiza
locate *v.t.* a situa
location *n.* locaţie
lock *n* zăvor
lock *n.* încuietoare
lock *v.t* a încuia
locker *n.* cufăr
locket *n.* medalion
locomotive *n.* locomotivă
locus *n.* loc geometric
locust *n.* lăcustă
locution *n.* locuţiune
lodge *n.* colibă
lodge *v.t.* a adăposti
lodging *n.* locuinţă
loft *n.* pod (de casă)
lofty *a.* semeţ
log *n.* butuc
logarithim *n.* logaritm
loggerhead *n.* bulgăre de răşină
logic *n.* logică
logical *a.* logic
logician *n.* logician
loin *n.* muşchi (de vită)
loiter *v.i.* a hoinări
loll *v.i.* a atârna
lollipop *n.* acadea
lone *a.* singuratic
loneliness *n.* singurătate

lonely *a.* singur
lonesome *a.* solitar
long *adv* vreme îndelungată
long *a.* lung
longevity *n.* longevitate
longing *n.* poftă nestăvilită
longitude *n.* longitudine
look *n* privire
look *v.i* a se uita(la)
loom *n* ţesătorie
loom *v.i.* a se întrezări
loop *n.* lupă
loop-hole *n.* portiţă de scăpare
loose *a.* nelegat
loose *v.t.* a dezlega
loosen *v.t.* a slăbi,
loot *n.* pradă
loot *v.i.* a lua ca pradă
lop *n.* vreascuri
lop *v.t.* a tăia
lord *n.* stăpân
lordly *a.* domnesc
lordship *n.* rang de lord
lore *n.* doctrină
lorry *n.* camion
lose *v.t.* a pierde
loss *n.* pierdere
lot *n* sorţi
lot *n.* mulţime
lotion *n.* loţiune
lottery *n.* loterie
lotus *n.* lotus
loud *a.* ţipător
lounge *n.* lenevire
lounge *v.i.* a tândăli
louse *n.* păduche
lovable *a.* amabil
love *n* iubire
love *v.t.* a iubi
lovely *a.* fermecător
lover *n.* amant
loving *a.* iubitor

low *adv.* redus
low *a.* scăzut
low *n.* jos
low *v.i.* a mugi
lower *v.t.* a coborî (vocea)
lowly *a.* smerit
loyal *a.* loial
loyalty *n.* loialitate
lubricant *n.* lubrifiant
lubricate *v.t.* a lubrifica
lubrication *n.* lubrificare
lucent *a.* transparent
lucerne *n.* lucernă
lucid *a.* lucid
lucidity *n.* luciditate
luck *n.* noroc
luckily *adv.* din fericire
luckless *a.* fără noroc
lucky *a.* norocos
lucrative *a.* profitabil
lucre *n.* profit
luggage *n.* bagaj
lukewarm *a.* călduţ
lull *n.* moment de linişte
lull *v.t.* a legăna
lullaby *n.* cântec de leagăn
luminary *n.* corp luminos
luminous *a.* liminos
lump *n.* bucată (fără formă
lump *v.t.* a aşeza grămadă
lunacy *n.* năzbâtie
lunar *a.* de semilună
lunatic *a.* lunatic
lunatic *n.* alienat mintal
lunch *v.i.* a prânzi
lunch *n.* prânz
lung *n* plămân
lunge *n.* pripon
lunge *v.i* a se repezi
lurch *n.* încurcătură
lurch *v.i.* a se împletici
lure *n.* momeală

lure *v.t.* a ademeni
lurk *v.i.* a sta la pândă
luscious *a.* pompos
lush *a.* luxuriant
lust *n.* desfrâu
lustful *a.* desfrânat
lustre *n.* lustră
lustrous *a.* sclipitor
lusty *a.* viguros
lute *n.* lut
luxuriance *n.* abundenţă
luxuriant *a.* luxuriant
luxurious *a.* luxos
luxury *n.* lux
lynch *v.t.* a linşa
lyre *n.* liră
lyric *n.* liric
lyric *a.* liric
lyrical *a.* liric

magical *a.* magic
magician *n.* magician
magisterial *a.* magistral
magistracy *n.* magistratură
magistrate *n.* magistratură
magnanimity *n.* mărinimie
magnanimous *a.* mărinimos
magnate *n.* magnat
magnet *n.* magnet
magnetic *a.* magnetc
magnetism *n.* magnetism
magnificent *a.* magnific
magnify *v.t.* a mări
magnitude *n.* magnitudine
magpie *n.* coţofană
mahogany *n.* mahon
mahout *n.* cameristă

maid *n.* fecioară
maiden *a* feciorelnic
maiden *n.* nume de fată
mail *n* armură
mail *n.* poştă
mail *v.t.* a expedia
main *a* principal
main *n* principal
mainly *adv.* în mare parte
mainstay *n.* sprijin
maintain *v.t.* a menţine
maintenance *n.* menţinere
maize *n.* porumb
majestic *a.* maiestuos
majesty *n.* majestate
major *a.* major
major *n* maior
majority *n.* majoritate
make *n* marcă
make *v.t.* a face
maker *n.* creator
maladroit *a.* neândemânatic
malaria *n.* malarie
malcontent *a.* nemulţumit
male *a.* bărbătesc
male *n* mascul
malediction *n.* afurisenie
malefactor *n.* răufăcător
malice *n.* pizmă
malign *a* malign
malign *v.t.* a vorbi de rău
malignancy *n.* reavoinţă
malignity *n.* reavoinţă
malleable *a.* maleabil
malnutrition *n.* subalimentare
malpractice *n.* neglijenţă (a unui medic)
malt *n.* malţ
mal-treatment *n.* maltratare
mamma *n.* mamă
mammal *n.* mamifer
mammary *a.* mamar

mammon *n.* Mamon
mammoth *a* mamut
mammoth *n.* monstruos
man *v.t.* a îmbărbăta
man *n.* bărbat
manage *v.t.* a administra
manageable *a.* uşor de mânuit
management *n.* conducere (de afaceri)
manager *n.* administrator
managerial *a.* directorial
mandate *n.* mandat
mandatory *a.* mandatorial
mane *n.* coamă
manes *n.* spiritele strămoşilor
manful *a.* bărbătesc
manganese *n.* mangan
manger *n.* iesle
mangle *v.t.* a sfâşia
mango *n* mando
manhood *n.* vârsta bărbăţiei
mania *n* manie
maniac *n.* maniac
manicure *n.* manichiură
manifest *a.* evident
manifest *v.t.* a scoate în evidenţă
manifestation *n.* manifestare
manifesto *n.* manifest
manifold *a.* variat
manipulate *v.t.* a manipula
manipulation *n.* manipulare
mankind *n.* omenire
manlike *a.* omenesc
manliness *n* bărbăţie
manly *a.* bărbătesc
mannerism *n.* manierism
mannerly *a.* manierat
manoeuvre *n.* manevră
manoeuvre *v.i.* a manevra
manor *n.* moşie
mansion *n.* casă mare
manual *a.* manual

manual *n* manual (carte)
manufacture *n* manufactură
manufacture *v.t.* a manufactura
manufacturer *n* fabricant
manumission *n.* eliberare
manure *n.* îngrăşământ
manure *v.t.* a îngrăşa (pământul)
manuscript *n.* manuscris
many *a.* mulţi
map *v.t.* a întocmi o hartă
map *n* hartă
mar *v.t.* a strica
marathon *n.* maraton
maraud *v.i.* a prăda
marauder *n.* prădător
marble *n.* marmură
march *n* (luna) martie
march *n.* marş
march *v.i* a mărşălui
mare *n.* iapă
margarine *n.* margarină
margin *n.* lizieră
marginal *a.* marginal
marigold *n.* gălbinele
marine *a.* marin
mariner *n.* matroz
marionette *n.* marionetă
marital *a.* marital
maritime *a.* maritim
mark *n.* marcă
mark *v.t* a marca
market *n* piaţă
market *v.t* a vinde pe piaţă
marketable *a.* care se poate vinde
marksman *n.* trăgător de elită
marl *n.* marnă
marmalade *n.* marmeladă
maroon *a* castaniu
maroon *n.* culoare castanie
maroon *v.t* a părăsi (pe cineva)
marriage *n.* căsătorie

marriageable *a.* de măritat
marry *v.t.* a se căsători
Mars *n* Marte
marsh *n.* baltă
marshal *n* mareşal
marshal *v.t* a rândui
marshy *a.* mlăştinos
mart *n.* sală de licitaţie
marten *n.* jder
martial *a.* marţial
martyr *n.* martir
martyrdom *n.* martiriu
marvel *n.* lucru minunat
marvel *v.i* a se minuna
marvellous *a.* uimitor
mascot *n.* mascotă
masculine *a.* masculin
mash *v.t* a face pireu
mash *n.* pastă
mask *n.* mască
mask *v.t.* a masca
mason *n.* zidar
masonry *n.* zidărie
masquerade *n.* mascaradă
mass *n.* majoritate
mass *v.i* a se strânge
massacre *n.* masacru
massacre *v.t.* a masacra
massage *n.* masaj
massage *v.t.* a masa
masseur *n.* maseor
massive *a.* masiv
massy *a.* greoi
mast *n.* catarg
master *n.* maestru
master *v.t.* a stăpâni
masterly *a.* de maestru
masterpiece *n.* capodoperă
mastery *n.* autoritate
masticate *v.t.* a mesteca
masturbate *v.i.* a se masturba
mat *n.* matroz

matador *n.* matador
match *n* potrivire
match *v.i.* a asorta
match *n.* chibrit
matchless *a.* fără egal
mate *n* (d. păsări) bărbătuş
mate *n.* tovarăş
mate *v.t.* a împerechea (păsări)
mate *v.t.* a uni
material *a.* material
material *n* materie
materialism *n.* materialism
materialize *v.t.* a materializa
maternal *a.* matern
maternity *n.* maternitate
mathematical *a.* matematic
mathematician *n.* matematician
mathematics *n* matematică
matinee *n.* matineu
matricide *n.* matricid
matriculate *v.t.* a înmatricula
matriculation *n.* înscriere (a
    unui student)
matrimonial *a.* matrimonial
matrimony *n.* viaţă conjugală
matrix *n* matriţă
matron *n.* matroană
matter *n.* chestiune
matter *v.i.* a avea importanţă
mattock *n.* târnăcop
mattress *n.* saltea
mature *a.* matur
mature *v.i* a maturiza
maturity *n.* maturitate
maudlin *a* plângăreţ
maul *n.* mai
maul *v.t* a sfâşia în bucăţi
maunder *v.t.* a vorbi aiurea
mausoleum *n.* mausoleu
mawkish *a.* fad
maxim *n.* maximă
maximize *v.t.* a maximiza

maximum *n* cel mai înalt grad
maximum *a.* maximă
May *n.* Mai
may *v* a putea
mayor *n.* primar
maze *n.* labirint
me *pron.* eu
mead *n.* hidromel
meadow *n.* fâneață
meagre *a.* uscățiv
meal *n.* masă
mean *v.t* a vrea
mean *a.* meschin
meander *v.i.* a șerpui
meaning *n.* semnificație
meaningful *a.* semnificativ
meaningless *a.* nesemnificativ
meanness *n.* meschinărie
means *n* avar
meanwhile *adv.* între timp
measles *n* pojar
measurable *a.* măsurabil
measure *v.t* a măsura
measure *n.* măsură
measureless *a.* fără măsură
measurement *n.* măsurătoare
meat *n.* carne
mechanic *a* mecanic
mechanic *n.* mecanic
mechanical *a.* lipsit de originalitate
mechanics *n.* mecanică
mechanism *n.* mecanism
medal *n.* medalie
median *a.* de mijloc
mediate *v.i.* a media
mediation *n.* mediație
mediation *n.* mediere
mediator *n.* mediator
medical *a.* medical
medicament *n.* medicament
medicinal *a.* medicinal

medicine *n.* medicament
medieval *a.* din evul mediu
medieval *a.* medieval
mediocre *a.* mediocru
mediocrity *n.* mediocritate
meditate *v.t.* a medita
meditative *a.* gânditor
medium *a* mijlociu
medium *n* mediu
meek *a.* blajin
meet *n.* întâlnire
meet *v.t.* a întâlni
meeting *n.* întrunire
megalith *n.* megalit
megaphone *n.* megafon
melancholic *a.* melancolic
melancholy *adj* melancolic
melancholy *n.* melancolie
melee *n.* încăierare
meliorate *v.t.* a (se) ameliora
mellow *a.* atenuat
melodious *a.* melodios
melodrama *n.* melodrama
melodramatic *a.* melodramatic
melody *n.* melodie
melon *n.* pepene
melt *v.i.* a se topi
member *n.* membru
membership *n.* calitate de membru
membrane *n.* membrană
memento *n.* memento
memoir *n.* memoriu
memorable *a.* memorabil
memorandum *n* memorandum
memorial *a* memorial
memorial *n.* memorial
memory *n.* amintire
menace *n* amenințare
menace *v.t* a amenința
mend *v.t.* a repara
mendacious *a.* fals

menial *a.* de servitor
menial *n* slugă
meningitis *n.* meningită
menopause *n.* menopauză
menses *n.* impregnat
menstrual *a.* menstrual
menstruation *n.* menstruație
mental *a.* mintal
mentality *n.* mentalitate
mention *n.* mențiune
mention *v.t.* a menționa
mentor *n.* mentor
menu *n.* meniu
mercantile *a.* negustoresc
mercenary *a.* interesat
merchandise *n.* marfă
merchant *n.* de comerț
merciful *a.* milos
merciless *adj.* nemilos
mercurial *a.* inconstant
mercury *n.* mercur
mercy *n.* milă
mere *a.* pur și simplu
merge *v.t.* a îmbina (două
   sisteme)
merger *n.* absorbire
meridian *a.* meridian
merit *n.* merit
merit *v.t* a merita
meritorious *a.* meritoriu
mermaid *n.* sirenă
merman *n.* triton
merriment *n.* veselie
   zgomotoasă
merry *a* vesel
mesh *n.* plasă
mesh *v.t* a prinde (pești etc.)
mesmerism *n.* hipnotism
mesmerize *v.t.* a hipnotiza
mess *n.* murdărie
mess *v.i* a murdări
message *n.* mesaj

messenger *n.* mesager
Messrs *n.* domnii
metabolism *n.* metabolism
metal *n.* metal
metallic *a.* metalic
metallurgy *n.* metalurgie
metamorphosis *n.* metamorfoză
metaphor *n.* metaforă
metaphysical *a.* metafizic
metaphysics *n.* metafizică
mete *v.t* a măsura
meteor *n.* meteor
meteoric *a.* meteoric
meteorologist *n.* meteorog
meteorology *n.* meteorologie
meter *n.* contor
method *n.* metodă
methodical *a.* metodic
metre *n.* metru
metric *a.* metric
metrical *a.* metric
metropolis *n.* metropolă
metropolitan *a.* metropolitan
metropolitan *n.* metropolitan
mettle *n.* ardoare
mettlesome *a.* înfocat
mew *n.* colivie de șoim
mew *v.i.* a întemnița
mezzanine *n.* mezanin
mica *n.* mică
micrometer *n.* micrometru
microphone *n.* microfon
microscope *n.* microscop
microscopic *a.* microscopic
microwave *n.* cuptor cu
   microunde
mid *a.* mijlociu
midday *n.* amiază
middle *n* mijloc
middle *a.* mijlociu
middleman *n.* mijlocitor
middling *a.* mediocru

midget *n.* miniatură
midland *n.* mijlocul ţării
midnight *n.* miezul nopţii
midriff *n.* diafragmă
midst *n* mijloc
midsummer *n.* mijloc al verii
midwife *n.* moaşă
might *n.* forţă
mighty *adj.* puternic
migrant *n.* migrator
migrate *v.i.* a migra
migration *n.* migraţiune
milch *a.* cu lapte
mild *a.* nu prea tare
mildew *n.* mucegai
mile *n.* milă
mileage *n.* distanţă în mile
milestone *n.* bornă din milă în milă
militant *a.* militant
military *a.* militar
military *n* militarii
militate *v.i.* a (se) lupta (pentru)
militia *n.* armată nepermanentă
milk *v.t.* a mulge
milk *n.* lapte
milky *a.* de lapte
mill *v.t.* a măcina
mill *n.* moară
miller *n.* morar
millet *n.* mei
milliner *n.* bărbat uşuratic
milliner *n.* modistă
millinery *n.* articole de mode
million *n.* milion
millionaire *n.* milionar
mime *n.* mim
mime *v.i* a mima
mimic *a.* imitativ
mimic *n* imitator
mimic *v.t* a imita
mimicry *n* imitaţie

minaret *n.* minaret
mince *v.t.* a toca
mind *v.t.* a se ocupa de
mind *n.* minte
mindful *a.* grijuliu (cu)
mindless *a.* neatent (la)
mine *n* mină
mine *pron.* al meu, a mea
miner *n.* miner
mineral *a* mineral
mineral *n.* mineral
mineralogy *n.* mineralogie
mingle *v.t.* a (se) amesteca
miniature *a.* în miniatură
miniature *n.* miniatură
minim *n.* doime
minimal *a.* minim
minimize *v.t.* a minimaliza
minimum *a* minim (al)
minimum *n.* minm
minion *n.* favorit
minister *v.i.* a sluji (la)
minister *n.* ministru
ministrant *a.* oficiant
ministry *n.* minister
mink *n.* nurcă
minor *n* minor
minor *a.* mai mic
minority *n.* minorotate
minster *n.* catedrală
mint *n* monetărie
mint *v.t.* a bate (monedă)
mint *n.* mentă
minus *a* negativ
minus *n* (semnul) minus
minus *prep.* minus
minuscule *a.* minuscul
minute *a.* minuţios
minute *n.* minut
minutely *adv.* în amănunt
minx *n.* ştrengăriţă
miracle *n.* miracol

miraculous *a.* miraculos
mirage *n.* miraj
mire *v.t.* a înnămoli
mire *n.* mocirlă
mirror *v.t.* a oglindi
mirror *n* oglindă
mirth *n.* veselie
mirthful *a.* vesel
misadventure *n.* întâmplare nefericită
misalliance *n.* mezalianță
misanthrope *n.* mizantrop
misapplication *n.* proastă folosire
misapprehend *v.t.* a înțelege greșit
misappropriate *v.t.* a deturna (fonduri)
misbehave *v.i.* a se purta urât
misbehaviour *n.* conduită necuviincioasă
misbelief *n.* părere greșită
miscalculate *v.t.* a calcula greșit
miscalculation *n.* calcul greșit
miscall *v.t.* a numi greșit
miscarriage *n.* avort (spontan)
miscarry *v.i.* a avorta
miscellaneous *a.* divers
miscellany *n.* amestec
mischance *n.* neșansă
mischief *n* nedreptate
mischievous *a.* neascultător
misconceive *v.t.* a interpreta fals
misconception *n.* concepție greșită
misconduct *n.* proastă administrare
misconstrue *v.t.* a se înșela asupra
miscreant *n.* ticălos
misdeed *n.* faptă rea
misdemeanour *n.* delict

misdirect *v.t.* a deruta
misdirection *n.* trimitere în direcție falsă
miser *n.* perforator în piatră
miserable *a.* vrednic de milă
miserly *a.* hrăpăreț
misery *n.* suferință
misfortune *n.* nenoroc
misgive *v.t.* a presimți rele
misgiving *n.* presimțire rea
misguide *v.t.* a călăuzi greșit
mishap *n.* pățanie
misjudge *v.t.* a judega gresit
mislead *v.t.* a abate din drum
misnomer *n.* eroare de nume
misplace *v.t.* a așeza greșit
misprint *n.* greșeală de tipar
misprint *v.t.* a tipări greșit
misrepresent *v.t.* a răstălmăci
misrule *n.* neorânduială
miss *v.t.* a-i fi dor de
miss *n.* domnișoară
missile *n.* proiectil
mission *n.* misiune
missionary *n.* misionar
missis, missus *n..* soția
missive *n.* depeșă
mist *n.* ceață
mistake *v.t.* a confunda
mistake *n.* greșeală
mister *n.* domnul
mistletoe *n.* vâsc
mistreat *v.t* a maltrata
mistress *n.* amantă
mistrust *v.t.* a nu avea încredere în
mistrust *n.* neâncredere
misty *a.* neguros
misunderstand *v.t.* a înțelege greșit
misunderstanding *n.* neânțelegere

misuse *n.* abuz
misuse *v.t.* a întrebuinţa greşit
mite *n* molie
mite *n.* para
mitigate *v.t.* a alina (suferinţa)
mitigation *n.* atenuare (a unei dureri)
mitre *n.* mitră (de episcop)
mitten *n.* mănuşi de box
mix *v.t* a amesteca
mixture *n.* amestec
moan *n.* geamăt
moan *v.i.* a spune gemând
moat *n.* groapă
mob *n.* gloată
mob *v.t.* a aclama
mobile *a.* mobil
mobility *n.* mobilitate
mobilize *v.t.* a mobiliza
mock *adj* contrafăcut
mock *v.i.* a-şi bate joc (de)
mockery *n.* batjocură
modality *n.* modalitate
mode *n.* mod
model *v.t.* a modela
model *n.* model
moderate *a.* moderat
moderate *v.t.* a modera
moderation *n.* moderaţie
modern *a.* modern
modernize *v.t.* a moderniza
modest *a.* modest
modesty *n* modestie
modicum *n.* crâmpei
modification *n.* modificare
modify *v.t.* a modifica
modulate *v.t.* a modula
moil *v.i.* a se trudi
moist *a.* umed
moisten *v.t.* a (se) umezi
moisture *n.* umiditate
molar *a* molar

molar *n.* molar
molasses *n* melasă
mole *n.* stăvilar
molecular *a.* molecular
molecule *n.* moleculă
molest *v.t.* a molesta
molestation *n.* molestare
molten *a.* produs prin topire
moment *n.* moment
momentary *a.* momentan
momentous *a.* important
momentum *n.* motrice
monarch *n.* monarh
monarchy *n.* monarhie
monastery *n.* mănăstire
Monday *n.* (ziua de) luni
monetary *a.* monetar
money *n.* bani
monger *n.* negustor
mongrel *a* fără rasă definită
monitor *n.* monitor
monk *n.* călugăr
monkey *n.* maimuţă
monochromatic *a.* monocrom
monocle *n.* monoclu
monody *n.* monodie
monogamy *n.* monogamie
monogram *n.* monogramă
monograph *n.* monografie
monolith *n.* monolit
monologue *n.* monolog
monopolist *n.* monopolist
monopolize *v.t.* a monopoliza
monopoly *n.* monopol
monosyllabic *a.* monosilabic
monosyllable *n.* monosilabă
monotheism *n.* monoteism
monotonous *a.* monoton
monotony *n* monotonie
monsoon *n.* muson
monster *n.* monstru
monstrous *a.* monstruos

month *n.* lună
monthly *adv* lunar
monthly *n* revistă lunară
monthly *a.* lunar
monument *n.* monument
monumental *a.* monumental
moo *v.i* a mugi
mood *n.* dispoziție
moody *a.* posac
moon *n.* (astr.) Lună
moor *n.* pârloagă
moor *v.t* a ancora (un vas)
moot *n.* adunare
mop *v.t.* a șterge podeaua
mop *n.* perie cu coadă
mope *v.i.* a fi mâhnit
moral *n.* morală
moral *a.* moral
morale *n.* moral (al unei armate)
moralist *n.* moralist
morality *n.* moralitate
moralize *v.t.* a face morală
 (cuiva)
morbid *a.* morbid
morbidity *n* morbiditate
more *adv* mai mult(ă)
more *a.* mai mult
moreover *adv.* de altfel
morganatic *a.* morganatic
morgue *n.* morgă
moribund *a.* muribund
morning *n.* dimineață
morose *a.* posomorât
morrow *n.* ziua următoare
morsel *n.* îmbucătură
mortal *n* muritor
mortal *a.* mortal
mortality *n.* mortalitate
mortar *v.t.* a lega cu mortar
mortgage *v.t.* a ipoteca
mortgage *n.* ipotecă
mortify *v.t.* a mortifica

mortuary *n.* morgă
mosaic *n.* mozaic
mosque *n.* moschee
mosquito *n.* țânțar
moss *n.* mlaștină
most *adv.* mai ales
most *a.* cea mai mare parte
most *n* cel mult
mote *n.* fir de praf
motel *n.* hotel cu garaj
moth *n.* fluture de noapte
mother *v.i* a îngriji ca o mamă
mother *n* mamă
motherhood *n.* maternitate
motherly *a.* de mamă
motion *v.i.* a face semn (cuiva)
motion *n.* gest
motionless *a.* fără mișcare
motivate *v* a motiva
motivation *n.* motivație
motive *n.* motiv
motley *a.* împestrițat
motor *v.i.* a călători cu
 automobilul
motor *n.* motor
motorist *n.* automobilist
mottle *n.* pată
motto *n.* deviză
mould *n* matriță
mould *n* pământ afânat
mould *v.t.* a se mucegăi
mould *n.* mucegai
mouldy *a.* mucegăit
moult *v.i.* a năpârli
mound *n.* movilă
mount *n* călărie
mount *v.t.* a urca
mount *n.* montură
mountain *n.* munte
mountaineer *n.* muntean
mountainous *a.* muntos
mourn *v.i.* a ține doliu

mourner *n.* bocitoare
mourning *n.* mâhnire
mouse *n.* şoarece
moustache *n.* mustaţă
mouth *v.t.* a apuca cu dinţii
mouth *n.* gură
mouthful *n.* îmbucătură
movable *a.* mişcător
movables *n.* bunuri mobile
move *n.* mişcare
move *v.t.* a mişca
movement *n.* mişcare
mover *n.* mobil prim
movies *n.* filme
mow *v.t.* a cosi
much *adv* (foarte) mult
much *a* mult
mucilage *n.* vâscozitate
muck *n.* lucru dezgustător
mucous *a.* mucilaginos
mucus *n.* mucozitate
mud *n.* noroi
muddle *v.t.* a ameţi,
muddle *n.* (stare de) confuzie
muffle *v.t.* bot (de porc)
muffler *n.* eşarfă
mug *n.* huligan
mulatto *n.* mulatru
mulberry *n.* dud(ă)
mule *n.* catâr
mull *n.* încurcătură
mull *v.t.* a încurca
mullion *n.* despărţire a cercevelei
multifarious *a.* multiplu
multiform *n.* multiform
multilateral *a.* multilateral
multiple *n* multiplu
multiple *a.* multiplu
multiplicand *n.* deânmulţit
multiplication *n.* multiplicare
multiply *v.t.* a multiplica
multitude *n.* multitudine

mum *a.* tăcut
mum *n* mamă
mumble *v.i.* a mormăi
mummer *n.* comediant
mummy *n* mamă
mummy *n.* mumie
mumps *n.* oreion
munch *v.t.* a amesteca
mundane *a.* lumesc
municipal *a.* municipal
municipality *n.* municipalitate
munificent *a.* foarte generos
mural *a.* pe perete
murder *n.* omor
murder *v.t.* a asasina
murderer *n.* asasin
murderous *a.* criminal
murmur *v.t.* a murmura
murmur *n.* şoaptă
muscle *n.* muşchi
muscular *a.* muscular
muse *n* muză
muse *v.i.* a medita,
museum *n.* muzeu
mush *n.* fiertură
mushroom *n.* ciupercă
music *n.* muzică
musical *a.* muzical
musician *n.* muzician
musk *n.* mosc
musket *n.* muschetă
musketeer *n.* muşchetar
muslin *n.* muselină
must *n* mucegăială
must *n.* must
must *v.* trebuie
mustache *n.* mustaţă
mustard *n.* muştar
muster *n* reuniune
muster *v.t.* a reuni
musty *a.* mucegăit
mutation *n.* mutaţie

mute *a.* mut
mute *n.* mut
mutilate *v.t.* a mutila
mutilation *n.* mutilare
mutinous *a.* răzvrătitor
mutiny *v. i* a se răscula
mutiny *n.* răscoală
mutter *v.i.* a bombăni
mutton *n.* carne de oaie
mutual *a.* reciproc
muzzle *v.t* a pune botniţă la
muzzle *n.* botniţă
my *a.* meu
myopia *n.* miopie
myriad *a* nenumărat
myriad *n.* mii şi mii
myrrh *n.* smirnă
myrtle *n.* mirt
myself *pron.* eu însumi
mysterious *a.* misterios
mystery *n.* mister
mystic *n* mistic
mystic *a.* mistic
mysticism *n.* misticism
mystify *v.t.* a înconjura de mister
myth *n.* mit
mythical *a.* mitic
mythological *a.* mitologic
mythology *n.* mitologie

nab *v.t.* a pune mâna pe
nabob *n.* bogătaş
nadir *n.* nadir
nag *v.t.* a sâcîi
nag *n.* căluţ
nagotiation *n.* negociere
nail *v.t.* a încuia (într-o discuţie)

nail *n.* nail
naive *a.* naiv
naivety *n.* naivitate
naked *a.* gol
name *n.* nume
name *v.t.* a numi
namely *adv.* anume
namesake *n.* omonim
nap *n* puf (stofă)
nap *n.* moţăială
nap *v.i.* a moţăi
nape *n.* ceafă
napkin *n.* şerveţel
narcissism *n.* narcisism
narcissus *n* narcisist
narcosis *n.* narcoz
narcotic *n.* narcotic
narrate *v.t.* a nara
narrative *a.* narativ
narrative *n.* nuvelă
narrator *n.* narator
narrow *v.t.* a strânge
narrow *a.* strâmt
nasal *a.* nazal
nascent *a.* în stare nativă
nasty *a.* obscen
natal *a.* natal
nation *n.* naţiune
national *a.* naţional
nationalism *n.* naţionaism
nationalist *n.* naţionalist
nationality *n.* naţionalitate
nationalization *n.* naţionalizare
nationalize *v.t.* a naţionaliza
native *n* nativ
native *a.* nativ
nativity *n.* naştere
natural *a.* natural
naturalist *n.* naturalist
naturalize *v.t.* a naturaliza
naturally *adv.* în mod natural
nature *n.* natură

naughty *a.* neascultător
nausea *n.* greață
nautic(al) *a.* nautic
naval *a.* naval
nave *n.* navă
navigable *a.* navigabil
navigate *v.i.* a naviga
navigation *n.* navigare
navigator *n.* navigator
navy *n.* flotă
nay *adv.* nu numai
near *adv.* în apropiere
near *prep.* aproape de
near *v.i.* a (se) apropia
nearly *adv.* îndeaproape
neat *a.* îngrijit
nebula *n.* albeață (pe ochi)
necessary *a* necesar
necessary *n.* necesar
necessitate *v.t.* a necesita
necessity *n.* necesitate
neck *n.* gât
necklace *n.* colier
necromancer *n.* necromant
necropolis *n.* necropol
nectar *n.* nectar
need *v.t.* a avea nevoie
need *n.* nevoie
needful *a.* necesar
needle *n.* ac (de cusut)
needless *a.* inutil
needs *adv.* numaidecât
needy *a.* nevoiaș
nefarious *a.* nemernic
negation *n.* negație
negative *n.* replică negativă
negative *v.t.* a contrazice
negative *a.* negativ
neglect *n* neglijare
neglect *v.t.* a neglija
negligence *n.* neglijență
negligent *a.* neglijent

negligible *a.* neglijabil
negotiable *a.* negociabil
negotiate *v.t.* a negocia
negotiator *n.* negociator
negress *n.* negresă
negro *n.* negru
neigh *n.* nechezat
neigh *v.i.* a necheza
neighbour *n.* vecin
neighbourhood *n.* cartier
neither *conj.* nici
neolithic *a.* neolitic
neon *n.* neon
nephew *n.* nepot
nepotism *n.* nepotism
Neptune *n.* Neptun
Nerve *n.* nerv
nerveless *a.* fără nervi
nervous *a.* nervos
nescience *n.* ignoranță
nest *n.* cuib
nest *v.t.* a cuibări
nestle *v.i.* a se cuibări
net *a* net
net *v.t.* a primi net
net *v.t.* a prinde în cursă
net *n.* năvod
nether *a.* inferior
nettle *n.* urzică
nettle *v.t.* a urzica
network *n.* rețea
neurologist *n.* neurolog
neurology *n.* neurologie
neurosis *n.* nevroză
neuter *a.* neutru
neuter *n* (genul) neutru
neutral *a.* imparțial
neutralize *v.t.* a neutraliza
neutron *n.* neutron
never *adv.* niciodata
nevertheless *conj.* cu toate
  acestea

new *a.* nou
news *n.* ştiri
next *adv.* următorul
next *a.* următor
nib *n.* cioc
nibble *n* ciupitură
nibble *v.t.* a ciupi
nice *a.* drăguţ
nicety *n.* precizie
niche *n.* nişă
nick *n.* crestătură (în lemn)
nickel *n.* nichel
nickname *v.t.* a porecli
nickname *n.* poreclă
nicotine *n.* nicotină
niece *n.* nepoată
niggard *n.* zgârcit
nigger *n.* om de rasă neagră
nigh *adv.* aproape
nigh *prep.* lângă
night *n.* noapte
nightingale *n.* privighetoare
nightly *adv.* în fiecare noapte
nightmare *n.* coşmar
nil *n.* nimic
nimble *a.* sprinten
nimbus *n.* nimb
nine *n.* numărul nouă
nineteen *n.* nouăsprezece
nineteenth *a.* al nouăsprezecelea
ninetieth *a.* al nouăzecilea
ninety *n.* nouăzeci
ninth *a.* al nouălea
nip *v.t* a pişca
nipple *n.* sfârc de sân
nitrogen *n.* azot
no *a.* nici un
no *adv.* nu
no *n* nu
nobility *n.* nobleţe
noble *a.* nobil
noble *n.* nobil

nobleman *n.* gentilom
nobody *pron.* nimeni
nocturnal *a.* nocturn
nod *v.i.* a-şi înclina capul
node *n.* nod
noise *n.* zgomot
noisy *a.* zgomotos
nomad *n.* nomad
nomenclature *n.* nomenclatură
nominal *a.* nominal
nominate *v.t.* a nominaliza
nomination *n.* nominalizare
nominee *n* nominalizat
nonchalance *n.* nepăsare
nonchalant *a.* indiferent
none *adv.* de loc
none *pron.* nici unul (dintre)
nonentity *n.* nonexistenţă
nonetheless *adv.* totuşi
nonpareil *n.* lucru fără pereche
nonpareil *a.* fără pereche
nonplus *v.t.* a băga în încurcătură
nonsense *n.* absurditate
nonsensical *a.* lipsit de sens
nook *n.* ungher
noon *n.* amiază
noose *n.* şnur
noose *v.t.* a prinde în laţ
nor *conj* şi nici
norm *n.* normă
norm *n.* regulă
normal *a.* normal
normalcy *n.* normalitate
normalize *v.t.* a normaliza
north *a* nordic
north *adv.* la nord
north *n.* nord
northerly *adv.* în nord
northerly *a.* de la nord
northern *a.* nordic
nose *v.t* a adulmeca
nose *n.* nas

nosegay *n.* buchet de flori
nostalgia *n.* nostalgie
nostril *n.* nară
nosy *a.* indiscret
not *adv.* nu
notability *n.* distincție
notable *a.* nabil
notary *n.* notar
notation *n.* notație
notch *n.* defileu
note *v.t.* a nota
note *n.* notiță
noteworthy *a.* demn de atenție
nothing *adv.* nicidecum
nothing *n.* nimic
notice *v.t.* a remarca
notice *n* înștiințare
notification *n.* notificare
notify *v.t.* a informa
notion *n.* noțiune
notional *a.* speculativ
notoriety *n.* notorietate
notorious *a.* notoriu
notwithstanding *adv.* în ciuda
nought *n.* nul
noun *n.* substantiv
nourish *v.t.* a nutri
nourishment *n.* hrană
novel *a.* inedit
novel *n* roman
novelette *n.* nuvelă
novelist *n.* romancier
novelty *n.* inovație
november *n.* noiembrie
novice *n.* novice
now *conj.* acum când
now *adv.* acum
nowhere *adv.* nicăieri
noxious *a.* nociv

nozzle *n.* cioc (de sculă
nuance *n.* nuanță
nubile *a.* nubil
nuclear *a.* nuclear
nucleus *n.* nucleu
nude *a.* dezbrăcat
nude` *n* nud
nudge *v.t.* a da cu cotul în
nudity *n.* ghiont
nugget *n.* bulgăre de aur
nuisance *n.* pagubă
null *a.* nul
nullification *n.* anulare
nullify *v.t.* a anula
numb *a.* amorțit
number *v.t.* a număra
number *n.* număr
numberless *a.* fără număr
numeral *a.* numeral
numerator *n.* numărător
numerical *a.* numeric
numerous *a.* numeros
nun *n.* călugări
nunnery *n.* mănăstire de
   călugărițe
nuptial *a.* nupțial
nurse *v.t* a crește (un copil)
nurse *n.* infirmieră
nursery *n.* infirmerie
nurture *v.t.* a educa
nurture *n.* creștere
nut *n* nuc
nutrition *n.* nutriție
nutritious *a.* hrănitor
nutritive *a.* nutritiv
nuzzle *v.i.* a râma
nylon *n.* nailon
nymph *n.* nimfă

O

oak *n.* stejar
oar *n.* vâslă
oarsman *n.* vâslaş
oasis *n.* oază
oat *n.* ovăz
oath *n.* jurământ
obduracy *n.* dârzenie
obdurate *a.* insensibil
obedience *n.* supunere
obedient *a.* supus
obeisance *n.* omagiu
obesity *n.* obezitate
obey *v.t.* a se supune
obituary *n* listă de decese
object *n.* obiect
object *v.t.* a obiecta
objection *n.* obiecţie
objective *a.* obiectiv
objective *n.* obiectiv
oblation *n.* ofradă
obligation *n.* obligaţie
obligatory *a.* obligatoriu
oblige *v.t.* a obliga
oblique *a.* oblic
obliterate *v.t.* a şterge
obliteration *n.* ştersătură
oblivion *n.* amnistie
oblivious *a.* uituc
oblong *a.* lunguieţ
oblong *n.* dreptunghi
obnoxious *a.* infam
obscene *a.* obscen
obscenity *n.* obscenitate
obscure *v.t.* a umbri
obscure *a.* obscur
obscurity *n.* obscuritate
observance *n.* refulă (a religiei)
observant *a.* care observă

observation *n.* observaţie
observatory *n.* observator
observe *v.t.* a observa
obsess *v.t.* a obseda
obsession *n.* obsesie
obsolete *a.* perimat
obstacle *n.* obstacol
obstinacy *n.* îndârjire
obstinate *a.* încăpăţânat
obstruct *v.t.* a astupa
obstruction *n.* obstrucţie
obstructive *a.* obstructiv
obtain *v.t.* a obţine
obtainable *a.* care se poate
    obţine
obtuse *a.* obtuz
obvious *a.* evident
occasion *v.t* a ocaziona
occasion *n.* ocazie
occasional *a.* ocazional
occasionally *adv.* ocazional
occident *n.* occident
occidental *a.* occidental
occult *a.* ocult
occupancy *n.* ocupaţie
occupant *n.* ocupant
occupation *n.* ocupaţie
occupier *n.* posesor
occupy *v.t.* a ocupa
occur *v.i.* a se întâmpla
occurrence *n.* întâmplare
ocean *n.* ocean
oceanic *a.* ioceanic
octagon *n.* octagon
octave *n.* octavă
October *n.* octombrie
ocular *a.* ocular
oculist *n.* oculist
odd *a.* bizar
oddity *n.* originalitate
odds *n.* şanse de succes
ode *n.* odă

odious *a.* odios
odour *n.* odor
offence *n.* jignire
offend *v.t.* a jigni
offender *n.* jignitor
offensive *n* ofensă
offensive *a.* ofensiv
offer *n* ofertă
offer *v.t.* a oferi
offering *n.* ofrandă
office *n.* birou
officer *n.* ofiţer
official *n* oficial
official *a.* oficial
officially *adv.* oficial
officiate *v.i.* a oficia
officious *a.* îndatoritor
offing *n.* largul mării
offset *n* compensaţie
offset *v.t.* a compensa
offshoot *n.* mlădiţă
offspring *n.* urmaş
oft *adv.* adesea
often *adv.* deseori
ogle *n* privire galeşă
ogle *v.t.* a privi galeş
oil *n.* ulei
oil *v.t* a impregna cu ulei
oily *a.* uleios
ointment *n.* unguent
old *a.* bătrân
oligarchy *n.* oligarhie
olive *n.* măslină
omen *n.* augur
ominous *a.* ameninţător
omission *n.* neglijare
omit *v.t.* a omite
omnipotence *n.* atotputernicie
omnipotent *a.* atotputernic
omnipresence *n.* omniprezenţă
omnipresent *a.* omniprezent
on *adv.* înainte

on *prep.* pe
once *adv.* o dată
one *pron.* o persoană oarecare
one *a.* unu(a)
oneness *n.* singularitate
onerous *a.* oneros
onion *n.* ceapă
only *adv.* doar
only *a.* singur
onset *n.* început
onslaught *n.* atac
onus *n.* obligaţie
onward *a.* înainte
ooze *v.i.* a se scurge încet
ooze *n.* scurgere lentă
opacity *n.* opacitate
opal *n.* opal
opaque *a.* opac
open *v.t.* a deschide
open *a.* deschis
opening *n.* deschidere
openly *adv.* (în mod) sincer
opera *n.* operă
operate *v.t.* a opera
operation *n.* operaţie
operative *a.* operativ
operator *n.* operator
opinion *n.* părere
opium *n.* opiu
opponent *n.* oponent
opportune *a.* oportun
opportunism *n.* oportunism
opportunity *n.* oportunitate
oppose *v.t.* a opune
opposite *a.* opus
opposition *n.* opoziţie
oppress *v.t.* a oprima
oppression *n.* opresion
oppressive *a.* opresiv
oppressor *n.* opresor
opt *v.t* a opta (pentru)
optic *a.* optic

optician *n.* optician
optimism *n.* optimism
optimist *n.* optimism
optimistic *a.* optimist
option *n.* opţiune
optional *a.* opţional
opulence *n.* abundenţă
opulent *a.* abundent
oracle *n.* oracol
oracular *a.* înţelept
oral *a.* oral
orange *a* portocaliu
orange *n.* portocală
oration *n.* discurs (solemn)
orator *n.* orator
oratorical *a.* oratoric
oratory *n.* retorică
orb *n.* orbită
orbit *n.* orbită
orchard *n.* livadă
orchestra *n.* orchestră
orchestral *a.* orchestral
ordeal *n.* încercare grea
order *v.t* a comanda
order *n.* ordin
orderly *n.* ordonanţă
orderly *a.* ordonat
ordinance *n.* decret
ordinary *a.* obişnuit
ordnance *n.* artilerie
ore *n.* minereu
organ *n.* organ
organic *a.* organic
organism *n.* organism
organization *n.* organizaţie
organize *v.t.* a organiza
orient *v.t.* a (se) orienta
orient *n.* orient
oriental *n* oriental
oriental *a.* oriental
orientate *v.t.* a orienta
origin *n.* origine

original *n* original
original *a.* original
originality *n.* originalitate
originate *v.t.* a produce
originator *n.* creator
ornament *n.* ornament
ornament *v.t.* a ornamenta
ornamental *a.* ornamental
orphan *n.* orfan
orphanage *n.* orfelinat
orthodox *a.* ortodox
orthodoxy *n.* ortodoxie
oscillate *v.i.* a oscila
oscillation *n.* oscilaţie
ossify *v.t.* a (se) osifica
ostracize *v.t.* a exila
ostrich *n.* struţ
other *pron.* altul, alta,
other *a.* alt, altă
otherwise *conj.* dacă nu
otherwise *adv.* altfel
otter *n.* vidră
ottoman *n.* divan
ounce *n.* uncie (28,35 g)
our *adj* nostru
oust *v.t.* a înlătura
out *adv.* afară
outbid *v.t.* a supralicita
outbreak *n.* revoltă (în masă)
outburst *n.* izbucnire
outcast *a* dat afară
outcast *n.* exilat
outcome *n.* consecinţă
outcry *n* strigăt de protest
outdo *v.t.* a epuiza
outdoor *a.* extern
outer *a.* de (din)afară
outfit *n.* echipament
outfit *v.t* a echipa
outgrow *v.t.* a creşte mai mare
outhouse *n.* şopron
outing *n.* excursie

outlandish *a.* străin
outlaw *v.t* a scoate în afara legii
outlaw *n.* persoană proscrisă
outline *v.t.* a contura
outline *n.* contur
outlive *v.i.* a supravieţui
outlook *n.* vigilenţă
outnumber *v.t.* a întrece ca
   număr
outpost *n.* avanpost
output *n.* randament
outrage *n.* ofensă
outrage *v.t.* a insulta
outright *a* complet
outright *adv.* în întregime
outrun *v.t.* a depăşi
outset *n.* început
outshine *v.t.* a întrece ca
   strălucire
outside *adv* din afară
outside *n* suprafaţă
outside *prep* afară din
outside *a.* afară de
outsider *n.* persoană din afară
outskirts *n.pl.* lizieră (a unei
   păduri)
outspoken *a.* spus clar
outstanding *a.* remarcabil
outward *a.* extern
outwardly *adv.* pe din afară
outwards *adv* (înspre) afară
outweigh *v.t.* a întrece în greutate
outwit *v.t.* a întrece
oval *n* oval
oval *a.* oval
ovary *n.* ovar
ovation *n.* ovaţie
oven *n.* cuptor
over *adv* terminat
over *prep.* peste
overact *v.t.* a şarja (un rol)
overall *adv* pretutindeni

overall *n.* halat
overboard *adv.* peste bord
overburden *v.t.* a supraîncărca
overcast *a.* acoperit cu nori
overcharge *n* preţ excesiv
overcharge *v.t.* a cere un preţ
   exagerat
overcoat *n.* pardesiu
overcome *v.t.* a învinge
overdo *v.t.* a depăşi limitele
overdose *v.t.* a lua supradoză
overdose *n.* supradoză
overdraft *n.* descoperit de cont
overdraw *v.t.* a exceda (creditul)
overdue *a.* expirat
overhaul *n.* cercetare
overhaul *v.t.* a controla din nou
overhear *v.t.* a auzi fără să vrea
overlap *v.t.* a acoperi parţial
overleaf *adv.* pe partea cealaltă
overload *n* supraîncărcare
overload *v.t.* a supraîncărca
overlook *v.t.* a trece cu vederea
overnight *adv.* peste noapte
overpower *v.t.* a domina
overrate *v.t.* a supraestima
overrule *v.t.* a fi mai puternic
   decât
overrun *v.t* a trece peste
oversee *v.t.* a nu observa
overseer *n.* supraveghetor
overshadow *v.t.* a pune în umbră
oversight *n.* supraveghere
overt *a.* clar
overtake *v.t.* a ajunge din urmă
overthrow *n* răsturnare
overthrow *v.t.* a da peste cap
overtime *n* muncă suplimentară
overtime *adv.* suplimentar
overture *n.* uvertură
overwhelm *v.t.* a copleşi
overwork *n.* muncă excesivă

overwork *v.i.* a (se) istovi
muncind
owe *v.t* a datora
owl *n.* bufniţă
own *v.t.* a poseda
own *a.* propriu
owner *n.* proprietar
ownership *n.* (drept de)
proprietate
ox *n.* bou
oxygen *n.* oxigen
oyster *n.* scoică

pace *v.i.* a merge în buiestru
pace *n* pas (măsură)
pacific *a.* paşnic
pacify *v.t.* a pacifica (o ţară)
pack *n.* pachet
pack *v.t.* a împacheta
package *n.* colet
packet *n.* pachet
packing *n.* împachetare
pact *n.* pact
pad *v.t.* a căptuşi cu perne
pad *n.* bloc cu foi detaşabile
padding *n.* vătuire
paddle *n* padelă
paddle *v.i.* a se bălăci
paddy *n.* orez nedecorticat
page *v.t.* a pagina
page *n.* pagină
pageant *n.* procesiune
pagoda *n.* pagodă
pail *n.* căldare
pain *v.t.* a supăra
pain *n.* durere
painful *a.* dureros

painstaking *a.* sârguincios
paint *v.t.* a vopsi
paint *n.* vopsea
painter *n.* pictor
painting *n.* tablou
pair *n.* pereche
pair *v.t.* a (se) împerechea
pal *n.* tovarăş
palace *n.* palat
palatable *a.* pe gustul (cuiva)
palatal *a.* palatal
palate *n.* gust delicat
pale *a* palid
pale *v.i.* a se îngălbeni (la faţă)
pale *n.* ţeapă
palette *n.* paletă
palm *n.* palmă
palm *n.* ramură de palmier
palm *v.t.* a atinge (cu palma)
palmistry *n.* chiromanţie
palpable *a.* palpabil
palpitate *v.i.* a palpita
palpitation *n.* palpitaţie
palsy *n.* paralizie
paltry *a.* fără valoare
pamper *v.t.* a răsfăţa
pamphlet *n.* pamflet
pamphleteer *n.* pamfletar
panacea *n.* panaceu
pandemonium *n.* infern
pane *n.* (ochi de) geam
panel *n.* panou
pang *n.* junghi (de durere)
panic *n.* panică
panorama *n.* panoramă
pant *n.* gâfîială
pant *v.i.* a gâfîi
pantaloon *n.* bufon
pantheism *n.* panteism
panther *n.* panteră
pantomime *n.* pantomimă
pantry *n.* cămară

papal *a.* papal
paper *n.* hârtie
par *n.* paritate
parable *n.* parabolă
parachute *n.* paraşută
parachutist *n.* paraşutist
parade *v.t.* a face paradă
parade *n.* paradă
paradise *n.* paradis
paradox *n.* paradox
paradoxical *a.* paradoxal
paraffin *n.* parafină
paragon *n.* model (de virtute etc.)
paragraph *n.* paragraf
parallel *v.t.* a compara
parallel *a.* paralel
parallelism *n.* paralelism
parallelogram *n.* paralelogram
paralyse *v.t.* a paraliza
paralysis *n.* paralizie
paralytic *a.* paralitic
paramount *n.* suprem
paramour *n.* suprem
paraphernalia *n. pl* podoabe
paraphrase *v.t.* a parafraza
paraphrase *n.* parafrază
parasite *n.* parazit
parcel *v.t.* a împărţi (în)
parcel *n.* parcelă
parch *v.t.* a (se) scoroji
pardon *n.* iertare
pardon *v.t.* a scuza
pardonable *a.* părinte
parent *n.* părinte
parentage *n.* ascendenţă (biologică)
parental *a.* părintesc
parenthesis *n.* paranteză
parish *n.* parohie
parity *n.* paritate
park *n.* parc

park *v.t.* a parca
parlance *n.* limbaj
parley *v.i* a duce tratative
parley *n.* tratativ
parliament *n.* parlament
parliamentarian *n.* parlamentar
parliamentary *a.* parlamentar
parlour *n.* vorbitor
parody *v.t.* a parodia
parody *n.* parodie
parole *n.* cuvânt (de onoare)
parricide *n.* trădător de ţară
parrot *n.* papagal
parry *n.* parare
parry *v.t.* a para (o lovitură)
parson *n.* paroh
part *v.t.* a separa
part *n.* parte
partake *v.i.* a participa la
partial *a.* parţial
partiality *n.* părtinire
participant *n.* participant
participate *v.i.* a participa
participation *n.* participare
particle *n* părticică
particular *n.* particularitate
particular *a.* particular
partiotism *n.* patriotism
partisan *n.* partizan
partition *v.t.* a diviza în părţi
partition *n.* repartiţie
partner *n.* partener
partnership *n.* parteneriat
party *n.* petrecere
pass *n* trecătoare
pass *v.i.* a trece
passage *n.* pasaj
passenger *n.* pasager
passion *n.* pasiune
passionate *a.* pasionat
passive *a.* pasiv
passport *n.* paşaport

past *n.* trecut
past *prep.* dincolo de
past *a.* trecut
paste *v.t.* a afişa
paste *n.* pastă
pastel *n.* pastel
pastime *n.* recreaţie
pastoral *a.* ciobănesc
pasture *v.t.* a paşte
pasture *n.* păşunat
pat *adv* potrivit
pat *n* gest de mângâiere
pat *v.t.* a mângâia
patch *n* petic
patch *v.t.* a petici
patent *n* brevet
patent *v.t.* a breveta
patent *a.* brevetat
paternal *a.* patern
path *n.* potecă
pathetic *a.* patetic
pathos *n.* înflăcărare
patience *n.* răbdare
patient *n* pacient
patient *a.* răbdător
patricide *n.* patricid
patrimony *n.* patrimoniu
patriot *n.* patriot
patriotic *a.* patriotic
patrol *n* patrulă
patrol *v.i.* a patrula
patron *n.* protector
patronage *n.* patronaj
patronize *v.t.* a patrona
pattern *n.* tipar (pt. croit)
paucity *n.* cantitate mică (de)
pauper *n.* cerşetor
pause *v.i.* a pune pauză
pause *n.* pauză
pave *v.t.* a pava
pavement *n.* pavaj
pavilion *n.* pavilion

paw *v.t.* a lovi cu laba
paw *n.* labă
pay *n* plată
pay *v.t.* a plăti
payable *a.* plătibil
payment *n.* sumă plătită
pea *n.* mazăre
peace *n.* pace
peaceable *a.* paşnic
peaceful *a.* liniştit
peach *n.* piersică
peacock *n.* păun
peahen *n.* păuniţă
peak *n.* pisc
pear *n.* pară
pearl *n.* perlă
peasant *n.* ţăran
peasantry *n.* ţărănime
pebble *n.* pietricică
peck *v.i.* a ciuguli
peck *n.* ciugueală
peculiar *a.* specific
peculiarity *n.* trăsătură caracteristică
pecuniary *a.* pecuniar
pedagogue *n.* pedagog
pedagogy *n.* pedagogie
pedal *n.* pedală
pedal *v.t.* a pedala
pedant *n.* pedant
pedantic *n.* pedant
pedantry *n.* pedanterie
pedestal *n.* piedestal
pedestrian *n.* pieton
pedigree *n.* rasă (de animale)
peel *n.* coajă
peel *v.t.* a curăţa de coajă
peep *n* apariţie
peep *v.i.* a apărea
peer *n.* aristocrat
peerless *a.* incomparabil
peg *v.t.* a jalona

peg *n.* cui de lemn
pelf *n.* haos
pell-mell *adv.* talmeş-balmeş
pen *v.t.* a scrie/redacta
pen *n.* stilou
penal *a.* penal
penalize *v.t.* a penaliza
penalty *n.* amendă
pencil *v.t.* a scrie cu creionul
pencil *n.* creion
pending *a* nehotărât
pending *prep.* până la
pendulum *n.* pendul
penetrate *v.t.* a penetra
penetration *n.* penetrare
penis *n.* penis
penniless *a.* fără nici un ban
penny *n.* monedă div. engleză
pension *v.t.* a pensiona
pension *n.* pensie
pensioner *n.* pensionar
pensive *a.* gânditor
pentagon *n.* pentagon
people *v.t.* a popula
people *n.* oameni de rând
pepper *n.* piper
pepper *v.t.* a pipera
per *prep.* pe
per cent *adv.* la sută
perambulator *n.* cărucior (de copil)
perceive *v.t.* a pricepe
percentage *n.* procentaj
perceptible *adj* perceptibil
perception *n.* percepţie
perceptive *a.* perceptiv
perch *v.i.* a se cocoţa
perch *n.* prăjină
perennial *n.* plantă vivace
perennial *a.* peren
perfect *a.* perfect
perfect *v.t.* a perfecta

perfection *n.* perfecţiune
perfidy *n.* perfidie
perforate *v.t.* a perfora
perforce *adv.* în mod necesar
perform *v.t.* a interpreta (un rol)
performance *n.* performanţă
performer *n.* executant
perfume *n.* parfum
perfume *v.t.* a parfuma
perhaps *adv.* poate
peril *v.t.* a primejdui
peril *n.* primejdie
perilous *a.* primejdios
period *n.* perioadă
periodical *a.* periodic
periodical *n.* publicaţie periodică
periphery *n.* periferie
perish *v.i.* a pieri
perishable *a.* pieritor
perjure *v.t* a jura fals
perjury *n.* jurământ fals
permanence *n.* permanenţă
permanent *a.* permanent
permissible *a.* permis
permission *n.* permisiune
permit *n.* autorizaţie
permit *v.t.* a permite
permutation *n.* permutare
pernicious *a.* pernicios
perpendicular *a.* perpendicular (pe)
perpendicular *n.* perpendiculară
perpetual *a.* perpetuu
perpetuate *v.t.* a perpetua
perplex *v.t.* a lăsa perplex
perplexity *n.* perplexitate
persecute *v.t.* a persecuta
persecution *n.* persecuţie
perseverance *n.* perseverenţă
persevere *v.i.* a persevera
persist *v.i.* a persista

persistence *n.* persistenţă
persistent *a.* persistent
person *n.* persoană
personage *n.* personaj
personal *a.* personal
personality *n.* personalitate
personification *n.* personificare
personify *v.t.* a personifica
personnel *n.* personal
perspective *n.* perspectivă
perspiration *n.* transpiraţie
perspire *v.i.* a transpira
persuade *v.t.* a convinge (de)
persuasion *n.* convingere
pertain *v.i.* a aparţine (de)
pertinent *a.* pertinent
perturb *v.t.* a perturba
perusal *n.* examinare atentă
peruse *v.t.* a examina cu grijă
pervade *v.t.* a se infiltra în
perverse *a.* pervers
perversion *n.* perversiune
perversity *n.* perversitate
pervert *v.t.* a perverti
pessimism *n.* pesimism
pessimist *n.* pesimist
pessimistic *a.* pesimist
pest *n.* parazit
pesticide *n.* pesticid
pestilence *n.* molimă
pet *v.t.* a mângâia
pet *n.* animal favorit
petal *n.* petală
petition *v.t.* a solicita prin petiţie
petition *n.* petiţie
petitioner *n.* petiţionar
petrol *n.* benzină
petroleum *n.* petrol
petticoat *n.* jupon
petty *a.* mărunt
petulance *n.* susceptibilitate
phantom *n.* fantomă

pharmacy *n.* farmacie
phase *n.* fază
phenomenal *a.* fenomenal
phenomenon *n.* fenomen
phial *n.* fiolă
philanthropic *a.* filantropic
philanthropist *n.* filantrop
philanthropy *n.* filantropie
philological *a.* folologic
philologist *n.* foilolog
philology *n.* filologie
philosopher *n.* filozof
philosophical *a.* filozofic
philosophy *n.* filozofie
phone *n.* telefon
phonetic *a.* fonetic
phonetics *n.* fonetică
phosphate *n.* fosfat
phosphorus *n.* fosfor
photo *n* fotografie
photograph *n* fotografie
photograph *v.t.* a fotografia
photographer *n.* fotograf
photographic *a.* fotografic
photography *n.* fotografie
phrase *v.t.* a exprima
phrase *n.* frază
phraseology *n.* frazeologie
physic *v.t.* a droga
physic *n.* medicament
physical *a.* fizic
physician *n.* medic
physicist *n.* fizician
physics *n.* fizică
physiognomy *n.* fizionomie
physique *n.* fizic
pianist *n.* pianist
piano *n.* pian
pick *n.* alegere
pick *v.t.* a alege
picket *v.t.* a posta pichete
picket *n.* pichet

pickle *v.t* a pune la saramură
pickle *n.* murătură
picnic *v.i.* a face un picnic
picnic *n.* picnic
pictorial *a.* pitoresc
picture *v.t.* a descrie
picture *n.* pictură
picturesque *a.* pitoresc
piece *n.* bucată
piece *v.t.* a asambla
pierce *v.t.* a găuri
piety *n.* pietate
pig *n.* porc
pigeon *n.* porumbel
pile *v.t.* a grămadi
pile *n.* grămadă
piles *n.* grămezi
pilfer *v.t.* a fura
pilgrim *n.* pelerin
pilgrimage *n.* pelerinaj
pill *n.* pilulă
pillar *n.* stâlp
pillow *v.t.* a servi ca pernă
pillow *n* pernă
pilot *v.t.* a pilota
pilot *n.* pilot
pimple *n.* coş (pe faţă)
pin *v.t.* a înţepa cu un ac
pin *n.* ac cu gămălie
pinch *n* ciupeală
pinch *v.t.* a ciupi
pine *v.i.* a lâncezi
pine *n.* pin
pineapple *n.* ananas
pink *a* roz
pink *n.* culoarea roz
pinnacle *n.* apogeu
pioneer *v.t.* a deschide căi noi
pioneer *n.* pionier
pious *a.* cucernic
pipe *n.* ţeavă
pipe *v.i* a cânta din fluier

piquant *a.* picant
piracy *n.* piraterie
pirate *v.t* a jefui
pirate *n.* pirat
pistol *n.* pistol
piston *n.* piston
pit *v.t.* a scoate sâmburii
pit *n.* sâmbure
pitch *n.* păcură
pitch *v.t.* a unge cu smoală
pitcher *n.* oală (de pământ)
piteous *a.* deplorabil
pitfall *n.* capcană
pitiable *a.* vrednic de milă
pitiful *a.* compătimitor
pitiless *a.* neândurător
pitman *n.* miner
pittance *n.* remuneraţie mică
pity *v.t.* a-i fi milă de
pity *n.* păcat
pivot *n.* pivot
pivot *v.i* a pivota
place *v.t.* a aşeza
place *n.* loc
plague *n* ciuma
plain *a.* simplu
plain *n.* şes
plan *v.t.* a planifica
plan *n.* plan
plane *a.* plan
plane *n* rindea
plane *v.t.* a zbura cu avionul
plane *n.* avion
planet *n.* planetă
planetary *a.* planetar
plank *n.* dulap
plant *n.* plantă
plant *v.t.* a planta
plantation *n.* plantaţie
plaster *v.t.* a aplica un plasture pe
plaster *n.* plasture
plate *n.* farfurie

platform *n.* platformă
platonic *a.* platonic
play *v.i.* a juca
playcard *n.* carte de joc
player *n.* jucător
plead *v.i.* a pleda
pleasant *a.* plăcut
pleasantry *n.* joacă
please *v.t.* a mulţumi
pleasure *n.* plăcere
plebiscite *n.* plebiscit
pledge *v.t.* a amaneta
pledge *n.* amanet
plenty *n.* belşug
plight *n.* stare
pliteness *n.* politeţe
plod *v.i.* a toci
plot *v.t.* a pune la cale
plot *n.* parcelă
plough *v.i* a face zbârcituri
plough *n.* plug
ploughman *n.* plugar
pluck *n* jumulire
pluck *v.t.* a jumuli
plug *v.t.* a astupa
plug *n.* cep
plum *n.* prună
plumber *n.* instalator
plunder *n* pradă
plunder *v.t.* a prăda
plural *a.* plural
plurality *n.* pluralitate
plus *a.* plus
plus *n* semnul adunării
ply *n* cută
ply *v.t.* a îmbia (cu)
pneumonia *n* pneumonie
pocket *v.t.* a băga în buzunar
pocket *n.* buzunar
pod *n.* teacă
poem *n.* poem
poesy *n.* poezie

poet *n.* poet
poetaster *n.* poet mediocru
poetess *n.* poetă
poetic *a.* poetic
poetics *n.* artă poetică
poetry *n.* poezie
poignant *a.* zguduitor
point *v.t.* a puncta
point *n.* punct
poise *n* echilibru
poise *v.t.* a ţine în echilibru
poison *v.t.* a otrăvi
poison *n.* otravă
poisonous *a.* otrăvitor
poke *n.* ghiont
poke *v.t.* a îmboldi
polar *n.* polar
pole *n.* pol
police *n.* poliţie
policeman *n.* poliţist
policy *n.* poliţă
polish *n* lustru
polish *v.t.* a lustrui
polite *a.* politicos
politic *a.* politic
political *a.* politic
politician *n.* politician
politics *n.* politică
polity *n.* organizare socială
poll *v.t.* a înscrie ca alegător
poll *n.* scrutin
pollen *n.* polen
pollute *v.t.* a polua
pollution *n.* poluare
polygamous *a.* poligam
polygamy *n.* poligamie
polyglot1 *n.* poliglot
polyglot2 *a.* poliglot
polytechnic *a.* politehnic
polytechnic *n.* şcoală politehnică
polytheism *n.* politeism
pomp *n.* pompă

pomposity *n.* înfumurare
pompous *a.* pompos
pond *n.* liră sterlină
ponder *v.t.* a cugeta
pontentiality *n.* potenţialitate
pony *n.* ponei
poor *a.* sărac
pop *n* băutură gazoasă
pop *v.i.* a pocni
pope *n.* preot (ortodox)
poplar *n.* plop
poplin *n.* poplin
populace *n.* gloată
popular *a.* popular
popularity *n.* popularitate
popularize *v.t.* a populariza
populate *v.t.* a popula
population *n.* populaţie
populous *a.* populat
porcelain *n.* porţelan
porch *n.* portic
pore *n.* por
pork *n.* carne de porc
porridge *n.* terci de ovăz
port *n.* ţinută
portable *a.* portabil
portage *n.* preţ de transport
portal *n.* portal
portend *v.t.* a prevesti
porter *n.* hamal
portfolio *n.* potofoliu
portico *n.* portic
portion *n* porţie
portion *v.t.* a împărţi
portrait *n.* portret
portraiture *n.* portret
portray *v.t.* a zugrăvi
portrayal *n.* zugrăvire
pose *n.* ţinută (a corpului)
pose *v.i.* a poza
position *n.* poziţie
position *v.t.* a poziţiona

positive *a.* pozitiv
possess *v.t.* a poseda
possession *n.* posesie
possibility *n.* posibilitate
possible *a.* posibil
post *n* stâlp
post *n.* poştă
post *v.t.* a lipi (un afiş)
post *v.t.* a posta o scrisoare
postage *n.* timbrare
postal *a.* poştal
poster *n.* afiş
posthumous *a.* postum
postman *n.* factor poştal
postmaster *n.* director al poştei
post-mortem *a.* postmortem
post-office *n.* oficiu poştal
postpone *v.t.* a amâna
postponement *n.* amânare
postscript *n.* postscriptum
posture *n.* postură
pot *n.* vas
pot *v.t.* a conserva in oală
potash *n.* potasă
potassium *n.* potasiu
potato *n.* cartof
potency *n.* potent
potent *a.* potent
potential *n.* potenţial
potential *a.* potenţial
potter *n.* olar
pottery *n.* olărie
pouch *n.* pungă
poultry *n.* păsări de curte
pounce *n* gheară
pounce *v.i.* a se repezi
pound *n.* ţarc
pound *v.t.* a pisa
pour *v.t* a turna
poverty *n.* sărăcie
powder *v.t.* a pudra
powder *n.* pudră

power *n.* putere
powerful *a.* puternic
practicability *n.* practicabilitate
practicable *a.* practicabil
practical *a.* practic
practice *n.* practică
practise *v.t.* a exersa
practitioner *n.* liber-profesionist
pragmatic *a.* pragmatic
pragmatism *n.* pragmatism
praise *n.* elogiu
praise *v.t.* a elogia
prank *n.* festă
prattle *n.* gângurit (de copil)
pray *v.i.* a se ruga
prayer *n.* rugăciune
preach *v.i.* a predica
preacher *n.* predicator
preamble *n.* preambul
precaution *n.* precauţie
precede *v.* a preceda
precedence *n.* precedenţă
precedent *n.* precedent
precept *n.* somaţie
preceptor *n.* preceptor
precious *a.* preţios
precis *n.* rezumat
precise *n.* precis
precision *n.* precizie
precursor *n.* precursor
predecessor *n.* predecesor
predestination *n.* predestinare
predicament *n.* categorie
predicate *n.* a predica
predict *v.t.* a prezice
prediction *n.* predicţie
predominance *n.* superioritate
predominant *a.* predominant
predominate *v.i.* a predomina
preface *n.* prefaţă
preface *v.t.* a scrie o prefaţă la
prefect *n.* prefect

prefer *v.t.* a prefera
preference *n.* preferinţă
preferential *a.* privilegiat
prefix *n.* prefix
prefix *v.t.* a prefixa
pregnancy *n.* sarcină
pregnant *a.* însărcinată
prehistoric *a.* preistoric
prejudice *n.* prejudiciu
prelate *n.* prelat
preliminary *a.* preliminar
preliminary *n* măsură preliminară
prelude *n.* preludiu
prelude *v.t.* a preluda
premature *a.* prematur
premeditate *v.t.* a premedita
premeditation *n.* premeditare
premier *a.* de prim rang
premier *n* premier
premiere *n.* premieră
premium *n.* primă
premonition *n.* premoniţie
preoccupation *n.* preocupare
preoccupy *v.t.* a preocupa
preparation *n.* preparare
preparatory *a.* preparator
prepare *v.t.* a prepara
preponderance *n.* preponderenţă
preponderate *v.i.* a prepondera
preposition *n.* prepoziţie
prerogative *n.* prerogativă
prescribe *v.t.* a prescrie
prescription *n.* reţetă
presence *n.* prezenţă
present *a.* prezent
present *n.* cadou
present *v.t.* a prezenta
presentation *n.* prezentare
presently *adv.* numaidecât
preservation *n.* păstrare
preservative *a.* care conservă
preservative *n.* conservant

preserve *n.* teritoriu rezervat
preserve *v.t.* a conserva
preside *v.i.* a prezida
president *n.* preşedinte
presidential *a.* prezidenţial
press *n* presă
press *v.t.* a presa
pressure *n.* presiune
prestige *n.* prestigiu
prestigious *a.* prestigios
presume *v.t.* a presupune
presumption *n.* presupunere
pretence *n.* pretenţie (la)
pretend *v.t.* a simula (ceva)
pretentious *a.* pretenţios
pretext *n* pretext
pretty *a* drăguţ
pretty *adv.* destul de
prevail *v.i.* a domina
prevalent *a.* predominant
prevent *v.t.* a împiedica
prevention *n.* prevenire
preventive *a.* preventiv
previous *a.* precedent
prey *n.* victimă
prey *v.i.* a chinui
price *n.* preţ
price *v.t.* a evalua
prick *v.t.* a înţepa
prick *n.* împunsătură
pride *n.* mândrie
pride *v.t.* a se mândri (cu)
priest *n.* preot
primary *a.* primar
prime *a.* prim
prime *n.* începere
primer *n.* noţiune de bază
primeval *a.* primitiv
primitive *a.* primitiv
prince *n.* prinţ
princely *a.* princiar
princess *n.* prinţesă

principal *a* principal
principal *n.* director (de şcoală)
principle *n.* principiu
print *n* imprimare
print *v.t.* a imprima
printer *n.* imprimanta
prior *a.* anterior
prior *n* stareţ
priority *n.* prioriotate
prison *n.* închisoare
prisoner *n.* prizonier
privacy *n.* taină
private *a.* privat
privation *n.* privaţiune
privilege *n.* privilegiu
prize *n.* premiu
prize *v.t.* a premia
probability *n.* probabilitate
probable *a.* verosimil
probably *adv.* probabil
probation *n.* probă
probe *n* sondă
probe *v.t.* a sonda
problem *n.* problemă
problematic *a.* problematic
procedure *n.* procedură
proceed *v.i.* a proceda
proceeding *n.* procedeu
process *n.* proces
procession *n.* defilare
proclaim *v.t.* a proclama
proclamation *n.* proclamaţie
proclivity *n.* înclinaţie
procrastinate *v.i.* a amâna
procure *v.t.* a procura
procurement *n.* achiziţie
prodigal *a.* risipitor
prodigality *n.* risipă
produce *n.* producţie
produce *v.t.* a produce
product *n.* produs
production *n.* producţie

productive *a.* productiv
productivity *n.* productivitate
profane *v.t.* a profana
profane *a.* profan
profess *v.t.* a profesa
profession *n.* profesie
professional *a.* profesional
professor *n.* profesor
proficiency *n.* dibăcie
proficient *a.* priceput
profile *n.* profil
profile *v.t.* a profila
profit *n.* profit
profit *v.t.* a profita de
profitable *a.* profitabil
profiteer *n.* speculant
profiteer *v.i.* a specula
profligate *a.* desfrânat
profound *a.* profund
profundity *n.* profunzime
profuse *a.* extravagant
profusion *n.* somptuozitate
progeny *n.* progenitură
programme *n.* program
progress *n.* progres
progress *v.i.* a progresa
progressive *a.* progresiv
prohibit *v.t.* a interzice
prohibition *n.* interzicere
prohibitive *a.* prohibitiv
project *n.* proiect
project *v.t.* a proiecta
projectile *a* proiectare
projectile *n.* proiectil
projection *n.* proiectare
prolific *a.* prolific
prolong *v.t.* a prelungi
prominence *n.* proeminență
prominent *a.* proeminent
promise *v.t* a promite
promise *n* promisiune
promising *a.* promițător

promissory *a.* care promite
promote *v.t.* a promova
promotion *n.* promovare
prompt *a.* prompt
prompt *v.t.* a îndemna (să)
prompter *n.* sufler
prone *a.* întins
pronoun *n.* pronume
pronounce *v.t.* a pronunța
pronunciation *n.* pronunțare
proof *a* care rezistă (la)
proof *n.* dovadă
prop *n.* proptea
prop *v.t.* a susține
propaganda *n.* propagandă
propagandist *n.* propagandist
propagate *v.t.* a propaga
propel *v.t.* a propulsa
proper *a.* decent
property *n.* propietate
prophecy *n.* profeție
prophesy *v.t.* a prezice
prophet *n.* profet
prophetic *a.* profetic
proportion *n.* proporție
proportion *v.t.* a proporționa
proportional *a.* proporțional
proportionate *a.* proporționat
proposal *n.* prpunere
propose *v.t.* a propune
proposition *n.* propunere
propound *v.t.* a propune
proprietary *a.* de proprietate
proprietor *n.* proprietar
propriety *n.* bună-cuviință
prorogue *v.t.* a proroga
prosaic *a.* prozaic
prose *n.* proză
prosecute *v.t.* a exercita
prosecution *n.* urmărire judiciară
prosecutor *n.* reclamant
prosody *n.* prozodie

prospect *n.* perspectivă
prospective *a.* în perspectivă
prosper *v.i.* a prospera
prosperity *n.* prosperitate
prosperous *a.* prosper
prostitute *n.* prostituată
prostitute *v.t.* a prostitua
prostitution *n.* prostituţie
prostrate *a.* sleit
prostrate *v.t.* doborî
protagonist *n.* protagonist
protect *v.t.* a proteja
protection *n.* protecţie
protective *a.* protector
protector *n.* ocrotitor
protein *n.* proteină
protest *n.* protest
protest *v.i.* a protesta
protestation *n.* protestaţie
prototype *n.* prototip
proud *a.* mândru
prove *v.t.* a dovedi
proverb *n.* proverb
proverbial *a.* proverbial
provide *v.i.* a procura (pt. cineva)
providence *n.* providenţă
provident *a.* prevăzător
province *n.* provincie
provincial *a.* din provincie
provincialism *n.* provincialism
provision *n.* aprovizionare
provisional *a.* provizoriu
proviso *n.* clauză condiţională
provocation *n.* provocare
provocative *a.* provocator
provoke *v.t.* a provoca
prowess *n.* bravură
proximate *a.* aproximativ
proximity *n.* aproximare
proxy *n.* locţiitor
prude *n.* mironosiţă
prudence *n.* prudenţă

prudent *a.* prudent
prune *v.t.* prună uscată
pry *v.i.* a se uita pe furiş
psalm *n.* psalm
pseudonym *n.* pseudonim
psychiatrist *n.* psihiatru
psychiatry *n.* psihiatrie
psychic *a.* psihic
psychological *a.* psihologic
psychologist *n.* psiholog
psychology *n.* psihologie
psychopath *n.* psihopat
psychosis *n.* psihoză
puberty *n.* pubertate
public *a.* public
public *n.* public
publication *n.* publicaţie
publicity *n.* publicitate
publicize *v.t.* a face reclamă
publish *v.t.* a publica
publisher *n.* editor
pudding *n.* budincă
puddle *n.* baltă
puddle *v.t.* a tulbura (apa)
puerile *a.* pueril
puff *n.* suflare (de vânt, fum)
puff *v.i.* a sufla
pull *n.* tragere
pull *v.t.* a trage
pulley *n.* scripete
pulp *n.* pulpă (de fructe)
pulp *v.t.* a transforma în pastă
pulpit *n* amavon
pulpy *a.* cărnos
pulsate *v.i.* a pulsa
pulsation *n.* pulsaţie
pulse *n* mişcare ritmică
pulse *n.* puls
pulse *v.i.* a pulsa
pump *n.* pompă
pump *v.t.* a pompa
pumpkin *n.* dovleac

pun *n.* joc de cuvinte
pun *v.t* a face un clambur
punch *n.* lovitură de pumn
punch *v.t.* a lovi cu pumnul
punctual *a.* punctual
punctuality *n.* punctualitate
punctuate *v.t.* a întrerupe
punctuation *n.* punctuaţie
puncture *n.* înţepătură
puncture *v.t.* a înţepa
pungent *a.* spinos
punish *v.t.* a pedepsi
punishment *n.* pedeapsă
punitive *a.* penal
puny *a.* neânsemnat
pupil *n.* şcolar
puppet *n.* marionetă
puppy *n.* căţeluş
purblind *a* aproape orb
purchase *v.t.* a achiziţiona
purchase *n.* cumpărătură
pure *a* pur
purgation *n.* purgaţie
purgative *a* purgative
purgative *n.* purgativ
purgatory *n.* purgatoriu
purge *v.t.* e epura
purification *n.* purificare
purify *v.t.* a purifica
purist *n.* purist
purity *n.* puritate
purple *adj./n.* culoarea mov
purport *n.* semnificaţie
purport *v.t.* a da de înţeles
purpose *n.* ţel
purpose *v.t.* a-si propune
purposely *adv.* înadins
purr *n.* tors (de pisică)
purr *v.i.* a toarce
purse *v.t.* a încreţi (fruntea)
purse *n.* pungă
pursuance *n.* urmare

pursue *v.t.* a urmări
pursuit *n.* goană
purview *n.* privire de ansamblu
pus *n.* puroi
push *n.* împingere
push *v.t.* a împinge
put *v.t.* a pune
puzzle *n.* încurcătură
puzzle *v.t.* a încurca
pygmy *n.* pigmeu
pyramid *n.* piramidă
pyre *n.* rug funerar
python *n.* piton

quack *n* măcăit de raţă
quack *v.i.* a măcăi
quackery *n.* şarlatanie
quadrangle *n.* patrulater
quadrilateral *a. & n.* patrulater
quadruped *n.* patruped
quadruple *a.* cvadruplu
quadruple *v.t.* a împătri
quail *n.* pitpalac
quaint *a.* ciudat
quake *n* cutremure (de pământ)
quake *v.t.* a se cutremura
qualification *n.* calificare
qualify *v.i.* a se califica
qualitative *a.* calitativ
quality *n.* calitate
quandary *n.* dificultate
quantitative *a.* cantitativ
quantity *n.* cantitate
quantum *n.* cuantum
quarrel *v.i.* a se certa (cu)
quarrel *n.* neânţelegere
quarrelsome *a.* certăreţ

quarry *v.t.* a extrage
quarry *n.* sursă
quarter *v.t.* a intra (într-un pătrar)
quarter *n.* sfert
quarterly *a.* trimestrial
queen *n.* regină
queer *a.* cherchelit
quell *v.t.* a calma
quench *v.t.* a înăbuși (o dorință)
query *v.t* a se îndoi de
query *n.* semn de întrebare
quest *v.t.* a adulmeca
quest *n.* cercetare
question *v.t.* a întreba
question *n.* întrebare
questionable *a.* discutabil
questionnaire *n.* chestionar
queue *n.* rând
quibble *v.i.* a vorbi în echivocuri
quibble *n.* calambur
quick *n* punct sensibil
quick *a.* repezit
quicksand *n.* nisip mișcător
quicksilver *n.* argint viu
quiet *n.* liniște
quiet *v.t.* a liniști
quiet *a.* tăcut
quilt *n.* plapumă
quintessence *n.* chintesență
quit *v.t.* a înceta
quite *adv.* cu totul
quiver *v.i.* a tremura (de)
quiver *n.* tremurare
quiz *v.t.* a râde de
quiz *n.* întrebare absurdă
quorum *n.* cvorum
quota *n.* cotă
quotation *n.* citare
quote *v.t.* a fixa (un preț)
quotient *n.* cât

R

rabate *n.* rabat
rabbit *n.* iepure
rabies *n.* turbare
race *v.i* a se întrece în viteză
race *n.* alergare
racial *a.* de rasă
racialism *n.* rasism
rack *n.* scaun de tortură
rack *v.t.* a slei de puteri
racket *n.* rachetă (de tenis)
radiance *n.* strălucire
radiant *a.* strălucitor
radiate *v.t.* a radia
radiation *n.* radical
radical *a.* radical
radio *n.* radio
radio *v.t.* a radiotelegrafia
radish *n.* ridiche
radium *n.* radiu
radius *n.* rază
rag *v.t.* a tachina
rag *n.* cârpă
rage *v.i.* a turba
rage *n.* mânie
raid *v.t.* a face o razie
raid *n.* razie
rail *v.t.* a trasporta cu trenul
rail *n.* șină
raillery *n.* zeflemire
railway *n.* cale ferată
rain *n* ploaie
rain *v.i.* a ploua
rainy *a.* ploios
raise *v.t.* ridicare
raisin *n.* stafidă
raling *n.* grilaj
rally *n* regrupare de trupe
rally *v.t.* a regrupa (trupe)

ram *v.t.* a îndesa
ram *n.* pinten
ramble *n* hoinăreală
ramble *v.t.* a hoinări,
rampage *n.* ieşire violentă
rampage *v.i.* face tărăboi
rampant *a.* exuberant
rampart *n.* meterez
rancour *n.* ranchiună
random *a.* întâmplător
range *n.* sferă (de cunoştinţe)
range *v.t.* a aşeza în rând
ranger *n.* pădurar
rank *a* murdar
rank *v.t.* a aşeza în rânduri
rank *n.* grad
ransack *v.t.* a scotoci
ransom *v.t.* a răscumpăra
ransom *n.* răscumpărare
raparable *a.* reparabil
rape *v.t.* a viola
rape *n.* viol
rapid *a.* rapid
rapidity *n.* rapiditate
rapier *n.* spadă
rapport *n.* raport
rapt *a.* absorbit
rapture *n.* răpire
rare *a.* rar
rascal *n.* pungaş
rash *a.* năvalnic
rat *n.* şobolan
rate *n.* rată
rate *v.t.* a evalua
rather *adv.* mai degrabă
ratify *v.t.* a ratifica
ratio *n.* proporţie
ration *n.* raţie
rational *a.* raţional
rationale *n.* raţiune fundamentală
rationality *n.* raţiune
rationalize *v.t.* a raţionaliza

rattle *n* trăncăneală
rattle *v.i.* a turui
ravage *v.t.* a devasta
ravage *n.* ravagiu
rave *v.i.* a şuiera
raven *n.* corb
ravine *n.* prăpastie
raw *a.* crud
ray *n.* licărire
razor *n.* brici
reach *v.t.* a ajunge
react *v.i.* a reacţiona
reaction *n.* reacţie
read *v.t.* a citi
reader *n.* cititor
readily *adv.* fără greutate
readiness *n.* promptitudine
ready *a.* pregătit
real *a.* real
realism *n.* realism
realist *n.* realist
realistic *a.* realist
reality *n.* realitate
realization *n.* realizare
realize *v.t.* a realiza
really *adv.* cu adevărat
realm *a.* domeniu
ream *n.* top
reap *v.t.* a recolta
reaper *n.* culegător
rear *v.t.* a construi (o clădire)
rear *n.* coada (unei coloane
reason *v.i.* a raţiona
reason *n.* cauză
reasonable *a.* rezonabil
reassure *v.t.* a reasigura
rebel *v.i.* a se răscula
rebel *n.* rebel
rebellion *n.* rebeliune
rebellious *a.* răsculat
rebound *n.* salt
rebound *v.i.* a face o săritură

rebuff *v.t.* a respinge
rebuff *n.* insucces
rebuke *n.* mustrare
rebuke *v.t.* a mustra
recall *n.* rechemare
recall *v.t.* a rechema
recede *v.i.* a se depărta
receipt *n.* chitanţă
receive *v.t.* a primi
receiver *n.* destinatar
recent *a.* recent
recently *adv.* recent
reception *n.* recepţie
receptive *a.* receptive
recess *n.* nişă
recession *n.* recesiune
recipe *n.* reţetă
recipient *n.* recipient
reciprocal *a.* reciproc
reciprocate *v.t.* a răsplăti
recital *n.* recital
recitation *n.* recitare
recite *v.t.* a recita
reckless *a.* nepăsător
reckon *v.t.* a aprecia
reclaim *v.t.* a revendica
reclamation *n* reclamaţie
recluse *n.* pustnic
recognition *n.* recunoaştere
recognize *v.t.* a recunoaşte
recoil *n* destindere (a unui arc)
recoil *v.i.* a se feri
recollect *v.t.* a-şi aminti
recollection *n.* amintire
recommend *v.t.* a recomanda
recommendation *n.* recomandare
recompense *n.* recompensă
recompense *v.t.* a recompensa
reconcile *v.t.* a reconcilia
reconciliation *n.* reconciliere
record *n.* adeverinţă

record *v.t.* a înregistra
recorder *n.* magnetofon
recount *v.t.* a nara
recoup *v.t.* a redobândi
recourse *n.* recurs
recover *v.t.* a recupera
recovery *n.* recuperare
recreation *n.* recreaţie
recruit *v.t.* a recruta
recruit *n.* recrut
rectangle *n.* dreptunghi
rectangular *a.* dreptunghiular
rectification *n.* rectificare
rectify *v.i.* a rectifica
rectum *n.* rectificare
recur *v.i.* a se reproduce
recurrence *n.* recidivă
recurrent *a.* periodic
red *n.* roşu
red *a.* roşu
redden *v.t.* a (se) înroşi
reddish *a.* roşiatic
redeem *v.t.* a strânge (bani)
redemption *n.* compensare
redouble *v.t.* a îndoi
redress *n* corectare
redress *v.t.* a îndrepta
reduce *v.t.* a reduce
reduction *n.* reducere
redundance *n.* surplus
redundant *a.* surplus
reel *n.* bobină
reel *v.i.* a ţârîi
refer *v.t.* a raporta (la)
referee *n.* arbitru
reference *n.* referinţă
referendum *n.* referendum
refine *v.t.* a (se) rafina
refinement *n.* rafinare
refinery *n.* rafinărie
reflect *v.t.* a reflecta
reflection *n.* reflectare

reflective *a.* care reflectă
reflector *n.* reflector
reflex *a* reflex
reflex *n.* reflex
reflexive *a* reflexiv
reform *n.* reformă
reform *v.t.* a (se) reforma
reformation *n.* reformare
reformatory *n.* casă de corecţie
reformatory *a* reformator
reformer *n.* reformator
refrain *n* refren
refrain *v.i.* a reţine
refresh *v.t.* a se învoira
refreshment *n.* aliment răcoritor
refrigerate *v.t.* aliment răcoritor
refrigeration *n.* răcire
refrigerator *n.* frigider
refuge *n.* refugiu
refugee *n.* refugiat
refulgence *n.* splendoare
refulgent *a.* splendid
refund *n.* restituire
refund *v.t.* a restitui
refusal *n.* refuz
refuse *n.* rebut
refuse *v.t.* a refuza
refutation *n.* refutare
refute *v.t.* a respinge
regal *a.* regal
regard *n.* privinţă
regard *v.t.* a avea legătură cu
regenerate *v.t.* a regenera
regeneration *n.* regenerare
regicide *n.* regicid
regime *n.* regim
regiment *n.* regiment
regiment *v.t.* a face un regiment
region *n.* regiune
regional *a.* regional
register *n.* registru
register *v.t.* a înregistra

registrar *n.* registrator
registration *n.* înregistrare
registry *n.* registru
regret *n* regret
regret *v.i.* a regreta
regular *a.* regulat
regularity *n.* regularitate
regulate *v.t.* a regula
regulation *n.* regulament
regulator *n.* regulator
rehabilitate *v.t.* a reabilita
rehabilitation *n.* reabilitare
rehearsal *n.* repetiţie
rehearse *v.t.* a repeta
reign *n* domnie
reign *v.i.* a domni
reimburse *v.t.* a rambursa
rein *v.t.* a ţine frâu
rein *n.* frâu
reinforce *v.t.* a întări
reinforcement *n.* întărire
reinstate *v.t.* a restabili
reinstatement *n.* restabilire
reiterate *v.t.* a repeta
reiteration *n.* repetare
reject *v.t.* a respinge
rejection *n.* rebut
rejoice *v.i.* a se bucura
rejoin *v.t.* a reântâlni
rejoinder *n.* replică
rejuvenate *v.t.* a întineri
rejuvenation *n.* întinerire
relapse *n.* recidivă
relapse *v.i.* a recădea
relate *v.t.* a relata
relation *n.* legatură
relative *n.* relativ
relative *a.* relativ
relax *v.t.* a se relaxa
relaxation *n.* relaxare
relay *n.* schimb
relay *v.t.* a transmite prin releu

release *n* punere în libertate
release *v.t.* a pune în libertate
relent *v.i.* a se înduioşa
relentless *a.* implacabil
relevance *n.* relevanţă
relevant *a.* relevant
reliable *a.* de nădejde
reliance *n.* sprijin
relic *n.* moaşte
relief *n.* uşurare
relieve *v.t.* a uşura
religion *n.* religie
religious *a.* religios
relinquish *v.t.* a da drumul la
relish *n* vocaţie
relish *v.t.* a da gust (unei
    mâncări)
reluctance *n.* rezistenţă
reluctant *a.* care se împotriveşte
rely *v.i.* a se încrede (în)
remain *v.i.* a rămâne
remainder *n.* rămăşiţă
remand *n* rechemare
remand *v.t.* a rechema
remark *v.t.* a remarca
remark *n.* remarcă
remarkable *a.* remarcabil
remedy *n.* remediu
remedy *v.t* a remedia
remember *v.t.* a-şi aminti
remembrance *n.* aducere aminte
remind *v.t.* a aminti
reminder *n.* memento
reminiscence *n.* reminiscenţă
reminiscent *a.* care (îşi)
    aminteşte
remission *n.* atenuare (a unei
    boli)
remit *v.t.* a potoli (o durere)
remittance *n.* remitere (de bani)
remorse *n.* remuşcare
remote *a.* vag

removable *a.* detaşabil
removal *n.* scoatere
remove *v.t.* a scoate
remunerate *v.t.* a remunera
remuneration *n.* remuneraţie
remunerative *a.* care răsplăteşte
renaissance *n.* renaştere
render *v.t.* a înapoia
rendezvous *n.* loc de întâlnire
renew *v.t.* a reânnoi
renewal *n.* reânnoire
renounce *v.t.* a renunţa
renovate *v.t.* a renova
renovation *n.* renovare
renown *n.* renume
renowned *a.* renumit
rent *v.t.* a închiria
rent *n.* chirie
renunciation *n.* renunţare
repair *n.* reparare
repair *v.t.* a repara
repartee *n.* ripostă
repatriate *n* repatriere
repatriate *v.t.* a repatria
repatriation *n.* repatriere
repay *v.t.* a răsplăti
repayment *n.* răsplată
repeal *n* revocare
repeal *v.t.* a revoca
repeat *v.t.* a repeta
repel *v.t.* a combate
repellent *a.* impermeabil
repent *v.i.* a-i părea rău (de)
repentance *n.* căinţă
repentant *a.* care se căieşte,
repercussion *n.* repercursiune
repetition *n.* repetiţie
replace *v.t.* a înlocui
replacement *n.* înlocuitor
replenish *v.t.* a reaproviziona
replete *a.* sătul (de)
replica *n.* duplicat

reply *n* replică
reply *v.i.* a replica la
report *n.* raport
report *v.t.* a reporta
reporter *n.* reporter
repose *v.i.* a se sprijini pe
repose *n.* repaus
repository *n.* prăvălie
represent *v.t.* a reprezenta
representation *n.* reprezentare
representative *a.* reprezentativ
representative *n.* reprezentant
repress *v.t.* a reprima
repression *n.* reprimare
reprimand *v.t.* a mustra
reprimand *n.* mustrare
reprint *n.* retipărire
reprint *v.t.* a retipări
reproach *n.* reproş
reproach *v.t.* a reproşa
reproduce *v.t.* a reproduce
reproduction *n* reproducere
reproductive *a.* reproductiv
reproof *n.* imputare
reptile *n.* reptilă
republic *n.* republică
republican *n* republican
republican *a.* republican
repudiate *v.t.* a repudia
repudiation *n.* repudiere
repugnance *n.* antipatie
repugnant *a.* antipatic
repulse *n.* refuz
repulse *v.t.* a refuza
repulsion *n.* repulsie
repulsive *a.* repulsiv
reputation *n.* reputaţie
repute *n.* reputaţie
repute *v.t.* a fi socotit
request *n* solicitare
request *v.t.* a cere
requiem *n.* recviem

require *v.t.* a cere insistent
requirement *n.* cerinţă
requisite *a.* trebuincios
requisition *n.* rechiziţie
requisition *v.t.* a rechiziţiona
requiste *n* lucru necesar
requite *v.t.* a răsplăti
rescue *n* salvare
rescue *v.t.* a salva
research *n* cercetare
research *v.i.* a cerceta
resemblance *n.* asemănare
resemble *v.t.* a semăna cu
resent *v.t.* a lua în nume de rău
resentment *n.* resentiment
reservation *n.* rezervare
reserve *v.t.* a rezerva
reservoir *n.* rezervor
reside *v.i.* a locui
residence *n.* reşedinţă
resident *a.* permanent
resident *n* rezident
residual *a.* rezidual
residue *n.* reziduu
resign *v.t.* a demisiona
resignation *n.* demisie
resist *v.t.* a rezista la
resistance *n.* rezistenţă
resistant *a.* rezistent
resolute *a.* ferm
resolution *n.* rezoluţie
resolve *v.t.* a rezolva
resonance *n.* rezonanţă
resonant *a.* rezonant
resort *n* resursă
resort *v.i.* a recurge (la)
resound *v.i.* a răsuna
resource *n.* resursă
resourceful *a.* plin de resurse
respect *n.* respect
respect *v.t.* a respecta
respectful *a.* respectuos

respective *a.* respectiv
respiration *n.* respiraţie
respire *v.i.* a respira
resplendent *a.* strălucitor
respond *v.i.* a răspunde
respondent *n.* pârît
response *n.* răspuns
responsibility *n.* responsabilitate
responsible *a.* responsabil
rest *n* odihnă
rest *v.i.* a se odihni
restaurant *n.* restaurant
restive *a.* îndărătnic
restoration *n.* restabilire
restore *v.t.* a reconstitui
restrain *v.t.* a reţine
restrict *v.t.* a limita
restriction *n.* restricţie
restrictive *a.* restrictiv
result *n.* rezultat
result *v.i.* a rezulta
resume *n.* rezultat
resume *v.t.* a rezuma
resumption *n.* reluare
resurgence *n.* renaştere
retail *adv.* cu amănuntul
retail *n.* amănunt
retail *v.t.* a vinde cu amănuntul
retailer *n.* vânzător cu amănuntul
retain *v.t.* a reţine
retaliate *v.i.* a se răzbuna
retaliation *n.* revanşă
retard *v.t.* a întârzia
retardation *n.* întârziere
retention *n.* reţinere
retentive *a.* care reţine
reticence *n.* reticenţă
reticent *a.* reticent
retina *n.* retină
retinue *n.* suită
retire *v.i.* a se retrage
retirement *n.* retragere

retort *n.* retortă
retort *v.t.* a distila
retouch *v.t.* a retuşa
retrace *v.t.* a reconstitui
retread *v.t.* a merge din nou pe
retreat *v.i.* a se retrage
retrench *v.t.* a suprima
retrenchment *n.* suprimare
retrieve *v.t.* a repara
retrospect *n.* retrospectivă
retrospection *n.* retrospect
retrospective *a.* retrospectiv
return *n.* întoarcere
revel *n.* sărbătoare
revel *v.i.* a se înapoia
revelation *n.* revelaţie
reveller *n.* chefliu
revenge *n.* răzbunare
revenge *v.t.* a se răzbuna
revengeful *a.* răzbunător
revenue *n.* venit
revere *v.t.* a venera
reverence *n.* reverenţă
reverend *n* preot
reverent *a.* smerit
reverie *n.* reverie
reversal *n.* inversare
reverse *a.* contrar
reverse *n* revers
reverse *v.t.* a inversa
reversible *a.* reversibil
revert *v.i.* a reveni
review *n* revizuire
review *v.t.* a revizui
revise *v.t.* a revizui
revision *n.* revizie
revival *n.* redeşteptare
revive *v.i.* a reânvia
revocable *a.* revocabil
revocation *n.* revocare
revoke *v.t.* a revoca
revolt *n.* revoltă

revolt *v.i.* a se revolta
revolution *n.* revoluţie
revolutionary *a.* revoluţionar
revolutionary *n* revoluţionar
revolve *v.i.* a se învârti
revolver *n.* revolver
reward *n.* recompensă
reward *v.t.* a recompensa
rhetoric *n.* retoric
rhetorical *a.* retoric
rheumatic *a.* reumatic
rheumatism *n.* reumatism
rhinoceros *n.* rinocer
rhyme *n.* rimă
rhyme *v.i.* a rima
rhymester *n.* poetastru
rhythm *n* ritm
rhythmic *a.* ritmic
rib *n.* coastă
ribbon *n.* fâşie
rice *n.* orez
rich *a.* bogat
riches *n.* bogăţie
richness *n* abundenţă
rickets *n.* rahitism
rickety *a.* rahitic
rickshaw *n.* rişcă
rid *v.t.* a scăpa
riddle *n.* sită
riddle *v.i.* a vorbi în parabole
ride *n* cursă
ride *v.t.* a călări
rider *n.* călăreţ
ridge *n.* muchie
ridicule *n.* batjocură
ridicule *v.t.* a ridiculiza
ridiculous *a.* ridicol
rifle *n* a trage (cu, carabina)
rifle *v.t.* carabină
rift *n.* fisură
right *a.* drept
right *adv* drept

right *n* drept
right *v.t.* a pune în ordine
righteous *a.* îndreptăţit
rigid *a.* rigid
rigorous *a.* riguros
rigour *n.* rigoare
rim *n.* obadă
ring *n.* inel
ring *v.t.* a pune un inel
ringlet *n.* cârlionţ
ringworm *n.* bube dulci
rinse *v.t.* a clăti
riot *n.* dezordine
riot *v.t.* a face dezordine
rip *v.t.* a spinteca
ripe *a* copt
ripen *v.i.* a se coace
ripple *n.* buclă (de păr)
ripple *v.t.* a ondula
rise *n.* mărire
rise *v.i.* a răsări
risk *n.* risc
risk *v.t.* a risca
risky *a.* ricant
rite *n.* ritual
ritual *n.* ritual
rival *n.* rival
rival *v.t.* a rivaliza cu
rivalry *n.* rivalitate
river *n.* râu
rivet *n.* nit
rivet *v.t.* a nitui
rivulet *n.* râuleţ
road *n.* drum
roam *v.i.* a colinda
roar *n.* răget
roar *v.i.* a rage
roast *a* fript
roast *n* friptură
roast *v.t.* a frige
rob *v.t.* a jefui
robber *n.* tâlhar

robbery *n.* jaf
robe *n.* robă
robe *v.t.* a se îmbrăca în robă
robot *n.* robot
robust *a.* robust
rock *n.* stâncă
rock *v.t.* a legăna
rocket *n.* rachetă
rod *n.* baston
rodent *n.* rozător
roe *n.* icre
rogue *n.* buruiană
roguery *n.* pungăşie
roguish *a.* pungăşesc
role *n.* rol
roll *n.* rulou
roll *v.i.* a se rostogoli
roller *n.* cilindru
romance *n.* romanţă
romantic *a.* romantic
romp *n.* hărmălaie
romp *v.i.* a se juca zgomotos
rood *n.* crucifix
roof *n.* acoperiş
roof *v.t.* a adăposti
rook *n.* pungaş
rook *v.t.* a trişa
room *n.* cameră
roost *n.* cracă
roost *v.i.* a se cocoţa
root *n.* rădăcină
root *v.i.* a prinde rădăcini
rope *n.* frânghie
rope *v.t.* a lega cu funie
rosary *n.* mătănii
rose *n.* trandafir
rostrum *n.* tribună
rosy *a.* trandafiriu
rot *n.* carie
rot *v.i.* a se caria
rotary *a.* rotativ
rotate *v.i.* a se roti

rotation *n.* rotaţie
rote *v.t* a învăţa pe dinafară
rouble *n.* rublă
rough *a.* aspru
round *a.* rotund
round *adv.* circular
round *n.* rond
round *v.t.* a rotunji
rouse *v.i.* a se deştepta
rout *n* debandadă
rout *v.t.* a scormoni
route *n.* rută
routine *a* curent
routine *n.* rutină
rove *v.i.* a vagabonda
rover *n.* vagabond
row *n* plimbare cu barca
row *n.* şir
row *v.t.* a duce cu o barcă
row *n.* încăierare
rowdy *a.* violent
royal *a.* regal
royalist *n.* regalist
royalty *n.* regalitate
rub *n* frecare
rub *v.t.* a freca
rubber *n.* cauciuc
rubbish *n.* gunoi
rubble *n.* moloz
ruby *n.* rubin
rude *a.* prost crescut
rudiment *n.* organ rudimentar
rudimentary *a.* rudimentar
rue *v.t.* a regreta
rueful *a.* jalnic
ruffian *n.* brută
ruffle *v.t.* a agasa
rug *n.* pled
rugged *a.* ursuz
ruin *n.* ruină
ruin *v.t.* a ruina
rule *n.* regulă

rule *v.t.* a dirija
ruler *n.* conducător
ruling *n.* ordonanţă
rum *a* suveran
rum *n.* rom
rumble *n.* huruit
rumble *v.i.* a hurui
ruminant *a.* rumegător
ruminant *n.* rumegător
ruminate *v.i.* a rumega
rumination *n.* rumegare
rummage *n* scotocire
rummage *v.i.* a răscoli
rummy *n.* bizar
rumour *n.* zvon
rumour *v.t.* a răspândi zvonuri
run *n.* fugă
run *v.i.* a fugi
rung *n.* treaptă
runner *n.* alergător
rupture *v.t.* a rupe
rupture *n.* rupere
rural *a.* rural
rush *n* papură
rush *n.* grabă
rush *v.t.* a se grăbi
rust *n.* rugină
rust *v.i* a (se) rugini
rustic *a.* rustic
rustic *n* sătean
rusticate *v.t.* a trimite la ţară
rusticity *n.* bădărănie
rusty *a.* ruginit
rut *n.* făgaş
ruthless *a.* crunt
rye *n.* secară

S

sabbath *n.* sabat
sabotage *n.* sabotaj
sabotage *v.t.* a sabota
sabre *n.* cicatrice
sack *n.* prădare
sack *v.t.* a prăda
sacrament *n.* sfinţire
sacred *a.* sacru
sacrifice *n.* sacrificiu
sacrifice *v.t.* a sacrifica
sacrilege *n.* sacrilegiu
sad *a.* trist
sadden *v.t.* a întrista
saddle *n.* şa
saddle *v.t.* a înşeua
safe *a.* în stare bună
safe *n.* seif
safeguard *n.* pază
safety *n.* siguranţă
sagacious *a.* perspicace
sagacity *n.* perspicacitate
sage *a.* înţelept
sage *n.* salbie
sail *v.i.* a naviga
sail *n.* călătorie pe mare
sailor *n.* marinar
saint *n.* sfânt
sake *n.* drag
salad *n.* salată
salary *n.* salariu
sale *n.* vânzare
salesman *n.* vânzător
salient *a.* proeminent
saline *a.* salin
salinity *n.* salinitate
saliva *n.* salivă
sally *n.* escapadă
saloon *n.* salon

salt *n.* sare
salt *v.t* a săra
salty *a.* sărat
salutary *a.* salutar
salutation *n.* salutare
salute *n* salut
salute *v.t.* a saluta
salvage *n.* salvare
salvage *v.t.* a salva
salvation *n.* salvare
same *a.* acelasi
sample *n.* mostră
sample *v.t.* a lua o mostră din
sanatorium *n.* sanatoriu
sanctify *v.t.* a sfinți
sanction *n.* sancțiune
sanction *v.t.* a ratifica o lege
sanctuary *n.* sanctuar
sand *n.* nisip
sandal *n.* sandală
sandalwood *n.* copac parfumat
sandwich *n.* sandviș
sandy *a.* nisipos
sane *a.* cu mintea sănătoasă
sanguine *a.* sanguin
sanitary *a.* sanitar
sanity *n.* judecată sănătoasă
sap *n.* sevă
sap *v.t.* a săpa
sapphire *n.* safir
sarcasm *n.* sarcasm
sarcastic *a.* sarcastic
sardonic *a.* răutăcios
satchel *n.* tolbă
satellite *n.* satelit
satiate *v.t.* a sătura până la refuz
satiety *n.* saturare
satire *n.* satiră
satirical *a.* satiric
satirist *n.* (scriitor) satiric
satirize *v.t.* a satiriza
satisfaction *n.* satisfacție

satisfactory *a.* satisfăcător
satisfy *v.t.* a satisface
saturate *v.t.* a satura
saturation *n.* saturație
Saturday *n.* sâmbătă
sauce *n.* sos
saucer *n.* farfurioară
saunter *v.t.* a hoinări
savage *a.* necivilizat
savage *n* sălbatic
savagery *n.* bădărănie
save *prep* afară de
save *v.t.* a salva
saviour *n.* salvator
savour *n.* savoare
savour *v.t.* a savura
saw *n.* ferăstrău
saw *v.t.* a tăia cu ferăstrăul
say *n.* vorbă
say *v.t.* a spune
scabbard *n.* teacă
scaffold *n.* schelă
scale *n.* scară
scale *v.t.* a cântări
scalp *n* scalp
scamper *v.i* a o lua la sănătoasa
scan *v.t.* a scanda (versuri)
scandal *n* scandal
scandalize *v.t.* a scandaliza
scant *a.* limitat
scanty *a.* insuficient
scapegoat *n.* țap ispășitor
scar *n* cicatrice
scarce *a.* neîndestulător
scarcely *adv.* abia
scarcity *n.* speriat
scare *n.* sperietură
scare *v.t.* a speria
scarf *n.* eșarfă
scatter *v.t.* a împrăștia
scavenger *n.* măturător de stradă
scene *n.* scenă

scenery *n.* cadru
scenic *a.* dramatic
scent *n.* mireasmă
scent *v.t.* a parfuma
sceptic *n.* sceptic
sceptical *a.* sceptic
scepticism *n.* scepticism
sceptre *n.* sceptru
schedule *n.* orar
schedule *v.t.* a planifica
scheme *n.* schemă
scheme *v.i.* a face schema
schism *n.* schizmă
scholar *n.* discipol
scholarly *a.* competent
scholarship *n.* bursă
scholastic *a.* şcolar
school *n.* şcoală
science *n.* ştiinţă
scientific *a.* ştiinţific
scientist *n.* om de ştiinţă
scintillate *v.i.* a scânteia
scintillation *n.* scânteiere
scissors *n.* foarfece
scoff *v.i.* a zeflemisi
scold *v.t.* a certa cu asprime
scooter *n.* trotinetă
scope *n.* scop
scorch *v.t.* a pârli
score *n.* scor
score *v.t.* a câştiga
scorer *n.* golgeter
scorn *n.* indignare
scorn *v.t.* a dispreţui
scorpion *n.* scorpion
Scot *n.* scoţian
scotch *a.* scoţian
scotch *n.* whisky scoţian
scot-free *a.* teafăr
scoundrel *n.* derbedeu
scourge *n.* bici
scourge *v.t.* a biciui

scout *n.* cercetaş
scout *v.i* a inspecta
scowl *n.* privire posomorâtă
scowl *v.i.* a se încrunta
scramble *n.* escaladare pe brânci
scramble *v.i.* a merge pe brânci
scrap *n.* fragment
scratch *n.* zgârietură uşoară
scratch *v.t.* a zgâria
scrawl *v.t.* a mâzgăli
scream *n.* ţipăt
scream *v.i.* a ţipa
screen *v.t.* a ecraniza
screen *n.* ecran
screw *v.t.* a înşuruba
screw *n.* şurub
scribble *n.* mâzgălitură
scribble *v.t.* a mâzgăli
script *n.* scenariu
scripture *n.* scriptură
scroll *n.* sul
scrutinize *v.t.* a verifica scrutinul
scrutiny *n.* verificare a
  scrutinului
scuffle *v.i.* a se încăiera
scuffle *n.* încăierare
sculptor *n.* sculptor
sculpture *n.* sculptură
scythe *n.* coasă
sea *n.* mare
seal *n.* focă
seal *v.t.* a sigila
seal *n.* sigiliu
seam *v.t.* a coase
seam *n.* cusătură
seamy *a.* cusut
search *v.t.* a căuta
search *n.* căutare
season *v.t.* a aclimatiza
season *n.* anotimp
seasonable *a.* de sezon
seasonal *a.* sezonier

seat *v.t.* a se aşeza
seat *n.* scaun
secede *v.i.* a se separa
secession *n.* sciziune
secessionist *n.* secesionist
seclude *v.t.* a izola (o persoană)
secluded *a.* izolat
seclusion *n.* izolare
second *a.* de gradul al doilea
second *n* secundă
second *v.t.* a secunda (pe cineva)
secondary *a.* secundar
secrecy *n.* taină
secret *n.* secret
secret *a.* secret
secretariat (e) *n.* secretariat
secretary *n.* secretară
secrete *v.t.* a secreta
secretion *n.* tăinuire
secretive *a.* discret
sect *n.* sectă
sectarian *a.* sectarist
section *n.* secţiune
sector *n.* sector
secure *a.* asigurat
secure *v.t.* a asigura
security *n.* securitate
sedan *n.* automobil închis
sedate *v.t.* a seda
sedate *a.* potolit
sedative *n* calmant
sedative *a.* calmant
sedentary *a.* sedentar
sediment *n.* sediment
seditious *a.* sediţios
seduce *v.t* a seduce
seduction *n.* seducţie
seductive *a* seducător
see *v.t.* a vedea
seed *n.* sămânţă
seek *v.t.* a căuta
seem *v.i.* a părea

seemly *a.* convenabl
seep *v.i.* a se prelinge
seer *n.* profet
seethe *v.i.* a clocoti
segment *n.* segment
segregate *v.t.* a separa
segregation *n.* separare
seismic *a.* seismic
seize *v.t.* a sesiza
seizure *n.* confiscare
seldom *adv.* (a)rareori
select *a* selectat
select *v.t.* a selecta
selection *n.* selecţie
selective *a.* selectiv
self *n.* individualitate
selfish *a.* egoist
sell *v.t.* a vinde
seller *n.* vânzător
semblance *n.* similitudine
semester *n.* semestru
seminar *n.* seminar
senate *n.* senat
senator *n.* senator
send *v.t.* a trimite
senile *a.* senil
senility *n.* senilitate
senior *n.* senior
senior *a.* senior
seniority *n.* calitatea de senior
sensation *n.* senzaţie
sensational *a.* senzaţional
sense *v.t.* a intui
sense *n.* simţ
senseless *a.* fără simţire
sensibility *n.* sensibilitate
sensible *a.* sensibil
sensitive *a.* sensibil
sensual *a.* senzual
sensuality *n.* senzualitate
sensuous *a.* voluptuos
sentence *v.t.* a condamna

sentence *n.* propoziție
sentient *a.* simțitor
sentiment *n.* sentiment
sentimental *a.* sentimental
sentinel *n.* santinelă
sentry *n.* strajă
separable *a.* separabil
separate *a.* separat
separate *v.t.* a separa
separation *n.* separare
September *n.* septembrie
septic *a.* septic
sepulchre *n.* mormânt
sepulture *n.* înhumare
sequel *n.* urmare
sequence *n.* secvență
sequester *v.t.* a sechestra
serene *a.* senin
serenity *n.* seninătate
serf *n.* șerb
serge *n.* serj
sergeant *n.* sergent
serial *n.* serial
serial *a.* serial
series *n.* serie
serious *a* serios
sermon *n.* predică
serpent *n.* șarpe
serpentine *n.* serpentină
servant *n.* servitor
serve *n.* servă
serve *v.t.* a servi
service *v.t* a depana
service *n.* ntreținere automobile
serviceable *a.* utilizabil
servile *a.* slugarnic
session *n.* sesiune
set *a* fixat
set *n* configurație
set *v.t* a fixa
settle *v.i.* a se statornici
settlement *n.* stabilire

settler *n.* argument
seven *n.* șapte
seventeen *n.*, a șaptesprezece
seventeenth *a.* al
  șaptisprezecelea
seventh *a.* al șaptelea
seventy *n.*, a șaptezeci
sever *v.t.* a despărți
several *a* mai mulți
severe *a.* sever
severity *n.* severitate
sew *v.t.* a coase
sewage *n.* apă de canal
sewer *n* persoană care coase
sewerage *n.* sistem de canalizare
sex *n.* sex
sexual *a.* sexual
sexuality *n.* sexualitate
shabby *a.* ordinar
shackle *v.t.* a încătușa
shackle *n.* cataramă
shade *v.t.* a umbri
shade *n.* umbră
shadow *v.t* a umbri
shadow *n.* umbră
shadowy *a.* umbrit
shaft *n.* mâner
shake *n* zdruncinătură
shake *v.i.* a se clătina
shaky *a.* tremurător
shallow *a.* puțin adânc
sham *a* simulat
sham *n* prefăcătorie
sham *v.i.* a simula
shame *v.t.* a face de rușine
shame *n.* rușine
shameful *a.* rușinos
shameless *a.* nerușinat
shampoo *v.t.* a șampona
shampoo *n.* șampon
shanty *n* baracă
shape *v.t* a modela

shape *n.* formă
shapely *a.* simetric
share *n* acţiune
share *v.t.* a împărţi
share *n.* parte
shark *n.* rechin
sharp *adv.* exact
sharp *a.* ascuţit
sharpen *v.t.* a ascuţi
sharpener *n.* ascuţitoare
sharper *n.* escroc
shatter *v.t.* a sfărâma
shave *n* bărbierit
shave *v.t.* a bărbieri
shawl *n.* şal
she *pron.* ea
sheaf *n.* snop
shear *v.t.* a jumuli
shears *n. pl.* tunsori
shed *n* grajd
shed *v.t.* a revărsa
sheep *n.* oaie
sheepish *a.* sfios
sheer *a.* veritabil
sheet *v.t.* a acoperi cu o pânză
sheet *n.* cearşaf
shelf *n.* raft
shell *v.t.* a coji
shell *n.* coajă
shelter *v.t.* a adăposti
shelter *n.* adăpost
shelve *v.t.* a fi înclinat
shepherd *n.* păstor
shield *v.t.* a blinda
shield *n.* blindaj
shift *n* schimb de tură
shift *v.t.* a înlocui
shifty *a.* viclean
shilling *n.* monedă englezească
shilly-shally *v.i.* a fi nehotărât
shin *n.* tibie
shine *n* strălucire

shine *v.i.* a străluci
shiny *a.* strălucitor
ship *v.t.* a îmbarca
ship *n.* vapor
shipment *n.* încărcătură
shirk *v.t.* a se sustrage de la
shirt *n.* cămaşă
shiver *v.i.* a tremuta (de frig, etc)
shoal *n* teanc
shoal *n.* puzderie
shock *v.t.* a şoca
shock *n.* şoc
shoe *v.t.* a încălţa
shoe *n.* pantof
shoot *n* tir
shoot *v.t.* a trage (cu o armă)
shop *v.i.* a face cumpărături
shop *n.* magazin
shore *n.* ţărm
short *adv.* brusc
short *a.* scurt
shortage *n.* insuficienţă
shortcoming *n.* insuficienţă
shorten *v.t.* a scurta
shortly *adv.* pe scurt
shot *n.* împuşcătură
shoulder *v.t.* a lua pe umăr
shoulder *n.* umăr
shout *v.i.* a striga
shout *n.* strigăt
shove *n.* brânci
shove *v.t.* a îmbrânci
shovel *v.t.* a lua cu lopata
shovel *n.* lingură
show *n.* arătare
show *v.t.* a arăta
shower *v.t.* a face duş
shower *n.* duş
shrew *n.* femeie îndărătnică
shrewd *a.* dibaci
shrill *a.* strident
shrine *n.* moaşte

shrink *v.i* a se micşora
shroud *v.t.* a înfăşura în giulgiu
shroud *n.* giulgiu
shrub *n.* arbust
shrug *v.t.* a ridica din umeri
shudder *n* fior
shudder *v.i.* a se înfiora
shuffle *n.* mers târşât
shuffle *v.i.* a amesteca (cărţile)
shun *v.t.* a se feri de
shunt *v.t.* a manevra (un tren)
shut *v.t.* a închide
shutter *n.* oblon
shuttle *v.t.* a se fâstâci
shuttle *n.* suveică
shuttlecock *n.* minge cu pene
shy *v.i.* a se ruşina
shy *n.* timid
sick *a.* bonlav
sickle *n.* seceră
sickly *a.* bolnăvicios
sickness *n.* boală
side *v.i.* a fi de partea cuiva
side *n.* parte
siege *n.* asediu
sieve *v.t.* a cerne
sieve *n.* ciur
sift *v.t.* a iscodi
sigh *v.i.* a suspina
sigh *n.* suspin
sight *v.t.* a zări
sight *n.* vedere
sightly *a.* vizibil
sign *v.t.* a semna
sign *n.* semn
signal *a.* însemnat
signal *v.t.* a da un semnal
signal *n.* semnal
signatory *n.* semnatar
signature *n.* semnătură
significance *n.* semnificaţie
significant *a.* semnificativ

signification *n.* semnificaţie
signify *v.t.* a semnifica
silence *v.t.* a reduce la tăcere
silence *n.* tăcere
silencer *n.* surdină
silent *a.* tăcut
silhouette *n.* siluetă
silk *n.* mătase
silken *a.* mătăsos
silky *a.* mătăsos
silly *a.* prostuţ
silt *v.t.* a (se) înnămoli
silt *n.* nămol
silver *a* argintiu
silver *n.* argint
similar *a.* similar
similarity *n.* similaritate
similitude *n.* similitudine
simmer *v.i.* a mocni
simple *a.* simplu
simpleton *n.* nătărău
simplicity *n.* simplitate
simplification *n.* simplificaţie
simplify *v.t.* a simplifica
simultaneous *a.* simultan
sin *v.i.* a păcătui
sin *n.* păcat
since *adv.* de atunci
since *conj.* de când
since *prep.* de la
sincere *a.* sincer
sincerity *n.* sinceritate
sinful *a.* păcătos
sing *v.i.* a cânta
singe *v.t.* a arde
singer *n.* cântăreţ
single *n.* simplu
single *v.t.* a distinge
single *a.* celibatar(ă)
singular *a.* singular
singularity *n.* particularitate
sinister *a.* sinistru

sink *n* chiuvetă
sink *v.i.* a se scufunda
sinner *n.* păcătos
sinuous *a.* păcătos
sip *n.* sorbitură
sip *v.t.* a sorbi
sir *n.* domn
siren *n.* sirenă
sister *n.* soră
sit *v.i.* a lua loc
site *n.* poziție
situation *n.* situație
six *n., a* șase
sixteen *n., a.* șaisprezece
sixteenth *a.* al șaisprezecelea
sixth *a.* al șaselea
sixtieth *a.* al șaizecilea
sixty *n., a.* șaizeci
size *n.* mărime
size *v.t.* a orândui
sizzle *v.i.* a sfârâi (la prăjit)
skate *n.* patina
skate *v.t.* a patina
skein *n.* scul
skeleton *n.* schelet
sketch *v.t.* a schița
sketch *n.* schiță
sketchy *a.* sumar
skid *n* sabot de frână
skid *v.t* a face să derapeze
skilful *a.* descurcăreț
skill *n.* dibăcie
skin *v.t* a jupui
skin *n.* piele
skip *v.i.* a omite
skipper *n.* comandant de vas
skirmish *v.t.* a se hărțui
skirmish *n.* încăierare
skirt *n.* fustă
skit *n.* satiră
skull *n.* craniu
sky *n.* cer

slab *n.* lespede
slack *a.* slăbit
slacken *v.t.* a reduce
slake *v.t.* a potoli (setea)
slam *n* zgomot (de ușă trântită)
slam *v.t.* a trânti (ușa)
slander *n.* clevetire
slander *v.t.* a cleveti
slang *n.* jargon
slant *n* pantă
slant *v.t.* a fi oblic
slap *v.t.* a pălmui
slap *n.* palmă
slash *n* tăietură
slash *v.t.* a cresta
slate *n.* ardezie
slattern *n.* femeie neângrijită
slaughter *v.t.* a măcelări
slaughter *n.* măcel
slave *v.i.* a robi
slave *n.* sclav
slavery *n.* sclavie
slavish *a.* servil
slay *v.t.* a asasina
sleek *a.* unsuros
sleep *n.* somn
sleep *v.i.* a dormi
sleeper *n.* vagon de dormit
sleepy *a.* somnoros
sleeve *n* mânecă
sleight *n.* dexteritate
slender *n.* subțire
slice *v.t.* a tăia (ceva) în felii
slice *n.* felie
slick *a* alunecos
slide *n* alunecare
slide *v.i.* a aluneca
slight *v.t.* a desconsidera
slight *a.* plăpând
slim *v.i.* a subția
slim *a.* subțire
slime *n.* mocirlă

slimy *a.* vâscos
sling *n.* praştie
slip *n.* alunecare
slip *v.i.* a aluneca
slipper *n.* papuc
slippery *a.* alunecos
slipshod *a.* scâlciat
slit *v.t.* a (se) despica
slit *n.* şliţ
slogan *n.* lozincă
slope *v.i.* a fi în pantă
slope *n.* diferenţă de nivel
sloth *n.* trândăvie
slough *v.t.* a năpârli
slough *n.* mlaştină
slough *n.* piele de şarpe năpârlită
slow *v.i.* a reduce viteza
slow *a* încet
slowly *adv.* lent
sluggard *n.* leneş
sluggish *a.* apatic
sluice *n.* stăvilar
slum *n.* mahala
slumber *n.* picoteală
slumber *v.i.* a dormita
slump *v.i.* a scădea brusc
slump *n.* scădere a preţurilor
slur *n.* dezaprobare
slush *n.* zăpadă fleşcăită
slut *n.* târfă
sly *a.* şiret
smack *n* palmă
smack *n.* iz
smack *v.i.* a da impresia (de)
smack *v.t.* a face să pocnească
smack *n.* trosnitură
small *n* indispensabili
small *a.* mic
smallpox *n.* variolă
smart *n* suferinţă
smart *v.i* a ustura
smart *a.* inteligent

smash *n* sfărâmare
smash *v.t.* a zdrobi
smear *n.* mâzgălitură
smear *v.t.* a murdări
smell *v.t.* a mirosi
smell *n.* miros
smelt *v.i.* a topi (un minereu)
smile *v.i.* a zâmbi
smile *n.* zâmbet
smith *n.* fierar
smog *n.* ceaţă şi fum
smoke *v.i.* a fuma
smoke *n.* fum
smoky *a.* de fum
smooth *v.t.* a netezi
smooth *a.* neted
smother *v.t.* a asfixia
smoulder *v.i.* a mocni
smug *a.* îngust la minte
smuggle *v.t.* a introduce pe furiş
smuggler *n.* contrabandist
snack *n.* gustare
snag *n.* buturugă
snail *n.* melc
snake *v.i.* a şerpui
snake *n.* şarpe
snap *a* neprevăzut
snap *n* pocnet
snap *v.t.* a pocni
snare *n.* laţ
snarl *v.i.* a mârîi
snarl *n.* mârîit
snatch *n.* înşfăcare
snatch *v.t.* a înşfăca
sneak *n* netrebnic
sneak *v.i.* a se furişa
sneer *n* rânjet
sneer *v.i* a rânji
sneeze *n* strănut
sneeze *v.i.* a strănut
sniff *n* inspiraţie
sniff *v.i.* a inspira

snob *n.* snob
snobbery *n.* snobism
snore *n* sforăit
snore *v.i.* a sforăi
snort *n.* sforăială
snout *n.* a pufni
snow *v.i.* a ninge
snow *n.* zăpadă
snowy *a.* de zăpadă
snub *n.* dojană
snub *v.t.* a dojeni
snuff *n.* tutun de prizat
snug *a.* comod
so *adv.* aşa
so *conj.* deci
soak *v.t.* a uda
soap *v.t.* a (se) săpuni
soap *n.* săpun
soar *v.i.* a se avânta
sob *n* hohot de plâns
sob *v.i.* hohot de plâns
sober *a.* care n-a băut
sobriety *n.* sobrietate
sociability *n.* sociabilitate
sociable *a.* sociabil
social *n.* social
socialism *n* socialism
socialist *n,a* socialist
society *n.* societate
sociology *n.* sociologie
sock *n.* şosetă
socket *n.* cavitate
sod *n.* gazon
sofa *n.* canapea
soft *n.* moale
soften *v.t.* a moleşi
soil *v.t.* a îngrăşa (pământul)
soil *n.* pământ
sojourn *n* loc de şedere
sojourn *v.i.* a rămâne undeva
solace *n.* consolare
solace *v.t.* a consola

solar *a.* solar
solder *v.t.* a suda
solder *n.* sudură
soldier *v.i.* a fi militar
soldier *n.* soldat
sole *a* singur
sole *v.t* a pingeli
sole *n.* pingea
solemn *a.* solemn
solemnity *n.* solemnitate
solicit *v.t.* a solicita
solicitation *n.* solicitare
solicitor *n.* avocat
solicitude *n.* solicitudine
solid *n* corp solid
solid *a.* solid
solidarity *n.* solidariate
solitary *a.* solitar
solitude *n.* singurătate
solo *a.* singur
solo *n* solo
soluble *a.* solubil
solution *n.* soluţie
solve *v.t.* a rezolva
solvency *n.* solvabilitate
solvent *n* disolvant
solvent *a.* solvabil
sombre *a.* întunecat
some *pron.* câţiva
some *a.* vreun
somebody *n.* o personalitate
somebody *pron.* cineva
somehow *adv.* cumva
someone *pron.* careva
somersault *v.i.* a face o tumbă
somersault *n.* săritură
something *adv.* puţin
something *pron.* ceva
sometime *adv.* cândva
sometimes *adv.* câteodată
somewhat *adv.* oarecum
somewhere *adv.* undeva

somnambulist *n.* somnambul
somnolence *n.* somnolenţă
somnolent *n.* somnolent
son *n.* fiu
song *n.* cântec
songster *n.* pasăre cântătoare
sonnet *n.* sonet
sonority *n.* sonoritate
soon *adv.* curând
soot *v.t.* a acoperi cu funingine
soot *n.* funingine
soothe *v.t.* a potoli
sophism *n.* sofism
sophisticate *v.t.* a corupe
sophisticated *a.* rafinat
sophistication *n.* rafinament
sorcerer *n.* vrăjitor
sorcery *n.* vrăjitorie
sordid *a.* josnic
sore *n* rană
sore *a.* dureros
sorrow *v.i.* necaz
sorrow *n.* necaz
sorry *a.* căruia îi pare rău
sort *n.* soi
sort *v.t* a sorta
soul *n.* suflet
sound *n* sunet
sound *v.i.* a suna
sound *a.* sănătos
soup *n.* supă
sour *v.t.* a acri
sour *a.* acru
source *n.* sursă
south *a* sudic
south *adv* spre sud
south *n.* sud
southerly *a.* sudic
southern *a.* sudic
souvenir *n.* suvenir
sovereign *a* suveran
sovereign *n.* suveran

sovereignty *n.* suveranitate
sow *n.* scroafă
sow *v.t.* a semăna
space *v.t.* a spaţia
space *n.* spaţiu
spacious *a.* spaţios
spade *v.t.* a săpa
spade *n.* sapă
span *v.t.* a măsura cu palma
span *n.* scurt răstimp
Spaniard *n.* spaniol
spaniel *n.* (om) linguşitor
Spanish *n.* limba spaniolă
Spanish *a.* spaniolesc
spanner *n.* cheie de piuliţă
spare *a* de rezervă
spare *v.t.* a scuti
spark *n.* licărire
spark *v.i.* a scânteia
spark *n.* scânteie
sparkle *n.* scânteiere
sparkle *v.i.* a scânteia
sparrow *n.* vrabie
sparse *a.* răzleţit
spasm *n.* spasm
spate *n.* revărsare
spatial *a.* spaţial
spawn *v.i.* a depune icre
spawn *n.* icre
speak *v.i.* a vorbi
speaker *n.* vorbitor
spear *v.t.* a străpunge cu lancea
spear *n.* lance
special *a.* deosebit
specialist *n.* specialist
speciality *n.* specialitate
specialization *n.* specializare
specialize *v.i.* a specializa
species *n.* specie
specific *a.* specific
specification *n.* specificaţie
specify *v.t.* a specifica

specimen *n.* speciment
speck *n.* strop
spectacle *n.* spectacol
spectacular *a.* spectaculos
spectator *n.* spectator
spectre *n.* spectru
speculate *v.i.* a specula
speculation *n.* speculație
speech *n.* discurs
speed *v.i.* a merge repede
speed *n.* viteză
speedy *a.* repede
spell *n* interval de timp
spell *v.t.* a pronunța
spell *n.* vrajă
spend *v.t.* a cheltui
spendthrift *n.* om cheltuitor
sperm *n.* spermă
sphere *n.* sferă
spherical *a.* sferic
spice *v.t.* a condimenta
spice *n.* condiment
spicy *a.* condimentat
spider *n.* păianjen
spike *v.t.* a străpunge
spike *n.* vârf ascuțit
spill *n* cădere
spill *v.i.* a vărsa
spin *n.* rotire
spin *v.i.* a învârti
spinach *n.* spanac
spinal *a.* spinal
spindle *n.* fus
spine *n.* ghimpe
spinner *n.* titirez
spinster *n.* fată bătrână
spiral *a.* în spirală
spiral *n.* spirală
spirit *n.* spirit
spirited *a.* spiritual
spiritual *a.* spiritual
spiritualism *n.* spiritualism

spirituality *n.* spiritualitate
spit *n* scuipat
spit *v.i.* a scuipa
spite *n.* pică
spittle *n* salivă
spittoon *n.* scuipătoare
splash *n* stropire
splash *v.i.* a țâșni
spleen *n.* splină
splendid *a.* splendid
splendour *n.* splendoare
splinter *v.t.* a rupe
splinter *n.* așchie
split *n* despicare
split *v.i.* a despica
spoil *n* jaf
spoil *v.t.* a strica
spoke *n.* spiță (de roată)
spokesman *n.* purtător de cuvânt
sponge *v.t.* a suge cu buretele
sponge *n.* burete
sponsor *v.t.* a sponsoriza
sponsor *n.* sponsor
spontaneity *n.* spontaneitate
spontaneous *a.* spontan
spoon *n.* lingură
spoon *v.t.* a mânca cu lingura
spoonful *n.* lingură (conținut)
sporadic *a.* sporadic
sport *v.i.* a face sport
sport *n.* sport
sportive *a.* sportiv
sportsman *n.* sportiv
spot *v.t.* a păta
spot *n.* pată
spotless *a.* fără pete
spouse *n.* soț, soție
spout *v.i.* a țâșni
spout *n.* burlan
sprain *n.* luxație
sprain *v.t.* a luxa
spray *n* pulverizator

spray *v.t.* a pulveriza (un lichid)
spray *n.* apă pulverizată
spread *n.* răspândire
spread *v.i.* a răspândi
spree *n.* zburdălnicie
sprig *n.* primăvară
sprightly *a.* zburdalnic
spring *n* primăvară
spring *v.i.* a încovoia
sprinkle *v. t.* a presăra (cu)
sprint *n* cursă de viteză
sprint *v.i.* a sprinta
sprout *n* germen
sprout *v.i.* a încolţi
spur *v.t.* a da pinteni (calului)
spur *n.* pinten
spurious *a.* falsificat
spurn *v.t.* a respinge cu dispreţ
spurt *n* efort de viteză
spurt *v.i.* a face un efort de viteză
spy *v.i.* a spiona
spy *n.* spion
squad *n.* grupă de soldaţi
squadron *n.* batalion
squalid *a.* murdar
squander *v.t.* a cheltui nebuneşte
square *a* pătrat
square *v.t.* a ridica la pătrat
square *n.* pătrat
squash *n* strivire
squash *v.t.* a strivi
squat *v.i.* a se instala
squeak *n* chiţăit
squeak *v.i.* a chiţăi
squeeze *v.t.* a stoarce
squint *n* privire saşie
squint *v.i.* a se uita saşiu
squire *n.* scutier
squirrel *n.* veveriţă
stab *n.* lovitură de cuţit
stab *v.t.* a înjunghia

stability *n.* stabilitate
stabilization *n.* stabilizare
stabilize *v.t.* a stabiliza
stable *n* grajd
stable *v.t.* a băga în grajd
stable *a.* a stabiliza
stadium *n.* stadion
staff *v.t.* a înzestra cu personal
staff *n.* personal
stag *n.* cerb
stage *v.t.* a pune în scenă
stage *n.* scenă
stagger *n.* clătinare
stagger *v.i.* a se clătina
stagnant *a.* stagnant
stagnate *v.i.* a stagna
stagnation *n.* stagnare
staid *a.* cumpătat
stain *v.t.* pată
stain *n.* pată
stainless *a.* nepătat
stair *n.* treaptă
stake *v.t.* a juca
stake *n* miză
stale *v.t.* a se învechi
stale *a.* stătut
stalk *n* picior (de pahar)
stalk *v.i.* a păşi cu aroganţă
stalk *n.* coş de fabrică
stall *v.t.* a bloca (un motor)
stall *n.* magherniţă
stallion *n.* armăsar
stalwart *a.* viguros
stalwart *n* membru al unui partid
stamina *n.* vigoare
stammer *n* bâlbâire
stammer *v.i.* a se bâlbâi
stamp *v.i.* a timbra
stamp *n.* timbru
stampede *v.i* a fi cuprins de panică
stampede *n.* panică

stand *n.* oprire
stand *v.i.* a sta (în picioare)
standard *a* etalon
standard *n.* etalon
standardize *v.t.* a standardiza
standing *n.* poziţie în picioare
standpoint *n.* punct de vedere
standstill *n.* punct mort
stanza *n.* strofă
staple *a* a prevedea cu zăvor
staple *n.* agrafă
star *v.t.* a înstela
star *n.* stea
starch *v.t.* a apreta
starch *n.* scrobeală
stare *n.* privire fixă
stare *v.i.* a se holba (la)
stark *adv.* pe de-a-ntregul
stark *a.* desăvârşit
starry *a.* înstelat
start *n* început
start *v.t.* a începe
startle *v.t.* a înfiora
starvation *n.* înfometare
starve *v.i.* a răbda de foame
state *v.t* a declara
state *n.* stat
stateliness *n.* comunicat
statesman *n.* om de stat
static *n.* paraziţi atmosferici
statics *n.* statică
station *n.* post de radio
station *v.t.* a plasa
stationary *a.* staţionar
stationer *n.* vânzător (de hârtie)
stationery *n.* papetărie
statistical *a.* statistic
statistics *n.* statistică
statue *n.* statuie
stature *n.* statură
status *n.* statut legal
statute *n.* act emis de parlament

statutory *a.* statutar
staunch *a.* devotat
stay *n* şedere
stay *v.i.* a sta
steadfast *a.* constant
steady *v.t.* a consolida
steady *a.* neclintit
steal *v.i.* a fura
steam *n* abur
steam *v.i.* a răspândi aburi
steamer *n.* vapor
steed *n.* bidiviu
steel *n.* oţel
steep *v.t.* a pune la muiat
steep *a.* abrupt
steeple *n.* turlă
steer *v.t.* a cârmi
stellar *a.* stelar
stem *v.i.* a stăvili
stem *n.* tulpină
stench *n.* duhoare
stencil *v.i.* a vopsi
stencil *n.* şablon
stenography *n.* stenografie
step *v.i.* a păşi
step *n.* pas
steppe *n.* stepă
stereotype *a.* stereotip
stereotype *n.* clişeu
sterile *a.* steril
sterility *n.* sterilitate
sterilization *n.* sterilizare
sterilize *v.t.* a steriliza
sterling *n.* monedă engleză
sterling *a.* veritabil
stern *n.* pupă
stern *a.* rigid
stethoscope *n.* stetoscop
stew *v.t.* a fierbe înăbuşit
stew *n.* tocană
steward *n.* intendent
stick *v.t.* a înfige

stick *n.* băţ
stickler *n.* enigmă
sticky *a.* lipicios
stiff *a.* ţeapăn
stiffen *v.t.* a înţepeni
stifle *v.t.* a sufoca
stigma *n.* stigmat
still *adv.* încă
still *n.* calm
still *v.t.* a distila
still *a.* nemişcat
stimulant *n.* stimulent
stimulate *v.t.* a stimula
stimulus *n.* stimul
sting *n.* înţepătură
sting *v.t.* a înţepa
stingy *a.* zgârcit
stink *n* duhoare
stink *v.i.* a puţi
stipend *n.* stipendiu
stipulate *v.t.* a stipula
stipulation *n.* stipulare
stir *v.i.* a agita (un lichid)
stirrup *n.* scară de şa
stitch *v.t.* a coase
stitch *n.* copcă
stock *v.t.* a aproviziona
stock *n.* stoc
stocking *n.* ciorap
stoic *n.* stoic
stoke *v.t.* a încărca
stoker *n.* fochist
stomach *v.t.* a suporta
stomach *n.* stomac
stone *v.t.* a pava
stone *n.* piatră
stony *a.* de piatră
stool *n.* taburet
stoop *n* poziţie încovoiată
stoop *v.i.* a se încovoia
stop *n* oprire
stop *v.t.* a opri

stoppage *n* întrerupere
storage *n.* înmagazinare
store *v.t.* a stoca
store *n.* provizie
storey *n.* etaj
stork *n.* barză
storm *v.i.* a se dezlănţui
storm *n.* furtună
stormy *a.* furtunos
story *n.* povestire
stout *a.* corpolent
stove *n.* sobă
stow *v.t.* a rândui
straggle *v.i.* a se abate
straight *adv.* direct
straight *a.* drept
straighten *v.t.* a îndrepta
straightforward *a.* de încredere
strain *n* încordare
strain *v.t.* a încorda
strait *n.* strâmtoare
straiten *v.t.* a strâmta
strand *n* ţărm
strand *v.i.* a eşua
strange *a.* straniu
stranger *n.* (om) străin
strangle *v.t.* a strangula
strangulation *n.* strangulare
strap *n.* curea
strategic *a.* strategic
strategist *n.* strategie
strategy *n.* strategie
stratum *n.* strat
straw *n.* pai
strawberry *n.* căpşună
stray *a* pierdut
stray *n* animal rătăcit
stray *v.i.* a rătăci
stream *v.i.* a izvorî
stream *n.* fluviu
streamer *n.* fascicul
street *n.* stradă

strength *n.* forţă
strengthen *v.t.* a întări
strenuous *a.* energic
stress *v.t* a stresa
stress *n.* stres
stretch *n* întindere
stretch *v.t.* a întinde
stretcher *n.* extensor
strew *v.t.* a răspândi
strict *a.* strict
stricture *n.* obiecţie
stride *n* pas mare
stride *v.i.* a umbla prin
strident *a.* strident
strife *n.* conflict
strike *n* lovitură
strike *v.t.* a izbi
striker *n.* grevist
string *v.t.* a lega cu sfoară
string *n.* şnur
stringency *n.* severitate
stringent *a.* strict
strip *v.t.* a dezgoli
strip *n.* fâşie
stripe *n.* dungă
strive *v.i.* a se strădui
stroke *n* atac
stroke *v.t.* a dezmierda
stroke *n.* lovitură
stroll *n* plimbare (scurtă)
stroll *v.i.* a hoinări
strong *a.* puternic
stronghold *n.* fortăreaţă
structural *a.* structural
structure *n.* structură
struggle *n* străduinţă
struggle *v.i.* a se zbate
strumpet *n.* târfă
strut *n* umblet ţanţoş
strut *v.i.* a merge ţanţoş
stub *n.* buştean
stubble *n.* mirişte

stubborn *a.* încăpăţânat
stud *v.t.* a împodobi cu cuie
stud *n.* crampon
student *n.* elev
studio *n.* atelier
study *n.* studiu
study *v.i.* a studia
stuff *v.t.* a îndopa
stuff *n.* baliverne
stuffy *a.* îmbâcsit
stumble *n.* poticnire
stumble *v.i.* a se poticni
stump *v.t* a estompa
stump *n.* butuc
stun *v.t.* a năuci
stunt *n* tur de forţă
stunt *v.t.* a opri creşterea
stupefy *v.t.* a stupefia
stupendous *a.* uimitor
stupid *a* stupid
stupidity *n.* stupiditate
sty *n.* urcior (la ochi)
style *n.* stil
subdue *v.t.* a subjuga
subject *a* subjugat
subject *n.* subiect
subject *v.t.* a subjuga
subjection *n.* subjugare
subjective *a.* subiectiv
subjugate *v.t.* a subjuga
subjugation *n.* subjugare
sublet *v.t.* a subânchiria
sublimate *v.t.* a sublima
sublime *a.* sublim
sublimity *n.* sublimitate
submarine *a* submarin
submarine *n.* submarin
submerge *v.i.* a cufunda în apă
submission *n.* supunere
submissive *a.* supus
submit *v.t.* a supune
subordinate *a.* subordonat

subordinate *n* subordonare
subordinate *v.t.* s subordona
subordination *n.* subordonare
subscribe *v.t.* a iscăli
subscription *n.* iscălitură
subsequent *a.* care urmează
subservient *a.* folositor (pentru)
subside *v.i.* a se sedimenta
subsidiary *a.* auxiliar
subsidize *v.t.* a subvenționa
subsidy *n.* subvenție
subsist *v.i.* a subzista
subsistence *n.* trai
substance *n.* substanță
substantial *a.* substanțial
substantially *adv.* sunstanțial
substitute *n.* locțiitor
subterranean *a.* subteran
subtle *n.* subtil
subtlety *n.* subtilitate
subtract *v.t.* a scădea
subtraction *n.* scădere
suburb *n.* suburbie
subvert *v.t.* a răstuna (un sistem)
succeed *v.i.* a succeda
success *n.* succes
successful *a* de succes
succession *n.* succesiune
successive *a.* succesiv
successor *n.* succesor
succour *v.t.* a sprijini (pe cineva)
succour *n.* ajutor
succumb *v.i.* a cade prada
such *a.* atât de
suck *n.* supt
suck *v.t.* a suge
suckle *v.t.* a alăpta (un copil)
sudden *n.* lucru năprasnic
suddenly *adv.* pe neașteptate
sue *v.t.* a da în judecată
suffer *v.t.* a suferi
suffice *v.i.* a ajunge

sufficiency *n.* suficiență
sufficient *a.* suficient
suffix *n.* sufix
suffocate *v.t* a sufoca
suffocation *n.* sufocare
suffrage *n.* drept de vot
sugar *v.t.* a zaharisi
sugar *n.* zahăr
suggest *v.t.* a sugera
suggestion *n.* sugestie
suggestive *a.* sugestiv
suicidal *a.* sinucigaș
suicide *n.* a se sinucide
suit *v.t.* a adapta
suit *n.* costum de haine
suitable *a.* potrivit
suite *n.* suită
suitor *n.* pretendent
sullen *a.* morocănos
sulphur *n.* sulf
sulphuric *a.* sulfuric
sultry *a.* înăbușitor
sum *v.t.* a aduna
sum *n.* sumă
summarily *adv.* sumar
summarize *v.t.* a sumariza
summary *a* sumar
summary *n.* sumar
summer *n.* vară
summit *n.* culme
summon *v.t.* a soma
summons *n.* citație
sumptuous *a.* somptuos
sun *n.* soare
Sunday *n.* duminică
sunder *v.t.* a separa
sunny *a.* însorit
sup *v.i.* a cina
superb *a.* superb
superficial *a.* superficial
superficiality *n.* superficialitate
superfluity *n.* suplus

superfluous *a.* de prisos
superintend *v.t.* a supraveghea
superintendent *n.* supraveghetor
superior *a.* superior
superiority *n.* superioritate
superlative *n.* superlativ
superlative *a.* superlativ
superman *n.* supraom
supernatural *a.* supranatural
supersede *v.t.* a suprima
supersonic *a.* supersonic
superstition *n.* superstiție
superstitious *a.* superstițios
supertax *n.* suprataxă
supervise *v.t.* a controla
supper *n.* cină
supple *a.* suplu
supplement *n.* supliment
supplement *v.t.* a suplimenta
supplementary *a.* suplimentar
supplier *n.* furnizor
supply *n* aprovizionare
supply *v.t.* a aproviziona
support *n.* sprijin
support *v.t.* a sprijini
suppose *v.t.* a presupune
supposition *n.* presupunere
suppress *v.t.* a suprima
supremacy *n.* supremație
supreme *a.* suprem
surcharge *v.t.* a supraâncărca
surcharge *n.* surplus
sure *a.* sigur
surely *adv.* cu siguranță
surety *n.* siguranță
surf *n.* valuri
surface *n.* suprafață
surface *v.i* a polei
surfeit *n.* saturație
surge *v.i.* a fi furioasă
surge *n.* talaz
surgeon *n.* chirurg

surgery *n.* chirurgie
surmise *v.t.* a presupune
surmise *n.* presupunere
surmount *v.t.* a trece peste
surname *n.* nume de familie
surpass *v.t.* a depăși
surplus *n.* surplus
surprise *v.t.* a surprinde
surprise *n.* surpriză
surrender *n* predare
surrender *v.t.* a preda
surround *v.t.* a înconjura
surroundings *n.* împrejurimi
surtax *n.* suprataxă
surveillance *n.* inspecție
survey *n.* vedere generală
survey *v.t.* a examina detaliatv.t
survival *n.* supraviețuire
survive *v.i.* a supraviețui
suspect *n* suspect
suspect *a.* suspect
suspect *v.t.* a suspecta
suspend *v.t.* a suspenda
suspense *n.* suspensie
suspension *n.* suspendare
susperhuman *a.* supraomenesc
suspicion *n.* bănuială
suspicious *a.* bănuitor
sustain *v.t.* a susține
sustenance *n.* susținere
swagger *n* lăudăroșenie
swagger *v.i.* a se făli,
swallow *n.* înghițitură
swallow *n.* rândunică
swallow *v.t.* a înghiți
swamp *v.t.* a umple cu apă
swamp *n.* mlaștină
swan *n.* lebădă
swarm *v.i.* a escalada
swarm *n.* mulțime
swarthy *a.* oacheș
sway *n* balansare

sway *v.i.* a se balansa
swear *v.t.* a jura
sweat *v.i.* a asuda
sweat *n.* sudoare
sweater *n.* pulover
sweep *n.* măturat
sweep *v.i.* a mătura
sweeper *n.* măturătoare mecanică
sweet *n* dulciuri
sweet *a.* dulce
sweeten *v.t.* a îndulci
sweetmeat *n.* bomboană
sweetness *n.* dulceață
swell *n* umflătură
swell *v.i.* a se umfla
swift *a.* prompt
swim *n* înot
swim *v.i.* a înota
swimmer *n.* înotător
swindle *n.* escrocherie
swindle *v.t.* a escroca
swindler *n.* escroc
swine *n.* porc
swing *n* leagăn
swing *v.i.* a se legăna
swiss *n.* elvețian
switch *v.t.* a schimba
switch *n.* comutator
swoon *v.i* a leșina
swoon *n.* leșin
swoop *v.i.* a se repezi (la)
sword *n.* sabie
sycamore *n.* sicomor
sycophant *n.* parazit
syllabic *a.* silabic
syllable *n.* silabă
syllabus *n.* plan
sylvan *a.* de pădure
symbol *n.* simbol
symbolic *a.* simbolic
symbolism *n.* simbolism
symbolize *v.t.* a simboliza

symmetrical *a.* simetric
symmetry *n.* simetrie
sympathetic *a.* simpatic
sympathize *v.i.* a simpatiza
sympathy *n.* simpatie
symphony *n.* simfonie
symposium *n.* simpozion
symptom *n.* simptom
synonym *n.* sinonim
synonymous *a.* sinonim (cu)
syntax *n.* sintaxă
synthesis *n.* sinteză
synthetic *n* sintetic
synthetic *a.* sintetic
syringe *n.* seringă
syrup *n.* sirop
system *n.* sistem
systematic *a.* sistematic
systematize *v.t.* a sistematiza

T

table *n.* masă
tablet *n.* tabletă
taboo *a* interzis
taboo *v.t.* a interzice
taboo *n.* tabu
tabular *a.* tabelar
tabulate *v.t.* a cataloga
tacit *a.* tăcut
tackle *v.t.* a înhăța
tackle *n.* unealtă
tact *n.* tact
tactful *a.* cu tact
tactics *n.* tactică
tactile *a.* tactil
tag *n.* etichetă
tag *v.t.* a eticheta
tail *n.* coadă

tailor *v.t.* a croi
tailor *n.* croitor
taint *v.t.* a păta
taint *n.* pată
take *v.t* a lua
tale *n.* basm
talent *n.* talent
talisman *n.* talisman
talk *n* conversaţie
talk *v.i.* a vorbi
talkative *a.* vorbăreţ
tall *a.* înalt
tallow *n.* unsoare
tally *v.t.* a socoti
tally *n.* duplicat
tame *v.t.* a îmblânzi
tame *a.* îmblânzit
tamper *v.i.* a îmblânzi
tan *n., a.* bronz
tan *v.i.* a bronza
tangent *n.* tangent
tangible *a.* tangibil
tangle *v.t.* a încurca
tangle *'n.* nod
tank *n.* rezervor
tanker *n.* autocisternă
tanner *n.* tăbăcar
tantamount *a.* echivalent (cu)
tap *n.* lovitură uşoară
tap *v.t.* a lovi uşor
tape *n.* bandă
taper *n* lumânare de ceară
taper *v.i.* a fi ascuţit
tapestry *n.* tapiserie
tar *v.t.* a gudrona
tar *n.* gudron
target *n.* ţintă
tariff *n.* tarif
tarnish *v.t.* a lua lustrul
task *v.t.* a pune la treabă
task *n.* sarcină
taste *v.t.* a gusta

taste *n.* gust
tasty *a.* savuros
tatter *n.* zdreanţă
tattoo *v.i.* a tatua
tattoo *n.* tatuaj
taunt *n* dojană
taunt *v.t.* a dojeni
tavern *n.* tavernă
tax *v.t.* a taxa
tax *n.* taxă
taxable *a.* taxabil
taxation *n.* taxare
taxi *n.* taxi
tea *n* ceai
teach *v.t.* a preda
teacher *n.* profesor
team *n.* echipă
tear *n.* lacrimă
tear *v.t.* a rupe
tease *v.t.* a cicăli
teat *n.* sfârc (de sân)
technical *n.* tehnic
technicality *n.* tehnicalitate
technician *n.* tehnician
technique *n.* tehnică
technological *a.* tehnologic
technologist *n.* tehnolog
technology *n.* tehnologie
tedious *a.* anost
tedium *n.* plictiseală
teem *v.i.* a forfoti
teenager *n.* adolescent
teens *n. pl.* adolescenţi
teethe *v.i.* a-i da dinţii
teetotaller *n.* abstinent
telecast *n.* emisiune de
    televiziune
telecast *v.t.* a transmite televizat
telecommunications *n.*
    telecomunicare
telegram *n.* telegramă
telegraph *n.* telegraf

telegraphy *n.* telegrafie
telepathic *a.* telepatic
telepathy *n.* telepatie
telephone *n.* telefon
telephone *v.t.* a telefona
telescope *n.* telescop
telescopic *a.* telescopic
televise *v.t.* a televiza
television *n.* televiziune
tell *v.t.* a spune
teller *n.* povestitor
temper *v.t.* a tempera
temper *n.* temperament
temperament *n.* temperament
temperamental *a.*
temperamental
temperance *n.* temperanţă
temperate *a.* temperat
temperature *n.* temperatură
tempest *n.* furtună
tempestuous *a.* violent
temple *n* tâmplă
temple *n.* templu
temporal *a.* temporal
temporary *a.* temporar
tempt *v.t.* a tenta
temptation *n.* tentaţie
ten *n., a* zece
tenable *a.* care poate fi apărat
tenacious *a.* tenace
tenacity *n.* tenacitate
tenancy *n.* stăruinţă
tenant *n.* chiriaş
tend *v.i.* a îngriji
tendency *n.* tendinţă
tender *a* fraged
tender *n* păzitor
tender *v.t.* a oferi
tender *n* tandru
tenet *n.* doctrină
tennis *n.* tenis
tense *a.* încordat

tense *n.* timp
tension *n.* tensiune
tent *n.* cort
tentative *a.* tentativă
tenure *n.* posesiune
term *n.* termen
term *v.t.* a califica
terminable *a.* terminabil
terminal *n* punct terminus
terminal *a.* terminal
terminate *v.t.* a termina
termination *n.* terminare
terminology *n.* terminologie
terminus *n.* staţie finală
terrace *n.* terasă
terrible *a.* teribil
terrier *n.* (câine) terier
terrific *a.* terifiant
terrify *v.t.* a terifia
territorial *a.* teritorial
territory *n.* teritoriu
terror *n.* teroare
terrorist *n.* terorism
terrorize *v.t.* a teroriza
terse *a.* concis
test *n* test
test *v.t.* a testa
testament *n.* testament
testicle *n.* testicul
testify *v.i.* a mărturisi
testimonial *n.* certificat
testimony *n.* mărturie
tether *v.t.* a priponi
tether *n.* pripon
text *n.* text
textile *n* textilă
textile *a.* textil
textual *n.* textual
texture *n.* textură
thank *v.t.* a mulţumi
thankful *a.* recunoscător
thanks *n.* mulţumire

that *adv.* atât de
that *conj.* (pentru) ca să
that *dem. pron.* acela
that *rel. pron.* pe care
that *a.* acel
thatch *v.t.* a acoperi cu paie
thatch *n.* păr des
thaw *n* dezgheţ
thaw *v.i* a dezgheţa
theatre *n.* teatru
theatrical *a.* teatral
theft *n.* furt
their *a.* lor
theirs *pron.* a lor
them *pron.* ei
thematic *a.* tematic
theme *n.* temă
then *a* de atunci
then *adv.* atunci
thence *adv.* de acolo
theologian *n.* teolog
theological *a.* teologic
theology *n.* teologie
theorem *n.* teoremă
theoretical *a.* teoretic
theory *n.* teorie
therapy *n.* terapie
there *adv.* acolo
thereabouts *adv.* cam pe acolo
thereby *adv.* astfel
therefore *adv.* prin urmare
thermal *a.* termal
thermometer *n.* termometru
thermos (flask) *n.* termos
thesis *n.* teză
thick *a.* gros
thick *n.* parte mai densă
thicken *v.i.* a îngroşa
thicket *n.* bilet
thief *n.* hoţ
thigh *n.* coapsă
thimble *n.* degetar

thin *v.t.* a subţia
thin *a.* subţire
thing *n.* lucru
think *v.t.* a gândi
thinker *n.* gânditor
third *n.* treime
third *a.* al treilea
thirst *v.i.* a-i fi sete
thirst *n.* sete
thirsty *a.* însetat
thirteen *a* treisprezece
thirteen *n.* treisprezece
thirteenth *a.* al treisprezecelea
thirtieth *n* a treizecea
thirtieth *a.* al treizecilea
thirty *a* treizeci
thirty *n.* treizeci
thistle *n.* ciulin
thither *adv.* acolo
thorn *n.* spin
thorny *a.* ţepos
thorough *a* amănunţit
thoroughfare *n.* pasaj
though *adv.* totuşi
though *conj.* cu toate că
thought *n* gând
thoughtful *a.* gânditor
thousand *a* mie
thousand *n.* mie
thrall *n.* iobag
thralldom *n.* iobăgie
thrash *v.t.* a chelfăni
thread *v.t* a înşira
thread *n.* tăiş
threadbare *a.* jerpelit
threat *n.* ameninţare
threaten *v.t.* a ameninţa
three *a* trei
three *n.* trei
thresh *v.t.* a treiera (cereale)
thresher *n.* treierător
threshold *n.* prag

thrice *adv.* de trei ori
thrift *n.* economie
thrifty *a.* cumpătat
thrill *v.t.* a face să tresară
thrill *n.* tresărire
thrive *v.i.* a prospera
throat *n.* gâtlej
throaty *a.* gutural
throb *n.* palpitaţie
throb *v.i.* a bate puternic
throne *n.* tron
throng *n.* aglomeraţie
throng *v.t.* a se îmbulzi
throttle *v.t.* a obtura
throttle *n.* trahee
through *a* direct
through *adv.* prin mijlocul
through *prep.* printre
throughout *prep.* pretutindeni
throughout *adv.* în lung şi-n lat
throw *n.* aruncare
throw *v.t.* a arunca
thrust *n* brânci
thrust *v.t.* a vârî
thud *v.i.* a cădea su zgomot surd
thud *n.* zgomot surd
thug *n.* ucigaş
thumb *n.* deget mare
thunder *v.i.* a tuna
thunder *n.* tunet
Thursday *n.* joi
thus *adv.* astfel
tick *v.i.* a ticăi
tick *n.* tic-tac
ticket *n.* bilet
tickle *v.t.* a gâdila
ticklish *a.* care se gâdilă
tidal *a.* privitor la maree
tide *n.* maree
tidiness *n.* ordine
tidings *n. pl.* noutăţi
tidy *v.t.* a pune în ordine

tidy *a.* ordonat
tie *n* cravată
tie *v.t.* a lega
tier *n.* întăritură
tiger *n.* tigru
tight *a.* strâmt
tighten *v.t.* a strânge
tigress *n.* tigroaică
tile *v.t.* a acoperi cu ţigle
tile *n.* ţiglă
till *n. conj.* până când să
till *v.t.* a ara
till *prep.* până (la)
tilt *n.* pantă
tilt *v.i.* a se apleca
timber *n.* cherestea
time *v.t.* a calcula durata
time *n.* timp
timely *a.* de actualitate
timid *a.* timid
timidity *n.* timiditate
timorous *a.* sperios
tin *v.t.* a conserva în cutii
tin *n.* cutie de conserve
tincture *v.t.* a nuanţa
tincture *n.* tinctură
tinge *v.t.* a nuanţa
tinge *n.* nuanţă
tinker *n.* cârpaci
tinsel *n.* bătător la ochi
tint *v.t.* a haşura
tint *n.* tentă
tiny *a.* minuscul
tip *n.* extremitate
tip *n.* sfat
tip *v.t.* a da
tip *v.t.* a da bacşiş (cuiva)
tip *v.t.* a sfătui
tip *n.* bacşiş
tipsy *a.* afumat
tirade *n.* afumat
tire *v.t.* a extenua

tiresome *a.* obositor
tissue *n.* ţesătură
titanic *a.* titanic
tithe *n.* zeciuială
title *n.* titlu
titular *a.* titular
toad *n.* broască râioasă
toast *v.t.* a toasta
toast *n.* pâine prăjită
today *n.* azi
today *adv.* astăzi
toe *n.* deget de la picior
toffee *n.* caramelă
together *adv.* împreună
toil *v.i.* a trudi
toil *n.* mreajă
toilet *n.* toaletă
token *n.* semn
tolerable *a.* tolerabil
tolerance *n.* toleranţă
tolerant *a.* tolerant
tolerate *v.t.* a tolera
toleration *n.* toleranţă
toll *n* uium
toll *v.t.* a trage
toll *n.* impozit
tomato *n.* roşie
tomb *n.* cavou
tomboy *n.* băieţoi
tome *n.* volum
tomorrow *adv.* mâine
tomorrow *n.* mâine
ton *n.* tonă
tone *n.* ton
tone *v.t.* a acorda
tongs *n. pl.* cleşte
tongue *n.* limbă
tonic *n.* tonic
tonic *a.* tonic
tonight *adv.* astă seară
to-night *n.* noapte a zilei de azi
tonsil *n.* amigdală

tonsure *n.* tonsură
too *adv.* prea
tool *n.* instrument
tooth *n.* dinte
top *n.* suprafaţă
top *v.t.* a acoperi (cu)
top *n.* vârf
topic *n.* subiect (de conversaţie
topical *a.* de actualitate
topography *n.* topografie
topple *v.i.* a răsturna
torch *n.* torţă
torment *n.* tortură
torment *v.t.* a tortura
tornado *n.* tornadă
torpedo *v.t.* a torpila
torpedo *n.* torpilă
torrent *n.* torent
torrential *a.* torenţial
torrid *a.* torid
tortoise *n.* broască ţestoasă
tortuous *a.* întortocheat
torture *v.t.* a totura
torture *n.* tortură
toss *n* azvârlitură
toss *v.t.* a zgâlţâi
total *n.* total
total *v.t.* a aduna
total *a.* total
totality *n.* totalitate
touch *n* atingere
touch *v.t.* a atinge
touchy *a.* susceptibil
tough *a.* tare
toughen *v.t.* a (se) întări
tour *v.i.* a face un tur
tour *n.* tur
tourism *n.* turism
tourist *n.* turist
tournament *n.* campionat
towards *prep.* către
towel *n.* prosop

tower *v.i.* a se înălţa
tower *n.* turn
town *n.* oraş
toy *v.i.* a se juca
toy *n.* jucărie
trace *v.t.* a urmări
trace *n.* urmă
track *v.t.* a urmări
track *n.* pistă
tract *n* întindere (de pământ)
tract *n.* pamflet
traction *n.* tracţiune
tractor *n.* tractor
trade *v.i* a face comerţ (cu)
trade *n.* comerţ
trader *n.* ocupaţie
tradesman *n.* comerciant
tradition *n.* tradiţie
traditional *a.* tradiţional
traffic *v.i.* a face trafic
traffic *n.* trafic
tragedian *n.* tragedian
tragedy *n.* tragedie
tragic *a.* tragic
trail *v.t.* a târî
trail *n.* potecă
train *v.t.* a dresa
train *n.* tren
training *n.* antrenament
trait *n.* trăsătură (de caracter)
traitor *n.* trădător
tram *n.* tramvai
trample *v.t.* a dispreţui
trance *n.* transă
tranquil *a.* calm
tranquility *n.* calimitate
tranquillize *v.t.* a linişsti
transact *v.t.* a negocia
transaction *n.* tranzacţie
transcribe *v.t.* a transcrie
transcription *n.* a transcrie
transfer *v.t.* a transfera

transfer *n.* transfer
transferable *a.* transferabiol
transfiguration *n.* transfiguraţie
transfigure *v.t.* a transfigura
transform *v.t* a transforma
transformation *n.* transformare
transgress *v.t.* a încălca (o lege)
transit *n.* tranzit
transition *n.* tranziţie
transitive *n.* tranzitiv
transitory *n.* trecător
translate *v.t.* a traduce
translation *n.* traducere
transmigration *n.* transmigraţie
transmission *n.* trasmisie
transmit *v.t.* a transmite
transmitter *n.* transmiţător
transparent *a.* transparent
transplant *v.t.* a transplanta
transport *n.* transport
transport *v.t.* a transporta
transportation *n.* transportare
trap *v.t.* a prinde in capcană
trap *n.* capcană
trash *n.* boarfe
travel *n* călătorie
travel *v.i.* a călători
traveller *n.* călător
tray *n.* tavă
treacherous *a.* trădător
treachery *n.* trădare
tread *n* zgomot de paşi
tread *v.t.* a merge pe
treason *n.* trădare
treasure *v.t.* a preţui
treasure *n.* comoară
treasurer *n.* trezorier
treasury *n.* tezaur public
treat *n* desfătare
treat *v.t.* desfătare
treatise *n.* tratat
treatment *n.* tratament

treaty *n.* tratat
tree *n.* copac
tremble *v.i.* a tremura
tremendous *a.* îngrozitor
tremor *n.* tremur
trench *v.t.* a se îndrepta (spre)
trench *n.* şanţ
trend *n.* tendinţa
trespass *n.* delict
trespass *v.i.* a abuza (de)
trial *n.* judecată
triangle *n.* triunghi
triangular *a.* triunghiular
tribal *a.* tribal
tribe *n.* trib
tribulation *n.* suferinţă
tribunal *n.* tribunal
tributary *a.* tributar
tributary *n.* tributar
trick *v.t.* a înşela
trick *n* truc
trickery *n.* şiretlic
trickle *v.i.* a se prelinge
trickster *n.* şmenar
tricky *a.* şiret
tricolour *n* tricolor
tricolour *a.* tricolor
tricycle *n.* tricicletă
trifle *v.i* a glumi (cu)
trifle *n.* fleac
trigger *n.* trăgaci
trim *n* ţinută
trim *v.t.* a curăţa (de crengi)
trim *a.* îngrijit
trio *n.* trio
trip *n.* excursie
trip *v.t.* a face să cadă
triple *a.* triplu
triple *v.t.,* a întrei
tripod *n.* trepied
triumph *v.i.* a triumfa
triumph *n.* triumf

triumphal *a.* triumfal
triumphant *a.* triumfant
trivial *a.* banal
troop *v.i* a mărşălui
troop *n.* trupă (de actori)
trooper *n.* cavalerist
trophy *n.* trofeu
tropic *n.* tropic
tropical *a.* tropical
trot *n* trap
trot *v.i.* a tropăi
trouble *v.t.* a tulbura
trouble *n.* tulburare
troublesome *a.* supărător
troupe *n.* trupă
trousers *n.* *pl* pantaloni
trowel *n.* mistrie
truce *n.* armistiţiu
truck *n.* platformă
true *a.* adevărat
trump *v.t.* a trage pe sfoară
trump *n.* atu
trumpet *v.i.* a suna din trâmbiţă
trumpet *n.* trompetă
trunk *n.* trunchi
trust *v.t* a avea încredere în
trust *n.* încredere
trustee *n.* epitrop
trustful *a.* încrezător
trustworthy *a.* demn de
   încredere
trusty *n.* om cu comportare bună
truth *n.* adevăr
truthful *a.* sincer
try *n* încercare
try *v.i.* a încerca
trying *a.* apăsător
tub *n.* cadă
tube *n.* metroul
tuberculosis *n.* turculoză
tubular *a.* cilindric
tug *v.t.* a remorca

tuition *n.* învăţământ
tumble *n.* cădere bruscă
tumble *v.i.* a cădea brusc
tumbler *n.* pahar mare
tumour *n.* tumoare
tumult *n.* tumult
tumultuous *a.* tumultos
tune *v.t.* a acorda
tune *n.* melodie
tunnel *n.* tunel
turban *n.* turban
turbine *n.* turbină
turbulence *n.* turbulenţă
turbulent *a.* turbulent
turf *n.* ţarină
turkey *n.* curcan
turmoil *n.* harababura
turn *n* rând
turn *v.i.* a se învârti
turner *n.* strungar
turnip *n.* nap (turcesc)
turpentine *n.* terebentină
turtle *n.* broasca ţestoasă
tusk *n.* colţ
tutor *n.* meditator
twelfth *n.* al doisprezecelea
twelfth *a.* al doisprezecelea
twelve *n* doisprezece
twelve *n.* twelve
twentieth *n* douăzecime
twentieth *a.* al douăzecilea
twenty *n* douăzeci
twenty *a.* douăzeci
twice *adv.* de două ori
twilight *n* crepuscul
twin *a* îngemănat
twin *n.* geamăn
twinkle *n.* licărire
twinkle *v.i.* a licări
twist *n.* (ră)sucire
twist *v.t.* a răsuci
twitter *v.i.* a ciripi

twitter *n.* stare de nervozitate
two *a.* două
two *n.* doi
type *v.t.* a dactilografia
type *n.* tip
typhoid *n.* febră tifoidă
typhoon *n.* taifun
typhus *n.* tifos exantematic
typical *a.* tipic
typify *v.t.* a personifica
typist *n.* dactilograf(ă)
tyranny *n.* tiranie
tyrant *n.* tiran
tyre *n.* cauciuc

udder *n.* uger
ugliness *n.* urâţenie
ugly *a.* urât
ulcer *n.* ulcer
ulcerous *a.* ulceros
ulterior *a.* ulterior
ultimate *a.* ultim
ultimately *adv.* la urmă
ultimatum *n.* ultimatum
umbrella *n.* umbrelă
umpire *n.* arbitru
umpire *v.t.,* a arbitra
unable *a.* incapabil
unanimity *n.* unanimitate
unawares *adv.* din neatenţie
unburden *v.t.* a despovăra
uncanny *a.* misterios
uncertain *a.* nesigur
uncle *n.* unchi
uncouth *a.* necivilizat
under *adv* sub
under *prep.* sub

undercurrent *n.* curent submarin
undergo *v.t.* a îndura
undergraduate *n.* student
underhand *a.* clandestin
underline *v.t.* a sublinia
underneath *adv.* dedesubt
underneath *prep.* dedesubt
understand *v.t.* a înțelege
undertake *v.t.* a lua asupra sa
underwear *n.* lenjerie de corp
underworld *n.* lumea interlopă
undo *v.t.* a desface
undue *a.* inoportun
undulate *v.i.* a ondula
undulation *n.* ondulare
unearth *v.t.* a exhuma
uneasy *a.* incomod
unfair *a* nedrept
unfold *v.t.* a desfășura
unfortunate *a.* ghinionist
ungainly *a.* neândemânatic
unhappy *a.* nefericit
unification *n.* unificare
union *n.* uniune
unionist *n.* unionist
unique *a.* unic
unison *n.* acord
unit *n.* unitate
unite *v.t.* a uni
unity *n.* unitate
universal *a.* universal
universality *n.* universalitate
universe *n.* univers
university *n.* universitate
unjust *a.* nedrept
unless *conj.* dacă nu
unlike *a* neasemănător
unlikely *a.* improbabil
unmannerly *a* nemanierat
unprincipled *a.* fără scrupule
unreliable *a.* nedemn de
   încredere

unrest *n* frământare
unruly *a.* nesupus
until *conj* până când să
until *prep.* până (la)
untoward *a.* impropriu
unwell *a.* suferind
unwittingly *adv.* involuntar
up *adv.* (în) sus
up *prep.* în susul
upbraid *v.t* a dojeni
upheaval *n.* ridicare a straturilor
uphold *v.t* a susține
upkeep *n* întreținere
uplift *n* înălțare
uplift *v.t.* a înălța
upon *prep* pe
upper *a.* superior
upright *a.* drept
uprising *n.* răzvrătire
uproar *n.* zarvă
uproot *v.t.* a dezrădăcina
upset *v.t.* a supăra
upshot *n.* concluzie
upstart *n.* parvenit
up-to-date *a.* actual
upward *a.* îndreptat în sus
upwards *adv.* în sus
urban *a.* urban
urbane *a.* urban
urbanity *n.* urbanitate
urchin *n.* puști
urge *n* imbold
urge *v.t* a îmboldi
urgency *n.* urgență
urgent *a.* urgent
urinal *n.* urinal
urinary *a.* urinal
urinate *v.i.* a urina
urination *n.* urinare
urine *n.* urină
urn *n* urnă
usage *n.* folosință

use *n.* folos
use *v.t.* a folosi
useful *a.* folositor
usher *n.* plasator
usher *v.t.* a introduce
usual *a.* obişnuit
usually *adv.* de obicei
usurer *n.* cămătar
usurp *v.t.* a uzurpa
usurpation *n.* usurpare
usury *n.* cămătărie
utensil *n.* ustensilă
uterus *n.* uter
utilitarian *a.* utilitar
utility *n.* utilitate
utilization *n.* utilizare
utilize *v.t.* a utiliza
utmost *a.* cel mai depărtat
utter *a* total
utter *v.t.* a rosti
utterance *n.* dicţiune
utterly *adv.* dicţiune

vacancy *n.* vacanţă
vacant *a.* vacant
vacate *v.t.* a elibera
vacation *n.* vacanţă
vaccinate *v.t.* a vaccina
vaccination *n.* vaccinare
vaccinator *n.* vaccinator
vaccine *n.* vaccin
vacillate *v.i.* a se clătina
vacuum *n.* vid
vagabond *a* vagabond
vagabond *n.* vagabond
vagary *n.* toană
vagina *n.* vagin

vague *a.* vag
vain *a.* inutil
vainglorious *a.* vanitos
vainglory *n.* vanitate
vale *n.* vâlcea
valiant *a.* viteaz
valid *a.* valid
validate *v.t.* a valida
validity *n.* validitate
valley *n.* vale
valour *n.* valoare
valuable *a.* valoros
valuation *n.* evaluare
value *v.t.* a valora
value *n.* valoare
valve *n.* valvă
van *n.* dubă
vanish *v.i.* a dispărea
vanity *n.* vanitate
vanquish *v.t.* a înfrânge
vaporize *v.t.* a se evapora
vaporous *a.* vaporos
vapour *n.* vapor
variable *a.* variabil
variance *n.* variaţie
variation *n.* variaţie
varied *a.* variat
variety *n.* varietate
various *a.* felurit
varnish *v.t.* a smălţui
varnish *n.* smalţ
vary *v.t.* a varia
vasectomy *n.* vasectomie
vaseline *n.* vaselină
vast *a.* vast
vault *n.* pivniţă
vault *v.i.* a bolti
vault *n.* săritură
vegetable *a.* de legume
vegetable *n.* legumă
vegetarian *a* vegetarian
vegetarian *n.* vegetarian

vegetation *n.* vegetație
vehemence *n.* vehemență
vehement *a.* vehement
vehicle *n.* vehicul
vehicular *a.* vehicular
veil *v.t.* a învălui
veil *n.* voal
vein *n.* venă
velocity *n.* iuțeală
velvet *n.* catifea
velvety *a.* catifelat
venal *a.* corupt
venality *n.* corupție
vendor *n.* vânzător
venerable *a.* venerabil
venerate *v.t.* a venera
veneration *n.* venerare
vengeance *n.* răzbunare
venom *n.* venin
venomous *a.* veninos
vent *n.* deschizătură
ventilate *v.t.* a ventila
ventilation *n.* ventilație
ventilator *n.* ventilator
venture *v.t.* a cuteza
venture *n.* acțiune riscantă
venturesome *a.* îndrăzneț
venue *n.* loc(alitate)
veracity *n.* veracitate
verb *n.* verb
verbal *a.* verbal
verbally *adv.* verbal
verbatim *a.* textual
verbose *a.* prolix
verbosity *n.* prolixitate
verdant *a.* înverzit
verdict *n.* verdict
verge *n.* margine
verification *n.* verificare
verify *v.t.* a verifica
verisimilitude *n.* verisimilitudine
veritable *a.* veritabil

vernacular *a.* indigen
vernacular *n.* dialect local
vernal *a.* tineresc
versatile *a.* versat
versatility *n.* versatilitate
verse *n.* vers
versed *a.* versat
versification *n.* versificare
versify *v.t.* a versifica
version *n.* versiune
versus *prep.* contra
vertical *a.* vertical
verve *n.* vervă
very *a.* foarte
vessel *n.* vas
vest *v.t.* a învesti
vest *n.* vestă
vestige *n.* semn
vestment *n.* veșmânt
veteran *a.* veteran
veteran *n.* veteran
veterinary *a.* veterinar
veto *v.t.* a vota contra
veto *n.* veto
vex *v.t.* a necăji
vexation *n* necăjire
via *prep.* prin
viable *a.* viabil
vibrate *v.i.* a vibra
vibration *n.* vibrație
vicar *n.* paroh
vicarious *a.* prin împuternicire
vice *n.* viciu
viceroy *n.* vicerege
vice-versa *adv.* vice-versa
vicinity *n.* apropiere
vicious *a.* vicios
vicissitude *n.* vicisitudine
victim *n.* victimă
victimize *v.t.* a victimiza
victor *n.* învingător
victorious *a.* victorios

victory *n.* victorie
victuals *n. pl* alimente
vie *v.i.* a rivaliza (cu)
view *n.* privire
view *v.t.* a privi
vigil *n.* veghe
vigilance *n.* vigilenţă
vigilant *a.* vigilent
vigorous *a.* viguros
vile *a.* fără valoare
vilify *v.t.* a defăima
villa *n.* vilă
village *n.* sat
villager *n.* sătean
villain *n.* nemernic
vindicate *v.t.* a susţine
vindication *n.* apărare
vine *n.* viţă de vie
vinegar *n.* oţet
vintage *n.* culesul viilor
violate *v.t.* a viola
violation *n.* violare
violence *n.* violenţă
violent *a.* violent
violet *n.* viorea
violin *n.* violină
violinist *n.* violonist
virgin *n* fecioară
virgin *n.* virgin
virginity *n.* virginitate
virile *a.* viril
virility *n.* virilitate
virtual *a* virtual
virtue *n.* virtute
virtuous *a.* virtuos
virulence *n.* virulenţ
virulent *a.* virulenţă
virus *n.* virus
visage *n.* figură
visibility *n.* vizibilitate
visible *a.* vizibil
vision *n.* viziune

visionary *n.* vizionar
visionary *a.* vizionar
visit *n.* vizită
visit *v.t.* a vizita
visitor *n.* vizitator
vista *n.* perspectivă
visual *a.* vizual
visualize *v.t.* a vizualiza
vital *a.* vital
vitality *n.* vitalitate
vitalize *v.t.* a vitaliza
vitamin *n.* vitamină
vitiate *v.t.* a vicia
vivacious *a.* vivace
vivacity *n.* vivacitate
vivid *a.* însufleţit
vocabulary *n.* vocabular
vocal *a.* vocal
vocalist *n.* vocalist
vocation *n.* vocaţie
vogue *n.* vogă
voice *v.t.* a sonoriza
voice *n.* voce
void *n.* gol
void *a.* gol
volcanic *a.* vulcanic
volcano *n.* vulcan
volition *n.* voinţă
volley *v.t* a relua (mingea)
volt *n.* volt
voltage *n.* voltaj
volume *n.* volum
voluminous *a.* voluminos
voluntarily *adv.* voluntar
voluntary *a.* voluntar
volunteer *v.t.* a voluntaria
volunteer *n.* voluntar
voluptuous *a.* voluptos
vomit *n* vomitat
vomit *v.t.* a vomita
voracious *a.* lacom
votary *n.* adept

vote *v.i.* a vota
vote *n.* vot
voter *n.* alegător
vouch *v.t* a confirma
voucher *n.* garant
vouchsafe *v.t.* a binevoi să acorde
vow *v.t.* a făgădui (solemn)
vow *n.* făgăduială (solemnă)
vowel *n.* vocală
voyage *n.* voiaj
voyager *n.* pasager
vulgar *a.* vulgar
vulgarity *n.* vulgaritate
vulnerable *a.* vulnerabil
vulture *n.* vultur

waddle *v.i.* a merge legănat
wade *v.i.* a avansa cu greu
waft *n* suflare
waft *v.t.* a purta
wag *v.i.* a agita
wage *n.* salariu
wage *v.t.* a duce
wager *v.t* a paria pe
wager *n.* rămăşag
wagon *n.* căruţă
wail *n* geamăt
wail *v.i.* a se tângui
wain *n.* car
waist *n.* talie
waistcoat *n.* vestă
wait *n.* aşteptare
wait *v.i.* a aştepta
waiter *n.* ospătar
waitress *n.* ospătăriţţ
waive *v.t.* a renunţa la
wake *n* priveghi

wake *n* trezire
wake *v.t.* a trezi
wakeful *a.* treaz
walk *n* mers
walk *v.i.* a merge pe jos
wall *v.t.* a zidi
wall *n.* perete
wallet *n.* portofel
wallop *v.t.* a bate
wallow *v.i.* a se desfăta
walnut *n.* nuc
walrus *n.* morsă
wan *a.* palid
wand *n.* baghetă
wander *v.i.* a pribegi
wane *n* declin
wane *v.i.* a descreşte
want *n* lipsă
want *v.t.* a vrea
wanton *a.* poznaş
war *v.i.* a se război
war *n.* război
warble *v.i.* a cânta în triluri
ward *v.t.* a străjui
ward *n.* strajă
warden *n.* santinelă
wardrobe *n.* şifonier
ware *n.* marfă
warehouse *v.t* a depozita
warfare *n.* ostilităţi
warlike *a.* de război
warm *v.t.* a încălzi
warm1 *a.* cald
warmth *n.* căldură
warn *v.t.* a preveni
warning *n.* avetizment
warrant *v.t.* a garanta
warrant *n.* garanţie
warranty *n.* garanţie
warrior *n.* războinic
wart *n.* neg
wary *a.* circumspect

wash *n* spălare
wash *v.t.* a spăla
washable *a.* de spălat
washer *n.* saiba
wasp *n.* viespe
waste *n.* risipă
waste *v.t.* a irosi
waste *a.* de prisos
wasteful *a.* risipitor
watch *n.* pândă
watch *v.t.* a păzi
watchful *a.* atent
watchword *n.* parolă
water *v.t.* a iriga
water *n.* apă
waterfall *n.* cascadă
water-melon *n.* pepene
waterproof *n* impermeabil
waterproof *a.* impermeabil
watertight *a.* ermetic
watery *a.* apos
watt *n.* watt
wave *v.t.* a face unde
wave *n.* val
waver *v.i.* a oscila
wax *v.t.* a da cu ceară
wax *n.* ceară
way *n.* cale
wayfarer *n.* drumeț
waylay *v.t.* a pândi
wayward *a.* capricios
weak *a.* firav
weaken *v.t. & i* a slăbi
weakling *n.* om plăpând
weakness *n.* slăbiciune
weal *n.* bunăstare
wealth *n.* bogăție
wealthy *a.* bogat
weapon *n.* armă
wear *v.t.* a fi îmbrăcat cu
weary *a.* plicticos
weary *v.t.* a obosi

weary *v.t. & i* a se sătura
weary *a.* obositor
weather *n* vreme
weather *v.t.* a măcina
weave *v.t.* a țese
weaver *n.* țesător(-oare)
web *n.* membrană
wed *v.t.* a lua în căsătorie
wedding *n.* nuntă
wedge *v.t.* a înțepeni
wedge *n.* pană
wedlock *n.* căsătorie
Wednesday *n.* miercuri
weed *v.t.* a plivi
weed *n.* iarbă
week *n.* săptămână
weekly *adv.* săptămânal
weekly *a.* săptămânal
weep *v.i.* a plânge
weigh *v.t.* a cântări
weight *n.* greutate
weighty *a.* greu
weir *n.* baraj
weird *a.* ciudat
welcome *n* primire călduroasă
welcome *v.t* a ura bun venit
welcome *a.* binevenit
weld *n* sudură
weld *v.t.* a (se) suda
welfare *n.* bunăstare
well *adv.* favorabil
well *n.* bine
well *v.i.* a țâșni
well *a.* bine
well-known *a.* cunoscut
well-read *a.* citit
well-to-do *a.* bine situat
welt *n.* ramă (la încălțăminte)
welter *n.* harababură
wen *n.* cucui
wench *n.* femeie tânără
west *a.* vestic

west *adv.* la vest
west *n.* vest
westerly *adv.* dinspre vest
westerly *a.* înspre vest
western *a.* occidental
wet *v.t.* a uda
wet *a.* ud
wetness *n.* umezeală
whack *v.t.* a lovi cu putere
whale *n.* balenă
what *a.* ce
what *interj.* ce?
what *pron.* ceea ce
whatever *pron.* orice
wheat *n.* grâu
wheedle *v.t.* a linguşi
wheel *v.t.* a învârti
wheel *n.* roată
whelm *v.t.* a scufunda
whelp *n.* pui
when *conj.* îndată ce
when *adv.* când
whence *adv.* de unde
whenever *adv. conj* oricând
where *conj.* unde?
where *adv.* unde
whereabout *adv.* pe unde?
whereas *conj.* întrucât
whereat *conj.* la care?
wherein *adv.* în care
whereupon *conj.* după care
wherever *adv.* oriunde
whet *v.t.* a da la tocilă
whether *conj.* fie că
which *a* care?
which *pron.* pe care?
whichever *pron* ori(şi)care
whiff *n.* adiere
while *conj.* în timp ce
while *v.t.* a trece
while *n.* răstimp
whim *n.* moft

whimper *v.i.* a scânci
whimsical *a.* cu toane
whine *n* cu toane
whine *v.i.* cu toane
whip *n.* bici
whip *v.t.* a biciui
whipcord *n.* sfoară pentru bici
whir *n.* freamăt
whirl *n* rotire
whirl *v.i.* a roti
whirligig *n.* piruetă
whirlpool *n.* vârtej de apă
whisk *n* pămătuf
whisk *v.t.* a şterge praful
whisker *n.* favoriţi
whisky *n.* whisky
whisper *n* şoaptş
whisper *v.t.* a şopti
whistle *n* fluier
whistle *v.i.* a fluiera
white *n* alb
white *a.* alb
whiten *v.t.* a înălbi
whitewash *v.t.* a vărui
whitewash *n.* văruire
whither *adv.* destinaţie
whittle *v.t.* a ciopli
whiz *v.i.* a vâjîi
who *pron.* cine?
whoever *pron.* oricine
whole *a.* integral
wholesale *a* cu ridicata
wholesale *n.* vânzare angro
wholesome *a.* prielnic
wholly *adv.* în întregime
whom *pron.* cine?
whore *n.* târfă
whose *pron.* al cui?
why *adv.* de ce?
wick *n.* fitil
wicked *a.* imoral
wicker *n.* imoral

wicket *n.* ghişeu
wide *adv.* departe
wide *a.* larg
widen *v.t.* a lărgi
widespread *a.* (larg) răspândit
widow *v.t.* a văduvi
widow *n.* fereastră
widower *n.* văduv
width *n.* lărgime
wield *v.t.* a stăpâni
wife *n.* soţie
wig *n.* perucă
wight *n.* individ
wild *a.* sălbatic
wilderness *n.* sălbăticie
wile *n.* viclenie
will *v.t.* a vrea
will *n.* voinţă
willing *a.* dispus
willingness *n.* bunăvoinţă
willow *n.* salcie
wily *a.* şiret
wimble *n.* burghiu
wimple *n.* haină călugărească
win *n* victorie
win *v.t.* a câştiga
wince *v.i.* a se strâmba
winch *n.* manivelă
wind *v.t.* a sufla
wind *n.* vânt
wind *v.t.* a înfăşa
winder *n.* vârtelniţă
windlass *n* scripete
windmill *n.* moară de vânt
window *n.* fereastră
windy *a.* vântos
wine *n.* vin
wing *n.* aripă
wink *n* clipire
wink *v.i.* a face cu ochiul
winner *n.* câştigător
winnow *v.t.* a vântura

winsome *a.* fermecător
winter *v.i* a ierna
winter *n.* iarnă
wintry *a.* de iarnă
wipe *n.* batistă
wipe *v.t.* a şterge
wire *v.t.* a telegrafia
wire *n.* cablu
wireless *n* radiogramă
wireless *a.* fără fir
wisdom *n.* înţelepciune
wise *a.* înţelept
wish *v.t.* a-şi dori
wish *n.* dorinţă
wishful *a.* doritor
wisp *n.* mănunchi
wistful *a.* visător
wit *n.* agerime
witch *n.* vrăjitoare
witchery *n.* vrăjitorie
with *prep.* cu
withal *adv.* în acelaşi timp
withdraw *v.t.* a retrage
withdrawal *n.* retragere
withe *n.* nuia de salcie
wither *v.i.* a se ofili
withhold *v.t.* a reţine
within *adv.* în interior
within *n.* parte interioară
within *prep.* înăuntrul
without *adv.* fără
without *conj.* fără ca să
without *prep.* afară de
withstand *v.t.* a se împotrivi la
witless *a.* imbecil
witness *v.i.* a fi martor
witness *n.* martor
witticism *n.* cuvânt de duh
witty *a.* spiritual
wizard *n.* scamator
wobble *v.i* a se clătina
woe *n.* nenorocire

woeful *a* trist
wolf *n.* lup
woman *n.* femeie
womanhood *n.* feminitate
womanise *v.t.* a afemeia
womanish *n.* femeiesc
womb *n.* pântece
wonder *v.i.* a se mira
wonder *n* minune
wonderful *a.* minunat
wont *n* deprindere
wonted *a.* obişnuit
woo *v.t.* a curta (o fată)
wood *n.* lemn
wooden *a.* de lemn
woodland *n.* regiune păduroasă
woods *n.* pădure
woof *n.* bătătură
wool *n.* lână
woollen *n* lânărie
woollen *a.* de lână
word *v.t* a exprima în cuvinte
word *n.* cuvânt
wordy *a.* verbal
work *v.t.* a lucra
work *n.* muncă
workable *a.* executabil
workaday *a.* de lucru
worker *n.* muncitor
workman *n.* lucrător
workmanship *n.* îndemânare
workshop *n.* atelier
world *n.* lume
worldly *a.* lumesc
worm *n.* vierme
wormwood *n.* pelin
worn *a.* avertizment
worry *v.i.* a se îngrijora
worry *n.* grijă
worsen *v.t.* a înrăutăţi
worship *v.t.* a venera
worship *n.* veneraţie

worst *a* cel mai rău
worst *n.* partea cea mai rea
worst *v.t.* a învinge
worsted *n.* lână toarsă
worth *a* care merită osteneala
worth *n.* merit
worthy *a.* care merită
would-be *a.* pretins
wound *v.t.* a se răni
wound *n.* rană
wrack *n.* algă marină
wraith *n.* vedenie
wrangle *n.* ciorăvăială
wrangle *v.i.* a se ciondăni
wrap *n* pătură
wrap *v.t.* a înveli
wrapper *n.* învelitoare
wrath *n.* furie
wreath *n.* coroană
wreathe *v.t.* a încununa
wreck *v.t.* a ruina
wreck *n.* epavă
wreckage *n.* rămăşiţe
wrecker *n.* distrugător
wren *n.* pitulice
wrench *v.t.* a smuci
wrench *n.* smucire
wrest *v.t.* a smulge
wrestle *v.i.* a se lua la trântă (cu)
wretch *n.* sărman
wretched *a.* nefericit
wriggle *n* răsucire
wriggle *v.i.* a se răsuci
wring *v.t* a frânge
wrinkle *v.t.* a se rida
wrinkle *n.* rid
wrist *n.* încheietură a mâinii
writ *n.* scriptură
write *v.t.* a scrie
writer *n.* scriitor
writhe *v.i.* a se crispa
wrong *adv.* greşit

wrong *v.t.* a nedreptăți
wrong *a.* greşit
wrongful *a.* nedrept
wry *a.* strâmb

xerox *n.* xerox
xerox *v.t.* a xeroxa
Xmas *n.* Crăciun
x-ray *n.* rază X
x-ray *v.t.* a radiografia
xylophone *n.* xilofon

yacht *n.* iaht
yap *n* chelălăit
yap *v.i.* a chelălăi
yard *n.* curte
yarn *n.* fir tors
yawn *n.* căscat
yawn *v.i.* a căsca
year *n.* an
yearly *a.* an de an
yearly *adv.* anual
yearn *v.i.* a tânji (după)
yeast *n.* drojdie de bere
yell *n* ţipăt
yell *v.i.* a urla
yellow *a.* galben
yellow *n* galben
yellow *v.t.* a îngălbeni
yellowish *a.* gălbui
Yen *n.* Yen
yeoman *n.* răzeş

yes *adv.* da
yesterday *adv.* ieri
yesterday *n.* ieri
yet *adv.* deocamdată
yet *conj.* încă
yield *n* producţie
yield *v.t.* a produce
yoke *n.* jug
yoke *v.t.* a înjuga (boi)
yolk *n.* gălbenuş (de ou)
young *a.* tânăr
young *n* tânăr
youngster *n.* pici
youth *n.* tinereţe
youthful *a.* plin de tinereţe

zany *n* măscărici
zeal *n.* zel
zealot *n.* fanatic
zebra *n.* zebră
zenith *n.* apogeu
zephyr *n.* adiere
zero *n.* zero
zest *n.* savoare
zigzag *a.* în zigzag
zigzag *n.* drum în zigzag
zinc *n.* zinc
zip *n.* şuierat
zip *v.t.* a şuiera
zodiac *n* zodiac
zone *n.* zonă
zoo *n.* grădină zoologică
zoological *a.* zoologic
zoologist *n.* zoologist
zoology *n.* zoologie
zoom *v.i.* a face "lumânarea"

ROMANIAN-ENGLISH

A

a abandona *v.t* abandon
a abate *v.t* avert
a abate din drum *v.t* mislead
a abdica *v.t* abdicate
a abroga *v.t* abrogate
a absolvi *v.i* graduate
a absolvi *v.t* absolve
a absorbi *v.t* engross
a absorbi *v.t* absorb
a abunda *v.i* abound
a abuza *v.t* abuse
a abuza de *v.i* trespass
a accelera *v.t* accelerate
a accentua *v.t* accent
a accepta *v.t* accept
a achita *v.t* acquit
a achiziţiona *v.t* purchase
a aclama *v.t* mob
a aclimatiza *v.t* season
a acompania *v.t* accompany
a acoperi *v.t* cover
a acoperi *v.t* mantle
a acoperi cu *v.t* top
a acoperi cu bale *v.t* beslaver
a acoperi cu funingine *v.t* soot
a acoperi cu o pânză *v.t* sheet
a acoperi cu paie *v.t* thatch
a acoperi cu ţigle *v.t* tile
a acoperi parţial *v.t* overlap
a acorda *v.t* award
a acorda *v.t* grant
a acorda *v.t* tone
a acorda *v.t* tune
a acorda drept de vot *v.t* enfranchise
a acri *v.t* sour
a acţiona *v.i* act
a activa *v.t* activate

a acumula *v.t* accumulate
a acuza *v.t* accuse
a adăposti *v.t* harbour
a adăposti *v.t* house
a adăposti *v.t* lodge
a adăposti *v.t* roof
a adăposti *v.t* shelter
a adapta *v.t* suit
a adapta *v.t* adapt
a adapta la *v.t* accommodate
a adăuga *v.t* add
a ademeni *v.t* allure
a ademeni *v.t* lure
a adera *v.i* adhere
a adjudeca *v.t* adjudge
a administra *v.t* administer
a administra *v.t* manage
a admira *v.t* admire
a admite *v.t* avow
a admite *v.t* acknowledge
a adopta *v.t* adopt
a adora *v.t* adore
a aduce *v.t* bring
a aduce dovezi *v.t* adduce
a adulmeca *v.t* nose
a adulmeca *v.t* quest
a aduna *v.t* amass
a aduna *v.t* gather
a aduna *v.t* sum
a aduna *v.t* total
a afecta *v.t* affect
a afemeia *v.t* womanise
a afirma *v.t* affirm
a afirma *v.t* assert
a afişa *v.i* paste
a agasa *v.t* ruffle
a agita *v.t* agitate
a agita *v.i* wag
a agita un lichid *v.i* stir
a agrava *v.t* aggravate
a ajunge *v.t* get
a ajunge *v.t* reach

a **ajunge** *v.i* suffice
a **ajunge din urmă** *v.t* overtake
a **ajunge la un acord** *v.i*
   compound
a **ajusta** *v.t* adjust
a **ajuta** *v.t* aid
a **ajuta** *v.t* help
a **alăpta** *v.t* suckle
a **alarma** *v.t* alarm
a **alătura** *v.t* adjoin
a **alătura** *v.t* enclose
a **alcătui** *v.t* compile
a **alege** *v.t* choose
a **alege** *v.t* elect
a **alege** *v.t* pick
a **alia** *v.t* ally
a **alina** *v.t* allay
a **alina suferinţa** *v.t* mitigate
a **alinia** *v.t* align
a **alinia** *v.t* line
a **alitera** *v.t* alliterate
a **aloca** *v.t* allocate
a **alterna** *v.t* alternate
a **altoi** *v.t* graft
a **aluneca** *v.t* glide
a **aluneca** *v.i* slide
a **aluneca** *v.i* slip
a **amalgama** *v.t* amalgamate
a **amâna** *v.t* adjourn
a **amâna** *v.t* postpone
a **amâna** *v.i* procrastinate
a **amaneta** *v.t* pledge
a **amărâ** *v.t* embitter
a **ameliora** *v.t* meliorate
a **ameliora** *v.t* ameliorate
a **amenda** *v.t* amend
a **amenda** *v.t* fine
a **ameninţa** *v.t* menace
a **ameninţa** *v.t* threaten
a **amesteca** *v.t* intermingle
a **amesteca** *v.t* mingle
a **amesteca** *v.t* blend

a **amesteca** *v.t* mix
a **amesteca** *v.t* munch
a **amesteca, cărţile** *v.i* shuffle
a **ameţi,** *v.t* muddle
a **aminti** *v.t* remind
a **amplifica** *v.t* amplify
a **amuza** *v.t* amuse
a **analiza** *v.t* analyse
a **ancora un vas** *v.t* moor
a **anexa** *v.t* annex
a **anexa la** *v.t* append
a **angaja** *v.t* employ
a **anima** *v.t* animate
a **ansambla** *v.t* assemble
a **anticipa** *v.t* antedate
a **anticipa** *v.t* anticipate
a **anula** *v.t* abolish
a **anula** *v.t* annul
a **anula** *v.t* cancel
a **anula** *v.t* nullify
a **anunţa** *v.t* announce
a **apăra** *v.t* defend
a **apărea** *v.i* appear
a **apărea** *v.i* peep
a **aparţine** *v.i* belong
a **aparţine de** *v.i* pertain
a **apela** *v.t* appeal
a **aplauda** *v.t* acclaim
a **aplauda** *v.t* applaud
a **aplica** *v.t* apply
a **aplica o etichetă etc.** *v.t* adhibit
a **aplica un plasture pe** *v.t* plaster
a **aprecia** *v.t* appreciate
a **aprecia** *v.t* reckon
a **apreta** *v.t* starch
a **aprinde un foc** *v.t* light
a **aproba** *v.t* approbate
a **aproba** *v.t* approve
a **apropia** *v.i* near
a **aproviziona** *v.t* stock
a **aproviziona** *v.t* supply
a **apuca** *v.t* grab

a apuca *v.t* grip
a apuca cu dinţii *v.t* mouth
a ara *v.t* till
a aranja *v.t* arrange
a aranja *v.t* concert2
a arăta *v.t* show
a arbitra *v.t* arbitrate
a arbitra *v.t* umpire
a arcui *v.t* arch
a arde *v.t* burk
a arde *v.i* singe
a arde cu flăcări *v.i* blaze
a aresta *v.t* arrest
a arunca *v.t* discard
a arunca *v.t* hurl
a arunca *v.t* throw
a arunca o privire *v.i* glance
a asalta *v* assail
a asalta *v.t* assault
a asambla *v.t* piece
a asasina *v.t* assassinate
a asasina *v.t* murder
a asasina *v.t* slay
a asculta *v.i* listen
a ascunde *v.t* hide
a ascuţi *v.t* sharpen
a asedia *v.t* besiege
a aşeza *v.t* place
a aşeza grămadă *v.t* lump
a aşeza greşit *v.t* misplace
a aşeza în rând *v.t* range
a aşeza în rânduri *v.t* rank
a aşeza pe pernă *v.t* cushion
a asfixia *v.t* smother
a asigura *v.t* assure
a asigura *v.t* ensure
a asigura *v.t* insure
a asigura *v.t* secure
a asimila *v* assimilate
a asista *v.t* assist
a asista *v.t* attend
a asocia *v.t* associate

a asorta *v.i* match
a aspira *v.t* aspire
a aştepta *v.t* await
a aştepta *v.t* bide
a aştepta *v.i* wait
a astupa *v.t* obstruct
a astupa *v.t* plug
a asuda *v.i* sweat
a ataca *v.t* attack
a atârna *v.t* hang
a atârna *v.i* loll
a ataşa *v.t* attach
a ataşa chesonul *v.t* limber
a ateriza *v.i* land
a atinge *v.t* attain
a atinge *v.t* touch
a atinge cu degetul *v.t* finger
a atinge cu palma *v.t* palm
a atinge în medie *v.t* average
a aţîţa *v.t* abet
a atrage *v.t* attract
a atrage asupra sa *v.t* incur
a atribui *v.t* ascribe
a atribui *v.t* attribute
a auri *v.t* gild
a autoriza *v.t* authorize
a autoriza *v.t* license
a auzi *v.t* hear
a auzi fără să vrea *v.t* overhear
a avansa *v.t* advance
a avansa cu greu *v.i* wade
a avantaja *v.t* advantage
a avea *v.t* have
a avea grijă *v.i* care
a avea importanţă *v.i* matter
a avea încredere în *v.t* trust
a avea legătură cu *v.t* regard
a avea nevoie *v.t* need
a avertiza *v.t* caution
a avertiza *v.t* forewarn
a avorta *v.i* abort
a avorta *v.i* miscarry

a **azvârli** v.t fling
a **azvârli cu putere** v.t dash
a **băga cu forţa în** v.t intrude
a **băga în buzunar** v.t pocket
a **băga în grajd** v.t stable
a **băga în încurcătură** v.t nonplus
a **bandaja** v.t bandage
a **bântui** v.t haunt
a **bara** v.t bar
a **bărbieri** v.t shave
a **bate** v.t beat
a **bate** v.t wallop
a **bate monedă** v.t mint
a **bate puternic** v.i throb
a **bate toba** v.i drum
a **bate zdravăn** v.t belabour
a **bâzâi** v.i buzz
a **bea** v.t drink
a **bea într-una** v.i booze
a **behăi** v.i bleat
a **beneficia** v.t benefit
a **biciui** v.t flog
a **biciui** v.t scourge
a **biciui** v.t whip
a **binecuvânta** v.t bless
a **binevoi să acorde** v.t vouchsafe
a **blama** v.t impeach
a **blestema** v.t curse
a **blestema** v.t damn
a **blinda** v.t shield
a **bloca** v.t block
a **bloca un motor** v.t stall
a **boicota** v.t boycott
a **bolborosi** v.i gabble
a **bolti** v.i vault
a **bombăni** v.i mutter
a **bombarda** v.t bomb
a **bombarda** v.t bombard
a **boteza** v.t baptize
a **breveta** v.t patent
a **bronza** v.i tan
a **burniţa** v.i drizzle

a **cade prada** v.i succumb
a **cădea** v.i fall
a **cădea brusc** v.i tumble
a **cădea cu zgomot** v.i thud
a **călări** v.t ride
a **călători** v.i journey
a **călători** v.i travel
a **călători cu auto** v.i motor
a **călăuzi** v.t guide
a **călăuzi greşit** v.t misguide
a **călca** v,t iron
a **calcula** v.t calculate
a **calcula** v.t compute
a **calcula durata** v.t time
a **calcula greşit** v.t miscalculate
a **califica** v.t term
a **calma** v.t calm
a **calma** v.t quell
a **calomnia** v.t backbite
a **calomnia** v.i calumniate
a **calomnia** v.t libel
a **campa** v.i camp
a **cânta** v.i sing
a **cânta cucurigu** v.i crow
a **cânta din fluier** v.i pipe
a **cânta în triluri** v.i warble
a **cânta la flaut** v.i flute
a **cântări** v.t scale
a **cântări** v.t weigh
a **căpăta luciu** v.t glaze
a **capitula** v.t capitulate
a **captiva** v.t captivate
a **captura** v.t capture
a **căptuşi cu perne** v.t pad
a **căra** v.t carry
a **cârmi** v.t steer
a **căsca** v.i gape
a **căsca** v.i yawn
a **câştiga** v.t earn
a **câştiga** v.t gain
a **câştiga** v.t score
a **câştiga** v.t win

a castra *v.t* geld
a cataloga *v.t* tabulate
a căuta *v.t* search
a căuta *v.t* seek
a căuta pe bâjbâite *v.t* grope
a cauza *v.t* cause
a celebra *v.t* celebrate
a cenzura *v.t* censor
a cenzura *v.t* censure
a cerceta *v.i* research
a cere *v.t* request
a cere insistent *v.t* require
a cere un preţ exagerat *v.t* overcharge
a cerne *v.t* sieve
a cerşi *v.t* beg
a cerşi *v.i* cadge
a certa cu asprime *v.t* scold
a certifica *v.t* certify
a chefui *v.i* feast
a chelălăi *v.i* yap
a chelfăni *v.t* thrash
a cheltui *v.t* expend
a cheltui *v.t* spend
a cheltui nebuneşte *v.t* squander
a chema *v.t* beckon
a chema *v.t* call
a chicoti *v.i* chuckle
a chicoti *v.i* giggle
a chinui *v.t* agonize
a chinui *v.i* prey
a chiţăi *v.i* squeak
a cicăli *v.t* tease
a cimenta *v.t* cement
a cina *v.i* sup
a ciocăni *v.t* hammer
a ciocăni *v.t* knock
a ciocni *v.t* clash
a ciopârţi *v.t* hack
a ciopârţi *v.t* lacerate
a ciopli *v.t* carve
a ciopli *v.t* chop

a ciopli *v.t* whittle
a circula *v.i* circulate
a ciripi *v.t* chatter
a ciripi *v.t* chirp
a ciripi *v.i* prattle
a ciripi *v.i* twitter
a cita *v.t* cite
a citi *v.t* read
a ciuguli *v.i* peck
a ciupi *v.t* nibble
a ciupi *v.t* pinch
a civiliza *v.t* civilize
a clădi *v.t* build
a clarifica *v.t* clarify
a clarifica *v.t* clear
a clasa *v.t* file
a clasa *v.t* grade
a clasifica *v.t* classify
a clăti *v.t* rinse
a cleveti *v.t* slander
a clipi *v.t* blink
a cloci ouă *v.i* incubate
a clocoti *v.i* seethe
a coace *v.t* bake
a coase *v.t* seam
a coase *v.t* sew
a coase *v.t* stitch
a coborî *v.i* alight
a coborî *v.i* descend
a coborî vocea *v.t* lower
a cocoloşi *v.t* cocker
a coexista *v.i* co-exist
a coincide *v.i* coincide
a coji *v.t* shell
a colabora *v.i* collaborate
a colecta *v.t* collect
a colinda *v.i* roam
a comanda *v.t* command
a comanda *v.t* order
a combate *v.t* combat
a combate *v.t* repel
a combate cu dovezi *v.t* confute

a **combina** *v.t* combine
a **comemora** *v.t* commemorate
a **comenta** *v.i* comment
a **comite** *v.t* commit
a **comite o gafă** *v.i* blunder
a **compara** *v.t* compare
a **compara** *v.t* parallel
a **compătimi** *v.t* commiserate
a **compensa** *v.t* compensate
a **compensa** *v.t* offset
a **complica** *v.t* complicate
a **complimenta** *v.t* compliment
a **comprima** *v.t* compress
a **compromite** *v.t* compromise
a **compune** *v.t* compose
a **comunica** *v.t* communicate
a **comuta** *v.t* commute
a **concedia** *v.t* dismiss
a **concentra** *v.t* concentrate
a **concepe** *v.t* conceive
a **concura** *v.i* compete
a **concura cu** *v.t* contest
a **condamna** *v.t* condemn
a **condamna** *v.t* convict
a **condamna** *v.t* sentence
a **condensa** *v.t* condense
a **condimenta** *v.t* spice
a **conduce** *v.t* drive
a **conduce** *v.t* head
a **conduce** *v.t* lead
a **conecta** *v.t* connect
a **conferi** *v.i* confer
a **confirma** *v.t* confirm
a **confirma** *v.t* corroborate
a **confirma** *v.i* vouch
a **confisca** *v.t* confiscate
a **confunda** *v.t* mistake
a **conjuga** *v.t* conjugate
a **conjura** *v.i* conjure
a **consacra** *v.t* consecrate
a **consemna** *v.t* consign
a **conserva** *v.t* can

a **conserva** *v.t* conserve
a **conserva** *v.t* preserve
a **conserva în cutii** *v.t* tin
a **conserva in oală** *v.t* pot
a **considera** *v.t* consider
a **considera ca** *v.t* account
a **consimți** *v.t* accede
a **consimți la** *v.i* acquiesce
a **consimți la** *v.i* assent
a **consola** *v.t* comfort
a **consola** *v.t* console
a **consola** *v.t* solace
a **consolida** *v.t* consolidate
a **consolida** *v.t* steady
a **conspira** *v.i* conspire
a **consta în** *v.i* consist
a **constitui** *v.t* constitute
a **constrânge** *v.t* compel
a **construi** *v.t* construct
a **construi o clădire** *v.t* rear
a **consulta** *v.t* consult
a **consuma** *v.t* consume
a **contacta** *v.t* contact
a **contamina** *v.t* contaminate
a **contempla** *v.t* contemplate
a **contempla** *v.t* gaze
a **conține** *v.t* contain
a **continua** *v.i* continue
a **contracara** *v.t* counteract
a **contracta** *v.t* constrict
a **contracta** *v.t* contract
a **contramanda** *v.t* countermand
a **contrasemna** *v.t* countersign
a **contrasta** *v.t* contrast
a **contraveni la** *v.t* infringe
a **contrazice** *v.t* contradict
a **contrazice** *v.t* gainsay
a **contrazice** *v.t* negative
a **contribui** *v.t* contribute
a **controla** *v.t* check
a **controla** *v.t* control
a **controla** *v.t* supervise

a **controla din nou** *v.t* overhaul
a **contura** *v.t* outline
a **contuziona** *v.t* contuse
a **conversa** *v.t* converse
a **converti** *v.t* convert
a **convieţui** *v.t* cohabit
a **convinge** *v.t* convince
a **convinge** *v.t* induce
a **convinge de** *v.t* persuade
a **convoca** *v.t* convene
a **convoca** *v.t* convoke
a **coopera** *v.i* co-operate
a **coordona** *v.t* co-ordinate
a **copia** *v.t* copy
a **copleşi** *v.t* overwhelm
a **corecta** *v.t* correct
a **corespunde** *v.i* correspond
a **corupe** *v.t* corrupt
a **corupe** *v.t* sophisticate
a **corupe prin mită** *v.t* fit
a **cosi** *v.t* mow
a **costa** *v.t* cost
a **cotcodăci** *v.i* cackle
a **crăpa** *v.i* crack
a **crea** *v.t* create
a **crede** *v.t* believe
a **crede** *v.i* deem
a **cresta** *v.t* slash
a **creşte** *v.t* foster
a **creşte** *v.t* grow
a **creşte mai mare** *v.t* outgrow
a **creşte un copil** *v.t* nurse
a **critica** *v.t* criticize
a **critica aspru** *v.t* castigate
a **croi** *v.t* tailor
a **croncăni** *v.i* caw
a **cuceri** *v.t* conquer
a **cufunda** *v.i* duck
a **cufunda în apă** *v.i* submerge
a **cugeta** *v.t* ponder
a **cuibări** *v.t* nest
a **culca** *v.t* lay

a **culmina** *v.i* culminate
a **cultiva** *v.t* cultivate
a **cumpăra** *v.t* buy
a **curăţa** *v.t* clean
a **curăţa de coajă** *v.t* peel
a **curăţa de crengi** *v.t* trim
a **curge** *v.i* flow
a **curge** *v.i* leak
a **curge şiroaie** *v.i* flush
a **curta** *v.t* court
a **curta o fată** *v.t* woo
a **cuteza** *v.t* venture
a **da** *v.t* give
a **da** *v.t* tip
a **da bacşiş** *v.t* tip
a **da cu ceară** *v.t* wax
a **da cu cotul în** *v.t* nudge
a **da cu împrumut** *v.t* loan
a **da de înţeles** *v.t* purport
a **da din nou** *v.i* backslide
a **da drumul la** *v.t* relinquish
a **da gust la mâncăre** *v.t* relish
a **da impresia de** *v.i* smack
a **da în grija** *v.t* custody
a **da în judecată** *v.t* sue
a **da în litigiu** *v.t* litigate
a **da la tocilă** *v.t* whet
a **da o lovitură** *v.t* inflict
a **da peste** *v.t* encounter
a **da peste cap** *v.t* overthrow
a **da pinteni calului** *v.t* spur
a **da un semnal** *v.t* signal
a **dactilografia** *v.t* type
a **dansa** *v.t* dance
a **dărâma** *v.t* demolish
a **datora** *v.t* owe
a **de înclina** *v.i* lean
a **debita** *v.t* debit
a **decădea** *v.i* decay
a **decădea** *v.i* ebb
a **decădea** *v.i* lapse
a **decapita** *v.t* behead

a **deceda** *v.i* decease
a **decide** *v.t* decide
a **decima** *v.t* decimate
a **declanşa o armă** *v.t* fire
a **declara** *v.t* declare
a **declara** *v.t* state
a **deconecta** *v.t* disconnect
a **decora** *v.t* decorate
a **decreta** *v.i* decree
a **decreta** *v.t* enact
a **dedica** *v.t* dedicate
a **deduce din** *v.t* infer
a **defăima** *v.t* defame
a **defăima** *v.t* vilify
a **defini** *v.t* define
a **deforma** *v.t* distort
a **degenera** *v.t* depauperate
a **deghiza** *v.t* disguise
a **degrada** *v.t* degrade
a **dejuca** *v.t* forestall
a **delega** *v.t* delegate
a **delega** *v.t* depute
a **delibera** *v.i* deliberate
a **demisiona** *v.t* resign
a **demite** *v.t* depose
a **demonetiza** *v.t* demonetize
a **demonraliza** *v.t* demoralize
a **demonstarte** *v.t* demonstrate
a **denota** *v.i* denote
a **denunţa** *v.t* denounce
a **depana** *v.t* service
a **depăşi** *v.t* foil
a **depăşi** *v.t* outrun
a **depăşi** *v.t* surpass
a **depăşi cu** *v.t* exceed
a **depăşi limitele** *v.t* overdo
a **depinde** *v.i* depend
a **deplânge** *v.t* bewail
a **deplasa** *v.t* displace
a **deporta** *v.t* deport
a **depozita** *v.t* deposit
a **depozita** *v.t* warehouse

a **deprecia** *v.t* depreciate
a **deprima** *v.t* deject
a **deprima** *v.t* depress
a **deprinde** *v.t* habituate
a **depune icre** *v.i* spawn
a **depune în bancă** *v.t* bank
a **deraia** *v.t* derail
a **deranja** *v.t* bother
a **deruta** *v.t* baffle
a **deruta** *v.t* misdirect
a **descalifica** *v.t* disqualify
a **descărca** *v.t* discharge
a **deschide** *v.t* open
a **deschide căi noi** *v.t* pioneer
a **desconsidera** *v.t* slight
a **descoperi** *v.t* ascertain
a **descoperi** *v.t* discover
a **descoperi** *v.t* unsheathe
a **descreşte** *v.t* decrease
a **descreşte** *v.t* wane
a **descrie** *v.t* depict
a **descrie** *v.t* describe
a **descrie** *v.t* picture
a **descuraja** *v.t* discourage
a **descuraja** *v.t* dishearten
a **desface** *v.t* undo
a **desfăşura** *v.t* deploy
a **desfăşura** *v.t* expand
a **desfăşura** *v.t* unfold
a **despărţi** *v.t* divide
a **despărţi** *v.t* sever
a **despica** *v.t* slit
a **despica** *v.i* split
a **despica cu securea** *v.t* hew
a **despovăra** *v.t* unburden
a **destăinui** *v.t* confide
a **destina** *v.t* doom
a **detalia** *v.t* detail
a **detaşa** *v.t* detach
a **detecta** *v.t* detect
a **determina** *v.t* determine
a **detesta** *v.t* abhor

a **detrona** *v.t* dethrone
a **deturna fonduri** *v.t*
  misappropriate
a **devasta** *v.t* ravage
a **deveni** *v.i* become
a **devia** *v.i* deviate
a **devora** *v.t* devour
a **devota** *v.t* devote
a **dezamăgi** *v.t* disappoint
a **dezaproba** *v.t* disapprove
a **dezarma** *v.t* disarm
a **dezbate o problemă** *v.t* canvass
a **dezerta** *v.t* desert
a **dezgheţa** *v.i* thaw
a **dezgoli** *v.t* denude
a **dezgoli** *v.t* strip
a **dezlega** *v.t* loose
a **dezmierda** *v.t* dandle
a **dezmierda** *v.t* stroke
a **dezrădăcina** *v.t* uproot
a **dezvălui** *v.t* disclose
a **dezvolta** *v.t* develop
a **diagnostica** *v.t* diagnose
a **dicta** *v.t* dictate
a **diferi** *v.i* differ
a **digera** *v.t* digest
a **dilua** *v.t* dilute
a **diminua** *v.t* diminish
a **direcţiona** *v.t* direct
a **dirija** *v.t* conduct
a **dirija** *v.t* rule
a **discuta** *v.t* discuss
a **diseca** *v.t* dissect
a **dispărea** *v.i* disappear
a **dispărea** *v.i* vanish
a **dispera** *v.i* despair
a **dispersa** *v.t* disperse
a **dispreţ** *v.t* disdain
a **dispreţui** *v.t* despise
a **dispreţui** *v.t* scorn
a **dispreţui** *v.t* trample
a **dispune** *v.t* dispose

a **distila** *v.t* distil
a **distila** *v.t* retort
a **distila** *v.t* still
a **distinge** *v.i* distinguish
a **distinge** *v.t* single
a **distinge din, dintre** *v.t*
  discriminate
a **distra** *v.t* entertain
a **distrage** *v.t* divert
a **distribui** *v.t* allot
a **distribui** *v.t* distribute
a **distruge** *v.t* destroy
a **diviza în părţi** *v.t* partition
a **divorţa** *v.t* divorce
a **divulga** *v.t* divulge
a **divulga fără să vrea** *v.t* blurt
a **dizolva** *v.t* dissolve
a **doborî** *v.t* down
a **dojeni** *v.t* chide
a **dojeni** *v.t* snub
a **dojeni** *v.t* taunt
a **dojeni** *v.t* upbraid
a **domina** *v.t* dominate
a **domina** *v.t* overpower
a **domina** *v.i* prevail
a **domni** *v.i* reign
a **dona** *v.t* donate
a **dori** *v.t* desire
a **dormi** *v.i* sleep
a **dormita** *v.i* slumber
a **dota** *v.t* endow
a **dovedi** *v.t* attest
a **dovedi** *v.t* prove
a **dresa** *v.t* train
a **droga** *v.t* physic
a **dubla** *v.t* double
a **dubla** *v.t* duplicate
a **duce** *v.t* bear
a **duce** *v.t* wage
a **duce cu o barcă** *v.t* row
a **duce tratative** *v.i* parley
a **dura** *v.i* last

a **durea** *v.i* ache
a **durea** *v.t* hurt
a **echilibra** *v.t* balance
a **echipa** *v.t* equip
a **echipa** *v.t* outfit
a **ecraniza** *v.t* screen
a **edita** *v.t* edit
a **educa** *v.t* educate
a **educa** *v.t* nurture
a **efectua** *v.t* effect
a **egala** *v.t* equal
a **egaliza** *v.t* equalize
a **elabora** *v.t* elaborate
a **electriza** *v.t* electrify
a **elibera** *v.t* free
a **elibera** *v.t* liberate
a **elibera** *v.t* vacate
a **elimina** *v.t* eliminate
a **elimina din şcoală** *v.t* expel
a **elogia** *v.t* laud
a **elogia** *v.t* praise
a **elucida** *v.t* elucidate
a **emite** *v.t* emit
a **enerva** *v.t* annoy
a **enumera** *v.t* enumerate
a **epuiza** *v.t* exhaust
a **epuiza** *v.t* outdo
a **eradica** *v.t* eradicate
a **eroda** *v.t* erode
a **erupe** *v.i* erupt
a **escalada** *v.i* swarm
a **escava** *v.t* excavate
a **escorta** *v.t* escort
a **escroca** *v.t* swindle
a **estima** *v.t* esteem
• a **estima** *v.t* estimate
a **estompa** *v.t* stump
a **eşua** *v.i* fail
a **eşua** *v.i* strand
a **eticheta** *v.t* label
a **eticheta** *v.t* tag
a **evacua** *v.t* evacuate

a **evada** *v.i* escape
a **evada** *v.t* evade
a **evalua** *v.t* appraise
a **evalua** *v.t* assess
a **evalua** *v.t* evaluate
a **evalua** *v.t* price
a **evalua** *v.t* rate
a **evapora** *v.i* evaporate
a **evita** *v.t* avoid
a **evita** *v.t* dodge
a **evita** *v.t* elude
a **evoca** *v.t* evoke
a **exagera** *v.t* exaggerate
a **examina** *v.t* audit
a **examina** *v.t* examine
a **examina cu grijă** *v.t* peruse
a **examina detaliat** *v.t* survey
a **exceda creditul** *v.t* overdraw
a **excela** *v.i* excel
a **excepta** *v.t* except
a **exclama** *v.i* exclaim
a **exclude** *v.t* exclude
a **exclude de la** *v.t* debar
a **excomunica** *v.t* excommunicate
a **executa** *v.t* execute
a **executa** *v.t* implement
a **exercita** *v.t* prosecute
a **exersa** *v.t* exercise
a **exersa** *v.t* practise
a **exhuma** *v.t* unearth
a **exila** *v.t* exile
a **exila** *v.t* ostracize
a **exista** *v.i* exist
a **expedia** *v.t* mail
a **expira** *v.i* expire
a **explica** *v.t* explain
a **exploata** *v.t* exploit
a **exploda** *v.t* explode
a **explora** *v.t* explore
a **exporta** *v.t* export
a **exprima** *v.t* express
a **exprima** *v.t* phrase

a exprima condoleanțe *v.i* condole

a exprima în cuvinte *v.t* word

a expune *v.t* display

a expune *v.t* exhibit

a expune *v.t* expose

a extenua *v.t* tire

a extinde *v.t* extend

a extrage *v.t* extract

a extrage *v.t* quarry

a exulta *v.i* exult

a ezita *v.t* demur

a ezita *v.i* hesitate

a face *v.t* do

a face *v.t* make

a face "lumânarea" *v.i* zoom

a face aluzie la *v.i* allude

a face asemănător cu *v.t* liken

a face canotaj *v.i* boat

a face cavaler *v.t* knight

a face comerț cu *v.i* trade

a face cu ochiul *v.i* wink

a face cumpărături *v.i* shop

a face curățenie *v.t* cleanse

a face de rușine *v.t* abash

a face de rușine *v.t* embarrass

a face de rușine *v.t* shame

a face dezordine *v.t* riot

a face duș *v.t* shower

a face ecou *v.t* echo

a face egal *v.t* equate

a face egal cu *v.t* even

a face față *v.i* cope

a face gălăgie *v.i* clamour

a face glume *v.i* jest

a face groapă *v.t* moat

a face legi *v.i* legislate

a face morală *v.t* lecture

a face morală *v.t* moralize

a face o croazieră *v.i* cruise

a face o infuzie de *v.t* infuse

a face o razie *v.t* raid

a face o săritură *v.i* rebound

a face o tumbă *v.i* somersault

a face paradă *v.t* parade

a face pe plac *v.t* indulge

a face pireu *v.t* mash

a face posibil *v.t* enable

a face reclamă *v.t* publicize

a face reclamă *v.t* advertise

a face să cadă *v.t* trip

a face să derapeze *v.t* skid

a face să devieze *v.t* deflect

a face să pocnească *v.i* smack

a face să tacă *v.i* hush

a face să tresară *v.t* thrill

a face schema *v.i* scheme

a face semn *v.i* beckon

a face semn cuiva *v.i* motion

a face șicane *v.t* cavil

a face socoteli *v.t* cast

a face sport *v.i* sport

a face spumă *v.t* foam

a face trafic *v.i* traffic

a face un clambur *v.t* pun

a face un efort de viteză *v.i* spurt

a face un picnic *v.i* picnic

a face un proiect *v.t* design

a face un regiment *v.t* regiment

a face un tur *v.i* tour

a face unde *v.t* wave

a face zarvă *v.i* fuss

a face zbârcituri *v.i* plough

a facilita *v.t* facilitate

a făgădui solemn *v.t* vow

a falsifica *v.t* adulterate

a fărâmița *v.t* crumble

a fascina *v.t* fascinate

a făta *v.t* breed

a făta *v.t* litter

a favoriza *v.t* befriend

a favoriza *v.t* favour

a felicita *v.t* felicitate

a felicita *v.t* congratulate

a feri *v.t* fend
a fermeca *v.t* charm
a fermeca *v.t* enrapture
a fermenta *v.t* brew
a fermenta *v.t* ferment
a fertiliza *v.t* fertilize
a fi *v.t* be
a fi ascuţit *v.i* taper
a fi cuprins de panică *v.i* stampede
a fi de acord *v.i* agree
a fi de acord *v.i* consent
a fi de partea cuiva *v.i* side
a fi furioasă *v.i* surge
a fi îmbrăcat cu *v.t* wear
a fi în conflict *v.i* conflict
a fi în pantă *v.i* slope
a fi înclinat *v.t* shelve
a fi întins *v.i* lie
a fi lipsit de *v.t* lack
a fi mâhnit *v.i* mope
a fi mai puternic decât *v.t* overrule
a fi martor *v.i* witness
a fi militar *v.i* soldier
a fi nehotărât *v.i* shilly-shally
a fi neliniştit *v.t* fret
a fi oblic *v.t* slant
a fi socotit *v.t* repute
a fierbe *v.i* boil
a fierbe înăbuşit *v.t* stew
a fierbe zahăr *v.t* candy
a filma *v.t* film
a filtra *v.t* filter
a filtra *v.t* leach
a finanţa *v.t* finance
a fixa *v.t* affix
a fixa *v.t* bind
a fixa *v.t* fasten
a fixa *v.t* set
a fixa un cablu *v.t* cable
a fixa un preţ *v.t* quote

a flata *v.t* flatter
a flecări *v.t* blab
a flecări *v.i* blether
a flirta *v.i* flirt
a fluiera *v.i* whistle
a flutura *v.t* flutter
a folosi *v.t* avail
a folosi *v.t* use
a fonda *v.t* found
a forfoti *v.i* teem
a forma *v.t* form
a formula *v.t* formulate
a forţa *v.t* force
a forţa *v.t* forge
a fortifica *v.t* fortify
a fotografia *v.t* photograph
a fractura *v.t* fracture
a frământa *v.t* churn
a frâna *v.t* brake
a frâna *v.t* curb
a frânge *v.t* wring
a freca *v.t* rub
a frige *v.t* burn
a frige *v.t* roast
a fronta *v.t* front
a frustra *v.t* frustrate
a fugi *v.i* run
a fugi cu iubitul/a *v.i* elope
a fugi de *v.i* flee
a fuma *v.i* smoke
a funcţiona *v.i* function
a fura *v.t* pilfer
a fura *v.i* steal
a gâdila *v.t* tickle
a gâfâi *v.i* gasp
a gâfîi *v.i* pant
a galopa *v.t* gallop
a galvaniza *v.t* galvanize
a gândi *v.t* think
a gânguri *v.i* babble
a gânguri *v.i* coo
a garanta *v.t* guarantee

a garanta v.t warrant
a gargarisi v.i gargle
a găsi v.t find
a găti v.t cook
a găuri v.t hole
a găuri v.t pierce
a geme v.i groan
a genera v.t beget
a genera v.t generate
a germina v.i germinate
a ghici v.i guess
a ghiftui v.t glut
a gira v.t endorse
a glorifica v.t glorify
a glumi v.i joke
a glumi cu v.i trifle
a glumi răutăcios v.i gibe
a goli v.t empty
a grăbi v.t hurry
a grămadi v.t pile
a grava v.t engrave
a gravita v.i gravitate
a greşi v.i err
a greşi ordinea v.t mismatch
a grohăi v.i grunt
a grupa v.t group
a grupa v.t assort
a gudrona v.t tar
a gusta v.t taste
a guverna v.t govern
a handicapa v.t handicap
a hărţui v.t harass
a haşura v.t tint
a hipnotiza v.t hypnotize
a hipnotiza v.t mesmerize
a hoinări v.i loaf
a hoinări v.i loiter
a hoinări v.t saunter
a hoinări v.i stroll
a hoinări, v.t ramble
a hrăni v.t feed
a huidui v.i hoot

a hurui v.i rumble
a idealiza v.t idealize
a identifica v.t identify
a ieftini v.t cheapen
a ierna v.i winter
a ierta v.t forgive
a ieşi la iveală v.i emerge
a ignora v.t ignore
a ilumina v.t illuminate
a ilustra v.t illustrate
a imagina v.t imagine
a îmbălmăsa v.t embalm
a îmbărbăta v.t man
a îmbarca v.t embark
a îmbarca v.t ship
a îmbia cu v.t ply
a îmbina două sisteme v.t merge
a îmblânzi v.t tame
a îmblânzi v.i tamper
a îmbogăţi v.t enrich
a îmboldi v.t poke
a îmboldi v.t urge
a îmboldi vitele v.t goad
a îmbrăca v.t attire
a îmbrăca v.t clothe
a îmbrăca v.t dress
a îmbrânci v.t jostle
a îmbrânci v.t shove
a îmbrăţişa v.t embrace
a îmbunătăţi v.t better
a îmbunătăţi v.t improve
a imigra v.i immigrate
a imita v.t imitate
a imita v.t mimic
a imortaliza v.t immortalize
a împăca v.t conciliate
a împacheta v.t pack
a împăduri v.t afforest
a împărtăşi v.t impart
a împărţi v.t bisect
a împărţi v.t portion
a împărţi v.t share

a împărţi în *v.t* parcel
a împătri *v.t* quadruple
a împerechea *v.t* pair
a împerechea păsări *v.t* mate
a împiedica *v.t* hinder
a împiedica *v.t* impede
a împiedica *v.t* inhibit
a împiedica *v.t* prevent
a împinge *v.t* push
a împleti *v.t* knit
a împleti din trestie *v.t* cane
a implica *v.t* implicate
a implica *v.t* imply
a implica *v.t* involve
a împlini *v.t* fulfil
a implora *v.t* implore
a împodobi *v.t* deck
a împodobi cu bijuterii *v.t* jewel
a împodobi cu cuie *v.t* stud
a importa *v.t* import
a împovăra *v.t* burden
a împovăra *v.t* encumber
a împovăra *v.t* impoverish
a împrăştia *v.t* bestrew
a împrăştia *v.t* scatter
a impregna cu ulei *v.t* oil
a impresiona *v.t* impress
a impresiona puternic *v.t* excite
a împreuna *v.t* link
a imprima *v.t* imprint
a imprima *v.t* print
a împrumuta *v.t* borrow
a împrumuta *v.t* lend
a impune *v.t* impose
a imputa *v.t* impute
a împuternici *v.t* accredit
a împuternici *v.t* empower
a imuniza *v.t* immunize
a înăbuşi o dorinţă *v.t* quench
a înainta *v.t* forward
a înălbi *v.t* blanch
a înălbi *v.i* bleach

a înălbi *v.t* whiten
a înălţa *v.t* exalt
a înălţa *v.t* heighten
a înălţa *v.t* uplift
a înapoia *v.t* render
a înarma *v.t* arm
a înarma din vreme *v.t* forearm
a inaugura *v.t* auspicate
a încălca *v.i* encroach
a încălca o lege *v.t* transgress
a încălţa *v.t* shoe
a încălzi *v.t* heat
a încălzi *v.t* warm
a încânta *v.t* delight
a încânta *v.t* enamour
a încânta *v.t* enchant
a încărca *v.t* charge
a încărca *v.t* lade
a încărca *v.t* load
a încărca *v.t* stoke
a încarna *v.t* incarnate
a încasa *v.t* cash
a încătuşa *v.t* handcuff
a încătuşa *v.t* shackle
a incedia *v.t* kindle
a începe *v.t* begin
a începe *v.t* commence
a începe *v.t* start
a încerca *v.t* attempt
a încerca *v.i* try
a încerca să întreacă *v.t* emulate
a încercui *v.t* encircle
a înceta *v.i* cease
a înceta *v.t* quit
a închega *v.t* clot
a încheia *v.t* conclude
a încheia cu nasturi *v.t* button
a închide *v.t* close
a închide *v.t* shut
a închide cu cheie *v.t* key
a închiria *v.t* hire
a închiria *v.t* lease

a închiria *v.t* rent
a incinera *v.t* cremate
a încinge *v.t* girdle
a incita *v.t* incite
a încleia *v.t* lime
a încleşta *v.t* interlock
a înclina *v.t* bias
a înclina *v.i* incline
a include *v.t* include
a încolţi *v.i* sprout
a înconjura *v.t* encompass
a înconjura *v.t* surround
a înconjura de mister *v.t* mystify
a încorda *v.t* strain
a încorona *v.t* crown
a încorpora *v.t* incorporate
a încovoia *v.i* spring
a încredinţa *v.t* entrust
a încredinţa cuiva *v.t* consign
a încreţi fruntea *v.t* purse
a incrimina *v.t* incriminate
a încuia *v.t* lock
a încuia într-o discuţie *v.t* nail
a inculca *v.t* inculcate
a încunoştinţa *v.t* acquaint
a încununa *v.t* wreathe
a încuraja *v.t* embolden
a încuraja *v.t* encourage
a încurca *v.t* confuse
a încurca *v.t* entangle
a încurca *v.t* mull
a încurca *v.t* puzzle
a încurca *v.t* tangle
a îndemna să *v.t* prompt
a îndesa *v.t* ram
a indica *v.t* indicate
a îndoi *v.t* bend
a îndoi *v.t* fold
a îndoi *v.t* redouble
a îndopa *v.t* cram
a îndopa *v.t* stuff
a îndrăgi *v.t* endear

a îndrăzni *v.i* dare
a îndrepta *v.t* redress
a îndrepta *v.t* straighten
a induce *v.t* induct
a îndulci *v.t* sweeten
a îndupleca *v.t* coax
a îndura *v.t* endure
a îndura *v.t* undergo
a îndurera *v.t* aggrieve
a îndurera *v.t* distress
a înfăşa *v.t* wind
a înfăşura *v.t* convolve
a înfăşura *v.t* furl
a înfăşura în giulgiu *v.t* shroud
a infecta *v.t* infect
a înfige *v.t* stick
a înfiora *v.t* startle
a înflăcăra *v.t* inflame
a înflori *v.i* bloom
a înflori *v.i* blossom
a înflori *v.i* flourish
a influenţa *v.t* influence
a informa *v.t* inform
a informa *v.t* notify
a înfrânge *v.t* defeat
a înfrânge *v.t* vanquish
a înfrumuseţa *v.t* adorn
a înfrumuseţa *v.t* beautify
a înfuria *v.t* enrage
a înfuria *v.t* infuriate
a îngălbeni *v.t* yellow
a îngenunchea *v.i* kneel
a îngheţa *v.i* freeze
a înghiţi *v.t* engulf
a înghiţi *v.t* swallow
a îngrădi *v.t* confine
a îngrădi *v.t* hedge
a îngrădi cu *v.t* fence
a îngrămădi *v.t* heap
a îngrăşa pământul *v.t* manure
a îngrăşa pământul *v.i* soil
a îngriji *v.i* tend

a îngriji ca o mamă *v.i* mother
a îngropa *v.t* bury
a îngroşa *v.i* thicken
a îngrozi *v.t* horrify
a inhala *v.i* inhale
a înhăma *v.t* harness
a înhăţa *v.t* tackle
a iniţia *v.t* initiate
a injecta *v.t* inject
a înjosi *v.t* abase
a înjosi *v.t* debase
a înjuga boi *v.t* yoke
a înjumătăţi *v.t* halve
a înjunghia *v.t* stab
a înlătura *v.t* oust
a înlocui *v.t* replace
a înlocui *v.t* shift
a înmâna *v.t* hand
a înmatricula *v.t* matriculate
a înmuia *v.t* dip
a înmuia *v.t* drench
a înmuia *v.t* immerse
a înnămoli *v.t* silt
a înnămoli *v.t* mire
a înnegri *v.t* blacken
a înnoda *v.t* knot
a inocula *v.t* inoculate
a înota *v.i* swim
a inova *v.t* innovate
a înrăma *v.t* frame
a înrăutăţi *v.t* worsen
a înregistra *v.t* record
a înregistra *v.t* register
a înregistra *v.t* tape
a înrobi *v.t* enslave
a înrola *v.t* enlist
a înrola *v.t* enrol
a înscrie *v.t* inscribe
a înscrie ca alegător *v.t* poll
a înşela *v.t* cheat
a înşela *v.t* deceive
a înşela *v.t* delude

a înşela *v.t* gull
a înşela *v.t* trick
a înşeua *v.t* saddle
a înşfăca *v.t* snatch
a insinua *v.t* insinuate
a înşira *v.t* thread
a insista *v.t* insist
a inspecta *v.t* inspect
a inspecta *v.i* scout
a inspira *v.t* inspire
a inspira *v.t* sniff
a instala *v.t* install
a înstela *v.t* star
a instiga *v.t* instigate
a înstrăina *v.t* alienate
a instructa *v.t* instruct
a instrui *v.t* drill
a însufleţi *v.t* enliven
a insulta *v.t* affront
a insulta *v.t* insult
a insulta *v.t* outrage
a înşuruba *v.t* screw
a întâlni *v.t* meet
a întâmpina *v.t* greet
a înţărca *v.t* ablactate
a întări *v.t* toughen
a întări *v.t* harden
a întări *v.t* reinforce
a întări *v.t* strengthen
a întârzia *v.t* delay
a întârzia *v.t* retard
a înţelege *v.t* comprehend
a înţelege *v.t* understand
a înţelege greşit *v.t* misapprehend
a înţelege greşit *v.t*
    misunderstand
a întemniţa *v.t* imprison
a întemniţa *v.i* mew
a intensifica *v.t* intensify
a intenţiona *v.t* intend
a intenţiona *v.t* mean
a înţepa *v.t* prick

a înţepa *v.t* puncture
a înţepa *v.t* sting
a înţepa cu un ac *v.t* pin
a înţepeni *v.t* stiffen
a înţepeni *v.t* wedge
a intercepta *v.t* intercept
a interesa *v.i* commend
a interesa *v.t* concern
a interna *v.t* intern
a interoga *v.t* interrogate
a interpreta *v.t* interpret
a interpreta fals *v.t* misconceive
a interpreta un rol *v.t* perform
a intersecta *v.t* intersect
a interveni *v.i* interfere
a interveni *v.i* intervene
a intervieva *v.t* interview
a interzice *v.t* ban
a interzice *v.t* forbid
a interzice *v.t* prohibit
a interzice *v.t* taboo
a intimida *v.t* bully
a intimida *v.t* cow
a intimida *v.t* intimidate
a întinde *v.t* stretch
a întineri *v.t* rejuvenate
a intitula *v.t* entitle
a întocmi o hartă *v.t* map
a intoxica *v.t* intoxicate
a intra *v.t* enter
a intra într-un pătrar *v.t* quarter
a întreba *v.t* ask
a întreba *v.t* question
a întrebuinţa greşit *v.t* misuse
a întrece *v.t* outwit
a întrece ca număr *v.t* outnumber
a întrece ca strălucire *v.t*
   outshine
a întrece în greutate *v.t* outweigh
a întrei *v.t* triple
a întrerupe *v.t* discontinue
a întrerupe *v.t* interrupt

a întrerupe *v.t* punctuate
a intriga *v.t* intrigue
a întrista *v.t* sadden
a introduce *v.t* insert
a introduce *v.t* usher
a introduce pe furiş *v.t* smuggle
a întrona *v.t* enthrone
a întruchipa *v.t* embody
a intui *v.t* sense
a întuneca *v.i* darkle
a întuneca *v.t* dim
a inunda *v.t* flood
a invada *v.t* invade
a invalida *v.t* invalidate
a învălmăşi *v.t* clutter
a învălui *v.t* envelop
a învălui *v.t* veil
a învârti *v.i* spin
a învârti *v.t* wheel
a învăţa *v.i* learn
a învăţa pe dinafară *v.t* rote
a înveli *v.t* wrap
a inventa *v.t* invent
a inversa *v.t* invert
a inversa *v.t* reverse
a înveseli *v.t* cheer
a înveşmânta *v.t* apparel
a înveşmânta *v.t* garb
a investi *v.t* invest
a învesti *v.t* vest
a investiga *v.t* investigate
a invidia *v.t* envy
a învinge *v.t* overcome
a învinge *v.t* worst
a învinovăţi *v.t* blame
a invita *v.t* invite
a invoca *v.t* invoke
a invoca spiritele *v.t* conjure
a înzestra *v.t* grace
a înzestra cu personal *v.t* staff
a ipoteca *v.t* mortgage
a iradia *v.i* irradiate

a **iriga** v.t irrigate
a **iriga** v.t water
a **irita** v.t irritate
a **irosi** v.t waste
a **iscăli** v.t subscribe
a **iscodi** v.t sift
a **ispăşi** v.i atone
a **iubi** v.t love
a **izbi** v.t strike
a **izbucni** v.i burst
a **izgoni** v.t banish
a **izgoni** v.t evict
a **izola** v.t insulate
a **izola** v.t isolate
a **izola o persoană** v.t seclude
a **izvorî** v.i stream
a **jalona** v.t peg
a **jefui** v.t pirate
a **jefui** v.t rob
a **jigni** v.t offend
a **jongla** v.t juggle
a **juca** v.t play
a **juca** v.t stake
a **juca pe bani** v.i game
a **juca zaruri** v.i dice
a **judeca** v.i judge
a **judega gresit** v.t misjudge
a **jumuli** v.t pluck
a **jumuli** v.i shear
a **jupui** v.t skin
a **jura** v.t swear
a **jura fals** v.t perjure
a **justifica** v.t justify
a **lamina** v.t laminate
a **lâncezi** v.i languish
a **lâncezi** v.i pine
a **lansa o navă la apă** v.t launch
a **lansa pe apă** v.i float
a **lărgi** v.t enlarge
a **lărgi** v.t widen
a **lăsa** v.t let
a **lăsa moştenire** v.t bequeath

a **lăsa perplex** v.t perplex
a **lătra** v.t bark
a **lega** v.t tie
a **lega cu funie** v.t rope
a **lega cu mortar** v.t mortar
a **lega cu sfoară** v.t string
a **lega în şnururi** v.t lace
a **lega la mijloc** v.t gird
a **lega la ochi** v.i blindfold
a **lega la ochi** v.t hoodwink
a **legaliza** v.t legalize
a **legăna** v.t dangle
a **legăna** v.t lull
a **legăna** v.t rock
a **lepăda** v.t cast
a **leşina** v.i faint
a **leşina** v.i swoon
a **licări** v.t flicker
a **licări** v.i twinkle
a **lichefia** v.t liquefy
a **lichida** v.t liquidate
a **licita** v.t bid
a **limita** v.t limit
a **limita** v.t restrict
a **linge** v.t lick
a **linguşi** v.t wheedle
a **linia** v.t line
a **linişti** v.t tranquillize
a **linişti** v.t appease
a **linişti** v.t quiet
a **linşa** v.t lynch
a **lipi un afiş** v.t post
a **lista** v.t list
a **livra** v.t deliver
a **localiza** v.t localize
a **locui** v.t inhabit
a **locui** v.i reside
a **logodi** v.t betroth
a **logodi** v.t engage
a **lor** pron theirs
a **lovi** v.t bang
a **lovi** v.t hit

a lovi cu bâta *v.i* bat
a lovi cu laba *v.t* paw
a lovi cu piciorul *v.t* kick
a lovi cu pumnul *v.t* cuff
a lovi cu pumnul *v.t* punch
a lovi cu putere *v.t* whack
a lovi uşor *v.t* tap
a lua *v.t* take
a lua asupra sa *v.t* undertake
a lua ca pradă *v.i* loot
a lua cu lopata *v.t* shovel
a lua în căsătorie *v.t* wed
a lua în nume de rău *v.t* resent
a lua în seamă *v.t* heed
a lua loc *v.i* sit
a lua lustrul *v.t* tarnish
a lua masa *v.t* dine
a lua o mostră din *v.t* sample
a lua pe umăr *v.t* shoulder
a lua supradoză *v.t* overdose
a lubrifica *v.t* lubricate
a luci *v.i* glow
a lucra *v.t* work
a lui *pron* his
a lumina *v.t* enlighten
a lumina *v.i* lighten
a lungi *v.t* lengthen
a lupta cu *v.i* battle
a lustrui *v.t* brighten
a lustrui *v.t* polish
a luxa *v.t* sprain
a măcăi *v.i* quack
a măcelări *v.t* butcher
a măcelări *v.t* slaughter
a măcina *v.t* mill
a măcina *v.t* weather
a mâhni *v.t* afflict
a maimuţări *v.t* ape
a maltrata *v.t* bedevil
a maltrata *v.t* mistreat
a mânca *v.t* eat
a mânca cu lingura *v.t* spoon

a manevra *v.i* manoeuvre
a manevra un tren *v.t* shunt
a mângâia *v.t* caress
a mângâia *v.t* fondle
a mângâia *v.t* pat
a mângâia *v.t* pet
a manipula *v.t* manipulate
a manufactura *v.t* manufacture
a mânui *v.t* handle
a mârâi *v.i* growl
a marca *v.t* mark
a mărgini *v.t* border
a mări *v.t* augment
a mări *v.t* magnify
a mârîi *v.i* snarl
a mărşălui *v.i* march
a mărşălui *v.i* troop
a mărturisi *v.t* confess
a mărturisi *v.i* testify
a masa *v.t* massage
a masacra *v.t* massacre
a masca *v.t* mask
a măsura *v.t* measure
a măsura *v.t* mete
a măsura cu palma *v.t* span
a materializa *v.t* materialize
a mătura *v.i* sweep
a maturiza *v.i* mature
a maximiza *v.t* maximize
a mâzgăli *v.t* jot
a mâzgăli *v.t* scrawl
a mâzgăli *v.t* scribble
a media *v.i* mediate
a medita *v.t* meditate
a medita, *v.i* muse
a menţine *v.t* maintain
a menţiona *v.t* mention
a merge *v.i* go
a merge din nou pe *v.t* retread
a merge în buiestru *v.i* pace
a merge în rând *v.i* file
a merge legănat *v.i* waddle

a **merge pe** v.t tread
a **merge pe brânci** v.i scramble
a **merge pe jos** v.i walk
a **merge repede** v.i speed
a **merge țanțoș** v.i strut
a **merita** v.t deserve
a **merita** v.t merit
a **mesteca** v.t chew
a **mesteca** v.t masticate
a **migra** v.i migrate
a **mima** v.i mime
a **minimaliza** v.t minimize
a **minți** v.i lie
a **mirosi** v.t smell
a **mişca** v.t move
a **mitui** v.t bribe
a **mobila** v.t furnish
a **mobiliza** v.t mobilize
a **mocni** v.i simmer
a **mocni** v.i smoulder
a **modela** v.t model
a **modela** v.t shape
a **modera** v.t moderate
a **moderniza** v.t modernize
a **modifica** v.t modify
a **modula** v.t modulate
a **moleşi** v.t soften
a **molesta** v.t molest
a **momi** v.t entice
a **monopoliza** v.t monopolize
a **mormăi** v.i grumble
a **mormăi** v.i mumble
a **mortifica** v.t mortify
a **moşteni** v.t inherit
a **moțăi** v.i doze
a **moțăi** v.i nap
a **motiva** v.t motivate
a **mugi** v.i low
a **mugi** v.i moo
a **mulge** v.t milk
a **multiplica** v.t multiply
a **mulțumi** v.t content

a **mulțumi** v.t please
a **mulțumi** v.t thank
a **murdări** v.i mess
a **murdări** v.t smear
a **muri** v.i die
a **murmura** v.t murmur
a **muşca** v.t bite
a **mustra** v.t admonish
a **mustra** v.t rebuke
a **mustra** v.t reprimand
a **mutila** v.t mutilate
a **năpârli** v.i moult
a **năpârli** v.t slough
a **nara** v.t narrate
a **nara** v.t recount
a **născoci** v.t devise
a **născoci** v.t fabricate
a **naşte** v born
a **naționaliza** v.t nationalize
a **naturaliza** v.t naturalize
a **năuci** v.t bemuse
a **năuci** v.t stun
a **naviga** v.ki navigate
a **naviga** v.i sail
a **necăji** v.t vex
a **necesita** v.t necessitate
a **necheza** v.t neigh
a **nedreptăți** v.t wrong
a **nega** v.t deny
a **neglija** v.t neglect
a **negocia** v.t negotiate
a **negocia** v.t transact
a **neliniști** v.t unsettle
a **nemulțumi** v.t displease
a **nemulțumi** v.t dissatisfy
a **nesocoti** v.i disregard
a **netezi** v.t smooth
a **neutraliza** v.t neutralize
a **nimici** v.t annihilate
a **ninge** v.t snow
a **nitui** v.t rivet
a **nivela** v.t level

a **nominaliza** *v.t* nominate
a **normaliza** *v.t* normalize
a **nota** *v.t* note
a **nu avea încredere în** *v.t*
   mistrust
a **nu fi de acord** *v.i* disagree
a **nu observa** *v.t* oversee
a **nu se supune** *v.t* disobey
a **nuanţa** *v.t* tincture
a **nuanţa** *v.t* tinge
a **număra** *v.t* count
a **număra** *v.t* number
a **numi** *v.t* appoint
a **numi** *v.t* name
a **numi greşit** *v.t* miscall
a **nutri** *v.t* nourish
a **o lua la sănătoasa** *v.i* scamper
a **obiecta** *v.t* object
a **obişnui cu** *v.t* accustom
a **obliga** *v.t* oblige
a **obloji** *v.t* foment
a **obosi** *v.t* fatigue
a **obosi** *v.t* weary
a **obseda** *v.t* obsess
a **observa** *v.t* observe
a **obţine** *v.t* achieve
a **obţine** *v.t* obtain
a **obtura** *v.t* throttle
a **ocaziona** *v.t* occasion
a **ocupa** *v.t* occupy
a **oferi** *v.t* offer
a **oferi** *v.t* tender
a **oferi un banchet** *v.t* banquet
a **oficia** *v.i* officiate
a **oglindi** *v.t* mirror
a **omite** *v.i* hop
a **omite** *v.t* omit
a **omite** *v.i* skip
a **ondula** *v.t* ripple
a **ondula** *v.i* undulate
a **onora** *v.t* dignify
a **onora** *v.t* honour

a **opera** *v.t* operate
a **opri** *v.t* stop
a **opri creşterea** *v.t* stunt
a **oprima** *v.t* oppress
a **opta pentru** *v.t* opt
a **opune** *v.t* oppose
a **orândui** *v.t* size
a **organiza** *v.t* organize
a **orienta** *v.t* orient
a **orienta** *v.t* orientate
a **ornamenta** *v.t* ornament
a **oscila** *v.i* oscillate
a **oscila** *v.i* waver
a **osifica** *v.t* ossify
a **oţeţi** *v.* acetify
a **otrăvi** *v.t* poison
a **păcăli** *v.t* beguile
a **păcăli** *v.t* hoax
a **păcătui** *v.i* sin
a **pacifica** *v.t* pacify
a **pagina** *v.t* page
a **pălmui** *v.t* slap
a **pâlpâi** *v.i* flare
a **palpita** *v.i* palpitate
a **pândi** *v.t* waylay
a **para o lovitură** *v.t* parry
a **parafraza** *v.t* paraphrase
a **paraliza** *v.t* paralyse
a **părăsi** *v.t* forsake
a **părăsi pe cineva** *v.t* maroon
a **parca** *v.t* park
a **pardosi** *v.t* floor
a **părea** *v.i* seem
a **parfuma** *v.t* perfume
a **parfuma** *v.t* scent
a **paria** *v.i* bet
a **paria pe** *v.t* wager
a **pârli** *v.t* scorch
a **parodia** *v.t* parody
a **participa** *v.i* participate
a **participa la** *v.i* partake
a **păşi** *v.t* step

a păşi cu aroganţă *v.i* stalk
a paşte *v.t* pasture
a păstra *v.t* keep
a păstra cu evlavie *v.t* enshrine
a păstra în suflet *v.t* cherish
a păta *v.t* blot
a păta *v.t* spot
a păta *v.t* taint
a patina skate
a patrona *v.t* patronize
a patrula *v.i* patrol
a pava *v.t* pave
a pava *v.t* stone
a păzi *v.i* guard
a păzi *v.t* watch
a pedala *v.t* pedal
a pedepsi *v.t* punish
a penaliza *v.t* penalize
a penetra *v.t* penetrate
a pensiona *v.t* pension
a percepe *v.t* apprehend
a percepe *v.t* levy
a perfecta *v.t* perfect
a perfora *v.t* perforate
a permite *v.t* allow
a permite *v.t* permit
a perpetua *v.t* perpetuate
a persecuta *v.t* persecute
a persevera *v.i* persevere
a persista *v.i* persist
a personifica *v.t* impersonate
a personifica *v.t* personify
a personifica *v.t* typify
a perturba *v.t* perturb
a perverti *v.t* pervert
a perveti *v.t* debauch
a pescui *v.i* fish
a petici *v.t* patch
a picura *v.i* drip
a pierde *v.t* forfeit
a pierde *v.t* lose
a pieri *v.i* perish

a pili *v.t* file
a pilota *v.t* pilot
a pingeli *v.t* sole
a pipera *v.t* pepper
a pisa *v.t* pound
a pişca *v.t* nip
a piui *v.t* cheep
a pivota *v.i* pivot
a plânge *v.i* cry
a plânge *v.i* weep
a planifica *v.t* plan
a planifica *v.t* schedule
a planta *v.t* plant
a plasa *v.t* station
a plăti *v.t* pay
a pleca *v.i* depart
a pleca *v.t* leave
a pleda *v.i* plead
a pleda pentru *v.t* advocate
a plictisi *v.t* bore
a plivi *v.t* weed
a plonja *v.i* dive
a ploua *v.i* rain
a ploua cu grindină *v.i* hail
a pocni *v.i* clap
a pocni *v.i* pop
a pocni *v.t* snap
a polei *v.i* surface
a polua *v.t* pollute
a pompa *v.t* pump
a popula *v.t* people
a popula *v.t* populate
a populariza *v.t* popularize
a porecli *v.t* nickname
a poseda *v.t* own
a poseda *v.t* possess
a posta o scrisoare *v.t* post
a posta pichete *v.t* picket
a posti *v.i* fast
a potoli *v.t* assuage
a potoli *v.t* soothe
a potoli o durere *v.t* remit

a **potoli setea** *v.t* slake
a **poza** *v.i* pose
a **poziţiona** *v.t* position
a **prăda** *v.i* maraud
a **prăda** *v.t* plunder
a **prăda** *v.t* sack
a **prăji** *v.i* fry
a **prânzi** *v.i* lunch
a **prăpădi** *v.i* blast
a **preceda** *v.t* precede
a **preda** *v.t* teach
a **preda** *v.t* surrender
a **predetermina** *v.t* predetermine
a **predica** *v.i* preach
a **predica** *v.t* predicate
a **predomina** *v.i* predominate
a **prefera** *v.t* prefer
a **prefixa** *v.t* prefix
a **pregăti** *v.t* concoct
a **preluda** *v.t* prelude
a **prelungi** *v.t* prolong
a **premedita** *v.t* premeditate
a **premia** *v.t* prize
a **preocupa** *v.t* preoccupy
a **prepara** *v.t* prepare
a **prepondera** *v.i* preponderate
a **presa** *v.t* press
a **presăra** *v.t* asperse
a **presăra cu** *v.t* sprinkle
a **prescrie** *v.t* prescribe
a **prescurta** *v.t* abbreviate
a **prescurta** *v.t* abridge
a **presimţi rele** *v.t* misgive
a **presiona** *v.t* pressurize
a **presupune** *v.t* conjecture
a **presupune** *v.t* presume
a **presupune** *v.t* suppose
a **presupune** *v.t* surmise
a **pretinde** *v.t* claim
a **pretinde** *v.t* demand
a **preţui** *v.t* treasure
a **prevedea** *v.t* foresee

a **prevedea cu zăvor** *v.t* staple
a **preveni** *v.t* apprise
a **preveni** *v.t* warn
a **prevesti** *v.t* portend
a **prezenta** *v.t* introduce
a **prezenta** *v.t* present
a **prezice** *v.t* foretell
a **prezice** *v.t* predict
a **prezice** *v.t* prophesy
a **prezida** *v.i* preside
a **pribegi** *v.i* wander
a **pricepe** *v.t* perceive
a **pricinui durere** *v.t* ail
a **primejdui** *v.t* endanger
a **primejdui** *v.t* imperil
a **primejdui** *v.t* jeopardize
a **primejdui** *v.t* peril
a **primi** *v.t* receive
a **primi net** *v.t* net
a **prinde** *v.t* catch
a **prinde in capcană** *v.t* trap
a **prinde în capcană** *v.t* entrap
a **prinde în cursă** *v.t* net
a **prinde în laţ** *v.t* noose
a **prinde peşti** *v.t* mesh
a **prinde rădăcini** *v.i* root
a **priponi** *v.t* tether
a **priva** *v.t* deprive
a **privi** *v.t* view
a **privi galeş** *v.t* ogle
a **proceda** *v.i* proceed
a **proclama** *v.t* proclaim
a **procura** *v.t* acquire
a **procura** *v.t* procure
a **procura pt. cineva** *v.i* provide
a **produce** *v.t* originate
a **produce** *v.t* produce
a **produce** *v.t* yield
a **profana** *v.t* profane
a **profesa** *v.t* profess
a **profila** *v.t* profile
a **profita de** *v.t* profit

a **prognoza** *v.t* forecast
a **programa** *v.t* programme
a **progresa** *v.i* progress
a **proiecta** *v.t* project
a **promite** *v.t* promise
a **promova** *v.t* promote
a **pronunţa** *v.t* pronounce
a **pronunţa** *v.t* spell
a **propaga** *v.t* propagate
a **proporţiona** *v.t* proportion
a **propulsa** *v.t* propel
a **propune** *v.t* propose
a **propune** *v.t* propound
a **proroga** *v.t* prorogue
a **prospera** *v.i* prosper
a **prospera** *v.i* thrive
a **prostitua** *v.t* prostitute
a **proteja** *v.t* protect
a **protesta** *v.i* protest
a **proveni** *v.t* derive
a **proveni din** *v.i* accrue
a **provoca** *v.t* challenge
a **provoca** *v.t* provoke
a **publica** *v.t* publish
a **pudra** *v.t* powder
a **pufni** *v.t* snout
a **pulsa** *v.i* pulsate
a **pulsa** *v.i* pulse
a **pulveriza un lichid** *v.t* spray
a **puncta** *v.t* dot
a **puncta** *v.t* point
a **pune** *v.t* encase
a **pune** *v.t* put
a **pune bazele** *v.t* base
a **pune botniţă la** *v.t* muzzle
a **pune de acord** *v.t* accord
a **pune în afara legii** *v.t* attaint
a **pune in corelaţie** *v.t* correlate
a **pune în fiare** *v.t* fetter
a **pune în libertate** *v.t* release
a **pune în ordine** *v.t* right
a **pune în ordine** *v.t* tidy

a **pune în scenă** *v.t* stage
a **pune în umbră** *v.t* overshadow
a **pune la cale** *v.t* plot
a **pune la încercare** *v.t* essay
a **pune la îndoială** *v.t* arraign
a **pune la muiat** *v.t* steep
a **pune la păstrare** *v.t* bestow
a **pune la saramură** *v.t* pickle
a **pune la treabă** *v.t* task
a **pune mâna pe** *v.t* nab
a **pune momeală** *v.t* bait
a **pune pauză** *v.i* pause
a **pune un capac** *v.t* cap
a **pune un inel** *v.t* ring
a **purifica** *v.t* purify
a **purta** *v.t* waft
a **putea** *v.t* can
a **putea** *v.aux* may
a **puţi** *v.t* stink
a **rabda** *v.t* abide
a **răbda de foame** *v.i* starve
a **răci** *v.i* cool
a **rade** *v.t* grate
a **râde** *v.i* laugh
a **râde de** *v.t* quiz
a **radia** *v.i* beam
a **radia** *v.t* radiate
a **radiografia** *v.t* x-ray
a **radiotelegrafia** *v.t* radio
a **rafina** *v.t* refine
a **râgâi** *v.t* belch
a **rage** *v.i* roar
a **râma** *v.i* nuzzle
a **rămâne** *v.i* remain
a **rămâne undeva** *v.i* sojourn
a **rambursa** *v.t* reimburse
a **rândui** *v.t* array
a **rândui** *v.t* marshal
a **rândui** *v.t* stow
a **răni** *v.t* harm
a **răni** *v.t* injure
a **rânji** *v.i* sneer

a **răpi** *v.t* abduct
a **răpi** *v.i* bereave
a **răpi** *v.t* kidnap
a **raporta la** *v.t* refer
a **răsări** *v.i* rise
a **răscoli** *v.t* rummage
a **răscumpăra** *v.t* ransom
a **răsfăţa** *v.t* pamper
a **răsfoi** *v.t* browse
a **rasoli** *v.t* botch
a **răspândi** *v.i* spread
a **răspândi** *v.t* strew
a **răspândi aburi** *v.i* steam
a **răspândi zvonuri** *v.t* rumour
a **răsplăti** *v.t* reciprocate
a **răsplăti** *v.t* repay
a **răsplăti** *v.t* requite
a **răspunde** *v.t* answer
a **răspunde** *v.i* respond
a **rastălmăci** *v.t* misrepresent
a **răstuna un sistem** *v.t* subvert
a **răsturna** *v.i* capsize
a **răsturna** *v.i* topple
a **răsuci** *v.i* twist
a **răsuna** *v.i* resound
a **rătăci** *v* astray
a **rătăci** *v.i* stray
a **ratifica** *v.t* ratify
a **ratifica o lege** *v.t* sanction
a **raţiona** *v.i* reason
a **raţionaliza** *v.t* rationalize
a **râvni** *v.t* covet
a **râvni la** *v.i* hanker
a **răzbuna** *v.t* avenge
a **reabilita** *v.t* rehabilitate
a **reacţiona** *v.i* react
a **realiza** *v.t* accomplish
a **realiza** *v.t* realize
a **reânnoi** *v.t* renew
a **reântâlni** *v.t* rejoin
a **reânvia** *v.t* revive
a **reaproviziona** *v.t* replenish

a **reasigura** *v.t* reassure
a **recădea** *v.i* relapse
a **rechema** *v.t* recall
a **rechema** *v.t* remand
a **rechiziţiona** *v.t* requisition
a **recita** *v.t* recite
a **recolta** *v.t* reap
a **recomanda** *v.t* recommend
a **recompensa** *v.t* recompense
a **recompensa** *v.t* reward
a **reconcilia** *v.t* reconcile
a **reconstitui** *v.t* retrace
a **reconstitui** *v.t* restore
a **recruta** *v.t* recruit
a **rectifica** *v.i* rectify
a **recunoaşte** *v.t* admit
a **recunoaşte** *v.t* concede
a **recunoaşte** *v.t* recognize
a **recupera** *v.t* recover
a **recurge la** *v.i* resort
a **redobândi** *v.t* recoup
a **reduce** *v.t* abate
a **reduce** *v.t* reduce
a **reduce** *v.t* slacken
a **reduce la tăcere** *v.t* silence
a **reduce viteza** *v.i* slow
a **reflecta** *v.t* reflect
a **reforma** *v.t* reform
a **refuza** *v.t* refuse
a **refuza** *v.t* repulse
a **regenera** *v.t* regenerate
a **regreta** *v.i* regret
a **regreta** *v.t* rue
a **regrupa trupe** *v.t* rally
a **regula** *v.t* regulate
a **reieşi din** *v.i* ensue
a **relata** *v.t* relate
a **relua mingea** *v.t* volley
a **remarca** *v.t* notice
a **remarca** *v.t* remark
a **remedia** *v.t* remedy
a **remorca** *v.t* tug

a **remunera** *v.t* remunerate
a **renega** *v.t* abnegate
a **renova** *v.t* renovate
a **renunţa** *v.t* renounce
a **renunţa la** *v.t* jack
a **renunţa la** *v.t* waive
a **repara** *v.t* fix
a **repara** *v.t* mend
a **repara** *v.t* repair
a **repara** *v.t* retrieve
a **repartiza** *v.t* apportion
a **repartiza** *v.t* assign
a **repatria** *v.t* repatriate
a **repeta** *v.t* rehearse
a **repeta** *v.t* reiterate
a **repeta** *v.t* repeat
a **replica la** *v.t* reply
a **reporta** *v.t* report
a **reprezenta** *v.t* represent
a **reprima** *v.t* repress
a **reproduce** *v.t* reproduce
a **reproşa** *v.t* reproach
a **repudia** *v.t* repudiate
a **respecta** *v.t* respect
a **respinge** *v.t* disprove
a **respinge** *v.t* rebuff
a **respinge** *v.t* reject
a **respinge** *v.t* refute
a **respinge cu dispreţ** *v.t* spurn
a **respira** *v.i* breathe
a **respira** *v.i* respire
a **restabili** *v.t* reinstate
a **restitui** *v.t* refund
a **reţine** *v.t* detain
a **reţine** *v.i* refrain
a **reţine** *v.t* restrain
a **reţine** *v.t* retain
a **reţine** *v.t* withhold
a **retipări** *v.t* reprint
a **retrage** *v.t* withdraw
a **retuşa** *v.t* retouch
a **reuni** *v.t* muster

a **revărsa** *v.i* shed
a **revendica** *v.t* reclaim
a **reveni** *v.i* return
a **reveni** *v.i* revert
a **revizui** *v.t* review
a **revizui** *v.t* revise
a **revoca** *v.t* repeal
a **revoca** *v.t* revoke
a **rezerva** *v.t* book
a **rezerva** *v.t* reserve
a **rezista la** *v.t* resist
a **rezolva** *v.t* resolve
a **rezolva** *v.t* solve
a **rezulta** *v.t* result
a **rezulta din** *v.i* issue
a **rezuma** *v.t* resume
a **ridica** *v.t* elevate
a **ridica** *v.t* erect
a **ridica** *v.t* hoist
a **ridica corturile** *v.i* decamp
a **ridica din umeri** *v.t* shrug
a **ridica în slăvi** *v.t* extol
a **ridica la pătrat** *v.t* square
a **ridiculiza** *v.t* banter
a **ridiculiza** *v.t* ridicule
a **rima** *v.i* rhyme
a **risca** *v.i* gamble
a **risca** *v.t* risk
a **risipi** *v.t* lavish
a **rivaliza cu** *v.i* vie
a **rivaliza cu** *v.t* rival
a **roade** *v.i* graze
a **robi** *v.i* slave
a **roşi** *v.i* blush
a **rosti** *v.t* utter
a **roti** *v.i* whirl
a **rotunji** *v.t* round
a **ruga stăruitor** *v.t* entreat
a **rugini** *v.i* rust
a **ruina** *v.t* ruin
a **ruina** *v.t* wreck
a **rumega** *v.i* ruminate

a **rupe** *v.t* break
a **rupe** *v.t* rupture
a **rupe** *v.t* splinter
a **rupe** *v.t* tear
a **rupe** *v.t* tear
a **sabota** *v.t* sabotage
a **sâcîi** *v.t* nag
a **sacrifica** *v.t* sacrifice
a **saluta** *v.t* salute
a **salva** *v.t* rescue
a **salva** *v.t* salvage
a **salva** *v.t* save
a **şampona** *v.t* shampoo
a **sângera** *v.i* bleed
a **şantaja** *v.t* blackmail
a **săpa** *v.t* dig
a **săpa** *v.t* sap
a **săpa** *v.t* spade
a **săpuni** *v.t* soap
a **săra** *v.t* salt
a **sări** *v.i* dap
a **sări** *v.i* jump
a **sări peste** *v.i* leap
a **şarja un rol** *v.t* overact
a **săruta** *v.t* kiss
a **satiriza** *v.t* satirize
a **satisface** *v.t* satisfy
a **satura** *v.t* saturate
a **sătura până la refuz** *v.t* satiate
a **savura** *v.t* savour
a **scădea** *v.t* decline
a **scădea** *v.t* deduct
a **scădea** *v.t* subtract
a **scădea brusc** *v.i* slump
a **scânci** *v.i* whimper
a **scanda versuri** *v.t* scan
a **scandaliza** *v.t* scandalize
a **scânteia** *v.i* glitter
a **scânteia** *v.i* scintillate
a **scânteia** *v.i* spark
a **scânteia** *v.i* sparkle
a **scăpa** *v.i* drop

a **scăpa** *v.t* rid
a **scârţâi** *v.i* creak
a **schilodi** *v.t* disable
a **schilodi** *v.t* lame
a **schimba** *v.t* change
a **schimba** *v.t* switch
a **schimba ceva pe** *v.t* exchange
a **schimba idei** *v.t* interchange
a **schiţa** *v.t* draft
a **schiţa** *v.t* figure
a **schiţa** *v.t* sketch
a **scoate** *v.t* bail
a **scoate** *v.t* eject
a **scoate** *v.t* remove
a **scoate de sub control** *v.t* decontrol
a **scoate în afara legii** *v.t* outlaw
a **scoate în evidenţă** *v.t* manifest
a **scoate sâmburii** *v.t* pit
a **scobi** *v.t* groove
a **scormoni** *v.t* rout
a **scotoci** *v.t* ransack
a **scrie** *v.t* write
a **scrie cu creionul** *v.t* pencil
a **scrie cu iniţiale** *v.t* initial
a **scrie o prefaţă la** *v.t* preface
a **scrie pamflete** *v.t* lampoon
a **scrie/redacta** *v.t* pen
a **scufunda** *v.t* whelm
a **scuipa** *v.i* spit
a **sculpta** *v.t* chisel
a **scurge** *v.t* elapse
a **scurge** *v.t* drain
a **scurta** *v.t* shorten
a **scuti** *v.t* spare
a **scuti de** *v.t* exempt
a **scuza** *v.t* excuse
a **scuza** *v.t* pardon
a **se abate** *v.i* straggle
a **se abţine** *v.i* abstain
a **se adresa** *v.t* address
a **se aduna** *v.i* cluster

a se aduna *v.i* flock
a se agăţa *v.i* cling
a se amesteca *v.t* jumble
a se apleca *v.i* tilt
a se apropia de *v.t* approach
a se aşeza *v.t* seat
a se aştepta *v.t* expect
a se ataşa unui grup *v.t* join
a se avânta *v.i* soar
a se bălăci *v.i* paddle
a se balansa *v.i* sway
a se bâlbâi *v.t* lisp
a se bâlbâi *v.i* stammer
a se bucura *v.i* rejoice
a se bucura de *v.t* enjoy
a se califica *v.i* qualify
a se caria *v.t* rot
a se căsători *v.t* marry
a se căţăra *v.i* clamber
a se căţăra *v.t* climb
a se cerceta pe sine *v.i* introspect
a se certa *v.t* argue
a se certa *v.i* dispute
a se certa cu *v.i* quarrel
a se ciocni *v.i* collide
a se ciondăni *v.t* wrangle
a se clătina *v.i* shake
a se clătina *v.i* stagger
a se clătina *v.i* vacillate
a se clătina *v.i* wobble
a se clinti *v.i* budge
a se coace *v.i* ripen
a se cocoţa *v.i* perch
a se cocoţa *v.i* roost
a se concentra *v.t* focus
a se consfătui cu *v.t* commune
a se crăpa de ziuă *v.i* dawn
a se crispa *v.i* writhe
a se cuibări *v.i* nestle
a se cupla *v.t* couple
a se curba *v.t* curve
a se cutremura *v.i* quake

a se dedica *v.t* addict
a se depărta *v.i* recede
a se deplasa *v. refl* ambulate
a se descompune *v.t* decompose
a se desfăta *v.i* wallow
a se deştepta *v.i* rouse
a se dezlănţui *v.t* storm
a se dezvolta *v.t* evolve
a se duce după *v.t* fetch
a se duela *v.i* duel
a se eschiva de la *v.t* absent
a se evapora *v.t* vaporize
a se făli *v.i* swagger
a se fâstâci *v.t* shuttle
a se fâţâi *v.i* fiddle
a se feri *v.i* recoil
a se feri de *v.t* shun
a se furişa *v.i* sneak
a se ghemui *v.i* cower
a se ghemui *v.i* crouch
a se grăbi *v.i* hasten
a se grăbi *v.i* rush
a se hărţui *v.t* skirmish
a se hazarda *v.t* hazard
a se holba la *v.i* stare
a se îmbarca *v.t* board
a se îmbrăca în robă *v.t* robe
a se îmbulzi *v.t* throng
a se împerechea *v.i* copulate
a se împletici *v.i* lurch
a se împotrivi la *v.t* withstand
a se înălţa *v.i* heave
a se înălţa *v.i* tower
a se înapoia *v.i* revel
a se încăiera *v.i* scuffle
a se încovoia *v.i* stoop
a se încrede în *v.i* rely
a se încreţi *v.t* crimple
a se încreţi *v.i* cockle
a se încrunta *v.i* frown
a se încrunta *v.i* scowl
a se îndoi de *v.i* doubt

a se îndoi de *v.t* query
a se îndopa *v.i* gobble
a se îndrepta spre *v.t* trench
a se înduioşa *v.i* relent
a se îneca *v.t* choke
a se îneca *v.i* drown
a se infiltra în *v.t* pervade
a se înfiora *v.i* shudder
a se informa despre *v.t* inquire
a se îngălbeni la faţă *v.i* pale
a se îngrijora *v.i* worry
a se înroşi *v.t* redden
a se înşela asupra *v.t* misconstrue
a se instala *v.i* squat
a se întâlni *v.t* date
a se întâmpla *v.t* happen
a se întâmpla *v.i* occur
a se întâmpla cuiva *v.t* befall
a se întrece în viteză *v.i* race
a se întrezări *v.i* loom
a se învârti *v.i* revolve
a se învârti *v.i* turn
a se învechi *v.t* stale
a se înveseli *v.t* gladden
a se înviora *v.t* refresh
a se istovi muncind *v.i* overwork
a se ivi *v.i* arise
a se juca *v.i* toy
a se juca zgomotos *v.i* romp
a se lamenta *v.i* lament
a se lăuda *v.i* brag
a se lăuda cu *v.i* boast
a se legăna *v.i* swing
a se lua la trântă cu *v.i* wrestle
a se lupta *v.t* fight
a se lupta *v.i* grapple
a se lupta pentru *v.i* militate
a se mândri cu *v.t* pride
a se masturba *v.i* masturbate
a se micşora *v.t* lessen
a se micşora *v.t* dwindle
a se micşora *v.i* shrink

a se minuna *v.i* marvel
a se mira *v.i* wonder
a se mucegăi *v.t* mould
a se necăji *v.t* grieve
a se ocupa de *v.i* cater
a se ocupa de *v.t* mind
a se odihni *v.i* rest
a se ofili *v.i* fade
a se ofili *v.i* wither
a se opri *v.t* halt
a se opune *v.t* antagonize
a se opune *v.t* counter
a se păzi de *v.i* beware
a se plânge *v.i* complain
a se ploconi *v.i* cringe
a se poticni *v.i* stumble
a se prăbuşi *v.i* collapse
a se prelinge *v.i* seep
a se prelinge *v.i* trickle
a se purta bine *v.i* behave
a se purta urât *v.i* misbehave
a se răni *v.t* wound
a se răscula *v.i* mutiny
a se răscula *v.i* rebel
a se răsuci *v.i* wriggle
a se război *v.i* war
a se răzbuna *v.i* retaliate
a se răzbuna *v.t* revenge
a se referi la *v* advert
a se relaxa *v.t* relax
a se repezi *v.i* lunge
a se repezi *v.i* pounce
a se repezi la *v.i* swoop
a se reproduce *v.i* recur
a se retrage *v.i* retire
a se retrage *v.i* retreat
a se revolta *v.i* revolt
a se rida *v.t* wrinkle
a se ridica *v.t* lift
a se ridica la *v.i* amount
a se rostogoli *v.i* bowl
a se rostogoli *v.i* roll

a se roti *v.i* rotate
a se ruga *v.i* pray
a se ruşina *v.t* shy
a se sătura *v.t* weary
a se scobi, *v.t* hollow
a se scoroji *v.t* parch
a se scotoci *v.i* fumble
a se scufunda *v.i* sink
a se scurge încet *v.i* ooze
a se sedimenta *v.i* subside
a se separa *v.i* secede
a se sfătui *v.t* counsel
a se simţi atras de *v.t* fancy
a se sinucide *v.t* suicide
a se spăla *v.t* bathe
a se sprijini pe *v.i* repose
a se statornici *v.i* settle
a se strădui *v.i* endeavour
a se strădui *v.i* strive
a se strâmba *v.i* wince
a se strânge *v.i* mass
a se supune *v.i* comply
a se supune *v.t* obey
a se supune cuiva *v.t* bow
a se sustrage *v.i* abscond
a se sustrage de la *v.t* shirk
a se tângui *v.i* wail
a se târî *v.t* crawl
a se ţine după *v.t* dog
a se tocmi *v.t* bargain
a se tocmi *v.i* haggle
a se topi *v.i* melt
a se topi *v.t* fuse
a se trezi *v.t* awake
a se trudi *v.i* moil
a se uita la *v.i* look
a se uita pe furiş *v.t* pry
a se uita saşiu *v.i* squint
a se umfla *v.i* billow
a se umfla *v.i* swell
a se zbate *v.i* struggle
a sechestra *v.t* sequester

a secreta *v.t* secrete
a secunda pe cineva *v.t* second
a seda *v.t* sedate
a seduce *v.t* seduce
a selecta *v.t* select
a semăna *v.t* sow
a semăna cu *v.t* resemble
a semna *v.t* sign
a semnifica *v.t* signify
a separa *v.t* part
a separa *v.t* segregate
a separa *v.t* separate
a separa *v.t* sunder
a şerpui *v.i* meander
a şerpui *v.i* snake
a servi *v.t* serve
a servi ca pernă *v.t* pillow
a sesiza *v.t* seize
a sfârâi la prăjit *v.i* sizzle
a sfărâma *v.t* crackle
a sfărâma *v.t* disrupt
a sfărâma *v.t* shatter
a sfârşi *v.t* end
a sfâşia *v.t* mangle
a sfâşia în bucăţi *v.t* maul
a sfătui *v.t* advise
a sfătui *v.t* tip
a sfătui să nu *v.t* dissuade
a sfinţi *v.t* hallow
a sfinţi *v.t* sanctify
a sforăi *v.i* snore
a sforăi *v.i* snore
a sigila *v.t* seal
a simboliza *v.t* symbolize
a simpatiza *v.i* sympathize
a simplifica *v.t* simplify
a simţi *v.t* feel
a simula *v.t* feign
a simula *v.i* sham
a simula ceva *v.t* pretend
a sistematiza *v.t* systematize
a situa *v.t* locate

a slăbi *v.t* enfeeble
a slăbi *v.t* weaken
a slăbi, *v.t* loosen
a slei de puteri *v.t* rack
a sluji la *v.i* minister
a smălțui *v.t* varnish
a smuci *v.t* wrench
a smulge *v.t* wrest
a șoca *v.t* shock
a socoti *v.t* tally
a solicita *v.t* solicit
a solicita prin petiție *v.t* petition
a solidifica *v.t*
a soma *v.t* summon
a sonda *v.t* fathom
a sonda *v.t* probe
a sonoriza *v.t* voice
a șopti *v.t* whisper
a sorbi *v.t* sip
a sorta *v.t* sort
a sosi *v.i* arrive
a șovăi *v.i* falter
a spăla *v.t* wash
a spăla și a călca *v.t* launder
a spația *v.t* space
a specializa *v.i* specialize
a specifica *v.t* specify
a specula *v.i* profiteer
a specula *v.i* speculate
a spera *v.t* hope
a speria *v.t* daunt
a speria *v.t* frighten
a speria *v.t* scare
a spinteca *v.t* rip
a spiona *v.i* spy
a sponsoriza *v.t* sponsor
a spori *v.t* increase
a sprijini *v.t* boost
a sprijini *v.t* support
a sprijini pe cineva *v.t* succour
a sprinta *v.i* sprint
a spune *v.t* say

a spune *v.t* tell
a spune gemând *v.i* moan
a spune pe nerăsuflate *v.t* jabber
a spurca *v.t* defile
a sta *v.i* stay
a sta cu fața spre *v.t* face
a sta în picioare *v.i* stand
a sta la pândă *v.i* lurk
a sta la soare *v.i* bask
a sta la taifas *v.i* chat2
a stabili *v.t* establish
a stabiliza *v.t* stabilize
a stabiliza *v.t* stable
a stagna *v.t* stagnate
a standardiza *v.t* standardize
a stăpâni *v.t* master
a stăpâni *v.t* wield
a stârni *v.t* arouse
a stârni invidia *v.t* jaundice
a stărui asupra *v.t* enforce
a stăvili *v.i* stem
a șterge *v.t* delete
a șterge *v.t* efface
a șterge *v.t* erase
a șterge *v.t* obliterate
a șterge *v.t* wipe
a șterge podeaua *v.t* mop
a șterge praful *v.t* dust
a șterge praful *v.t* whisk
a steriliza *v.t* sterilize
a ști *v.t* know
a stimula *v.t* stimulate
a stinge *v.t* extinguish
a stipula *v.t* stipulate
a stoarce *v.t* squeeze
a stoca *v.t* store
a străjui *v.t* ward
a străluci *v.i* shine
a străluci orbitor *v.t* dazzle
a străluci orbitor *v.i* glare
a strâmta *v.t* straiten
a strânge *v.t* grasp

a **strânge** v.t narrow
a **strânge** v.t tighten
a **strânge bani** v.t redeem
a **strânge într-un tot** v.t
   aggregate
a **strânge laolaltă** v.t accrete
a **strangula** v.t strangle
a **strănut** v.i sneeze
a **străpunge** v.t jab
a **străpunge** v.t spike
a **străpunge cu lancea** v.t spear
a **străpunge cu suliţa** v.t lance
a **stresa** v.t stress
a **strica** v.t bungle
a **strica** v.t damage
a **strica** v.t mar
a **strica** v.t spoil
a **striga** v.i shout
a **striga,** v.t hail
a **strivi** v.t jam
a **strivi** v.t squash
a **studia** v.i study
a **stupefia** v.t stupefy
a **subânchiria** v.t sublet
a **subjuga** v.t subdue
a **subjuga** v.t subject
a **subjuga** v.t subjugate
a **sublima** v.t sublimate
a **sublinia** v.t emphasize
a **sublinia** v.t underline
a **submina** v.t undermine
a **subţia** v.i slim
a **subţia** v.t thin
a **subvenţiona** v.t subsidize
a **subzista** v.i subsist
a **succeda** v.i succeed
a **suci capul cuiva** v.t infatuate
a **suda** v.t weld
a **suda** v.t solder
a **suferi** v.t suffer
a **sufla** v.i blow
a **sufla** v.i puff

a **sufla** v.t wind
a **sufoca** v.t stifle
a **sufoca** v.t suffocate
a **suge** v.t suck
a **suge cu buretele** v.t sponge
a **sugera** v.i hint
a **sugera** v.t intimate
a **sugera** v.t suggest
a **şuiera** v.i hiss
a **şuiera** v.i rave
a **şuiera** v.t zip
a **sumariza** v.t summarize
a **suna** v.i sound
a **suna din trâmbiţă** v.i trumpet
a **supăra** v.t pain
a **supăra** v.t upset
a **suplimenta** v.t supplement
a **suporta** v.t bare
a **suporta** v.t stomach
a **supraâncărca** v.t overburden
a **supraâncărca** v.t overload
a **supraâncărca** v.t surcharge
a **supraestima** v.t overrate
a **supralicita** v.t outbid
a **supraveghea** v.t invigilate
a **supraveghea** v.t superintend
a **supravieţui** v.i survive
a **supravieţui** v.t outlive
a **suprima** v.t retrench
a **suprima** v.t supersede
a **suprima** v.t suppress
a **supune** v.t submit
a **surprinde** v.t surprise
a **suspecta** v.t distrust
a **suspecta** v.t suspect
a **suspenda** v.t suspend
a **suspina** v.i sigh
a **susţine** v.t allege
a **susţine** v.t prop
a **susţine** v.t sustain
a **susţine** v.t uphold
a **susţine** v.t vindicate

a susține *v.i* contend
a susține o cauză *v.t* champion
a sustrage *v.t* abstract
a susura *v.t* bicker
a tachina *v.t* rag
a tăia *v.t* cut
a tăia *v.t* lop
a tăia ceva în felii *v.t* slice
a tăia cu ferăstrăul *v.t* saw
a tăia din *v.t* curtail
a tămâia *v.t* cense
a tămâia *v.t* incense
a tândăli *v.i* lounge
a tânji *v.t* crave
a tânji după *v.i* yearn
a tânji după ceva *v.i* long
a târî *v.t* drag
a târî *v.t* trail
a țârîi *v.i* reel
a țâșni *v.i* splash
a țâșni *v.i* spout
a țâșni *v.i* well
a tatua *v.i* tattoo
a taxa *v.t* tax
a telefona *v.t* telephone
a telegrafia *v.t* wire
a televiza *v.t* televise
a tempera *v.t* temper
a tencui *v.t* daub
a tenta *v.t* tempt
a terifia *v.t* terrify
a termina *v.t* complete
a termina *v.t* finish
a termina *v.t* terminate
a teroriza *v.t* terrorize
a țesăla un cal *v.t* groom
a țese *v.t* weave
a testa *v.t* test
a ticăi *v.i* tick
a timbra *v.i* stamp
a ține *v.t* hold
a ține doliu *v.i* mourn

a ține frâu *v.t* rein
a ține în echilibru *v.t* poise
a ține secret *v.t* conceal
a ținti *v.i* aim
a țipa *v.t* scream
a tipări greșit *v.t* misprint
a toarce *v.i* purr
a toasta *v.t* toast
a toca *v.t* mince
a toci *v.t* dull
a toci *v.i* plod
a tolera *v.t* tolerate
a topi un minereu *v.i* smelt
a torpila *v.t* torpedo
a tortura *v.t* torment
a totaliza *v* amount
a totura *v.t* torture
a trăda *v.t* betray
a traduce *v.t* translate
a trage *v.t* pull
a trage *v.t* toll
a trage cu o armă *v.t* shoot
a trage cu, carabina *v.t* rifle
a trage o cacealma *v.t* bluff
a trage o carte de joc *v.t* draw
a trage pe sfoară *v.t* bilk
a trage pe sfoară *v.t* trump
a trăi *v.i* dwell
a trăi *v.i* live
a trăi o întâmplare *v.t* experience
a trâmbița *v.t* blare
a trândăvi *v.i* dawdle
a trândăvi *v.i* laze
a transcrie *v.t* transcribe
a transcrie *v.t* transcription
a transfera *v.t* transfer
a transfigura *v.t* transfigure
a transforma *v.t* alter
a transforma *v.t* transform
a transforma în pastă *v.t* pulp
a transmite *v.t* broadcast
a transmite *v.t* convey

a **transmite** *v.t* transmit
a **transmite prin releu** *v.t* relay
a **transmite televizat** *v.t* telecast
a **transpira** *v.i* perspire
a **transplanta** *v.t* transplant
a **transporta** *v.t* transport
a **trânti la pământ** *v.t* fell
a **trânti uşa** *v.t* slam
a **trasporta cu trenul** *v.t* rail
a **trata despre ceva** *v.i* deal
a **traversa** *v.t* cross
a **trece** *v.i* pass
a **trece** *v.t* while
a **trece ca fulgerul** *v.i* flash
a **trece cu bacul** *v.t* ferry
a **trece cu vederea** *v.t* overlook
a **trece peste** *v.t* overrun
a **trece peste** *v.t* surmount
a **treiera cereale** *v.t* thresh
a **treizecea** *v.t* thirtieth
a **tremura** *v.i* tremble
a **tremura de** *v.i* quiver
a **tremuta de frig** *v.i* shiver
a **trezi** *v.t* wake
a **trimite** *v.t* send
a **trimite la ţară** *v.t* rusticate
a **trişa** *v.t* rook
a **triumfa** *v.i* triumph
a **tropăi** *v.i* trot
a **truca** *v.t* gag
a **trudi** *v.i* labour
a **trudi** *v.i* grind
a **trudi** *v.i* toil
a **tulbura** *v.t* disturb
a **tulbura** *v.i* trouble
a **tulbura apa** *v.t* puddle
a **tuna** *v.i* thunder
a **tunde o oaie** *v.t* fleece
a **turba** *v.i* rage
a **turna** *v.t* ladle
a **turna** *v.t* pour
a **turui** *v.i* rattle

a **tuşi** *v.i* cough
a **ucide** *v.t* kill
a **uda** *v.t* soak
a **uda** *v.t* wet
a **uimi** *v.t* amaze
a **uita** *v.t* forget
a **ului** *v.t* astonish
a **ului** *v.t* astound
a **ului** *v.t* daze
a **umaniza** *v.t* humanize
a **umbla prin** *v.i* stride
a **umbri** *v.t* obscure
a **umbri** *v.t* shade
a **umbri** *v.t* shadow
a **umezi** *v.t* moisten
a **umezi** *v.i* dabble
a **umezi** *v.t* damp
a **umili** *v.t* humiliate
a **umple** *v.t* fill
a **umple cu apă** *v.t* swamp
a **unge** *v.t* anoint
a **unge** *v.t* grease
a **unge cu smoală** *v.t* pitch
a **unge cu unt** *v.t* butter
a **uni** *v.t* mate
a **uni** *v.t* unite
a **ura bun venit** *v.t* welcome
a **urâţi** *v.t* uglify
a **urca** *v.t* ascend
a **urca** *v.t* mount
a **urgenta** *v.t* expedite
a **urî** *v.t* hate
a **urina** *v.i* urinate
a **urla** *v.t* howl
a **urla** *v.t* yell
a **urma** *v.t* follow
a **urmări** *v.t* chase1
a **urmări** *v.t* indict
a **urmări** *v.t* pursue
a **urmări** *v.t* track
a **urmări** *v.t* trace
a **urzica** *v.t* nettle

a usca *v.i* dry
a ustura *v.i* smart
a uşura *v.t* alleviate
a uşura *v.t* ease
a uşura *v.t* relieve
a utiliza *v.t* utilize
a uzurpa *v.t* usurp
a vaccina *v.t* vaccinate
a văduvi *v.t* widow
a vagabonda *v.i* rove
a vâjîi *v.i* whiz
a valida *v.t* validate
a valora *v.t* value
a vâna *v.t* hunt
a vântura *v.t* winnow
a vaporiza *v.t* aerify
a vârî *v.t* thrust
a vârî în sac *v.i* bag
a varia *v.t* vary
a vărsa *v.i* spill
a vărui *v.t* whitewash
a vedea *v.t* see
a venera *v.t* revere
a venera *v.t* venerate
a venera *v.t* worship
a veni *v.i* come
a ventila *v.t* ventilate
a verifica *v.t* verify
a verifica scrutinul *v.t* scrutinize
a versifica *v.t* versify
a vesti *v.t* herald
a vibra *v.i* vibrate
a vicia *v.t* vitiate
a victimiza *v.t* victimize
a vinde *v.t* sell
a vinde cu amănuntul *v.t* retail
a vinde pe *v.t* barter1
a vinde pe piaţă *v.t* market
a vindeca *v.t* cure
a vindeca *v.i* heal
a viola *v.t* rape
a viola *v.t* violate

a visa *v.i* dream
a vitaliza *v.t* vitalize
a vizita *v.t* visit
a vizualiza *v.t* visualize
a voluntaria *v.t* volunteer
a vomita *v.t* vomit
a vopsi *v.t* colour
a vopsi *v.t* dye
a vopsi *v.t* paint
a vopsi *v.i* stencil
a vorbi *v.i* speak
a vorbi *v.i* talk
a vorbi aiurea *v.t* maunder
a vorbi de rău *v.t* malign
a vorbi în echivocuri *v.i* quibble
a vorbi în parabole *v.i* riddle
a vota *v.i* vote
a vota contra *v.t* veto
a vrăji *v.t* bewitch
a vrea *v.t* mean
a vrea *v.t* want
a vrea *v.t* will
a xeroxa *v.t* xerox
a zăbovi *v.i* lag
a zăbovi *v.i* linger
a zaharisi *v.t* sugar
a zâmbi *v.i* smile
a zăngăni *v.i* jingle
a zăpăci *v.t* bewilder
a zări *v.t* behold
a zări *v.t* sight
a zăvorî *v.t* bolt
a zbiera *v.i* bellow
a zbiera *v.i* bray
a zbura *v.i* fly
a zbura cu avionul *v.t* plane
a zburda *v.i* frolic
a zdrobi *v.i* crash
a zdrobi *v.t* crush
a zdrobi *v.t* smash
a zdruncina *v.t* jog
a zdruncina *v.t* jolt

a zeflemisi *v.i* scoff
a zgâlțâi *v.t* toss
a zgâria *v.t* claw
a zgâria *v.t* scratch
a zidi *v.t* wall
a zori *v.t* bustle
a zugrăvi *v.t* portray
a zumzăi *v.i* hum
abanos *subs* ebony
abces *subs.* abscess
abdicare *subs.* abdication
abdomen *subs.* abdomen
abdominal *adj.* abdominal
aberatie *subs.* aberrance
abia *adv* barely
abia *adv* scarcely
abil *adj* deft
abis *subs.* abyss
abrupt *adj.* abrupt
abrupt *adj* steep
absent *adj.* absent
absența *subs* absence
absolut *adv.* absolutely
absolut *adj.* absolute
absorbire *subs* merger
absorbit *adj* rapt
abstinent *subs* teetotaller
abstract *adj.* abstract
abstracție *subs.* abstract
absurd *adj.* absurd
absurditate *subs.* absurdity
absurditate *subs* nonsense
abțipild *subs* sticker
abundent *adj* opulent
abundenta *subs.* abundance
abundenta *adj.* abundant
abundență *subs* luxuriance
abundență *subs* opulence
abundență *subs* richness
abur *subs* steam
abuz *subs.* abuse
abuz *subs* breach

abuz *subs* misuse
abuziv *adj.* abusive
ac cu gămălie *subs* pin
ac de cusut *subs* needle
acadea *subs* lollipop
academic *adj.* academic
academie *subs.* academy
accelerație *subs.* acceleration
accent *subs.* accent
accentuat *adj* emphatic
acceptabil *adj.* acceptable
acceptare *subs.* acceptance
acces *subs.* access
acces *subs.* admittance
acces *subs* fit
accesoriu *subs.* accessory
accident *subs.* accident
accident *subs* crash
acefal *adj.* acephalous
acel *adj* that
acela *pron* that
acelasi *adj* same
acesta, aceasta *pron* it
achitare a unei datorii *subs.* acquittal
achiziție *subs* procurement
achiziționare *subs.* acquest
acid *adj.* acid
acid *subs.* acid
aciditate *subs.* acidity
aclamație *subs.* acclamation
acnee *subs.* acne
acolo *adv* there
acolo *adv* thither
acomodare *subs.* accommodation
acoperiș *subs* roof
acoperit cu nori *adj* overcast
acord *subs* agreement
acord *subs* unison
acrobat *subs.* acrobat
acromatic *adj.* achromatic
acru *adj* sour

act *subs.* act
act emis de parlament *subs* statute
acţiune *subs* deed
acţiune *subs* share
acţiune riscantă *subs* venture
activ *adj.* active
activitate *subs.* activity
actor *subs.* actor
actriţă *subs.* actress
actual *adj.* actual
actual *adj* up-to-date
acum *adv* now
acum când *conj* now
acumulare *subs.* accumulation
acustic *adj.* acoustic
acustică *subs.* acoustics
acuzare *subs.* accusation
acuzare *subs* indictment
acuzat *subs.* accused
acuzat *subs* culprit
acuzat *subs* defendant
acvariu *subs* aquarium
adamant *subs.* adamant
adânc *adj* deep
adâncime *subs* depth
adaos *subs.* addition
adaos *subs* appendage
adaos la o carte *subs* appendix
adăpost *subs* lee
adăpost *subs* shelter
adaptare *subs.* adaptation
adecvat *adj.* adequate
adecvat *adj* appropriate
ademenire *subs* allurement
adept *subs* devotee
adept *subs* votary
aderare *subs.* adherence
aderent *adj.* adhesive
adesea *adv* oft
adevăr *subs* truth
adevărat *adj* true

adeverinţă *subs* record
adeziune *subs.* adhesion
adiere *subs* whiff
adiere *subs* zephyr
adio *interj.* adieu
adio! *interj* farewell
adjectiv *subs.* adjective
adjunct *subs.* adjunct
administrare *subs.* administration
administrare proastă *subs* mismanagement
administrativ *adj.* administrative
administrator *subs.* administrator
administrator *subs* manager
admirabil *adj.* admirable
admiraţie *subs.* admiration
admirator *subs* fan
admisibil *adj.* admissible
admitere *subs.* acknowledgement
adolescent *subs* teenager
adolescenţă *subs.* adolescence
adolescenţă *subs* boyhood
adolescenţi *subs* teens
adopţie *subs.* adoption
adorabil *adj.* adorable
adorare *subs.* adoration
adormit *adj* asleep
adresa *subs.* address
aducere aminte *subs* remembrance
adult *adj* adult
adult *subs.* adult
adulter *subs.* adultery
adunare *subs* moot
adverb *subs* adverb
adverbial *adj.* adverbial
advers *adj* adverse
adversar *subs* adversary
adversar *subs* antagonist
adversitate *subs* adversity
aer *subs* air
aerat *adj* airy

aerian *adj* aerial
aerodrom *subs* aerodrome
aeronautică *subs.* aeronautics
aeronavă *subs* aircraft
afacere *subs* business
afacere *subs* deal
afacerist *subs* businessman
afară *adv* outwards
afară *adv* out
afară de *prep* except
afară de *adj* outside
afară de *prep* save
afară de *prep* without
afară din *prep* outside
afectare *subs* affectation
afecțiune *subs* affection
afectuos *adj* affectionate
afiliere *subs* affiliation
afirmație *subs* affirmation
afirmativ *adj* affirmative
afiș *subs* poster
afluență *subs* influx
afumat *adj* tipsy
afumat *subs* tirade
afurisenie *subs* malediction
agendă *subs* agenda
agent *subs* agent
agent *subs* henchman
agent de schimb *subs* broker
agenție *subs* agency
ager *adj* alacrious
ager *asdj* brisk
agerime *subs* alacrity
agerime *subs* wit
agil *adj* agile
agilitate *subs* agility
agitare *subs* agitation
agitație *subs.* ado
agitație *subs* wag
aglomerație *subs* throng
agonie *subs.* agony
agorafobie *subs* agoraphobia

agrafă *subs* clasp
agrafă *subs* staple
agrar *adj* agrarian
agravare aggravation
agreabil *adj* agreeable
agresiune *subs* aggression
agresiv *adj* aggressive
agresor *subs* aggressor
agricol *adj* agricultural
agricultor *subs* agriculturist
agricultură *subs* agriculture
agricultură *subs* husbandry
agriș *subs* gooseberry
agronomie *subs* agronomy
a-i da dinții *v.i* teethe
a-i da fiori *v.i* creep
a-i displăcea *v.t* dislike
a-i face breton *v.t* fringe
a-i fi dor de *v.t* miss
a-i fi frică *v.i* fear
a-i fi groază de *v.t* dread
a-i fi milă de *v.t* pity
a-i fi sete *v.i* thirst
a-i fi silă *v.t* loathe
a-i părea rău (de) *v.i* repent
a-i plăcea *v,t* like
aici *adv* here
aisberg *subs* iceberg
ajustare *subs.* adjustment
ajutor *subs* aid
ajutor *subs* help
ajutor *subs* succour
al cui? *pron* whose
al doisprezecelea *adj* twelfth
al doisprezecelea *subs* twelfth
al douăzecilea *adj* twentieth
al ei *adj* her
a-l mânca pielea *v.i* itch
al meu, a mea *pron* mine
al nouălea *adj* ninth
al nouăsprezecelea *adj*
    nineteenth

al nouăzecilea *adj* ninetieth
al şaisprezecelea *adj* sixteenth
al şaizecilea *adj* sixtieth
al şaptelea *adj* seventh
al şaptisprezecelea *adj* seventeenth
al şaselea *adj* sixth
al treilea *adj* third
al treisprezecelea *adj* thirteenth
al treizecilea *adj* thirtieth
alarmă *subs* alarm
alăturat *adj.* adjacent
alături *adv.* abreast
alături *prep* beside
alături *adv* by
alb *adj* white
alb *subs* white
albastru *subs* blue
albastru *adj* blue
albeaţă pe ochi *subs* nebula
albină *subs* bee
Albion *subs* albion
album *subs* album
albumină *subs* albumen
alchimie *subs* alchemy
alchimist *adj.* adept
alcol *subs* alcohol
alee *subs* alley
alegaţie *subs* allegation
alegător *subs* voter
alegere *subs* choice
alegere *subs* election
alegere *subs* pick
alegeri suplimentare *subs* by-election
alegoric *adj* allegorical
alegorie *subs* allegory
alergare *subs* race
alergător *subs* runner
alergie *subs* allergy
alfa *subs* alpha
alfabet *subs* alphabet

alfabetic *adj* alphabetical
algă marină *subs* wrack
algebră *subs* algebra
aliaj *subs* alloy
alianţă *subs* alliance
alianţe *subs* in-laws
aliat *subs* ally
alibi *subs* alibi
alicot *subs* aliquot
alienat mintal *subs* lunatic
aligator *subs* alligator
aliment *subs* aliment
aliment răcoritor *subs* refreshment
aliment răcoritor *v.t* refrigerate
alimentaţie *subs* feed
alimente *subs* victuals
aliniere *subs* alignment
aliteraţie *subs* alliteration
almanah *subs* almanac
alocaţie *subs* allocation
alocaţie *subs* grant
alpinist *subs* alpinist
alt *adj* another
alt, altă *adj* other
altar *subs* altar
altceva *adj* else
altercaţie *subs* altercation
alternant *adj* alternate
alternanţă *subs* interchange
alternativ *adj* alternative
alternativă *subs* alternative
Alteţa *subs* Highness
altfel *adv* otherwise
altimetru *subs* altimeter
altitudine *subs* altitude
alto *subs* alto
altoi *subs* graft
altul, alta *pron* other
aluminiu *subs* aluminium
alunecare *subs* slide
alunecare *subs* slip

alunecos *adj* slick
alunecos *adj* slippery
aluzie *subs* allusion
amabil *adj* affable
amabil *adj* bland
amabil *adj* kind
amabil *subs* lovable
amăgire *subs* delusion
amalgam *subs* amalgam
amalgamare *subs* amalgamation
amânare *subs.* adjournment
amânare *subs* postponement
amânare *subs* procrastination
amândoi *adj* both
amanet *subs* pledge
amant *subs* lover
amantă *subs* mistress
amănunt *subs* retail
amănunţit *adj* thorough
amar *adj* bitter
amarnic *adj* grievous
amasadă *subs* embassy
amator *subs* amateur
amavon *subs* pulpit
ambasador *subs* ambassador
ambiant *adj* ambient
ambiguitate *subs* ambiguity
ambiguu *adj* ambiguous
ambiguu *adj* equivocal
ambii *pron* both
ambiţie *subs* ambition
ambiţios *adj* ambitious
ambreiaj *subs* clutch
ambulant *adj* ambulant
ambulanţă *subs* ambulance
ambuscadă *subs* ambush
ameliorare *subs* amelioration
amendă *subs* penalty
amendament *subs* amendment
ameninţare *subs* menace
ameninţare *subs* threat
ameninţător *adj* ominous

amestec *subs* blend
amestec *subs* compound
amestec *subs* miscellany
amestec *subs* mixture
ameţitor *adj* giddy
amfibiu *adj* amphibious
amfiteatru *subs* amphitheatre
amiabil *subs* amiable
amiabilitate *subs* amiability
amiază *subs* midday
amiază *subs* noon
amigdală *subs* tonsil
amin *interj.* amen
amintire *subs* keepsake
amintire *subs* memory
amintire *subs* recollection
amiral *subs.* admiral
amnezie *subs* amnesia
amnistie *subs* amnesty
amnistie *subs* oblivion
amoc *adv* amuck
amor *subs* amour
amoral *adj* amoral
amoros *adj* amorous
amorţit *adj* numb
amper *subs* ampere
amplificare *subs* amplification
amplificator *subs* amplifier
amploare *subs* breadth
amplu *adj* ample
amuletă *subs* amulet
amuzament *subs* amusement
an *subs* year
an de an *adj* yearly
anabaptism *subs* anabaptism
anacronism *subs* anachronism
anal *adj* anal
anale *subs pl* annals
analfabetism *subs* illiteracy
analitic *adj* analytical
analiză *subs* analysis
analog cu *adj* analogous

analogie *subs* analogy
anamneză *subs* anamnesis
ananas *subs* pineapple
anarhie *subs* anarchy
anarhism *subs* anarchism
anarhist *subs* anarchist
anatomie *subs* anatomy
ancestral *adj* ancestral
anchetă *subs* inquest
ancoră *subs* anchor
ancorare *subs* anchorage
anecdotă *subs* anecdote
anemie *subs* anaemia
anemometru *subs* anemometer
anestezic *suba* anaesthetic
anestezie *subs* anaesthesia
anexă *subs* enclosure
anexiune *subs* annexation
angajare *subs* employment
angajat *subs* employee
anghină *subs* angina
anghinare *subs* artichoke
animal *subs* animal
animal favorit *subs* pet
animal rătăcit *subs* stray
animalic *adj* beastly
animat *adj* animate
animaţie *subs* animation
animozitate *subs* animosity
aniversare *subs* anniversary
anomalie *subs* anomaly
anonim *adj* anonymous
anonimat *subs* anonymity
anormal *adj* abnormal
anormal *adj* anomalous
anost *adj* tedious
anotimp *subs* season
ansamblare *subs* assembly
antagonism *subs* antagonism
antarctic *adj* antarctic
antebraţ *subs* forearm
antecedent *subs* antecedent

antecedent *adj* antecedent
antenă *subs* aerial
antenă *subs* antennae
anterior *adj* former
anterior *adj* prior
anti *pref* anti
antiaerian *adj* anti-aircraft
antic *adj* ancient
antic *adj* antique
antichitate *subs* antiquity
anticipare *subs* anticipation
anticipare *subs* forethought
antidor *subs* antidote
antilopă *subs* antelope
antipatic *adj* repugnant
antipatie *subs* antipathy
antipatie *subs* dislike
antipatie *subs* repugnance
antipozi *subs*
antiseptic *subs* antiseptic
antiseptic *adj* antiseptic
antiteză *subs* antithesis
antologie *subs* anthology
antonim *subs* antonym
antrenament *subs* training
antrenor *subs* coach
antrenor *subs* trainee
antrepozit *subs* godown
antropoid *adj* anthropoid
anual *adj* annual
anual *adv* yearly
anuar *subs* directory
anuitate *subs* annuity
anulare *subs* cancellation
anulare *subs* nullification
anume *adv* namely
anunţ *subs* announcement
anus *subs* anus
apă *subs* water
apă de canal *subs* sewage
apă pulverizată *subs* spray
apărare *subs* defence

apărare *subs* deference
apărare *subs* vindication
aparat *subs* apparatus
aparat de fotografiat *subs*
   camera
aparent *adj* apparent
apariţie *subs* appearance
apariţie *subs* peep
apartament *subs* apartment
apartament *subs* flat
aparte *subs* aside
apartenenţă *subs* appurtenance
apăsător *adj* trying
apatic *adj* listless
apatic *adj* sluggish
apatie *subs* apathy
apeduct *subs* aqueduct
apel *subs* call
apendice *subs* appendix
apendicită *subs* appendicitis
aperitiv *subs* appetizer
apicultură *subs* apiculture
aplaudare *subs* clap
aplauze *subs.* acclaim
aplauze *subs* applause
aplecare *subs* bend
aplicabil *adj* applicable
aplicant *subs* applicant
aplicaţie *subs* application
apogeu *subs* pinnacle
apogeu *subs* zenith
apos *adj* watery
apostol *subs* apostle
apostrof *subs* apostrophe
apoteoză *subs* apotheosis
apreciabil *adj* appreciable
apreciere *subs* appreciation
aprins *adj.* ablaze
aprins *adv* aflame
aproape *adv* almost
aproape *adv* anigh
aproape *avd* nigh

aproape de *prep* near
aproape orb *adj* purblind
aprobare *subs* approbation
aprobare *subs* approval
apropiat *adj* close
apropiat *adj* near
apropiere *subs* approach
apropiere *subs* vicinity
apropiere *subs* zoom
aprovizionare *subs* provision
aprovizionare *subs* supply
aproximare *subs* proximity
aproximativ *adj* approximate
aproximativ *adj* proximate
apt de a moşteni *adj* heritable
aptitudine *subs* aptitude
apucare *subs* grip
arabil *adj* arable
aramă *subs* copper
aranjament *subs* arrangement
arătare *subs* show
arbitrar *adj* arbitrary
arbitrare *subs* arbitration
arbitru *subs* arbiter
arbitru *subs* arbitrator
arbitru *subs* referee
arbitru *subs* umpire
arbust *subs* shrub
arc *subs* arc
arc *subs* arch
arc *subs* bow
arcă *subs* ark
arcadă *subs* arcade
arcaş *subs* archer
arctic *subs* Arctic
ardezie *subs* slate
ardoare *subs* ardour
ardoare *subs* mettle
arenă *subs* arena
arestare *subs* arrest
arestare *subs* caption
argilă *subs* argil

argint *subs* silver
argint viu *subs* quicksilver
argintiu *adj* silver
argument *subs* settler
arhaic *adj* archaic
arhanghel *subs* archangel
arhiepiscop *subs* archbishop
arhitect *subs* architect
arhitectură *subs* architecture
arhive *subs* archives
aripă *subs* wing
aripioară înotătoare *subs* fin
aristocrat *subs* aristocrat
aristocrat *subs* peer
aristocraţie *subs* aristocracy
aritmetic *adj* arithmetical
aritmetică *subs* arithmetic
armă *subs* weapon
armament *subs* armament
armăsar *subs* stallion
armată *subs* army
armată nepermanentă *subs* militia
armistiţiu *subs* armistice
armistiţiu *subs* truce
armonie *subs* concord
armonie *subs* harmony
armonios *adj* harmonious
armoniu *subs* harmonium
armură *subs* armature
armură *subs* mail
arogant *adj* arrogant
aroganţă *subs* arrogance
aromă *subs* flavour
arsenal *subs* armoury
arsenal *subs* arsenal
arsenic *subs* arsenic
arsură *subs* burn
artă *subs* art
artă poetică *subs* poetics
arteră *subs* artery
articol *subs* article

articol *subs* item
articole de modе *subs* millinery
articulat *adj* articulate
articulaţie *subs* joint
artificial *adj* artificial
artificiu *subs* artifice
artilerie *subs* artillery
artilerie *subs* ordnance
artist *subs* artist
artistic *adj* artistic
artrită *subs* arthritis
aruncare *subs* throw
aruncătură de privire *subs* glance
arzător *adj* ardent
arzător *adj* fiery
as *subs.* ace
aşa *adv* so
asalt *subs* assault
asasin *subs* assassin
asasin *subs* murderer
asasinare *subs* assassination
ascendenţă biologică *subs* parentage
ascensiune *subs* ascent
ascentic *adj* ascetic
aşchie *subs* splinter
ascultător *adj* amenable
ascultător *subs* auditor
ascultător *subs* listener
ascuţit *adj* sharp
ascuţitoare *subs* sharpener
asediu *subs* siege
asemănare *subs* likeness
asemănare *subs* resemblance
asemănător *adj* alike
asemănător cu *adj* like
aşezământ *subs* establishment
aşezare *subs* locality
a-şi aminti *v.t* recollect
a-şi aminti *v.t* remember
a-şi asuma *v.t* assume

a-şi bate joc de *v.i* jeer
a-şi bate joc de *v.i* mock
a-şi cere scuze *v.i* apologize
a-şi dori *v.t* wish
a-şi înclina capul *v.i* nod
a-şi însuşi *v.t* appropriate
a-şi permite *v.t* afford
a-si propune *v.t* purpose
asigurare *subs* assurance
asigurare *subs* indemnity
asigurare *subs* insurance
asigurat *adj* secure
asimilare *subs* assimilation
asistare *subs* attendance
asistent *subs* assistant
asistenţă *subs* assistance
asociat *adj* associate
asociat *subs* associate
asociaţie *subs* association
aspect *subs* aspect
aspirant *subs* aspirant
aspiraţie *subs* aspiration
aspru *adj* harsh
aspru *adj* rough
astă seară *adv* tonight
astăzi *adv* today
aşteptare *subs* expectation
aşteptare *subs* wait
asterisc *subs* asterisk
aşternut *subs* bedding
asteroid *subs* asteroid
astfel *adv* thereby
astfel *adv* thus
astmă *subs* asthma
astrolog *subs* astrologer
astrologie *subs* astrology
astronaut *subs* astronaut
astronom *subs* astronomer
astronomie *subs* astronomy
asumare *subs* assumption
atac *subs* attack
atac *subs* onslaught

atac *subs* stroke
ataşament *subs* attachment
ataşat *subs* attache
atât de *adj* such
atât de *adv* that
ateism *subs* atheism
atelier *subs* studio
atelier *subs* workshop
atent *adj* attentive
atent *adj* watchful
atenţie *subs* attention
atenuare *subs.* abatement
atenuare a unei boli *subs*
    remission
atenuare a unei dureri *subs*
    mitigation
atenuat *adj* mellow
aterizare *subs* landing
ateu *subs* antitheist
ateu *subs* atheist
atingere *subs* touch
atitudine *subs* attitude
atlas *subs* atlas
atlet *subs* athlete
atletic *adj* athletic
atletism *subs* athletics
atmosferă *subs* atmosphere
atol *subs* atoll
atom *subs* atom
atomis *adj* atomic
atotputernic *adj* almighty
atotputernic *adj* omnipotent
atotputernicie *subs* omnipotence
atracţie *subs* appeal
atracţie *subs* attraction
atrăgător *adj* attractive
atrăgător *subs* sexy
atribut *subs* attribute
atroce *adj* atrocious
atrocitate *subs* atrocity
atu *subs* trump
atunci *adv* then

audibil *adj* audible
audienţă *subs* audience
auditiv *adj* auditive
auditoriu *subs* auditorium
augur *subs* omen
august *subs* August
aur *subs* gold
aurar *subs* goldsmith
aurire *subs* gilt
auriu *adj* golden
auroră *subs* aurora
autentic *adj* authentic
autobiografie *subs* autobiography
autobuz *subs* bus
autocisternă *subs* tanker
autocrat *subs* autocrat
autocrat *adj* autocratic
autocraţie *subs* autocracy
autograf *subs* autograph
automat *adj* automatic
automobil *subs* automobile
automobil *subs* car
automobil închis *subs* sedan
automobilist *subs* motorist
autonom *adj* autonomous
autor *subs* author
autoritar *adj* authoritative
autoritate *subs* authority
autoritate *subs* governance
autoritate *subs* mastery
autorizaţie *subs* permit
autostradă *subs* highway
auxiliar *adj* auxiliary
auxiliar *subs* auxiliary
auxiliar *adj* subsidiary
avanpost *subs* outpost
avans *subs.* advance
avansare *subs* advancement
avânt *subs* drive
avantaj *subs* advantage
avantaj *subs* boon
avantajos *adj* advantageous

avar *subs* means
avariţie *subs* avarice
aventura *subs* adventure
aventură amoroasă *subs* affair
aventurier *adj* venturous
aventuros *adj* adventurous
avere *subs* fortune
aversiune *subs* aversion
avertizment *adj* worn
avetizment *subs* warning
aviaţie *subs* aviation
aviator *subs* aviator
aviditate *subs* avidity
avion *subs* aeroplane
avion *subs* plane
avocat *subs.* advocate
avocat *subs* lawyer
avocat *subs* solicitor
avocat pledant *subs* barrister
avocatură *subs* advocacy
avort *subs* abortion
avort spontan *subs* miscarriage
axă *subs* axis
azbest *subs* asbestos
azi *subs* today
azil *subs* asylum
azot *subs* nitrogen
azvârlitură *subs* toss

B

bac *subs* ferry
băcan *subs* grocer
băcănie *subs* grocery
bacşiş *subs* gratuity
bacşiş *subs* tip
bactericid *subs* germicide
bacterie *subs* bacteria
bădăran *subs* churl

bădărănie *subs* rusticity
bădărănie *subs* savagery
bagaj *subs* baggage
bagaj *subs* luggage
băgare de seamă *subs* heed
baghetă *subs* wand
băiat *subs* boy
baie *subs* bath
băieţoi *subs* tomboy
baionetă *subs* bayonet
baladă *subs* ballad
balansare *subs* sway
balaur *subs* dragon
bâlbâire *subs* stammer
bâlci *subs* fair
balcon *subs* balcony
bălegar *subs* compost
bălegar *subs* dung
balenă *subs* whale
balet *subs* ballet
baliverne *subs* stuff
balon *subs* balloon
balon de săpun *subs* bubble
balot *subs* bale
balsam *subs* balm
balsam *subs* balsam
baltă *subs* marsh
baltă *subs* puddle
baltag *subs* hatchet
bambus *subs* bamboo
banal *adj* banal
banal *adj* commonplace
banal *adj* trivial
banană *subs* banana
bancă *subs* bank
bancă *subs* bench
bancher *subs* banker
banchet *subs* banquet
bandă *subs* tape
bandaj *subs* bandage
bandit *subs* bandit
bani *subs* money

bani gheaţă *subs* cash
banjo *subs* banjo
bănuială *subs* suspicion
bănuitor *adj* suspicious
bar *subs* bar
bară de protecţie *subs* bumper
baracă *subs* shanty
baraj *subs* barrage
baraj *subs* weir
barbă *subs* beard
barbar *adj* barbarian
barbar *subs* barbarian
barbar *adj* barbarous
barbarie *subs* barbarism
barbaritate *subs* barbarity
bărbat *subs* man
bărbat uşuratic *subs* milliner
bărbătesc *adj* male
bărbătesc *adj* manful
bărbătesc *adj* manly
bărbăţie *subs* manliness
bărbătuş *subs* mate
bărbie *subs* chin
bărbier *subs* barber
bărbierit *subs* shave
barcă *subs* boat
bârfă *subs* gossip
baricadă *subs* barricade
barieră *subs* barrier
barometru *subs* barometer
barză *subs* stork
bărzăun *subs* hornet
bas *subs* bass
băşică *subs* bleb
băşică de piele *subs* blister
basm *subs* tale
bastard *subs* bastard
baştinaş *subs.* aboriginal
baştinaşi *subs. pl* aborigines
baston *subs* baton
baston *subs* bulwark
baston *subs* rod

băţ *subs* stick
bâtă *subs* bat
bătaie de joc *subs* banter
bătălie *subs* battle
batalion *subs* battalion
batalion *subs* squadron
bătător la ochi *subs* tinsel
bătătură *subs* woof
baterie *subs* battery
batistă *subs* handkerchief
batistă *subs* wipe
batjocură *subs* mockery
batjocură *subs* ridicule
bătrân *adj* old
băutură *subs* beverage
băutură *subs* drink
băutură alcoolică *subs* liquor
băutură alcoolică *subs* intoxicant
băutură gazoasă *subs* pop
bază *subs* alkali
bază *subs* base
bază *subs* basis
bâzâit *subs* buzz
bazin *subs* basin
bec *subs* bulb
behăit *subs* bleat
belicos *adj* bellicose
beligerant *adj* belligerent
beligerant *subs* belligerent
beligeranţă *subs* belligerency
belşug *subs* affluence
belşug *subs* plenty
beneficiar *subs* incumbent
beneficiu *subs* benefit
benzină *subs* petrol
bere *subs* beer
bere englezească *subs* ale
bestie *subs* beast
beţie *subs* bout
beţiv *subs* bibber
beţivan *subs* drunkard
beton *subs* concrete

biblie *subs* bible
bibliograf *subs* bibliographer
bibliografie *subs* bibliography
bibliotecar *subs* librarian
bicentenar *adj* bicentenary
biceps *subs* biceps
bici *subs* scourge
bici *subs* whip
bicicletă *subs* bicycle
bidiviu *subs* steed
bienial *adj* biennial
bigamie *subs* bigamy
bigot *subs* bigot
bigotism *subs* bigotry
bijuterie *subs* jewel
bijuterii *subs* jewellery
bijutier *subs* jeweller
bilet *subs* thicket
bilet *subs* ticket
bilingv *adj* bilingual
bilunar *adj* bimonthly
binar *adj* binary
bine *adv* aright
bine *subs* good
bine *adj* well
bine *subs* well
bine situat *adj* well-to-do
binefacere *subs* benefaction
binevenit *adj* welcome
binevoitor *adj* benevolent
binevoitor *adj* compliant
binoclu *subs* binocular
biograf *subs* biographer
biografie *subs* biography
biolog *subs* biologist
biologie *subs* biology
birocrat *subs* bureaucrat
birocraţie *subs* Bureacuracy
birou *subs* bureau
birou *subs* desk
birou *subs* office
biscuit *subs* biscuit

biserică *subs* church
bisexual *adj* bisexual
bivol *subs* buffalo
bizar *adj* bizarre
bizar *adj* odd
bizar *subs* rummy
bizon *subs* bison
blajin *adj* meek
blam *subs* impeachment
blamare *ubs* censure
blană *subs* fur
blând *adj* benign
blestem *subs* curse
blestem *subs* damnation
blestemat *adj.* accursed
blindaj *subs* blindage
blindaj *subs* shield
blindaj de vas, de tanc *subs* armour
bloc cu foi detaşabile *subs* pad
blocadă *subs* blockade
bluză *subs* blouse
boabă *subs* kernel
boală *subs* ailment
boală *subs* disease
boală *subs* illness
boală *subs* sickness
boarfe *subs* trash
bobină *subs* reel
bocitoare *subs* mourner
bogat *adj* rich
bogat *adj* wealthy
bogătaş *subs* nabob
bogăţie *subs* riches
bogăţie *subs* wealth
boicot *subs* boycott
boiler *subs* boiler
bolnav *adj* ill
bolnăvicios *adj* sickly
bolovan *subs* boulder
boltă *subs* canopy
bombă *subs* bomb

bombardament *subs* bombardment
bombardier *subs* bomber
bomboană *subs* comfit
bomboană *subs* sweetmeat
bomboane *subs* candy
bonetă *subs* bonnet
bonlav *adj* sick
bonus *subs* bonus
borcan *subs* jar
bordel *subs* brothel
bornă din milă în milă *subs* milestone
bot de porc *v.t* muffle
botanică *subs* botany
botez *subs* baptism
botniţă *subs* muzzle
bou *subs* bullock
bou *subs* ox
box *subs* boxing
brânci *subs* shove
brânci *subs* thrust
brânză *subs* cheese
braţ *subs* arm
braţ de râu *subs* armlet
brăţară *subs* bangle
brăţară *subs* bracelet
brăţară pentru gleznă *subs* anklet
bravură *subs* prowess
brazdă *subs* furrow
breton *subs* fringe
brevet *subs* patent
brevetat *adj* patent
brichetă *adv* lighter
brici *subs* razor
brigadă *subs* brigade
briză *subs* breeze
broască *subs* frog
broască râioasă *subs* toad
broasca ţestoasă *subs* turtle
broască ţestoasă *subs* tortoise

broboadă *subs* kerchief
brocart *subs* brocade
brocoli *subs* broccoli
broderie *subs* embroidery
bronz *subs, adj* bronze
bronz *subs* tan
broşură *subs* booklet
broşură *subs* brochure
brun *adj* brown
brusc *adv* short
brut *subs* brute
brută *subs* ruffian
brutal *adj* brutal
brutar *subs* baker
brutărie *subs* bakery
bube dulci *subs* ringworm
bucată *subs* piece
bucată fără formă *subs* lump
bucătar *subs* cook
bucătarie *subs* cuisine
bucătărie *subs* kitchen
buchet *subs* bouquet
buchet de flori *subs* nosegay
buclă *subs* curl
buclă de păr *subs* ripple
bucurie *subs* joy
bucuros *adj* glad
bucuros *adj* joyful, joyous
budincă *subs* pudding
bufniţă *subs* owl
bufon *subs* buffoon
bufon *subs* pantaloon
bufonerie *subs* antic
buget *subs* budget
buimăcit *adj* haggard
bulă *subs* bull
buldog *subs* bulldog
buletin *subs* bulletin
buletin de vot *subs* ballot
bulevard *subs* avenue

bulgăre *subs* clod
bulgăre de aur *subs* nugget
bulgăre de răşină *subs*
    loggerhead
bulion *subs* broth
bumbac *subs* cotton
bun *subs* asset
bun *adj* good
bunăcuviinţă *subs* decorum
bună-cuviinţă *subs* propriety
bunăstare *subs* weal
bunăstare *subs* welfare
bunătate *subs* goodness
bunăvoinţă *subs* benevolence
bunăvoinţă *subs* compliance
bunăvoinţă *subs* goodwill
bunăvoinţă *subs* willingness
bunuri *subs* belongings
bunuri mobile *subs* movables
burete *subs* sponge
burghiu *subs* auger
burghiu *subs* wimble
burlan *subs* spout
burniţă *subs* drizzle
bursă *subs* scholarship
bursuc *subs* badger
burtă *subs* belly
buruiană *subs* rogue
busolă *subs* compass
buştean *subs* stub
busuioc *subs* basil
butoi *subs* barrel
butoi *subs* cask
butuc *subs* block
butuc *subs* log
butuc *subs* stump
buturugă *subs* snag
buză *v.t* lip
buzunar *subs* pocket

C

ca *conj* like
ca *conj* such
ca şi *conj* as
cabaret *subs* cabaret
cabină *subs* cabin
cabină de dormit *subs* bunk
cablu *subs* cable
cablu *subs* wire
cactus *subs* cactus
cadă *subs* tub
cadavru *subs* corpse
cădelniţă *subs* censer
cădere *subs* fall
cădere *subs* spill
cădere bruscă *subs* tumble
cadou *subs* gift
cadou *subs* present
cadran *subs* dial
cadru *subs* scenery
cafea *subs* cafe
cafea *subs* coffee
câine *subs* dog
căinţă *subs* repentance
caisă *subs* apricot
cal *subs* horse
cal de lemn *subs* hobby-horse
calambur *subs* quibble
calamitate *subs* calamity
călăreţ *subs* rider
călărie *subs* mount
călător *subs* traveller
călătorie *subs* journey
călătorie *subs* travel
călătorie pe mare *subs* sail
călău *subs* executioner
călăuzire *subs* guidance
călcâi *subs* heel
calciu *subs* calcium

calcul *subs* calculation
calcul greşit *subs* miscalculation
calculator *subs* calculator
cald *adj* warm1
căldare *subs* pail
căldură *subs* heat
căldură *subs* warmth
călduţ *adj* lukewarm
cale *subs* way
cale ferată *subs* railway
calendar *subs* calendar
calificare *subs* qualification
caligrafie *subs* calligraphy
calimitate *subs* tranquility
calitate *subs* quality
calitate de membru *subs*
    membership
calitatea de senior *subs* seniority
calitativ *adj* qualitative
calm *subs* calm
calm *subs* composure
calm *subs* still
calm *adj* tranquil
calmant *adj* calmative
calmant *adj* sedative
calmant *subs* sedative
calomnie *subs* libel
calomnie *subs* lick
calorie *subs* calorie
călugăr *subs* monk
călugări *subs* nun
căluţ *subs* nag
cam *prep.* about
cam pe acolo *adv* thereabouts
cămară *subs* pantry
cămaşă *subs* nightie
cămaşă *subs* shirt
cămătar *subs* usurer
cămătărie *subs* usury
cameră *subs* room
cameristă *subs* mahout
camfor *subs* camphor

cămilă *subs* camel
cămin *subs* hostel
camion *subs* lorry
câmp *subs* field
campanie *subs* campaign
campion *subs* champion
campionat *subs* tournament
canal *subs* canal
canal de scurgere *subs* culvert
canal de scurgere *subs* drain
canal tv *subs* channel
canalizare *subs* drainage
canapea *subs* couch
canapea *subs* sofa
cancelar *subs* chancellor
cancer *subs* cancer
când *adv* when
candidat *subs* candidate
candidat la examen *subs* examinee
candoare *subs* candour
cândva *adv* sometime
cânepă *subs* hemp
canistră *subs* canister
canon *subs* canon
canonadă *subs* cannonade
cântăreţ *subs* singer
cântec *subs* song
cântec de leagăn *subs* lullaby
cantină *subs* canteen
cantitate *subs* quantity
cantitate mai mică *subs* less
cantitate mică de *subs* paucity
cantitativ *adj* quantitative
cantonament *subs* cantonment
cap *subs* head
capă *subs* cape
capabil *adj.* able
capabil *adj* capable
capabilitate *subs* capability
capac *subs* lid
capacitate *subs* capacity

căpăstru *subs* bridle
capcană *subs* pitfall
capcană *subs* trap
capelă *subs* chapel
capitală *subs* capital
capitalist *subs* capitalist
capitalist *subs* financier
căpitan *subs* captain
căpitan de vas *subs* commander
capitol *subs* chapter
capodoperă *subs* masterpiece
capră *subs* goat
capricios *adj* capricious
capricios *adj* fitful
capricios *adj* wayward
capriciu *subs* caprice
capriciu *subs* fad
Capricorn *subs* Capricorn
căprioară *subs* doe
capsă *subs* eyelet
căpşună *subs* strawberry
captiv *subs* captive
captiv *adj* captive
captivitate *subs* captivity
captivitate *subs* confinement
captură *subs* capture
car *subs* wain
car de război *subs* chariot
carabină *v.t* rifle
caracter *subs* character
caracter de insulă *subs* insularity
caraghios *addj* foolish
caramelă *subs* toffee
cărămidă *subs* brick
carat *subs* carat
cărăuş *subs* carrier
cărăuşie *subs* cartage
caravană *subs* caravan
carbid *subs* carbide
carbon *subs* carbon
cărbune *subs* coal
cardiac *adj* cardiacal

cardinal *subs* cardinal
care *pron* as
care coboară *adj* down
care conservă *adj* preservative
care îşi aminteşte *adj* reminiscent
care leagă *adj* binding
care merită *adj* worthy
care merită osteneala *adj* worth
care n-a băut *adj* sober
care nu e grăbit *adj* leisurely
care observă *adj* observant
care poate fi apărat *adj* tenable
care promite *adj* promissory
care răsplăteşte *adj* remunerative
care reflectă *adj* reflective
care reţine *adj* retentive
care rezistă la *adj* proof
care se căieşte *adj* repentant
care se gâdilă *adj* ticklish
care se împotriveşte *adj* reluctant
care se poate obţine *adj* obtainable
care se poate vinde *adj* marketable
care urmează *adj* subsequent
care vor apărea *adj* forthcoming
care? *adj* which
careva *pron* someone
cariat *adj* carious
caricatură *subs* caricature
carie *subs* rot
carieră *subs* career
caritabil *adj* charitable
caritate *subs* charity
cârjă *subs* crook
cârjă *subs* crutch
cârlig *subs* crotchet
cârlig *subs* grapple
cârlig *subs* hook
carlingă *subs* cock-pit
cârlionţ *subs* ringlet
cârmă *subs* helm

carmin *subs* crimson
carnagiu *subs* carnage
carnaval *subs* carnival
carne *subs* flesh
carne *subs* meat
carne de oaie *subs* mutton
carne de porc *subs* pork
carne de vacă *subs* beef
cărnos *adj* pulpy
cârpă *subs* cloth
cârpă *subs* rag
cârpă de praf *subs* duster
cârpaci *subs* cobbler
cârpaci *subs* tinker
carte *subs* book
carte de joc *subs* card
carte de joc *subs* playcard
cartier *subs* neighbourhood
cartof *subs* potato
carton *subs* cardboard
cartuş *subs* cartridge
cărucior *subs* cart
cărucior de copil *subs* perambulator
căruia îi pare rău *adj* sorry
căruţă *subs* wagon
casă *subs* home
casă *subs* house
casă de corecţie *subs* reformatory
casă mare *subs* mansion
căsătorie *subs* marriage
căsătorie *subs* wedlock
cască *subs* helmet
cascadă *subs* cascade
cascadă *subs* waterfall
căscat *subs* yawn
casetă *subs* cassette
casier *subs* cashier
cast *adj* chaste
castă *subs* caste
castană *subs* chestnut
castaniu *adj* maroon

castel *subs* castle
câştig *subs* gain
câştigător *subs* winner
castitate *subs* chastity
castor *subs* beaver
castrat *adj* effeminate
castravete *subs* cucumber
castron *subs* bowl
căsuţă *subs* cottage
cât *subs* quotient
cât se poate de *adv* highly
catafalc *subs* bier
catalog *subs* catalogue
catâr *subs* mule
cataractă *subs* cataract
cataramă *subs* buckle
cataramă *subs* shackle
căţărare *subs* climb1
căţărătoare *subs* creeper
catarg *subs* mast
căţea *subs* bitch
catedrală *subs* cathedral
catedrală *subs* minster
categoric *adj* categorical
categorie *subs* category
categorie *subs* grade
categorie *subs* predicament
căţeluş *subs* puppy
câteodată *adv* sometimes
catifea *subs* velvet
catifelat *adj* velvety
câţiva *adj* few
câţiva *pron* some
catolic *adj* catholic
către *prep* towards
cătun *subs* hamlet
cătuşe *subs* handcuff
cauciuc *subs* rubber
cauciuc *subs* tyre
caustic *adj* caustic
căutare *subs* search
cauză *subs* cause

cauză *subs* reason
cauzal *adj* causal
cavaler *subs* knight
cavaleresc *adj* chivalrous
cavalerie *subs* cavalry
cavalerism *subs* chivalry
cavalerist *subs* trooper
cavernă *subs* cavern
cavitate *subs* cavity
cavitate *subs* socket
cavou *subs* tomb
caz *subs* case
cazarmă *subs* barrack
ce what
ce nu merită osteneala *adj*
   worthless
ce? *interj* what
cea mai mare parte *adj* most
ceafă *subs* nape
ceai *subs* tea
ceapă *subs* onion
ceară *subs* wax
cearşaf *subs* sheet
ceas *subs* clock
ceaşcă *subs* cup
ceaţă *subs* fog
ceaţă *subs* mist
ceaţă şi fum *subs* smog
ceaţă uşoară *subs* haze
cec *subs* check
cec *subs* cheque
cedru *subs* cedar
ceea ce *pron* what
cel mai depărtat *adj* utmost
cel mai înalt grad *subs* maximum
cel mai intim *adj* innermost
cel mai puţin *adj* least
cel mai puţin *adv* least
cel mai rău *adj* worst
cel mult *subs* most
celebritate *subs* celebrity
celibat *subs* celibacy

celibatar *subs* bachelor
celibatar/ă *adj* single
celulă *subs* cell
celular *adj* cellular
cent *subs* cent
centenar *subs* centenarian
centenar *subs* centenary
centenar *adj* centennial
centigrad *adj* centigrade
central *adj* central
centrifugal *adj* centrifugal
centru *subs* center
centru *subs* centre
centru *subs* hub
cenușă *subs* ash
cenzor *subs* censor
cenzură *subs* censorship
cep *subs* plug
cer *subs* sky
ceramică *subs* ceramics
cerb *subs* deer
cerb *subs* stag
cerc *subs* circle
cerc al țintei *adj* inner
cercetare *subs* inquiry
cercetare *subs* overhaul
cercetare *subs* quest
cercetare *subs* research
cercetaș *subs* scout
cereală *subs* cereal
cerealier *adj* cereal
cerebral *adj* cerebral
ceremonie *subs* ceremony
ceremonios *adj* ceremonious
ceresc *adj* celestial
cerință *subs* requirement
cerneală *subs* ink
cerșetor *subs* beggar
cerșetor *subs* pauper
certăreț *adj* quarrelsome
certificat *subs* certificate
certificat *subs* testimonial

cetățean *subs* citizen
cetățenesc *adj* civil
cetățenie *subs* citizenship
cețos *adj* hazy
ceva *pron* something
cheag *subs* clot
chefliu *subs* reveller
cheie *subs* key
cheie de piuliță *subs* spanner
chel *adj* bald
chelălăit *subs* yap
cheltuială *subs* expense
cheltuire *subs* expenditure
chemare *subs* calling
chenzină *subs* fort-night
cherchelit *adj* queer
cherestea *subs* timber
chestionar *subs* questionnaire
chestiune *subs* matter
chiar și *adv* even
chibrit *subs* match
chibzuit *adj* judicious
chimic *adj* chemical
chimicale *subs* chemical
chimie *subs* chemistry
chimist *subs* chemist
chin *subs* anguish
chintesență *subs* quintessence
chiparos *subs* cypher cypress
chiriaș *subs* tenant
chirie *subs* rent
chiromanție *subs* palmistry
chirpici *subs.* adobe
chirurg *subs* surgeon
chirurgie *subs* surgery
chițăit *subs* squeak
chitanță *subs* receipt
chitară *subs* guitar
chiuvetă *subs* sink
cicatrice *subs* sabre
cicatrice *subs* scar
ciclic *adj* cyclic

ciclist *subs* cyclist
ciclon *subs* cyclone
ciclu *subs* cycle
cifră *subs* digit
cifru *subs* cipher, cipher
cilindric *adj* tubular
cilindru *subs* cylinder
cilindru *subs* roller
ciment *subs* cement
cimitir *subs* cemetery
cimpanzeu *subs* chimpanzee
cimpoi *subs* bagpipe
cină *subs* dinner
cină *subs* supper
cinabru *subs* cinnabar
cinci *subs* five
cincizeci *subs* fifty
cine? *pron* who
cine? *pron* whom
cinema *subs* cinema
cineva *pron* somebody
cingătoare *subs* girdle
cinic *subs* cynic
cinsprezece *subs* fifteen
cinstit *adj* fair
cioară *subs* crow
ciobănesc *adj* pastoral
cioc *subs* nib
cioc (de sculă *subs* nozzle
cioc de pasăre *subs* beak
ciocan *subs* hammer
ciocârlie *subs* lark
ciocnire *subs* clash
ciocnire *subs* jostle
ciocolată *subs* chocolate
ciomag *subs* cudgel
ciorap *subs* stocking
ciorăvăială *subs* wrangle
ciorchine *subs* cluster
circ *subs* circus
circuit *subs* circuit
circular *adj* circular

circular *subs* circular
circular *adv* round
circulație *subs* circulation
circulație monetară *subs*
  currency
circumferință *subs*
  circumference
circumspect *adj* circumspect
circumspect *adj* wary
circumstanță *subs* circumstance
cireadă *subs* herd
ciripit *subs* chirp
citadelă *subs* citadel
citare *subs* quotation
citație *subs* summons
citit *adj* well-read
cititor *subs* reader
citric *adj* citric
ciudă *v.t* grudge
ciudat *adj* quaint
ciudat *adj* weird
ciuguleală *subs* peck
ciulin *subs* thistle
ciuma *subs* plague
ciupeală *subs* pinch
ciupercă *subs* fungus
ciupercă *subs* mushroom
ciupitură *subs* nibble
ciur *subs* sieve
civic *adj* civic
civică *subs* civics
civil *subs* civilian
civilizație *subs* civilization
clădire *subs* building
clamă *subs* brace
clandestin *adj* clandestine
clandestin *adj* underhand
clar *adj* clear
clar *adj* overt
clarificare *subs* clarification
clarificare *subs* clearance
claritate *subs* clarity

clasă *subs* class
clasic *adj* classic
clasic *subs* classic
clasic *adj* classical
clasificare *subs* classification
clătinare *subs* stagger
clauză *subs* clause
clauză condiţională *subs* proviso
clavn *subs* clown
clei de prins păsări *subs* lime
clemă *subs* clamp
cler *subs* clergy
clerical *adj* clerical
cleşte *subs* tongs
clevetire *subs* slander
client *subs* client
client *subs* customer
climă *subs* climate
clinchet *subs* clink
clinchet *subs* jingle
clinică *subs* clinic
clipire *subs* wink
clişeu *subs* stereotype
clopot *subs* bell
clor *subs* chlorine
cloroform *subs* chloroform
club *subs* club
coadă *subs* tail
coada (unei coloane *subs* rear
coajă *subs* peel
coajă *subs* shell
coaliţie *subs* coalition
coamă *subs* mane
coapsă *subs* thigh
coardă *subs* chord
coasă *subs* scythe
coastă *subs* coast
coastă *subs* rib
cobalt *subs* cobalt
coborâre *subs* descent
cobra *subs* cobra
cocă *subs* dough

cocaină *subs* cocaine
cocoaşă *subs* hunch
cocor *subs* crane
cocoş *subs* cock
cocoş din Bantam *subs* bantam
cocs *v.t* coke
cod *subs* code
codoaşă *subs* bawd
coeficient *subs* coefficient
coerent *adj* coherent
coexistenţă *subs* co-existence
cofetar *subs* confectioner
cofetărie *subs* confectionery
colaborare *subs* collaboration
colecţie *subs* collection
colecţionar antichităţi *subs* antiquarian
colectiv *adj* collective
colector *subs* collector
coleg *subs* colleague
colegiu *subs* college
colet *subs* package
colibă *subs* cot
colibă *subs* hut
colibă *subs* lodge
colier *subs* necklace
colindă *subs* carol
colir *subs* eyewash
colivie de şoim *subs* mew
coloană *subs* column
coloana vertebrală *subs* backbone
colon *subs* colon
colonel *subs* colonel
colonial *adj* colonial
colonie *subs* colony
colţ *subs* corner
colţ *subs* tusk
comă *subs* coma
comandă *subs* command
comandant *subs* commandant
comandant de brigadă *subs* brigadier

comandant de vas *subs* skipper
combatant *subs* combatant1
combinat *adj* conjunct
combinaţie *subs* combination
combustibil *subs* fuel
comediant *subs* comedian
comediant *subs* mummer
comedie *subs* comedy
comemorare *subs* commemoration
comentariu *subs* comment
comentariu *subs* commentary
comentator *subs* commentator
comercial *adj* commercial
comerciant *subs* tradesman
comerţ *subs* commerce
comerţ *subs* trade
comestibil *adj* eatable
comestibil *adj* edible
cometă *subs* comet
comfortabil *adj* cozy
comic *adj* comic
comic *subs* comic
comic *adj* comical
comic *adj* humorous
comision *subs* commission
comision *subs* errand
comisionar *subs* commissioner
comitet *subs* committee
comoară *subs* treasure
comod *adj* snug
comoditate *subs* commodity
compact *adj* compact
companie *subs* company
companion *subs* companion
comparaţie *subs* comparison
comparativ *adj* comparative
compartiment *subs* compartment
compasiune *subs* compassion
compătimitor *adj* pitiful
compensare *subs* redemption
compensaţie *subs* compensation

compensaţie *subs* offset
competent *adj* competent
competent *adj* scholarly
competent în *adj* conversant
competenţă *subs* competence
competiţie *subs* competition
competitiv *adj* competitive
complement *subs* complement
complementar *adj* complementary
complet *adj* complete
complet *adj* downright
complet *adv* full
complet *adj* outright
completare *subs* completion
complex *subs* complex
complicat *adj* complex
complicaţie *subs* complication
complice *subs.* accomplice
compliment *subs* compliment
complotare *subs* collusion
complotist *subs* conspirator
component *adj* component
comportament *subs* behaviour
compoziţie muzicală *subs* glee
compromis *subs* compromise
compunere *subs* composition
compus *subs* compound
compus *adj* compound
comun *adj* common
comunal *adj* communal
comunicare *subs* communication
comunicat *subs* communiqué
comunism *subs* communism
comunitate *subs* commonwealth
comunitate *subs* community
comutator *subs* switch
con *subs* cone
concav *adj* concave
concediere *subs* dismissal
concentrare *subs* concentration
concept *subs* concept

concepție *subs* conception
concepție greșită *subs* misconception
concert *subs* concert
concesie *subs* concession
concis *adj* concise
concis *adj* curt
concis *adj* terse
concizie *subs* brevity
concluzie *subs* conclusion
concluzie *subs* upshot
concret *adj* concrete
concubină *subs* concubine
concubinaj *subs* concubinage
concurs *subs* contest
condamnare *subs* condemnation
condamnat *subs* convict
condiment *subs* spice
condimentat *adj* spicy
condiție *subs* condition
condițional *adj* conditional
condoleanță *subs* condolence
conducător *subs* ruler
conducere *subs* lead
conducere de afaceri *subs* management
conduită *subs* conduct
conduită inacceptabilă *subs* misbehaviour
conexiune *subs* connection
conferențiar *subs* lecturer
conferință *subs* conference
confident *subs* confidant
confidențial *adj* confidential
configurație *subs* set
confirmare *subs* confirmation
confiscare *subs* confiscation
confiscare *subs* forfeit
confiscare *subs* forfeiture
confiscare *subs* seizure
conflict *subs* conflict
conflict *subs* strife

confluent *adj* confluent
conform legii *adj* lawful
conformitate *subs* conformity
confort *subs* comfort1
confortabil *adj* comfortable
confortabil *adj* cosy
confrerie *subs* confraternity
confruntare *subs* confrontation
confuzie *subs* muddle
confuzie *subs* confusion
congres *subs* congress
coniac *subs* brandy
conjugal *adj* conjugal
conjunctivă *subs* conjunctiva
conjunctură *subs* conjuncture
conopidă *subs* cauliflower
consecință *subs* consequence
consecință *subs* outcome
consecutiv *adj* consecutive
consecutiv *adv* consecutively
consecvență *subs* consistence,-cy
consemnare *subs* consignment
consens *subs* consensus
conservă *subs* can
conservant *subs* preservative
conservare *subs* conservative
conservator *adj* conservative
considerabil *adj* aconsiderable
considerație *subs* consideration
consilier *subs* councillor
consiliu *subs* council
consimțământ *subs.* accord
consimțământ *subs.* acquiescence
consimțământ *subs* assent
consimțământ *subs* consent
consistent *adj* consistent
consoană *subs* consonant
consolare *subs* consolation
consolare *subs* solace
consolidare *subs* consolidation
consonanță *subs* consonance

conspect *subs* conspectus
conspirație *subs* conspiracy
constant *adj* constant
constant *adj* steadfast
constelație *subs* constellation
conștient *adj* aware
conștient *adj* conscious
conștiincios *adj* dutiful
conștiință *subs* conscience
constipație *subs* constipation
constituție *subs* constitution
constitutiv *adj* constituent
constrângere *subs* compulsion
construcție *subs* build
construcție *subs* construction
construcție de lemn *subs* mantel
consultație *subs* consultation
consumație *subs* consumption
cont *subs.* account
contabil *subs.* accountant
contabil *subs* book-keeper
contabilitate *subs.* accountancy
contact *subs* contact
contagios *adj* contagious
contemplare *subs* contemplation
contemporar *adj* contemporary
contesă *subs* countess
context *subs* context
continent *subs* continent
continental *adj* continental
continuare *subs* continuation
continuitate *subs* continuity
conținut *subs* content
continuu *adj* continual
contor *subs* meter
contra *prep* contra
contra *prep* versus
contraacuzare *subs* countercharge
contrabandist *subs* smuggler
contracepție *subs* contraception
contract *subs* contract

contradicție *subs* contradiction
contrafăcut *adj* mock
contrar *adj* contrary
contrar *adj* reverse
contrast *subs* contrast
contribuție *subs* contribution
control *subs* control
controversă *subs* argument
controversă *subs* controversy
contur *subs* contour
contur *subs* outline
convenabil *adj* convenient
convenabl *adj* seemly
conveniență *subs* convenience
convenție *subs* convention
conversație *subs* conversation
conversație *subs* talk
convertit *subs* convert
convingător *adj* cogent
convingere *subs* conviction
convingere *subs* inducement
convingere *subs* persuasion
convocare *subs* convocation
convulsiv *adj* spasmodic
cooperare *subs* co-operation
cooperatist *adj* co-operative
coordonare *subs* co-ordination
coordonat *adj* co-ordinate
copac *subs* tree
copac parfumat *subs* sandalwood
copcă *subs* stitch
copertă *subs* cover
copie *subs* copy
copil *subs* bantling
copil *subs* child
copilăresc *adj* childish
copilărie *subs* childhood
copilaș *subs* baby
copită *subs* hoof
copoi *subs* hound
copt *adj* ripe
cor *subs* choir

cor *subs* chorus
coral *subs* coral
corb *subs* raven
corcit *adj* hybrid
corcitură *subs* hybrid
cordial *adj* cordial
corect *adv* aright
corect *adj* correct
corectare *subs* redress
corecție *subs* correction
corelație *subs* correlation
corespondent *subs* correspondent
corespondență *subs* correspondence
corespunzător *adv.* accordingly
coriandru *subs* coriander
coridor *subs* corridor
cormoran *subs* cormorant
corn *subs* horn
corn de cerb *subs* antler
cornee *subs* cornea
cornet *subs* cornet
coroană *subs* crown
coroană *subs* wreath
corosiv *adj* corrosive
corp *subs* body
corp de armată *subs* corps
corp electoral *subs* constituency
corp luminos *subs* luminary
corp solid *subs* solid
corpolent *adj* stout
corporal *adj* corporal
corporație *subs* corporation
corporativ *adj* corporate
corpul alegătorilor *subs* electorate
corsaj *subs* bodice
cort *subs* tent
corupt *adj* corrupt
corupt *adj* venal
corupție *subs* corruption
corupție *subs* venality

coș *subs* basket
coș de fabrică *subs* stalk
coș mare *subs* crate
coș pe față *subs* pimple
coșmar *subs* nightmare
cosmetic *subs* cosmetic
cosmetic *adj* cosmetic
cosmic *adj* cosmic
cost *subs* cost
costal *adj* costal
costisitor *adj* costly
costum *subs* costume
costum de haine *subs* suit
cot *subs* elbow
cotă *subs* quota
coteț *subs* kennel
cotidian *adj* daily
cotidian *subs* journal
coțofană *subs* magpie
covor *subs* carpet
crab *subs* crab
cracă *subs* limb
cracă *subs* roost
Crăciun *subs* Christmas
Crăciun *subs* Xmas
crâmpei *subs* modicum
crampon *subs* stud
crâng *subs* coppice
craniu *subs* skull
crăpătură *subs* crack
crăpătură *subs* cleft
cras *adj* crass
cravată *subs* tie
creastă *subs* crest
creație *subs* creation
creativ *adj* creative
creator *subs* creator
creator *subs* maker
creator *subs* originator
creatură *subs* creature
credibil *adj* credible
credință *subs* belief

credinţă *subs* confidence
credinţă *subs* faith
credit *subs* credit
creditor *subs* creditor
credul *subs* gull
credulitate *adj* credulity
creier *subs* brain
creion *subs* pencil
cremă de ouă *subs* custard
crepuscul *subs* dusk
crepuscul *subs* twilight
crescătorie de păsări *subs* aviary
crestătură în lemn *subs* nick
crestere *subs* growth
creştere *subs* nurture
creştin *subs* Christian
creştinătate *subs* Christendom
creştinesc *adj* Christian
creştinism *subs* Christianity
cretin *subs* moron
crez *subs* creed
crimă *subs* crime
criminal *subs* criminal
criminal *adj* criminal
criminal *adj* murderous
criptografie *subs* cryptography
cristal *subs* crystal
criteriu *subs* criterion
critic *subs* critic
critică *subs* criticism
criză *subs* crisis
crocant *adj* crisp
crocodil *subs* crocodile
croitor *subs* tailor
croncănit *subs* caw
cronic *adj* chronic
cronică *subs* chronicle
cronică *subs* cornicle
cronicar *subs* annalist
cronograf *subs* chronograph
cronologie *subs* chronology
cruce *subs* cross

cruciadă *subs* crusade
crucifix *subs* rood
cruciş *prep* athwart
crucişător *subs* cruiser
crud *adj* crude
crud *adj* raw
crunt *adj* ruthless
crustă *subs* crust
cruzime *subs* cruelty
cu *prep* with
cu adevărat *adv* really
cu amănuntul *adv* retail
cu desăvârşire *adv* fully
cu gentileţe *adv* kindly
cu greu *adv* hardly
cu greu *adj* ill
cu gura căscată *adv* agape
cu încetul *adv* leisurely
cu întârziere *adv* late
cu lapte *adj* milch
cu mintea sănătoasă *adj* sane
cu ochii holbaţi *adv* agaze
cu ridicata *adj* wholesale
cu siguranţă *adv* certainly
cu siguranţă *adv* surely
cu tact *adj* tactful
cu toane *adj* whimsical
cu toane *v.i* whine
cu toane *subs* whine
cu toate acestea *conj* nevertheless
cu toate că *conj* although
cu toate că *conj* though
cu totul *adv* all
cu totul *adv* altogether
cu totul *adv* quite
cuantum *subs* quantum
cub *subs* cube
cubic *adj* cubical
cuc *subs* cuckoo
cucerire *subs* conquest
cucernic *adj* pious
cucui *subs* wen

cufăr *subs* locker
cui de lemn *subs* peg
cuib *subs* nest
cuişor *subs* clove
culcat *adv* abed
culegător *subs* compositor
culegător *subs* reaper
culesul viilor *subs* vintage
culme *subs* apex
culme *subs* summit
culoar *subs* lobby
culoare *subs* colour
culoare a pielii *subs* complexion
culoare castanie *subs* maroon
culoarea liliacului *subs* lilac
culoarea mov *adj/subs* purple
culoarea roz *subs* pink
cult *subs* cult
cultură *subs* culture
cultură generală *subs* literacy
cultural *adj* cultural
cum *adv* how
cumpărător *subs* buyer
cumpărătură *subs* purchase
cumpătat *adj* staid
cumpătat *adj* thrifty
cumplit *adj* dire
cumva *adv* somehow
cunoscut *adj* well-known
cunoştinţa *subs.* acquaintance
cupă *subs* beaker
cupă *subs* goblet
Cupidon *subs* Cupid
cuplet *subs* couplet
cuplu *subs* couple
cupon *subs* coupon
cuprinzător *adj* comprehensive
cuptor *subs* kiln
cuptor *subs* oven
cuptor cu microunde *subs* microwave
curaj *subs* courage

curajos *adj* brave
curajos *adj* courageous
curând *adv* soon
curat *subs* clean
curaţare *subs.* ablution
curăţenie *subs* cleanliness
curativ *adj* curative
curbă *subs* curve
curcan *subs* turkey
curea *subs* belt
curea *subs* strap
curent *subs* current
curent *adj* current
curent *adj* routine
curent de aer *subs* draught
curent submarin *subs* undercurrent
curgere *subs* flow
curier *subs* courier
curios *adj* curious
curiozitate *subs* curiosity
curs *subs* course
cursă *subs* chaise
cursă *subs* ride
cursă de viteză *subs* sprint
curte *subs* yard
curtea bisericii *subs* churchyard
curtea casei *subs* courtyard
curtea de justiţie *subs* chancery
curtean *subs* courtier
curtenitor *adj* courteous
curtezană *subs* courtesan
curtoazie *subs* courtesy
cusătură *subs* seam
cuşcă *subs* cage
cuşetă *subs* berth
cusurgiu *adj* censorious
cusut *adj* seamy
cută *subs* fold
cută *subs* ply
cutie *subs* box
cutie de carton *subs* carton

cutie de conserve *subs* tin
cuţit *subs* knife
cutremur *subs* earthquake
cutremure de pământ *subs*
   quake
cuvânt *subs* word
cuvânt de duh *subs* witticism
cuvânt de onoare *subs* parole
cuvenit *adj* due
cuvertură *subs* coverlet
cvadruplu *adj* quadruple
cvorum *subs* quorum

da *adv* yes
dacă *conj* if
dacă nu *conj* otherwise
dacă nu *conj* unless
dactilograf/ă *subs* typist
dafin *subs* laurel
daltă *subs* chisel
damă *subs* dame
dans *subs* dance
dar *prep* but
darnic *adj* bountiful
dârzenie *subs* obduracy
dat afară *adj* outcast
datorie *subs* debt
datorie *subs* due
datornic *subs* debtor
dăunător pentru *adj* maleficent
de acolo *adv* thence
de actualitate *adj* timely
de actualitate *adj* topical
de acum încolo *adv* henceforth
de aici înainte *adv* hence
de ajutor *adj* helpful
de altfel *adv* moreover

de anticar *adj* antiquarian
de asemenea *adv* also
de asemenea *adv* either
de asemenea *adv* likewise
de atunci *adv* since
de atunci *adj* then
de azi înainte *adv* henceforward
de azi înainte *adv* hereafter
de când *conj* since
de ce? *adv* why
de ceremonie *adj* ceremonial
de comerţ *subs* merchant
de dantela turna *adj* lacy
de dinafară *adj* outer
de două ori *adv* twice
de fapt *adv.* actually
de fată *adj* girlish
de fum *adj* smoky
de gradul al doilea *adj* second
de iarnă *adj* wintry
de încredere *adj* straightforward
de invidiat *adj* enviable
de jos *adj* ignoble
de la *prep* from
de la *prep* since
de la nord *adj* northerly
de lână *adj* woollen
de lapte *adj* milky
de legume *adj* vegetable
de lemn *adj* wooden
de litoral *adj* littoral
de loc *adv* none
de lucru *adj* workaday
de maestru *adj* masterly
de maimuţă *adj* apish
de mamă *adj* motherly
de măritat *adj* marriageable
de mijloc *adj* median
de moşie *adj* manorial
de nădejde *adj* reliable
de neâmblânzit *adj* indomitable
de neânvins *adj* insurmountable

de neânvins *adj* invincible
de neauzit *adj* inaudible
de nedescris *adj* indescribable
de nepătruns *adj* impenetrable
de netrecut *adj* impassable
de obicei *adv* usually
de onoare *adj* honorary
de pădure *adj* sylvan
de pământ *adj* earthen
de partizan *adj* partisan
de piatră *adj* stony
de plumb *adj* leaden
de prim rang *adj* premier
de prisos *adj* superfluous
de prisos *adj* waste
de proprietate *adj* proprietary
de râs *adj* laughable
de rasă *adj* racial
de război *adj* warlike
de rezervă *adj* spare
de semilună *adj* lunar
de servitor *adj* menial
de sezon *adj* seasonable
de spălat *adj* washable
de succes *adj* successful
de tipar *adj* literal
de trei ori *adv* thrice
de unde *adv* whence
de zăpadă *adj* snowy
de-a lungul *prep.* along
deal *subs* hill
deânmulțit *subs* multiplicand
deasupra *avd.* above
debandadă *subs* rout
debil *adj* infirm
debilitate *subs* debility
debit *subs* debit
decadă *subs* decade
decadent *adj* decadent
decădere *subs* decay
decan *subs* dean
decembrie *subs* december

decent *adj* decent
decent *adj* proper
decență *subs* decency
decepție *subs* deception
deces *subs* decease
deci *conj* so
decisiv *adj* crucial
decisiv *adj* decisive
decizie *subs* decision
decizie pe loc *subs* bylaw, bye-law
declarație *subs* declaration
declarație *subs* statement
declarație sub jurământ *subs* affidavit
declin *subs* decline
declin *subs* wane
decorație *subs* decoration
decret *subs* decree
decret *subs* ordinance
dedesubt *adv* below
dedesubt *adv* underneath
dedesubt *prep* underneath
dedesubtul *prep* beneath
dedicație *subs* dedication
defăimare *subs* defamation
defect *subs* defect
defect *subs* demerit
defensiv *adj* defensive
deficient *adj* deficient
deficient *adj* faulty
deficit *subs* deficit
defilare *subs* procession
defileu *subs* notch
definiție *subs* definition
degajat *adj* casual
deget *subs* finger
deget arătător *subs* forefinger
deget de la picior *subs* toe
deget mare *subs* thumb
degetar *subs* thimble
deghizare *subs* disguise

degradare *subs.* abasement
deist *subs* deist
deja *adv* already
delectare *subs* enjoyment
delegare *subs* delegation
delegat *subs* deputy
delegație *subs* deputation
deliberare *subs* deliberation
delicat *adj* delicate
delicatese *subs* dainty
delicios *adj* delicious
delict *subs* misdemeanour
delict *subs* trespass
deltă a unui râu *subs* delta
delușor *subs* hillock
demarcație *subs* demarcation
demență *subs* insanity
demisie *subs* resignation
demn de atenție *adj* noteworthy
demn de încredere *adj*
trustworthy
demn de laudă *adj* creditable
demnitate *subs* dignity
democratic *adj* democratic
democrație *subs* democracy
demodat *adj* antiquated
demodat *adj* outmoded
demon *subs* demon
demonstrație *subs* demonstration
dens *adj* dense
densitate *subs* density
dentist *subs* dentist
denunțare *subs* denunciation
deocamdată *adv* yet
deoparte *adv* aside
deosebit *adj* special
departament *subs* department
departe *adv.* afar
departe *adv* away
departe *adv* far
departe *adv* wide
dependent *adj* dependant

dependent de *adj* dependent
dependență *subs* dependence
depeșă *subs* missive
deplinătate *subs* fullness
deplorabil *adj* deplorable
deplorabil *adj* piteous
depou *subs* depot
depozit *subs* deposit
depravare *subs* debauchery
depresie *subs* depression
deprimare *subs* dejection
deprindere *subs* wont
derbedeu *subs* scoundrel
dermă *subs* cutis
derutant *adj* elusive
desăvârșit *adj* stark
descalificare *subs* disqualification
descărcare *subs* discharge
descendent *subs* descendant
deschidere *subs* opening
deschis *adj* open
deschizătură *subs* vent
descompunere *subs*
decomposition
descoperire *subs* discovery
descoperit de cont *subs* overdraft
descreștere *subs* decrease
descriere *subs* description
descriptiv *adj* descriptive
descurcăreț *adj* skilful
desen animat *subs* cartoon
desenator *subs* drawer
desenator tehnic *subs* draftsman
deseori *adv* often
desfătare *v.t* treat
desfătare *subs* treat
desființare *subs.* abolition
desfrânat *adj* lustful
desfrânat *adj* profligate
desfrâu *subs* debauch
desfrâu *subs* lust
deși *conj* albeit

despăgubire *subs* amends
despărţire a cercevelei *subs* mullion
despicare *subs* split
despot *subs* despot
despre *adv.* about
deştept *adj* clever
destin *subs* destiny
destinatar *subs.* addressee
destinatar *subs* receiver
destinaţie *subs* destination
destinaţie *adv* whither
destindere *subs* laxity
destindere a unui arc *subs* recoil
destins *adj* lax
destrăbălat *subs* debauchee
destul *adj* enough
destul de *adv* fairly
destul de *adv* pretty
detaliu *subs* detail
detaliu *subs* retail
detaşabil *adj* removable
detaşament *subs* detachment
detectiv *adj* detective
detectiv *subs* detective
determinare *subs* determination
deţinător al autorizaţiei *subs* licensee
deturnare *subs* misappropriation
deviere *subs* deviation
deviză *subs* motto
devotament *subs* devotion
devotat *adj* staunch
devreme *adv* early
devreme *adj* early
dexteritate *subs* sleight
dezacord *subs* disagreement
dezacord *subs* discord
dezagreabil *adj* disagreeable
dezaprobare *subs* disapproval
dezaprobare *subs* slur
dezarmare *subs* disarmament

dezastru *subs* disaster
dezastru *subs* havoc
dezastruos *adj* disastrous
dezavantaj *subs* disadvantage
dezbate *v.t* debate
dezbatere *subs* debate
dezbrăcat *adj* nude
dezgheţ *subs* thaw
dezirabil *adj* desirable
dezonoare *v.t* dishonour
dezonoare *subs* dishonour
dezonoare *subs* disrepute
dezordine *subs* disorder
dezordine *subs* riot
dezumflare *subs* deflation
dezvoltare *subs* development
diabet *subs* diabetes
diacon *subs* deacon
diademă *subs* coronet
diafragmă *subs* midriff
diagnostic *subs* diagnosis
diagramă *subs* diagram
dialect *subs* dialect
dialect *subs* idiom
dialect *subs* lingo
dialect local *subs* vernacular
dialog *subs* dialogue
diamant *subs* diamond
diametru *subs* diameter
diaree *subs* diarrhoea
diavol *subs* devil
dibaci *adj* artful
dibaci *adj* shrewd
dibăcie *subs* proficiency
dibăcie *subs* skill
dictare *subs* dictation
dictator *subs* dictator
dicţie *subs* diction
dictincţie *subs* distinction
dicţionar *subs* dictionary
dicţiune *subs* utterance
dicţiune *adv* utterly

didactic *adj* didactic
dietă *subs* diet
diferenţă *subs* difference
diferenţă *subs* disparity
diferenţă de nivel *subs* slope
diferit *adj* different
diferit *adj* dissimilar
dificil *adj* arduous
dificil *adj* difficult
dificultate *subs* difficulty
dificultate *subs* hardship
dificultate *subs* quandary
digestie *subs* digestion
dilemă *subs* dilemma
diluat *adj* dilute
dimensiune *subs* dimension
dimineaţă *subs* morning
din afară *adv* outside
din belşug *adv* galore
din evul mediu *adj* medieval
din faţă *adj* forward
din fericire *adv* luckily
din neatenţie *adv* unawares
din nou *adv* afresh
din nou *adv* again
din provincie *adj* provincial
din toată inima *adv* heartily
dinam *subs* dynamo
dinamic *adj* dynamic
dinamică *subs* dynamics
dinamită *subs* dynamite
dinastie *subs* dynasty
dincolo *adv.* across
dincolo de *prep* past
dinspre vest *adv* westerly
dinte *subs* tooth
diplomă *subs* diploma
diplomat *subs* diplomat
diplomatic *adj* diplomatic
diplomaţie *subs* diplomacy
direct *adj* direct
direct *adv* straight

direct *adj* through
direcţie *subs* direction
direcţie *subs* leadership
director *subs* director
director al poştei postmaster
director de şcoală *subs* principal
directorial *adj* managerial
dirijor *subs* conductor
disc *subs* disc
discernământ *subs* discretion
disciplină *subs* discipline
discipol *subs* disciple
discipol *subs* scholar
discret *adj* secretive
discriminare *subs* discrimination
discurs *subs* speech
discurs solemn *subs* oration
discutabil *adj* questionable
disecţie *subs* dissection
disertaţie asupra *subs* discourse
disolvant *subs* solvent
dispariţie *subs* disappearance
dispensar *subs* dispensary
disperare *subs* despair
disperat *adj* desperate
disperat *adj* hopeless
disponibil *adj* available
dispoziţie *subs* mood
dispozitiv *subs* appliance
dispozitiv *subs* device
dispreţ *subs* disdain
dispunere *subs* disposal
dispus *adj* willing
dispută *subs* contention
dispută *subs* dispute
distant *adj* distant
distanţă *subs* distance
distanţă în mile *subs* mileage
distanţă mare *subs* far
distanţă mică *subs* little
distilerie *subs* distillery
distinct *adj* distinct

distincţie *subs* notability
distracţie *subs* entertainment
distribuţie *subs* distribution
district *subs* district
distrugător *subs* wrecker
distrugere *subs* destruction
divan *subs* ottoman
divers *adj* diverse
divers *adj* miscellaneous
divin *adj* divine
divin *adj* heavenly
divinitate *subs* divinity
divinitate *subs* godhead
diviziune *subs* division
divorţ *subs* divorce
dizenterie *subs* dysentery
doamnă *subs* lady
doar *adv* only
dobândire *subs.* achievement
doborî *v.t* prostrate
doc *subs* dock
doc *subs* jean
docil *adj* docile
doctor *subs* doctor
doctorat *subs* doctorate
doctrină *subs* doctrine
doctrină *subs* lore
doctrină *subs* tenet
document *subs* document
dogmă *subs* dogma
dogmatic *adj* dogmatic
dogoare *subs* fervour
doi *subs* two
doime *subs* minim
doisprezece *subs* twelve
dojană *subs* snub
dojană *subs* taunt
dolar *subs* dollar
dom *subs* dome
domeniu *subs* domain
domeniu *adj* realm
domestic *adj* domestic

domiciliu *subs.* abode
domiciliu *subs* domicile
dominant *adj* dominant
dominare *subs* domination
dominaţtie *subs* dominion
domn *subs* sir
domnesc *subs* lordly
domnie *subs* reign
domnii *subs* Messrs
domnişoară *subs* damsel
domnişoară *subs* miss
domnul *subs* mister
donaţie *subs* donation
donator *subs* donor
dop *subs* cork
dorinţă *subs* desire
dorinţă *subs* wish
dorinţă de *subs* appetite
doritor *adj* eager
doritor *adj* wishful
dornic *adj* desirous
dos al palmei *subs* backhand
dosar *subs* file
două *subs* two
două puncte *subs* colon
douăzeci *adj* twenty
douăzeci *subs* twenty
douăzecime *subs* twentieth
dovadă *subs* proof
dovleac *subs* pumpkin
doză *subs* dose
drag *adj* dear
drag *subs* sake
dragoste nebună *subs* infatuation
drăguţ *adj* darling
drăguţ *adj* nice
drăguţ *adj* pretty
dramă *subs* drama
dramatic *adj* dramatic
dramatic *adj* scenic
dramaturg *subs* dramatist
drastic *adj* drastic

drept *adj* just
drept *adj* right
drept *adv* right
drept *subs* right
drept *adj* straight
drept *adj* upright
drept de proprietate *subs* ownership
drept de vot *subs* suffrage
dreptunghi *subs* oblong
dreptunghi *subs* rectangle
dreptunghiular *adj* rectangular
droaie *subs* brood
drojdie de bere *subs* yeast
drum *subs* road
drum în zigzag *subs* zigzag
drumeţ *subs* wayfarer
dual *adj* dual
dubă *subs* van
dublu *adj* double
dublu *adj* duplicate
dublură *subs* double
dublură *subs* lining
duce *subs* duke
dud(ă) *subs* mulberry
duel *subs* duel
duh *subs* ghost
duhoare *subs* stench
duhoare *subs* stink
dulap *subs* cabinet
dulap *subs* closet
dulap *subs* cupboard
dulap *subs* plank
dulce *adj* sweet
dulceaţă *subs* jam
dulceaţă *subs* sweetness
dulciuri *subs* sweet
duminică *subs* Sunday
dungă *subs* crease
dungă *subs* stripe
după *prep.* after
după *prep* behind

după aceea *adv* after
după care *conj* whereupon
după ce *conj* after
duplicat *subs* duplicate
duplicat *subs* replica
duplicat *subs* tally
duplicitate *subs* duplicity
durabil *adj* durable
durabil *adj* lasting
durată *subs* duration
durere *subs.* ache
durere *subs* pain
durere de cap *subs* headache
durere de dinte *subs* toothache
dureros *adj* painful
dureros *adj* sore
duş *subs* shower
duşcă *subs* dram
duşman *subs* foe
duşmănie *subs.* acrimony
duşmănie animus
duşmănie *ssubs* enmity
duzină *subs* dozen

E

e epura *v.t* purge
ea *pron* she
echilateral *adj* equilateral
echilibru *subs* balance
echilibru *subs* poise
echipă *subs* team
echipaj *subs* crew
echipament *subs* equipment
echipament *subs* outfit
echitabil *adj* equitable
echivalent *adj* equivalent
echivalent (cu) *adj* tantamount
eclipsă *subs* eclipse

economic *adj* economic
economic *adj* economical
economie *subs* economics
economie *subs* thrift
economisire *subs* economy
ecou *subs* echo
ecran *subs* screen
ecterior *adv* outward
ecuație *subs* equation
ecuator *subs* equator
edificiu *subs* edifice
ediție *subs* edition
editor *subs* editor
editor *subs* publisher
editorial *adj* editorial
editorial *subs* editorial
educație *subs* education
efect *subs* effect
efective *adj* effective
eficacitate *subs* efficacy
eficient *adj* efficient
eficiență *subs* efficiency
efort *subs* effort
efort de viteză *subs* spurt
egal *adj* equal
egal *subs* equal
egal *adj* even
egalitate *subs* equality
ego *subs* ego
egoist *adj* selfish
egotism *subs* egotism
egretă *subs* aigrette
ei *pron* them
el *pron* he
el *pron* him
elaborat *adj* elaborate
elastic *adj* elastic
electric *adj* electric
electricitate *subs* electricity
elefant *subs* elephant
elegant *adj* elegant
eleganță *subs* elegance

elegie *subs* elegy
element *subs* element
element constitutiv *subs* constituent
elementar *adj* elementary
elev *subs* student
eliberare *subs* liberation
eliberare *subs* manumission
eliberator *subs* liberator
eligibil *adj* eligible
eliminare *subs* elimination
elocvent *adj* eloquent
elocvență *subs* eloquence
elogiu *subs* panegyric
elogiu *subs* praise
eludare *subs* elusion
elvețian *subs* swiss
elvețian *adj* swiss
emancipare *subs* emancipation
emblemă *subs* emblem
embrion *subs* embryo
emfază *subs* emphasis
eminent *adj* eminent
eminență *subs* eminance
emisar *subs* emissary
emisferă *subs* hemisphere
emisiune de televiziune *subs* telecast
emoție *subs* emotion
emoțional *adj* emotional
enciclopedie *subs* encyclopaedia
energetic *adj* energetic
energic *adj* strenuous
energie *subs* energy
enervare *subs* annoyance
engleză *subs* English
englezesc *adj* british
enigmă *subs* enigma
enigmă *subs* stickler
enorm *adj* enormous
entitate *subs* entity
entomologie *subs* entomology

entuziasm *subs* enthusiasm
entuziastic *adj* enthusiastic
epavă *subs* debris
epavă *subs* wreck
epică *subs* epic
epidemie *subs* epidemic
epigramă *subs* epigram
epilepsie *subs* epilepsy
epilog *subs* epilogue
episcop *subs* bishop
episod *subs* episode
epitaf *subs* epitaph
epitrop *subs* trustee
epocă *subs* epoch
eră *subs* era
erecție *subs* erection
ereditar *subs* hereditary
ereditate *subs* heredity
ermetic *adj* watertight
eroare *subs* fallacy
eroare de nume *subs* misnomer
eroic *adj* heroic
eroină *subs* heroine
eroism *subs* heroism
erotic *adj* erotic
erou *subs* hero
eroziune *subs* erosion
erupție *subs* eruption
erupție *subs* irruption
erupție a unui vulcan *subs* belch
eșarfă *subs* muffler
eșarfă *subs* scarf
escaladare pe brânci *subs* scramble
escapadă *subs* sally
escortă *subs* escort
escroc *subs* knave
escroc *subs* sharper
escroc *subs* swindler
escrocherie *subs* knavery
escrocherie *subs* swindle
eseist *subs* essayist

esență *subs* essence
esență *subs* gist
esențial *adj* essential
eseu *subs* essay
est *subs* east
estetic *adj* aesthetic
estetică *subs* aesthetics
estic *adj* eastern
estimare *subs* esteem
estimare *subs* estimation
estimație *subs* estimate
estival *adj* aestival
estradă *subs* dais
eșua *subs* failure
etaj *subs* storey
etalare *subs* array
etalon *subs* standard
etalon *adj* standard
etalonare *subs* standardization
eter *subs* ether
etern *adv* eternal
etern *adj* everlasting
eternitate *subs* eternity
etic *adj* ethical
etică *subs* ethics
etichetă *subs* etiquette
etichetă *subs* label
etichetă *subs* tag
etimilogie *subs* etymology
eu *pron* I
eu *pron* me
eu însumi *pron* myself
eunuc *subs* eunuch
evacuare *subs* evacuation
evadare *subs* escape
evaluare *subs* assessment
evaluare *subs* computation
evaluare *subs* valuation
evanghelie *subs* gospel
eveniment *subs* event
eventual *adv* eventually
eventualitate *subs* contingency

evident *adj* conspicuous
evident *adj* evident
evident *adj* manifest
evident *adj* obvious
evitare *subs* avoidance
evlavios *adj* godly
evoluție *subs* evolution
evreu *subs* Jew
exact *adj* exact
exact *adv* sharp
exagerare *subs* exaggeration
examen *subs* examination
examinare *subs* audit
examinare atentă *subs* perusal
examinator *subs* examiner
excavare *subs* excavation
excelent *adj* excellent
excelență *subs* excellence
excelență *subs* excellency
excepție *subs* exception
exces *subs* excess
exclamație *subs* exclamation
exclusiv *adj* exclusive
excursie *subs* excursion
excursie *subs* outing
excursie *subs* trip
executabil *adj* workable
executant *subs* performer
execuție *subs* execution
exemplu *subs* example
exemplu *subs* instance
exercițiu *subs* exercise
exil *subs* exile
exilare *subs* banishment
exilat *subs* outcast
existență *subs* existence
expansiune *subs* expansion
expediție *subs* expedition
experiență *subs* experience
experiență științifică *subs* experiment

expert *adj* expert
expert *subs* expert
expirare *subs* expiry
expirat *adj* overdue
explicație *subs* explanation
explicit *adj* explicit
exploatare *subs* exploit
explorare *subs* exploration
explozie *subs* explosion
exploziv *subs* explosive
exploziv *adj* explosive
exponat *subs* exhibit
exponent *subs* exponent
export *subs* export
expoziție *subs* exhibition
expres *adj* express
expresie *subs* countenance
expresie *subs* expression
expresiv *adj* expressive
expulzare *subs* expulsion
expunere *subs* display
extensor *subs* stretcher
extern *adj* external
extern *adj* outdoor
extern *adj* outward
extragere *subs.* abstraction
extragere *subs* drawing
extraordinar *adj* extraordinary
extras *subs* extract
extravagant *adj* extravagant
extravagant *adj* profuse
extravanță *subs* extravagance
extrem *adj* extreme
extremă *subs* extreme
extremist *subs* extremist
extremitate *subs* tip
exuberant *adj* rampant
ezitare *subs* demur
ezitare *subs* hesitation

F

fabrică *subs* factory
fabrică de bere *subs* brewery
fabricant *subs* manufacturer
fabulă *subs* fable
fabulos *adj* fabulous
face tărăboi *v.i* rampage
facial *adj* facial
facil *adj* facile
facilitate *subs* facility
facsimil *subs* fac-simile
factor *subs* factor
factor poştal *subs* postman
factură *subs* invoice
facultate *subs* faculty
fad *adj* mawkish
fag *subs* beech
făgăduială solemnă *subs* vow
făgaş *subs* groove
făgaş *subs* rut
faimă *subs* fame
faimos *adj* famous
făină *subs* flour
faliment *subs* bankruptcy
falit *subs* bankrupt
fals *adj* false
fals *adj* mendacious
falsificare *subs.* adulteration
falsificare *subs* forgery
falsificat *adj* counterfeit
falsificat *adj* spurious
falsificator *subs* counterfeiter
familiar *adj* familiar
familiarizat cu *adj* conversant
familie *subs* family
fân *subs* hay
fanatic *adj* fanatic
fanatic *subs* fanatic
fanatic *subs* zealot

fâneaţă *subs* meadow
fântână *subs* fountain
fantastic *adj* fantastic
fantomă *subs* phantom
fapt *subs* fact
faptă *subs.* action
faptă *subs* gesture
faptă rea *subs* misdeed
faptă vitejească *subs* feat
far *subs* beacon
fără *prep* less
fără *adv* without
fără apărare *adj* indefensible
fără ca să *conj* without
fără de lege *adj* lawless
fără egal *adj* matchless
fără fir *adj* wireless
fără forme legale *adj* informal
fără greutate *adv* readily
fără limită *adj* limitless
fără măsură *adj* measureless
fără mişcare *adj* motionless
fără nervi *adj* nerveless
fără nici un ban *adj* penniless
fără noroc *adj* luckless
fără număr *adj* numberless
fără pereche *adv* beyond
fără pereche *adj* nonpareil
fără pete *adj* spotless
fără putere legală *adj* invalid
fără rasă definită *adj* mongrel
fără scrupule *adj* unprincipled
fără simţire *adj* senseless
fără valoare *adj* paltry
fără valoare *adj* vile
fără viaţă *adj* lifeless
fărâmă *subs* bit
farfurie *subs* plate
farfurioară *subs* saucer
farmacie *subs* pharmacy
farmacist *subs* druggist
farmec *subs* charm1

farmec *subs* glamour
farsă *subs* farce
farsă *subs* jest
fascicul *subs* streamer
fascinaţie *subs* fascination
fâşie *subs* ribbon
fâşie *subs* strip
fasole *subs* bean
fată *subs* girl
faţa *subs* face
faţă *subs* front
fată bătrână *subs* spinster
fată frumoasă *subs* belle
faţadă *subs* facade
fatal *adj* fatal
faţetă *subs* facet
faună *subs* fauna
favoare *subs* favourl
favorabil *adj* auspicious
favorabil *adj* favourable
favorabil *adv* well
favorit *subs* darling
favorit *adj* favourite
favorit *subs* favourite
favorit *subs* minion
favoriţi *subs* whisker
fază *subs* phase
febră *subs* fever
febră tifoidă *subs* typhoid
februarie *subs* February
fecioară *subs* maid
fecioară *subs* virgin
feciorelnic *adj* maiden
federal *adj* federal
federaţie *subs* federation
felicitare *subs* congratulation
felie *subs* slice
felinar *subs* lantern
felurit *adj* various
femeie *subs* woman
femeie îndărătnică *subs* shrew
femeie neângrijită *subs* slattern

femeie tânără *subs* wench
femeiesc *subs* womanish
femelă *subs* female
feminin *adj* female
feminin *adj* feminine
feminitate *subs* womanhood
fenomen *subs* phenomenon
fenomenal *adj* phenomenal
ferăstrău *subs* saw
fereastră *subs* widow
fereastră *subs* window
fericire *subs* bliss
fericire *subs* happiness
fericit *adj* happy
ferm *adj* firm
ferm *adj* resolute
fermă *subs* farm
fermecător *adj* lovely
fermecător *adj* winsome
ferment *subs* ferment
fermentaţie *subs* fermentation
fermier *subs* farmer
feroce *adj* ferocious
fertil *adj* fertile
fertilitate *subs* fertility
fertilizator *subs* fertilizer
festă *subs* prank
festiv *adj* festive
festival *subs* festival
festivitate *subs* festivity
fetişcană *subs* lass
feudal *adj* feudal
fiare *subs* fetter
fiasco *subs* fiasco
fibră *subs* fibre
fibră de nucă de cocos *subs* coir
ficat *subs* liver
ficţiune *subs* fiction
fictiv *adj* fictitious
fidel *adj* faithful
fidelitate *subs* fidelity
fie că *conj* whether

fiecare *adj* each
fiecare *adj* every
fier de călcat *subs* iron
fierar *subs* blacksmith
fierar *subs* smith
fierbere *subs* boil
fierbinte *adj* fervent
fierbinte *adj* hot
fiere *subs* bile
fiertură *subs* mush
figură *subs* effigy
figură *subs* visage
fiică *subs* daughter
ființă *subs* being
filantrop *subs* philanthropist
filantropic *adj* philanthropic
filantropie *subs* philanthropy
fildeș *subs* ivory
filfizon *subs* dandy
film *subs* film
filme *subs* movies
filologic *adj* philological
filologie *subs* philology
filozof *subs* philosopher
filozofic *adj* philosophical
filozofie *subs* philosophy
filtru *subs* filter
fin *adj* fine
final *adj* conclusive
final *adj* final
financiar *adj* financial
finanțe *subs* finance
finit *adj* finite
fiolă *subs* phial
fior *subs* shudder
fir de praf *subs* mote
fir tors *subs* yarn
firav *adj* frail
firav *adj* weak
firimitură *subs* crumb
firmă *subs* firm
fiscal *adj* fiscal

fisură *subs* fissure
fisură *subs* rift
fitil *subs* fuse
fitil *subs* wick
fiu *subs* son
fixat *adj* set
fizic *adv* bodily
fizic *adj* physical
fizic *subs* physique
fizică *subs* physics
fizician *subs* physicist
fizionomie *subs* physiognomy
flacă *subs* flame
flăcău *subs* lad
flagrant *adj* flagrant
flămând *adj* hungry
flanelă *subs* flannel
flatare *subs* flattery
flaut *subs* flute
fleac *subs* trifle
fleșcăit *adj* flabby
flirt *subs* flirt
flixibil *adj* flexible
floare *subs* bloom
floare *subs* blossom
floare *subs* flower
floare *subs* heyday
floră *subs* flora
florar *subs* florist
flotă *subs* fleet
flotă *subs* navy
flotă de război *subs* armada
fluent *adj* fluent
fluid *adj* fluid
fluid *subs* fluid
fluier *subs* whistle
fluture *subs* butterfly
fluture de noapte *subs* moth
fluviu *subs* stream
foaie goală *subs* blank
foaie volantă *subs* handbill
foaie volantă *subs* leaflet

foame *subs* hunger
foamete *subs* dearth
foamete *subs* famine
foarfece *subs* scissors
foarte *adj* very
foarte generos *adj* munificent
foarte mult *adv* much
foc *subs* fire
focă *subs* seal
focal *adj* focal
focar *subs* focus
fochist *subs* stoker
foilolog *subs* philologist
folos *subs* use
folosinţă *subs* usage
folositor *subs* beneficial
folositor *adj* useful
folositor pentru *adj* subservient
fond *subs* fund
fonetic *adj* phonetic
fonetică *subs* phonetics
fontă *subs* cast-iron
forjă *subs* forge
formă *subs* form
formă *subs* shape
formal *adj* formal
formare *subs* formation
format *subs* format
formatie *subs* band
formidabil *adj* formidable
formulă *subs* formula
fort *subs* fort
forţă *subs* force
forţă *subs* might
forţă *subs* strength
fortăreaţă *subs* fortress
fortăreaţă *subs* stronghold
forte *subs* forte
forum *subs* forum
fosfat *subs* phosphate
fosfor *subs* phosphorus
fosilă *subs* fossil

fotograf *subs* photographer
fotografic *adj* photographic
fotografie *subs* photo
fotografie *subs* photograph
fotografie *subs* photography
fracţie *subs* fraction
fracţionist *adj* factious
fracţiune *subs* faction
fractură *subs* fracture
fraged *adj* tender
fragil *adj* brittle
fragil *adj* fragile
fragment *subs* fragment
fragment *subs* scrap
frământare *subs* unrest
frână *subs* brake
franciză *subs* frachise
frânghie *subs* rope
franţuzesc *adj* French
frate *subs* brother
fraternitate *subs* fraternity
frăţesc *adj* fraternal
frăţie *subs* brotherhood
fratricid *subs* fratricide
frâu *subs* curb
frâu *subs* rein
fraudă *subs* fraud
frază *subs* phrase
frazeologie *subs* phraseology
freamăt *subs* whir
freamăt de frunze *subs* lisp
frecare *subs* rub
frecvent *subs* frequent
frecvenţa *subs* frequency
frenezie *subs* frenzy
frică *subs* fear
fricţiune *subs* friction
frig *subs* cold
frigid *adj* frigid
frigider *subs* fridge
frigider *subs* refrigerator
frigorifer *subs* cooler

friguros *adj* chilly
fript *adj* roast
friptură *subs* roast
frişcă *subs* cream
frivol *adj* frivolous
frontal *adj* front
frontieră *subs* border
frontieră *subs* frontier
fruct *subs* fruit
frugal *adj* frugal
frumos *adj* beautiful
frumos *adj* handsome
frumuseţe *subs* beauty
frunte *subs* forehead
frunză *subs* leaf
frunziş *subs* foliage
frunzos *adj* leafy
frustrare *subs* frustration
fugă *subs* run
fugar *adj* fugitive
fugitiv *subs* fugitive
fum *subs* smoke
funcţia de căpitan *subs* captaincy
funcţie *subs* function
funcţionar *subs* clerk
funcţionar *subs* functionary
fund *subs* bottom
fundal *subs* background
fundamental *adj* basic
fundamental *adj* capital
fundamental *adj* fundamental
fundaţie *subs* foundation
fundătură *subs* deadlock
funie *subs* cord
funingine *subs* soot
furie *subs* anger
furie *subs* fury
furie *subs* ire
furie *subs* wrath
furios *adj* furious
furnal *subs* furnace
furnică *subs* ant

furnizor *subs* contractor
furnizor *subs* supplier
furt *subs* theft
furtun *subs* hose
furtună *subs* storm
furtună *subs* tempest
furtunos *adj* stormy
fus *subs* spindle
fustă *subs* skirt
fuziune *subs* fusion

gafă *subs* blunder
gâfiială *subs* pant
găină *subs* hen
gaiţă *subs* jay
gălăgie *subs* clamour
galant *adj* gallant
galanterie *subs* gallantry
galaxie *subs* galaxy
galben *adj* yellow
galben *subs* yellow
gălbenuş de ou *subs* yolk
gălbinele *subs* marigold
gălbui *adj* yellowish
găleată *subs* bucket
galerie *subs* gallery
galon *subs* gallon
galop *subs* gallop
galop mic *subs* canter
gând *subs* thought
gândac *subs* beetle
gândac *subs* bug
gândac de bucătărie *subs* cockroach
gânditor *adj* meditative
gânditor *adj* pensive
gânditor *subs* thinker

gânditor *adj* thoughtful
gangster *subs* gangster
gângurit *subs* babble
gângurit *subs* coo
gângurit de copil *subs* prattle
garaj *subs* garage
garant *subs* voucher
garantator *subs* warrantor
garanție *subs* guarantee
garanție *subs* warrant
garanție *subs* warrantee
garanție *subs* warranty
gard *subs* fence
gard viu *subs* hedge
gardă *subs* guard
gardian *subs* guardian
garnitură *subs* gasket
gașcă *subs* gang
gâscă *subs* goose
gâscan *subs* gander
gastric *adj* gastric
gât *subs* neck
gâtlej *subs* throat
gaură *subs* gap
gaură *subs* hole
gaz *subs* gas
gaz lampant *subs* kerosene
gazdă *subs* host
gazetă *subs* gazette
gazon *subs* sod
gazos *adj* aeriform
geamăn *subs* twin
geamandură *subs* buoy
geamăt *subs* groan
geamăt *subs* moan
geamăt *subs* wail
geambaș *subs* coper
geamgiu *subs* glazier
geană *subs* eyelash
geană *subs* lash
geantă *subs* bag
gelos *adj* jealous

gelozie *subs* jealousy
gen *subs* gender
gen *subs* kind
general *adj* general
general *adv* generally
generare *subs* generation
generator *subs* generator
generos *adj* generous
generozitate *subs* generosity
genil *adj* gentle
geniu *subs* genius
gentilom *subs* nobleman
gentleman *subs* gentleman
genunchi *subs* knee
geograf *subs* geographer
geografic *adj* geographical
geografie *subs* geography
geolog *subs* geologist
geologic *adj* geological
geologie *subs* geology
geometric *adj* geometrical
geometrie *subs* geometry
ger *subs* frost
germen *subs* germ
germen *subs* sprout
germinație *subs* germination
gerunziu *subs* gerund
gest *subs* motion
gest de mângâiere *subs* pat
gheară *subs* pounce
gheată *subs* boot
gheață *subs* ice
ghem *subs* clew
gheretă *subs* booth
gherilă *subs* guerilla
ghețar *subs* glacier
ghiceală *subs* guess
ghicitoare *subs* conundrum
ghid *subs* guide
ghimbir *subs* ginger
ghimpat *adj* barbed
ghimpe *subs* spine

ghindă *subs.* acorn
ghinionist *adj* unfortunate
ghiont *subs* nudity
ghiont *subs* poke
ghirlandă *subs* festoon
ghirlandă *subs* garland
ghişeu *subs* wicket
ghiveci *subs* hotchpotch
gibon *subs* gibbon
gigant *subs* giant
gigantic *adj* gigantic
gimnast *subs* gymnast
gimnastic *adj* gymnastic
gimnastică *subs* gymnastics
gimnaziu *subs* gymnasium
gingie *subs* gum
girafă *subs* giraffe
giulgiu *subs* shroud
glandă *subs* gland
gleznă *subs* ankle
glicerină *subs* glycerine
gloată *subs* mob
gloată *subs* populace
glob *subs* globe
global *adj* global
glonţ *subs* bullet
glorie *subs* glory
glorificare *subs* glorification
glorios *adj* glorious
glosar *subs* glossary
glucoză *subs* glucose
glugă *subs* hood
glumă *subs* joke
glumă răutăcioasă *subs* gibe
glumeţ *subs* joker
goană *subs* pursuit
goarnă *subs* bugle
goarnă *subs* clarion
gol *adj* bare
gol *adj* blank
gol *adj* empty
gol *adj* naked

gol *adj* void
gol *subs* void
golf *subs* bay
golf *subs* bight
golf *subs* golf
golf *subs* gulf
golgeter *subs* scorer
gong *subs* gong
gorilă *subs* gorilla
grabă *subs* haste
grabă *subs* hurry
grabă *subs* rush
grăbit *adj* hasty
grad *subs* degree
grad *subs* rank
gradaţie *subs* gradation
grădină *subs* garden
grădină zoologică *subs* zoo
grădinar *subs* gardener
grădiniţă *subs* kindergarten ;
gradual *adj* gradual
grafic *subs* graph
grafic *adj* graphic
grajd *subs* shed
grajd *subs* stable
gram *subs* gramme
grămadă *adv* aheap
grămadă *subs* pile
gramatică *subs* grammar
gramatician *subs* grammarian
grămezi *subs* piles
gramofon *subs* gramophone
grână *subs* grain
grandoare *subs* grandeur
graniţă *subs* boundary
gras *adj* fat
grăsime *subs* fat
grăsime *subs* grease
graţie *subs* grace
gratificaţie *subs* gratification
graţios *adj* gracious
gratis *adv* gratis

gratuit *adj* free
grâu *subs* wheat
grav *adv* badly
grav *adj* grave
gravitate *subs* gravity
gravitaţie *subs* gravitation
gravor de medalii *subs* medallist
greaţă *subs* nausea
grec *subs* Greek
grecesc *adj* Greek
greiere *subs* cricket
grenadă *subs* grenade
greoi *adj* massy
greşală *subs* error
greşeală *subs* mistake
greşeală de tipar *subs* misprint
greşit *adj* erroneous
greşit *adj* wrong
greşit *adv* wrong
greţos *adj* loath
greu *adj* hard
greu *adj* weighty
greutate *subs* weight
grevist *subs* striker
gri *adj* grey
grijă *subs* care
grijă *subs* worry
grijuliu *adj* careful
grijuliu cu *adj* mindful
grilaj *subs* raling
grindă *subs* beam
grindă *subs* girder
grindină *subs* hail
groapă *subs* moat
gros *adj* thick
grosolan *adj* coarse
grosolan *adj* gross
grotesc *adj* grotesque
grup *subs* batch
grup *subs* group
grupă de soldaţi *subs* squad
gudron *subs* tar

guler *subs* collar
gunoi *subs* garbage
gunoi *subs* rubbish
gură *subs* mouth
guşă *subs* craw
gust *subs* taste
gust delicat *subs* palate
gustare *subs* snack
gustos *adj* tasteful
gută *subs* gout
gutural *adj* guttural
gutural *adj* throaty
guvern *subs* government
guvernantă *subs* governess
guvernator *subs* governor

habitaţie *subs* habitation
haină *subs* coat
haină călugărească *subs* wimple
haine *subs* clothes
halat *subs* gown
halat *subs* overall
haltă *subs* halt
ham *subs* harness
hamal *subs* porter
hambar *subs* barn
han *subs* inn
handicap *subs* handicap
haos *subs* chaos
haos *subs* pelf
haotic *adv* chaotic
harababura *subs* turmoil
harababură *subs* welter
hărmălaie *subs* babel
hărmălaie *subs* romp
harpă *subs* harp
hartă *subs* chart

hartă *subs* map
hârtie *subs* paper
hărțuire *subs* harassment
hazard *subs* hazard
hazna *subs* cesspool
herig *subs* herring
hernie *subs* hernia
hidos *adj* hideous
hidrogen *subs* hydrogen
hidromel *subs* mead
hienă *subs* hyaena, hyena
hiperbolă *subs* hyperbole
hipnotism *subs* hypnotism
hipnotism *subs* mesmerism
hirbernare *subs* hibernation
hoardă *subs* horde
hochei *subs* hockey
hohot de plâns *v.i* sob
hohot de plâns *subs* sob
hoinar *subs* loafer
hoinăreală *subs* ramble
hol *subs* hall
holeră *subs* cholera
holocaust *subs* holocaust
homar *subs* lobster
homeopat *subs* homoeopath
homeopatie *subs* homeopathy
hop *subs* hitch
horticultură *subs* horticulture
hoț *subs* thief
hotărât *adj* definite
hotărât *adj* intent
hotel *subs* hotel
hotel cu garaj *subs* motel
hrană *subs* eatable
hrană *subs* nourishment
hrănitor *adj* nutritious
hrăpăreț *adj* miserly
Hristos *subs* Christ
huiduială *subs* hoot
huligan *subs* bully
huligan *subs* hooligan

huligan *subs* mug
huruit *subs* rumble

iad *adj* hell
iaht *subs* yacht
iapă *subs* mare
iarăși *adv* anew
iarbă *subs* grass
iarbă *subs* herb
iarbă *subs* weed
iarnă *subs* winter
iasomie *subs* jasmine, jessamine
ibric *subs* kettle
icre *subs* roe
icre *subs* spawn
ideal *adj* ideal
ideal *adj* ideal
idealism *subs* idealism
idealist *subs* idealist
idealist *adj* idealistic
idee *subs* idea
idee vagă *subs* inkling
identic *adj* identical
identificare *subs* indentification
identitate *subs* identity
idiomatical *adj* idiomatic
idiot *subs* idiot
idol *subs* idol
idolatru *subs* idolater
iederă *subs* ivy
ieftin *adj* cheap
ieftin *adj* inexpensive
iepure *subs* rabbit
iepure de câmp *subs* hare
ierarhie *subs* hierarchy
ieri *subs* yesterday
ieri *adv* yesterday

iertare *subs* condonation
iertare *subs* pardon
ieşire *subs* exit
ieşire violentă *subs* rampage
iesle *subs* manger
igienă *subs* hygiene
igienic *adj* hygienic
ignorant *adj* ignorant
ignoranţă *subs* ignorance
ignoranţă *subs* nescience
ilegal *adj* illegal
ilicit *adj* illicit
ilizibilitate *subs* illegibility
ilogic *adj* illogical
iluminare *subs* illumination
ilustrare *subs* illustration
iluzie *subs* illusion
imaginar *adj* imaginary
imaginaţie *subs* fancy
imaginaţie *subs* imagination
imaginativ *adj* imaginative
imagine *subs* image
imaterial *adj* immaterial
imatur *adj* immature
imaturitate *subs* immaturity
îmbâcsit *adj* stuffy
imbecil *adj* witless
îmbelşugat *adj* affluent
îmblânzit *adj* tame
imbold *subs* goad
imbold *subs* urge
îmbrăcăminte *subs* attire
îmbrăcăminte *subs* clothing
îmbrăcăminte *subs* garment
îmbrăcare *subs* dressing
îmbrăţişare *subs* embrace
îmbucătură *subs* morsel
îmbucătură *subs* mouthful
îmbujorat *adv.* ablush
îmbulzeală *subs* confluence
îmbunătăţire *subs* betterment
îmbunătăţire *subs* improvement

imediat *adv* anon
imediat *adj* immediate
imens *adj* huge
imens *adj* immense
imensitate *subs* immensity
imersiune *subs* immersion
imigrant *subs* immigrant
imigraţie *subs* immigration
iminent *adj* imminent
imitaţie *subs* imitation
imitaţie *subs* mimicry
imitativ *subs* mimic
imitator *subs* imitator
imitator *subs* mimic
imn *subs* anthem
imn de laudă *subs* laud
imn religios *subs* hymn
imoral *adj* gay
imoral *adj* immoral
imoral *adj* wicked
imoral *subs* wicker
imoralitate *subs* immorality
imortal *adj* immortal
imortalitate *subs* immortality
împachetare *subs* packing
impact *subs* impact
împărat *subs* emperor
împărăteasă *subs* empress
imparţial *adj* impartial
imparţial *adj* neutral
imparţialitate *subs* impartiality
impas *subs* impasse
impediment *subs* impediment
imperativ *adj* imperative
imperfect *adj* imperfect
imperfecţiune *subs* imperfection
imperial *adj* imperial
imperialism *subs* imperialism
imperiu *subs* empire
impermeabil *subs* repellent
impermeabil *adj* waterproof
impermeabil *subs* waterproof

impersonal *adj* impersonal
impertinent *adj* impertinent
impertinenţă *subs* impertinence
împestriţat *adj* motley
impetuos *adj* impetuous
impetuozitate *subs* impetuosity
împingere *subs* push
implacabil *adj* relentless
implicaţie *subs* implication
implicit *adj* implicit
împlinire *subs* fulfilment
implorare *subs.* adjuration
împodobit *adj* flowery
import *subs* import
important *adj* important
important *adj* momentous
importanţă *subs* importance
imposibil *adj* impossible
imposibilitate *subs* impossibility
impostor *subs* impostor
impostură *subs* imposture
împotriva *prep.* against
împovărător *adj* burdensome
impozit *subs* toll
impozit indirect *subs* excise
impractibilitate *subs*
  impracticability
impracticabil *adj* impracticable
impregnat *adj* ingrained
impregnat *subs* menses
împrejurimi *subs* surroundings
impresie *subs* impression
impresionant *adj* impressive
împreună *adv* together
impreună *adv* jointly
imprimanta *subs* printer
imprimare *subs* imprint
imprimare *subs* print
improbabil *adj* unlikely
impropriu *adj* untoward
imprudent *adj* imprudent
imprudenţă *subs* imprudence

împrumut *subs* loan
impuls *subs* impulse
impulsiv *adj* impulsive
impunător *adj* imposing
impunere *subs* imposition
impunitate *subs* impunity
împunsătură *subs* prick
impur *adj* impure
impuritate *subs* impurity
împuşcătură *subs* shot
imputare *subs* reproof
imun *adj* immune
imunitate *subs* immunity
în *prep* in
în *prep* into
în acelaşi timp *adv* withal
în amănunt *adv* minutely
în apropiere *adv* around
în apropiere *adv* near
în aşteptare *adj* agog
în avans *adv* beforehand
în care *adv* wherein
în ciuda *adv* notwithstanding
în faţa *prep* before
în fiecare noapte *adv* nightly
în flăcări *adj* aglow
în formă *adj* fit
în formă de capsulă *adj* capsular
în formă de inimă *adj* cordate
în interior *adv* inwards
în interior *adv* within
în întregime *adv* downright
în întregime *adv* entirely
în întregime *adv* outright
în întregime *adv* wholly
în jos *adv* downward
în jurul *prep* around
în lung şi-n lat *adv* throughout
în mare parte *adv* mainly
în mijlocul *prep.* amid
în miniatură *adj* miniature
în mişcare *adv* astir

în mod natural *adv* naturally
în mod necesar *adv* perforce
în nord *adv* northerly
în numele cuiva *subs* behalf
în perspectivă *adj* prospective
în picioare *adj* erect
în plus *adv* else
în plus *avd* extra
în sfârşit *adv* lastly
în spatele *adv* behind
în spirală *adj* spiral
în stare bună *adj* safe
în stare nativă *adj* nascent
în stare să *adj* apt
în sus *adv* aloft
în sus *adv* upwards
în susul *prep* up
în timp ce *conj* while
în timpul *prep* during
în ultimul timp *adv* lately
în urmă *adv* backward
în van *adv* vainly
în vârstă de *adj* aged
în viaţă *adj* live
în zigzag *adj* zigzag
inabilitate *subs* inability
înăbuşitor *adj* sultry
inactiv *adj* inactive
înadins *adv* purposely
inadmisibil *adj* inadmissible
înainte *adv* afore
înainte *adv* ahead
înainte *adv* along
înainte *adv* before
înainte *adv* forward
înainte *adv* on
înainte *adj* onward
înainte *adv* onwards
înainte cu *adv* ago
înainte de masă *subs* forenoon
înalt *adj* high
înalt *adj* tall

înălţare *subs* uplift
înălţime *subs* height
inamic *subs* enemy
inaplicabil *adj* inapplicable
înapoi *adv.* aback
înapoi *adv* back
înapoiat *adj* backward
inaugurare *subs* inauguration
inaugurat *adj* inaugural
înăuntru *adv* indoors
înăuntru *adv* inside
înăuntrul *prep* inside
înăuntrul *prep* within
încă *adv* still
încă *conj* yet
încăierare *subs* melee
încăierare *subs* row
încăierare *subs* scuffle
încăierare *subs* skirmish
încâlcit *adj.* addle
incalculabil *adj* incalculable
încântare *subs* delight
incapabil *adj* incapable
incapabil *adj* unable
incapacitate *v.t* disability
incapacitate *subs* incapacity
încăpăţânat *adj* headstrong
încăpăţânat *adj* obstinate
încăpăţânat *adj* stubborn
încăpător *adj* capacious
încărcare *subs* charge
încărcătură *subs* cargo
încărcătură *subs* load
încărcătură *subs* shipment
încarnare *subs* incarnation
încarnat *adj* incarnate
incendiere *subs* arson
începere *subs* prime
început *subs* beginning
început *subs* commencement
început *subs* inception
început *subs* onset

început *subs* outset
început *subs* start
încercare *subs* attempt
încercare *subs* try
încercare grea *subs* ordeal
încercare riscantă *subs* flutter
încet *adj* slow
încheiere *subs* closure
încheietură *subs* juncture
încheietură a mâinii *subs* wrist
închidere *subs* close
închipuit *adj* bogus
închiriere *subs* hire
închiriere *subs* lease
închisoare *subs* prison
inchiziție *subs* inquisition
incident *subs* incident
incidental *adj* incidental
incie *subs* inch
incinerare *subs* cremation
înclinare *subs* bent
înclinare *subs* lean
înclinat *adj* declivous
înclinat *adj* downward
înclinație *suns.* addiction
înclinație *subs* bias
înclinație *subs* inclination
înclinație *subs* proclivity
includere *subs* inclusion
inclus *adj* inclusive
încoace *adv* hither
incoerent *adj* incoherent
incomod *adj* inconvenient
incomod *adj* uneasy
incomparabil *adj* incomparable
incomparabil *adj* irrecoverable
incomparabil *adj* peerless
incompatibil *adj* irreconcilable
incompetent *adj* incompetent
incomplet *adj* incomplete
inconstant *adj* mercurial
inconvenient *subs* drawback

încordare *subs* strain
încordat *adj* tense
incorect *adj* incorrect
incorigibil *adj* incorrigible
încoronare *subs* coronation
incorporare *subs* incorporation
încorporat *adj* incorporate
încorporat *subs* increment
incoruptibil *adj* incorruptible
încredere *subs* trust
incredibil *adj* incredible
încrezător *adj* confident
încrezător *adj* hopeful
încrezător *adj* trustful
încruntare *subs* frown
încuietoare *subs* lock
incult *adj* illiterate
incurabil *adj* incurable
încurcat *adj* intricate
încurcătură *subs* fix
încurcătură *subs* lurch
încurcătură *subs* mull
încurcătură *subs* puzzle
încuviințare *subs* connivance
îndărătnic *adj* restive
îndârjire *subs* obstinacy
îndată ce *conj* when
îndatorat *adj* indebted
îndatorire *subs* duty
îndatoritor *adj* officious
îndeajuns *adv* enough
îndeaproape *adv* nearly
indecent *adj* indecent
indecență *subs* indecency
îndemânare *subs.* ability
îndemânare *subs* workmanship
îndemânatic *adj* handy
independent *adj* independent
independent de *adj* irrespective
independență *subs* independence
îndeplinire *subs.* accomplishment
index *subs* index

indian *adj* Indian
indicative *adj* indicative
indicator *subs* indicator
indiciu *subs* clue
indiciu *subs* hint
indiferent *adj* indifferent
indiferent *adj* nonchalant
indiferenţă *subs* indifference
indigen *adj* indigenous
indigen *adj* vernacular
indigest *adj* indigestible
indigestie *subs* indigestion
indignare *subs* scorn
indignat *adj* indignant
indignaţie *subs* indignation
indigo *subs* indigo
îndiguire *subs* embankment
indirect *adj* indirect
indisciplina *subs* insubordination
indisciplină *subs* indiscipline
indiscret *adj* indiscreet
indiscret *adj* nosy
indiscreţie *subs* indiscretion
indiscriminat *adj* indiscriminate
indiscutabil *adj* indisputable
indispensabil *adj* indispensable
indispensabili *subs* small
indispus *adj* indisposed
indistinct *adj* indistinct
individ *subs* fellow
individ *v.t* jack
individ *subs* wight
individual *adj* individual
individualism *subs* individualism
individualitate *subs* individuality
individualitate *subs* self
indivizibil *adj* indivisible
îndoială *subs* doubt
indolent *adj* indolent
îndrăzneală *subs* boldness
îndrăzneală *subs* daring
îndrăzneală *subs* hardihood

îndrăzneţ *adj* bold
îndrăzneţ *adj* daring
îndrăzneţ *adj* venturesome
îndreptat în sus *adj* upward
îndreptăţit *adj* righteous
inducere *subs* induction
indulgent *adj* indulgent
indulgent *adj* lenient
indulgenţă *subs* indulgence
indulgenţă *subs* lenience,
     leniency
industrial *adj* industrial
industrie *subs* industry
inedit *adj* novel
ineficace *adj* ineffective
inel *subs* ring
ineluş *subs* annulet
inerent *adj* inherent
inert *adj* inert
inerţie *subs* inertia
inestimabil *adj* invaluable
inevitabil *adj* inevitable
inexact *adj* inaccurate
inexact *adj* inexact
inexorabil *adj* inexorable
inexplicabil *adj* inexplicable
infailibil *adj* infallible
infam *adj* infamous
infam *adj* obnoxious
infamie *subs* infamy
infanterie *subs* infantry
infanterist *subs* grunt
infantil *adj* infantile
infecţie *subs* infection
infecţios *adj* infectious
inferior *adj* base
inferior *adj* inferior
inferior *adj* nether
inferioritate *subs* inferiority
infern *adj* infernal
infern *subs* pandemonium
infinit *adj* infinite

infinitate *subs* infinity
infirm *subs* cripple
infirm *adj* invalid
infirmerie *subs* nursery
infirmieră *subs* nurse
infirmitate *subs* infirmity
înflăcărare *subs* pathos
inflamabil *adj* inflammable
inflamaţie *subs* inflammation
inflamator *adj* inflammatory
inflaţie *subs* inflation
inflexibil *adj* inflexible
influent *adj* influential
influenţă *subs* influence
înfocat *adj* keen
înfocat *adj* mettlesome
înfometare *subs* starvation
informaţie *subs* information
informativ *adj* informative
informator *subs* informer
infracţiune *subs* infringement
înfrângere *subs* defeat
înfumurare *subs* pomposity
infuzie *subs* infusion
îngemănat *adj* twin
înger *subs* angel
îngheţat *adj* icy
înghiţitură *subs* gulp
înghiţitură *subs* swallow
inginer *subs* engineer
îngrăşământ *subs* manure
ingredient *subs* ingredient
îngrijit *adj* neat
îngrijit *adj* trim
îngrijitor *subs* keeper
îngroşat *adj* callous
îngrozitor *adj* tremendous
îngust la minte *adj* smug
inhibiţie *subs* inhibition
înhumare *subs* sepulture
inimă *subs* heart
inimitabil *adj* inimitable

iniţial *adj* initial
iniţială *subs* initial
iniţiativă *subs* initiative
injecţie *subs* injection
înlăcrimat *adj* tearful
înlocuitor *subs* replacement
înmagazinare *subs* storage
înmiresmat *adj* odorous
înmormântare *subs* burial
înmormântare *subs* funeral
înmuiere într-un lichid *subs* dip
înnăscut *adj* inborn
înnăscut *adj* innate
înnorat *adj* cloudy
inocent *adj* innocent
inocenţă *subs* innocence
inoculare *subs* inoculation
inoperant *adj* inoperative
inoportun *adj* inopportune
inoportun *adj* undue
înot *subs* swim
înotător *subs* swimmer
inovaţie *subs* innovation
inovaţie *subs* novelty
inovator *subs* innovator
înregistrare *subs* registration
înrudire *subs* affinity
înrudire *subs* kinship
înrudit *adj* akin
înrudit *adj* cognate
însărcinată *adj* pregnant
înscriere a unui student *subs*
    matriculation
inscripţie *subs* inscription
insectă *subs* insect
insecticid *subs* insecticide
înşelăciune *subs* bluff
înşelăciune *subs* cheat
înşelăciune *subs* deceit
însemnat *adj* signal
insensibil *adj* insensible
insensibil *adj* obdurate

insensibilitate *subs* insensibility
inseparabil *adj* inseparable
inserţie *subs* insertion
însetat *adj* athirst
însetat *adj* thirsty
înşfăcare *subs* snatch
insignă *subs* badge
insinuare *subs* insinuation
insipid *adj* insipid
insipiditate *subs* insipidity
insistent *adj* insistent
insistenţă *subs* insistence
insolenţă *subs* insolence
insoloent *adj* insolent
insolubil *subs* insoluble
insolvent *adj* insolvent
insolvenţă *subs* insolvency
însorit *adj* sunny
înspăimântat *adj* aghast
înspăimântător *adj* dread
înspăimântător *adj* fearful
inspecţie *subs* inspection
inspecţie *subs* surveillance
inspector *subs* inspector
inspiraţie *subs* inspiration
inspiraţie *subs* sniff
înspre vest *adj* westerly
instabilitate *subs* instability
instalaţie *subs* installation
instalator *subs* plumber
instant *subs* instant
instant *adj* instant
instantaneu *adj* instantaneous
instantaneu *adv* instantly
înstelat *adj* starry
instigare *subs.* abetment
instigare *subs* instigation
înştiinţare *subs* notice
instinct *subs* instinct
instinctiv *adj* instinctive
institut *subs* institute
instituţie *subs* institution

înstrăinat *adj* alien
instrucţie *subs* instruction
instructor *subs* instructor
instrument *subs* implement
instrument *subs* instrument
instrument *subs* tool
instrumental *adj* instrumental
instrumentalist *adj*
   instrumentalist
insucces *subs* rebuff
insuficient *adj* insufficient
insuficient *adj* scanty
insuficienţă *subs* shortage
insuficienţă *subs* shortcoming
însufleţit *adj* vivid
insulă *subs* island
insulă *subs* isle
insular *adj* insular
insultă *subs* affront
insultă *subs* insult
insuportabil *adj* insupportable
insurecţie *subs* insurrection
însuşire *subs* appropriation
însutit *adj* centuple
intact *adj* intact
întâi *adv* first
întâlnire *subs* date
întâlnire *subs* meet
întâlnire neprevăzută *subs*
   encounter
întâmplare *subs* happening
întâmplare *subs* occurrence
întâmplare nefericită *subs*
   misadventure
întâmplător *adj* haphazard
întâmplător *adj* random
intangibil *adj* intangible
întâplător *adv.* accidental
înţărcare *subs.* ablactation
întărire *subs* reinforcement
întăritură *subs* tier
întârziat *adj* belated

întârziere *subs* retardation
integral *adj* integral
integral *adj* whole
integritate *subs* integrity
intelect *subs* intellect
intelectual *adj* intellectual
intelectual *subs* intellectual
intelectualitate *subs* intelligentsia
înțelegere *subs* comprehension
înțelepciune *subs* wisdom
înțelept *adj* oracular
înțelept *adj* sage
înțelept *adj* wise
inteligent *adj* apprehensive
inteligent *adj* intelligent
inteligent *adj* smart
inteligență *subs* intelligence
inteligibil *adj* intelligible
întemeietor *subs* founder
intendent *subs* steward
intens *adj* intense
intensitate *subs* intensity
intensiv *adj* intensive
intenție *subs* intent
intenție *subs* intention
intenționat *adj* deliberate
intenționat *adj* intentional
înțepătură *subs* barb
înțepătură *subs* puncture
înțepătură *subs* sting
interceptare *subs* interception
interdependent *adj*
   interdependent
interdependență *subs*
   interdependence
interdicție *subs* ban
interes *subs* interest
interesant *adj* interesting
interesat *adj* interested
interesat *adj* mercenary
interferență *subs* interference
interior *adj* inland

interior *subs* inside
interior *adj* interior
interior *subs* interior
interjecție *subs* interjection
interludiu *subs* interlude
intermediar *subs* intermediary
intermediar *adj* intermediate
intermediar *subs* jobber
interminabil *adj* interminable
intern *adj* indoor
intern *adj* inside
intern *adj* internal
intern *adj* inward
internațional *adj* international
interogație *subs* interrogation
interogativ *adj* interrogative
interogativ *subs* interrogative
interpret *subs* interpreter
intersecție *subs* intersection
intersecție *subs* junction
interval *subs* interval
interval de timp *subs* spell
intervenție *subs* intervention
interviu *subs* interview
interzicere *subs* prohibition
interzis *adj* taboo
intestin *subs* bowel
intestin *subs* intestine
intestinal *adj* intestinal
inticație *subs* indication
intim *adj* intimate
intim *adj* intrinsic
intimidare *subs* intimidation
intimitate *subs* intimacy
întindere *subs* extent
întindere *subs* lay
întindere *subs* stretch
întindere de pământ *subs* tract
întinerire *subs* rejuvenation
întins *adj* prone
întoarcere *subs* return
intolerabil *adj* intolerable

intolerant *adj* intolerant
intoleranţă *subs* intolerance
întortocheat *adj* tortuous
întotdeauna *adv* always
intoxicaţie *subs* intoxication
într-adevăr *adv* indeed
intranzitiv *adj* intransitive
intrare *subs* entrance
intrare *subs* entry
între *prep.* amongst
între *prep* between
între timp *adv* meanwhile
întrebare *subs* question
întrebare absurdă *subs* quiz
întredeschis *adj* ajar
întreg *adj* entire
întreprindere *subs* enterprise
întrerupere *subs.* abruption
întrerupere *subs* interruption
întrerupere *subs* stoppage
întreţinere *subs* upkeep
intrigă *subs* intrigue
întristare profundă *subs* distress
într-o privinţă oarecare *adv* aught
introducere *subs* introduction
introductiv *adj* introductory
introspecţie *subs* introspection
întrucât *conj* whereas
întrucâtva *adv* any
întruchipare *subs* embodiment
întrunire *subs* meeting
intuiţie *subs* intuition
intuitiv *adj* intuitive
întunecat *adj* dark
întunecat *adj* sombre
întunecos *adj* dim
întunecos *adj* gloomy
întuneric *subs* dark
întuneric *subs* gloom
inuman *adj* inhuman
inundaţie *subs* flood

inutil *adj* futile
inutil *adj* needless
inutil *adj* vain
invalid *adj* disabled
invalid *subs* invalid
învălmăşeală *subs* hubbub
învăţământ *subs* tuition
învăţat *adj* learned
învăţătură *subs* learning
invazie *subs* invasion
învecinat *adj* neighbourly
invectivă *subs* invective
învelitoare *subs* casing
învelitoare *subs* jade
învelitoare *subs* wrapper
inventator *subs* inventor
invenţie *subs* invention
inventiv *adj* inventive
inversare *subs* reversal
înverzit *adj* verdant
înveselire *subs* cheer
investigaţie *subs* investigation
investiţie *subs* investment
invidie *subs* envy
invidios *adj* envious
învingător *subs* victor
inviolabil *adj* inviolable
invitaţie *subs* invitation
invizibil *adj* invisible
invocare *subs* invocation
involuntar *adv* unwittingly
înzestrat *adj* gifted
iobag *subs* thrall
iobăgie *subs* thralldom
ioceanic *adj* oceanic
iotă *subs* jot
ipocrit *subs* hypocrite
ipocrizie *subs* hypocrisy
ipotecă *subs* mortgage
ipotent *adj* impotent
ipotenţă *subs* impotence
ipotetic *adj* hypothetical

ipoteză *subs* hypothesis
irascibil *adj* cross
iraţional *subs* irrational
irefutabil *adj* irrefutable
irelevant *adj* irrelevant
iresponsabil *adj* irresponsible
irigare *subs* irrigation
iritabil *adj* irritable
iritant *adj* irritant
iritant *subs* irritant
iritare *subs* irritation
irlandez *adj* Irish
Irlandeză *subs* Irish
ironic *adj* ironical
ironie *subs* irony
iscălitură *subs* subscription
iscusit *adj* argute
ispăşire *subs* atonement
isteric *adj* hysterical
isterie *subs* hysteria
istoric *subs* historian
istoric *adj* historic
istoric *adj* historical
istorie *subs* history
istorisire *subs* narration
italian *adj* Italian
Italiană *subs* Italian
italic *adj* italic
iubire *subs* love
iubit *adj* beloved
iubitor *adj* loving
iută *subs* jute
iuţeală *subs* velocity
iz *subs* smack
izbitură *subs* dash
izbucnire *subs* burst
izbucnire *subs* outburst
izgonire *subs* eviction
izolare *subs* insulation
izolare *subs* isolation
izolare *subs* seclusion
izolat *adj* secluded
izolator *subs* insulator

J

jachetă *subs* jacket
jad *subs* jail
jaf *subs* robbery
jaf *subs* spoil
jalnic *adj* rueful
jargon *subs* jargon
jargon *subs* slang
jartieră *subs* garter
jder *subs* marten
jeleu *subs* jelly
jerpelit *adj* threadbare
jerseu *subs* jersey
jignire *subs* offence
jignitor *adj* injurious
jignitor *subs* offender
joacă *subs* pleasantry
joc *subs* game
joc combinat *subs* interplay
joc de cuvinte *subs* pun
joc de noroc *subs* gamble
joi *subs* Thursday
jongler *subs* juggler
jos *adv* down
jos *subs* low
josnic *adj* sordid
jovial *adj* convivial
jovial *adj* jolly
jovial *adj* jovial
jovialitate *subs* joviality
jucărie *subs* toy
jucător *subs* gambler
jucător *subs* player
jucător de basebal *subs* batsman
judecată *subs* trial
judecată *subs* judge
judecată *subs* judgement
judecată sănătoasă *subs* sanity
judeţ *subs* county

judiciar *adj* judicial
jug *subs* yoke
jumătate *subs* half
jumulire *subs* pluck
junghi de durere *subs* pang
junglă *subs* jungle
junior *adj* junior
junior *subs* junior
jupon *subs* petticoat
jurământ *subs* oath
jurământ fals *subs* perjury
jurat *subs* juror
jurat *subs* juryman
jurați *subs* jury
jurisdicție *subs* jurisdiction
jurisprudență *subs* jurisprudence
jurist *subs* jurist
jurnal *subs* diary
jurnalism *subs* journalism
jurnalist *subs* journalist
just *adv* justly
justificabil *adj* justifiable
justificare *subs* justification
justiție *subs* justice
juvenil *adj* juvenile

L

la *prep* at
la bord *adv.* aboard
la care? *conj* whereat
la distanță *adv* aloof
la fel *adv* alike
la mal *adv* ashore
la modă *adj* fashionable
la nord *adv* north
la revedere *interj* bye-bye
la revedere *interj* good-bye
la sută *adv* per cent

la timp *adv* duly
la urmă *adv* ultimately
la vale *adv* downwards
la vest *adv* west
labă *subs* paw
laba piciorului *subs* foot
labial *adj* labial
labirint *subs* labyrinth
labirint *subs* maze
laborant *subs* analyst
laborator *subs* laboratory
lac *subs* lake
lacheu *subs* lackey
lacom *adj* avid
lacom *subs* glutton
lacom *adj* greedy
lacom *adj* voracious
lăcomie *subs* cupidity
lăcomie *subs* gluttony
lăcomie *subs* greed
laconic *adj* laconic
lacrimă *subs* tear
lactometru *subs* lactometer
lactoză *subs* lactose
lacună *subs* lacuna
lăcustă *subs* locust
lada *subs* lama
lagună *subs* lagoon
laic *adj* lay
laic *subs* layman
lamă *subs* blade
lămâie *subs* lemon
lămâie mică *subs* lime
lament *subs* lament
lamentabil *adj* lamentable
lamentare *subs* lamentation
lână *subs* fleece
lână *subs* wool
lână toarsă *subs* worsted
lânărie *subs* woollen
lance *subs* javelin
lance *subs* spear

lăncier *subs* lancer
lângă *prep* by
lângă *prep* nigh
lansare a unei nave *subs* launch
lanţ *subs* chain
lanternă *subs* lamp
lanţetă *adj* lancet
lăptărie *subs* dairy
lapte *subs* milk
lapte prins *subs* curd
larg *adj* large
larg *adj* wide
larg răspândit *adj* widespread
largheţe *subs* largesse
lărgime *subs* width
largul mării *subs* offing
laş *subs* coward
lasciv *adj* lascivious
laşitate *subs* cowardice
lat *adj* broad
laţ *subs* snare
latent *adj* latent
latitudine *subs* latitude
lătrat *subs* bark
latrină *subs* latrine
laudă *subs* boast
lăudabil *adj* laudable
lăudăros *subs* bouncer
lăudăroşenie *subs* brag
lăudăroşenie *subs* swagger
lăuntric *adj* inmost
laureat *subs* laureate
lavă *subs* lava
laxativ *subs* laxative
laxativ *adj* laxative
leagăn *subs* swing
lebădă *subs* swan
lectică *subs* palanquin
lecţie *subs* lesson
lectură *subs* lecture
legal *adj* legal
legalitate *subs* legality

legat *subs* bound
legatură *subs* relation
legătură *subs* bond
legătură *subs* faggot
legătură *subs* liaison
lege *subs* law
legendă *subs* legend
legendar *adj* legendary
legionar *subs* legionary
legislaţie *subs* legislation
legislativ *adj* legislative
legislator *subs* legislator
legislatură *subs* legislature
legitim *adj* legitimate
legitimitate *subs* legitimacy
legiune *subs* legion
legumă *subs* vegetable
lemn *subs* wood
lene *subs* laziness
leneş *subs* idler
leneş *subs* sluggard
leneş *subs* lazy
lenevire *subs* lounge
lengerie de spălat *subs* laundry
lenjerie de corp *subs* underwear
lent *adv* slowly
lentilă *subs* lens
leoaică *subs* lioness
leonin *adj* leonine
leopard *subs* leopard
lepră *subs* leprosy
lepros *subs* leper
lepros *adj* leprous
leşcăit *adj* lank
leşin *adj* faint
leşin *subs* swoon
lespede *subs* slab
letal *adj* lethal
letargic *adj* lethargic
letargie *subs* lethargy
leu *subs* lion
leucoplast *subs.* adhesive

levănţică *subs* lavender
lexicografie *subs* lexicography
liberal *adj* liberal
liberalism *subs* liberalism
liberalitate *subs* liberality
liber-profesionist *subs*
   practitioner
libertate *subs* freedom
libertate *subs* liberty
libertin *subs* libertine
libertin *adj* licentious
librar *subs* book-seller
librărie *subs* library
licărire *subs* flicker
licărire *subs* ray
licărire *subs* spark
licărire *subs* twinkle
licenţă *subs* licence
lichid *adj* liquid
lichid *subs* liquid
lichidare *subs* liquidation
licitant *subs* bidder
licitare *subs* bid
licitaţie *subs* auction
lider *subs* leader
ligă *subs* league
lignit *subs* lignite
liliac *subs* bat
liliac *subs* lily
limbă *subs* tongue
limba franceză *subs* French
limba spaniolă *subs* Spanish
limbaj *subs* language
limbaj *subs* parlance
liminos *adj* luminous
limită *subs* limit
limitare *subs* limitation
limitat *adj* limited
limitat *adj* scant
limonadă *subs* lemonade
limpede *adv* clearly
lingual *subs* linguist

lingură *subs* shovel
lingură *subs* spoon
lingură conţinut *subs* spoonful
linguşire *subs.* adulation
lingvistic *adj* linguistic
lingvistică *subs* linguistics
linie *subs* line
linişte *subs* calm
linişte *subs* quiet
liniştit *adj* peaceful
linte *subs* lentil
lipici *subs* glue
lipicios *adj* sticky
lipitoare *subs* leech
lipsă *subs* default
lipsă *subs* lack
lipsă *subs* want
lipsă de experienţă *subs*
   inexperience
lipsă de importanţă *subs*
   insignificance
lipsă de modestie *subs*
   immodesty
lipsit de *adj* devoid
lipsit de artă *adj* artless
lipsit de culoare *adj* lacklustre
lipsit de originalitate *adj*
   mechanical
lipsit de sens *adj* nonsensical
liră *subs* lyre
liră sterlină *subs* pond
liric *adj* lyric
liric *subs* lyric
liric *subs* lyrical
lişiţă *subs* coot
listă *subs* list
listă de decese *subs* obituary
liste *subs* lists
literar *adj* literary
literatură *subs* literature
litigiu *subs* litigant
litigiu *subs* litigation

litru *subs* litre
liturgic *adj* liturgical
livadă *subs* orchard
livrare *subs* delivery
livrea *subs* livery
lizibil *adj* legible
lizieră *subs* margin
lizieră a unei păduri *subs.pl*
   outskirts
lob de frunză *subs* lobe
loc *subs* lieu
loc *subs* place
loc al unei acţiuni *subs* locale
loc al unei plante *subs* habitat
loc de întâlnire *subs* haunt
loc de întâlnire *subs* rendezvous
loc de şedere *subs* sojourn
loc geometric *subs* locus
local *adj* local
localitate *subs* venue
locatar *subs* inmate
locaţie *subs* location
locomotivă *subs* locomotive
locotenent *subs* lieutenant
locţiitor *subs* proxy
locţiitor *subs* substitute
locuibil *adj* habitable
locuibil *adj* inhabitable
locuinţă *subs* dwelling
locuinţă *subs* lodging
locuitor *subs* inhabitant
locuţiune *subs* locution
logaritm *subs* logarithim
logic *adj* logical
logică *subs* logic
logician *subs* logician
logodnă *subs* betrothal
logodnă *subs* engagement
loial *adj* loyal
loialitate *subs* loyalty
longevitate *subs* longevity
longitudine *subs* longitude

lor *adj* their
loterie *subs* lottery
loţiune *subs* lotion
lotus *subs* lotus
lovitură *subs* bang
lovitură *subs* beat
lovitură *subs* hit
lovitură *subs* strike
lovitură *subs* stroke
lovitură cu biciul *subs* lash
lovitură cu piciorul *subs* kick
lovitură de cuţit *subs* stab
lovitură de pumn *subs* punch
lovitură de stat *subs* coup
lovitură uşoară *subs* tap
lozincă *subs* slogan
lubrifiant *adj* lubricant
lubrificare *subs* lubrication
lucernă *subs* lucerne
lucid *adj* lucid
luciditate *subs* lucidity
lucios *adj* glossy
luciu *subs* glaze
luciu *subs* gloss
luciu *subs* glow
lucrător *subs* workman
lucru *subs* thing
lucru de mântuială *subs* bungle
lucru dezgustător *subs* muck
lucru fără pereche *subs*
   nonpareil
lucru minunat *subs* marvel
lucru năprasnic *subs* sudden
lucru necesar *subs* requiste
lucru schimbat pe altul *subs*
   exchange
lumânare *subs* candle
lumânare de ceară *subs* taper
lume *subs* world
lumea interlopă *subs* underworld
lumesc *adj* mundane
lumesc *adj* worldly

lumină *subs* light
lumină orbitoare *subs* dazzle
lumină oxihidrică *subs* limelight
Lună *subs* moon
lună *subs* month
lună de miere *subs* honeymoon
lunar *adj* monthly
lunar *adv* monthly
lunatic *adj* lunatic
lung *adj* lengthy
lung *adj* long
lungime *subs* length
lunguieţ *adj* oblong
luni *subs* Monday
lup *subs* wolf
lupă *subs* loop
luptă *subs* combat1
luptă *subs* fight
luptă *subs* fray
lustră *subs* lustre
lustru *subs* polish
lut *subs* clay
lut *subs* lute
lux *subs* luxury
luxaţie *subs* sprain
luxos *adj* luxurious
luxuriant *adj* lush
luxuriant *adj* luxuriant

măcăit de raţă *subs* quack
măcel *subs* bloodshed
măcel *subs* slaughter
măcelar *subs* butcher
măceş *subs* hawthorn
maestru *subs* master
mâgar *subs* donkey
măgar *subs* ass

magazie *subs* bunker
magazie secretă *subs* cache
magazin *subs* shop
magazin de tricotaje *subs* hosiery
magherniţă *subs* stall
magic *adj* magical
magician *subs* magician
magistral *adj* magisterial
magistratură *subs* magistracy
magistratură *subs* magistrate
magnat *subs* magnate
magnet *subs* magnet
magnet natural *subs* loadstone
magnetc *adj* magnetic
magnetism *subs* magnetism
magnetofon *subs* recorder
magnific *adj* magnificent
magnitudine *subs* magnitude
mahala *subs* slum
mâhnire *subs* affliction
mâhnire *subs* mourning
mahon *subs* mahogany
mai *subs* maul
Mai *subs* May
mai ales *adv* most
mai bine *adv* better
mai bun *adj* better
mai curând *conj* before
mai degrabă *adv* rather
mai departe *adv* forth
mai departe *adv* further
mai jos *prep* below
mai jos *adv* beneath
mai mare *adj* elder
mai mic *adv* lesser
mai mic *adj* minor
mai mult *adj* further
mai mult *adj* more
mai mult/ă *adv* more
mai mulţi *adj* several
mai presus de *prep* beyond

mai puțin *adj* less
mai puțin *adv* less
mai târziu *adj* latter
maiestuos *adj* majestic
maimuță *subs* ape
maimuță *subs* monkey
mâine *subs* tomorrow
mâine *adv* tomorrow
maior *subs* major
maistru *subs* foreman
majestate *subs* majesty
major *adj* major
majoritate *subs* majority
majoritate *subs* mass
malarie *subs* ague
• **malarie** *subs* malaria
maleabil *adj* malleable
malign *adj* malign
malț *subs* malt
maltratare *subs* mal-treatment
mamă *subs* mamma
mamă *subs* mum
mamă *subs* mummy
mamă *subs* mother
mamar *adj* mammary
mamifer *subs* mammal
Mamon *subs* mammon
mămos *subs* motherlike
mamut *adj* mammoth
mână *subs* hand
mânăstire *subs.* abbey
mănăstire *subs* cloister
mănăstire *subs* convent
mănăstire *subs* monastery
mănăstire de călugărițe *subs*
   nunnery
mâncare *subs* food
mâncărime *subs* itch
mandat *subs* innings
mandat *subs* mandate
mandatar *subs* assignee
mandatorial *adj* mandatory

mando *subs* mango
mândrie *subs* pride
mândru *adj* proud
mânecă *subs* sleeve
manechin *subs* mannequin
mâner *subs* handle
mâner *subs* shaft
manevră *subs* manoeuvre
mângâiere *subs* endearment
mangan *subs* manganese
maniac *subs* maniac
mâniat *adj* irate
manichiură *subs* manicure
manie *subs* mania
mânie *subs* rage
manieră *subs* manner
manierat *adj* mannerly
manierism *subs* mannerism
manifest *subs* manifesto
manifestare *subs* manifestation
manipulare *subs* manipulation
manivelă *subs* winch
manșetă *subs* cuff
mantie *subs* cloak
mantie *subs* mantle
manual *subs* handbook
manual *adj* manual
manual carte *subs* manual
manufactură *subs* manufacture
mănunchi *subs* bunch
mănunchi *subs* wisp
mănușă *subs* glove
mănușă de armură *subs* gauntlet
manuscris *subs* manuscript
mănuși de box *subs* mitten
măr *subs* apple
maraton *subs* marathon
marcă *subs* brand
marcă *subs* mark
marcă *subs* make
marcaj *subs* hallmark
marcator *subs* marker

mare *adj* big
mare *subs* sea
maree *subs* tide
mareşal *subs* marshal
măreţ *adj* august
măreţ *adj* grand
măreţ *adj* great
marfă *subs* freight
marfă *subs* merchandise
marfă *subs* ware
margaretă *subs* daisy
margarină *subs* margarine
mărgea *subs* bead
marginal *adj* marginal
margine *subs* brim
margine *subs* brink
margine *subs* edge
margine *subs* verge
mârîială *subs* growl
mârîit *subs* snarl
mărime *subs* size
mărime de intrare *subs* input
marin *adj* marine
marinar *subs* sailor
mărinimie *subs* bounty
mărinimie *subs* magnanimity
mărinimos *adj* magnanimous
marionetă *subs* puppet
marionetă *subs* marionette
mărire *subs* augmentation
mărire *subs* rise
marital *adj* marital
maritim *adj* maritime
marmeladă *subs* marmalade
marmură *subs* marble
marnă *subs* marl
maron *subs* brown
marş *subs* march
mârşav *adj* despicable
Marte *subs* Mars
marţial *adj* martial
martie *subs* march

martir *subs* martyr
martiriu *subs* martyrdom
martor *subs* witness
mărturie *subs* evidence
mărturie *subs* testimony
mărturisire *subs* confession
mărunt *adj* petty
măruntaie *subs* entrails
masă *subs* gross
masă *adj* meal
masă *subs* table
masacru *subs* massacre
masaj *subs* massage
mască *subs* mask
mascaradă *subs* masquerade
măscărici *subs* zany
mascotă *subs* mascot
mascul *subs* male
masculin *adj* masculine
maseor *subs* masseur
maşină de gătit *subs* cooker
maşină de pisat *subs* grinder
masiv *adj* massive
măslină *subs* olive
măsură *subs* measure
măsură preliminară *subs*
   preliminary
măsurabil *adj* measurable
măsură-standard *subs* gauge
măsurătoare *subs* measurement
matador *subs* matador
mătănii *subs* rosary
mătase *subs* silk
mătăsos *adj* silken
mătăsos *adj* silky
matematic *adj* mathematical
matematică *subs* mathematics
matematician *subs*
   mathematician
material *adj* material
materialism *subs* materialism
materie *subs* material

matern *adj* maternal
maternitate *subs* maternity
maternitate *subs* motherhood
matineu *subs* matinee
mătreață *subs* dandruff
matricid *subs* matricide
matrimonial *adj* matrimonial
matriță *subs* matrix
matriță *subs* mould
matroană *subs* matron
matroz *subs* mariner
matroz *subs* mat
matur *adj* mature
mătură *subs* broom
măturat *subs* sweep
măturătoare mecanică *subs* sweeper
măturător de stradă *subs* scavenger
maturitate *subs* maturity
mătușă *subs* aunt
mausoleu *subs* mausoleum
maxilar *subs* jaw
maxilar *subs* maxilla
maximă *subs* dictum
maximă *subs* maxim
maximă *adj* maximum
mazăre *subs* pea
mâzgălitură *subs* scribble
mâzgălitură *subs* smear
mecanic *subs* mechanic
mecanic *adj* mechanic
mecanică *subs* mechanics
mecanism *subs* mechanism
medalie *subs* medal
medalion *subs* locket
mediație *subs* mediation
mediator *subs* mediator
medic *subs* physician
medical *adj* medical
medicament *subs* drug
medicament *subs* medicament

medicament *subs* medicine
medicament *subs* physic
medicinal *adj* medicinal
medie *subs* average
mediere *subs* mediation
medieval *adj* medieval
mediocritate *subs* mediocrity
mediocru *adj* mediocre
mediocru *adj* middling
meditator *subs* tutor
mediu *adj* average
mediu *subs* environment
mediu *subs* medium
megafon *subs* megaphone
megalit *subs* megalith
mei *subs* millet
melancolic *adj* melancholic
melancolic *adj* melancholy
melancolie *subs* melancholia
melancolie *subs* melancholy
melasă *subs* molasses
melc *subs* snail
melodie *subs* melody
melodie *subs* tune
melodios *a* melodious
melodrama *subs* melodrama
melodramatic *adj* melodramatic
membrană *subs* membrane
membrană *subs* web
membru *subs* member
membru al unui partid *subs* stalwart
membru din stânga *subs* leftist
memento *subs* memento
memento *subs* reminder
memorabil *adj* memorable
memorandum *subs* memorandum
memorial *subs* memorial
memorial *adj* memorial
memoriu *subs* memoir
meningită *subs* meningitis

meniu *subs* menu
menopauză *subs* menopause
menstrual *adj* menstrual
menstruaţie *subs* menstruation
mentă *subs* mint
mentalitate *subs* mentality
menţinere *subs* maintenance
menţiune *subs* mention
mentor *subs* mentor
mercenar *subs* hireling
mercur *subs* mercury
meridian *adj* meridian
merit *subs* merit
merit *subs* worth
meritoriu *a* meritorious
mers *subs* gait
mers *subs* walk
mers târşât *subs* shuffle
mesager *subs* messenger
mesaj *subs* message
meschin *adj* mean
meschinărie *subs* meanness
meserie *subs* handicraft
mesia *subs* messiah
mesteacăn *subs* birch
meşteşug *subs* craft
meşteşugar *subs* artisan
meşteşugar *subs* craftsman
metabolism *subs* metabolism
metafizic *adj* metaphysical
metafizică *subs* metaphysics
metaforă *subs* metaphor
metal *subs* metal
metalic *adj* metallic
metalurgie *subs* metallurgy
metamorfoză *subs* metamorphosis
meteor *subs* meteor
meteoric *adj* meteoric
meteorog *subs* meteorologist
meteorologie *subs* meteorology
meterez *subs* rampart

metodă *subs* method
metodic *adj* methodical
metric *adj* metric
metric *adj* metrical
metropolă *subs* metropolis
metropolitan *adj* metropolitan
metropolitan *subs* metropolitan
metroul *subs* tube
metru *subs* metre
meu *adj* my
mezalianţă *subs* misalliance
mezanin *subs* mezzanine
mezin *subs* cadet
mic *adj* little
mic *adj* small
mic dejun *subs* breakfast
mică *subs* mica
mică nobilime *subs* gentry
microfilm *subs* microfilm
microfon *subs* microphone
micrometru *subs* micrometer
microscop *subs* microscope
microscopic *adj* microscopic
mie *subs* thousand
mie *adj* thousand
miel *subs* lamb
mieluşel *subs* lambkin
miercuri *subs* Wednesday
miere *subs* honey
miez *subs* core
miezul nopţii *subs* midnight
migdală *subs* almond
migraţiune *subs* migration
migrator *subs* migrant
migrenă *subs* migraine
mii şi mii *subs* myriad
mijloc *subs* middle
mijloc *subs* midst
mijloc al verii *subs* midsummer
mijlocitor *subs* middleman
mijlociu *adj* medium
mijlociu *adj* mid

mijlociu *adj* middle
mijlocul ţării *subs* midland
milă *subs* mile
milă *subs* mercy
mileniu *subs* millennium
miliard *subs* billion
milion *subs* million
milionar *subs* millionaire
militant *adj* militant
militant *subs* militant
militar *adj* military
militarii *subs* military
milos *adj* merciful
mim *subs* mime
mină *subs* mine
minaret *subs* minaret
mincinos *subs* liar
minciună *subs* lie
miner *subs* miner
miner *subs* pitman
mineral *subs* mineral
mineral *adj* mineral
mineralogie *subs* mineralogy
minereu *subs* ore
minge *subs* ball
minge cu pene *subs* shuttlecock
miniatură *subs* midget
miniatură *subs* miniature
minim *adj* minimal
minimal *adj* minimum
minister *subs* ministry
ministru *subs* minister
minm *subs* minimum
minor *subs* infant
minor *subs* minor
minorat *subs* infancy
minorotate *subs* minority
mintal *adj* mental
minte *subs* mind
minunat *adj* wonderful
minune *subs* wonder
minus *prep* minus

minuscul *adj* minuscule
minuscul *adj* tiny
minut *subs* minute
minuţios *adj* minute
miop *adj* myopic
miopie *subs* myopia
miracol *subs* miracle
miraculos *adj* miraculous
miraj *subs* mirage
mire *subs* bridegroom
mire *subs* groom
mireasă *subs* bride
mireasmă *subs* scent
miriapod *subs* centipede
mirişte *subs* stubble
mironosiţă *subs* prude
miros *subs* smell
mirt *subs* myrtle
mişcare *subs* move
mişcare *subs* movement
mişcare ritmică *subs* pulse
mişcător *adj* movable
misionar *subs* missionary
misiune *subs* mission
mister *subs* mystery
misterios *adj* mysterious
misterios *adj* uncanny
mistic *adj* mystic
mistic *subs* mystic
misticism *subs* mysticism
mistrie *subs* trowel
mit *subs* myth
mită *subs* bribe
mitic *adj* mythical
mitologic *adj* mythological
mitologie *subs* mythology
mitră de episcop *subs* mitre
miză *subs* stake
mizantrop *subs* misanthrope
mlădios *subs* limber
mlădiţă *subs* offshoot
mlaştină *subs* bog

mlaştină *subs* moss
mlaştină *subs* slough
mlaştină *subs* swamp
mlăştinos *adj* marshy
moale *subs* soft
moară *subs* mill
moară de vânt *subs* windmill
moarte *subs* death
moaşă *subs* midwife
moaşte *subs* relic
moaşte *subs* shrine
mobil *adj* mobile
mobil prim *subs* mover
mobilă *subs* furniture
mobilitate *subs* mobility
mocirlă *subs* mire
mocirlă *subs* slime
mod *subs* mode
modă *subs* fashion
modalitate *subs* modality
model *subs* model
model de virtute *subs* paragon
moderat *adj* considerate
moderat *adj* moderate
moderaţie *subs* moderation
modern *adj* modern
modernitate *subs* modernity
modest *adj* modest
modestie *subs* humility
modestie *subs* modesty
modificare *subs* modification
modistă *subs* milliner
moft *subs* whim
molar *subs* molar
molar *adj* molar
molâu *subs* laggard
moleculă *subs* molecule
molecular *adj* molecular
molestare *subs* molestation
molie *subs* mite
molimă *subs* pestilence
moloz *subs* rubble

momeală *subs* bait
momeală *subs* lure
moment *subs* moment
moment de linişte *subs* lull
momentan *adj* momentary
monarh *subs* monarch
monarhie *subs* monarchy
monedă *subs* coin
monedă div. engleză *subs* penny
monedă engleză *subs* sterling
monedă englezească *subs*
   shilling
monetar *adj* monetary
monetărie *subs* mint
monitor *subs* monitor
monoclu *subs* monocle
monocrom *adj* monochromatic
monodie *subs* monody
monogamie *subs* monogamy
monografie *subs* monograph
monogramă *subs* monogram
monolit *subs* monolith
monolog *subs* monologue
monopol *subs* monopoly
monopolist *subs* monopolist
monosilabă *subs* monosyllable
monosilabic *adj* monosyllabic
monoteism *subs* monotheism
monoton *adj* humdrum
monoton *adj* inanimate
monoton *adj* monotonous
monotonie *subs* monotony
monstru *subs* monster
monstruos *subs* mammoth
monstruos *adj* monstrous
montură *subs* mount
monument *subs* monument
monumental *adj* monumental
moral *adj* moral
moral al unei armate *subs*
   morale
morală *subs* moral

moralist *subs* moralist
moralitate *subs* morality
morar *subs* miller
morbid *adj* morbid
morbiditate *subs* morbidity
morcov *subs* carrot
morgă *subs* morgue
morgă *subs* mortuary
morganatic *adj* morganatic
morman *subs* heap
mormânt *subs* grave
mormânt *subs* sepulchre
morocănos *adj* sullen
morsă *subs* walrus
mort *adj* dead
mortal *adj* deadly
mortal *adj* mortal
mortalitate *subs* mortality
mosc *subs* musk
moschee *subs* mosque
moscovit *subs* muscovite
moşie *subs* estate
moşie *subs* manor
moştenire *subs* heritage
moştenire *subs* inheritance
moştenitor *subs* heir
mostră *subs* sample
moţăială *subs* doze
moţăială *subs* nap
moţăială *subs* nap
motiv *subs* motive
motivaţie *subs* motivation
motor *subs* motor
motor de maşină *subs* engine
motrice *subs* momentum
movilă *subs* mound
mozaic *subs* mosaic
mreajă *subs* toil
mucegai *subs* mildew
mucegai *subs* mould
mucegăială *subs* must
mucegăit *adj* mouldy

mucegăit *adj* musty
muchie *subs* ridge
mucilaginos *adj* mucous
mucozitate *subs* mucus
mugur *subs* bud
mulatru *subs* mulatto
mult *adj* much
mulţi *adj* many
multiform *subs* multiform
multilateral *adj* multilateral
mulţime *subs* crowd
mulţime *subs* lot
mulţime *subs* swarm
multiplicare *subs* multiplication
multiplu *adj* multifarious
multiplu *adj* multiple
multiplu *subs* multiple
multitudine *subs* multitude
mulţumire *subs* content
mulţumire *subs* thanks
mulţumit *adj* content
mulţumit de sine *adj* complacent
mumie *subs* mummy
muncă *subs* work
muncă excesivă *subs* overwork
muncă manuală *subs* handiwork
muncă suplimentară *subs* overtime
muncitor *subs* worker
municipal *adj* municipal
municipalitate *subs* municipality
muniţie *subs* ammunition
munte *subs* mountain
muntean *subs* mountaineer
muntos *adj* mountainous
murătură *subs* pickle
murdar *adj* dirty
murdar *adj* filthy
murdar *adj* foul
murdar *adj* rank
murdar *adj* squalid
murdărie *subs* dirt

murdărie *subs* filth
murdărie *subs* mess
muribund *adj* moribund
muritor *subs* mortal
musafir *subs* guest
muscă *subs* fly
mușcătură *subs* bite
muschetă *subs* musket
mușchetar *subs* musketeer
mușchi *subs* muscle
mușchi de vită *subs* loin
muscular *adj* muscular
muselină *subs* muslin
muson *subs* monsoon
must *subs* must
muștar *subs* mustard
mustață *subs* moustache
mustață *subs* mustache
mustrare *subs.* admonition
mustrare *subs* rebuke
mustrare *subs* reprimand
mut *subs* mute
mut *subs* mute
mutație *subs* mutation
mutativ *adj* mutative
mutilare *subs* mutilation
muză *subs* muse
muzeu *subs* museum
muzică *subs* music
muzical *adj* musical
muzician *subs* musician

nabil *adj* notable
nadir *subs* nadir
nail *subs* nail
nailon *subs* nylon
naiv *adj* naive

naivitate *subs* naivety
nămol *subs* silt
nap turcesc *subs* turnip
nară *subs* nostril
narativ *adj* narrative
narator *subs* narrator
narcisă galbenă *subs* daffodil
narcisism *subs* narcissism
narcisist *subs* narcissus
narcotic *subs* narcotic
narcoz *subs* narcosis
nas *subs* nose
născocire *subs* concoction
născocire *subs* fabrication
născocire *subs* figment
naștere *subs* birth
naștere *subs* nativity
nasture *subs* button
natal *adj* natal
nătâng *subs* blockhead
nătâng *subs* dunce
nătărău *subs* simpleton
naționaism *subs* nationalism
național *adj* national
naționalist *subs* nationalist
naționalitate *subs* nationality
naționalizare *subs* nationalization
națiune *subs* nation
nativ *adj* native
nativ *subs* native
natură *subs* nature
natural *adj* natural
naturalist *subs* naturalist
nautic *adj* nautic(al)
navă *subs* nave
naval *adj* naval
năvalnic *adj* rash
navigabil *adj* navigable
navigare *subs* navigation
navigator *subs* navigator
năvod *subs* net
nazal *adj* nasal

năzbâtie *subs* lunacy
neam *subs* ancestry
neam *subs* kin
neâncetat *adj* ceaseless
neâncetat *adj* continuous
neâncredere *subs* mistrust
neândemânatic *adj* maladroit
neândemânatic *adj* ungainly
neândestulător *adj* scarce
neândurător *adj* pitiless
neânfricat *adj* dauntless
neânsemnat *adj* puny
neânțelegere *subs* misunderstanding
neânțelegere *subs* quarrel
neântemeiat *adj* baseless
neascultător *adj* mischievous
neascultător *adj* naughty
neasemănător *adj* unlike
neatent *adj* inattentive
neatent *adj* inauspicious
neatent *adj* unaware
neatent la *adj* mindless
nebun *adj* crazy
nebun *adj* insane
nebunesc *adj* frantic
necăjire *subs* vexation
necaz *subs* grief
necaz *subs* sorrow
necaz *v.i* sorrow
necesar *subs* necessary
necesar *adj* necessary
necesar *adj* needful
necesitate *subs* necessity
nechezat *subs* neigh
nechibzuit *adj* injudicious
necinste *subs* dishonesty
necinstit *adj* dishonest
necinstit *adj* fraudulent
neciteț *adj* illegible
necivilizat *adj* savage
necivilizat *adj* uncouth

neclintit *adj* steady
necromant *subs* necromancer
necropol *subs* necropolis
nectar *subs* nectar
necuviință *subs* impropriety
nedefinit *adj* indefinite
nedemn de încredere *adj* unreliable
nedisciplinat *adj* insubordinate
nedrept *adj* unfair
nedrept *adj* unjust
nedrept *adj* wrongful
nedreptate *subs* injustice
nedreptate *subs* mischief
nefericit *adj* unhappy
nefericit *adj* wretched
neg *subs* wart
negare *subs* denial
negație *subs* negation
negativ *adj* minus
negativ *adj* negative
neglijabil *adj* negligible
neglijare *subs* neglect
neglijare *subs* omission
neglijent *adj* careless
neglijent *adj* negligent
neglijență *subs* negligence
neglijență a unui medic *subs* malpractice
negociabil *adj* negotiable
negociator *subs* negotiator
negociere *subs* nagotiation
negresă *subs* negress
negru *adj* black
negru *subs* negro
neguros *adj* misty
negustor *subs* dealer
negustor *subs* monger
negustor ambulant *subs* hawker
negustoresc *adj* mercantile
nehotărâre *subs* indecision
nehotărât *adj* pending

neîncredere *subs* distrust
nelalocul lui *adv* amiss
nelegat *subs* loose
nelegitim *adj* bastard
nelegitim *adj* illegitimate
nelinişte *subs* anxiety
nelinişte *subs* discomfort
nelinişte *subs* disquiet
nelinişte *subs* fret
neliniştit *adj* anxious
neloial *adj* disloyal
nemanierat *adj* unmannerly
nemăsurat *adj* immeasurable
nemernic *adj* nefarious
nemernic *subs* villain
nemilos *adj* cruel
nemilos *adj* merciless
nemişcare *subs* inaction
nemişcare *subs* stillness
nemişcat *adj* immovable
nemişcat *adj* still
nemulţumire *subs* discontent
nemulţumire *subs* displeasure
nemulţumire *subs* dissatisfaction
nemulţumire *subs* malcontent
nemulţumit *adj* malcontent
nenoricit *subs* jerk
nenoroc *subs* misfortune
nenorocire *subs* bereavement
nenorocire *subs* woe
nenorocit *adj.* abject
nenorocit *adj* baleful
nenumărat *adj* countless
nenumărat *adj* innumerable
nenumărat *adj* myriad
neolitic *adj* neolithic
neon *subs* neon
neorânduială *subs* misrule
neospitalier *adj* inhospitable
nepăsare *subs* nonchalance
nepăsător *adj* reckless
nepătat *adj* stainless

nepieritor *adj* imperishable
nepoată *subs* niece
nepoliteţe *subs* disrespect
nepoliticos *adj* discourteous
nepoliticos *adj* impolite
nepot *subs* nephew
nepotism *subs* nepotism
nepotrivit *adj* improper
neprevăzut *adj* snap
Neptun *subs* Neptune
neputincios *adj* helpless
nerăbdare *subs* impatience
nerăbdător *adj* impatient
nerecunoscător *adj* thankless
nerecunoştinţă *subs* ingratitude
neregularitate *subs* irregularity
neregulat *adj* irregular
neruşinare *subs* brass
neruşinat *adj* lewd
neruşinat *adj* shameless
nerv *subs* Nerve
nervos *adj* nervous
neşansă *subs* mischance
nesătul *adj* insatiable
nesemnificativ *adj* insignificant
nesemnificativ *adj* meaningless
neseriozitate *subs* flippancy
nesigur *adj* insecure
nesigur *adj* uncertain
nesiguranţă *subs* insecurity
nesincer *adj* insincere
nesinceritate *subs* insincerity
nesocotire *subs* disregard
nesocotit *adj* inconsiderate
nestemată *subs* gem
nesupus *adj* unruly
net *adj* net
neted *adj* smooth
netrebnic *subs* sneak
neurolog *subs* neurologist
neurologie *subs* neurology
neutron *subs* neutron

neutru *subs* neuter

neutru *adj* neuter

nevoiaş *adj* needy

nevoie *subs* need

nevroză *subs* neurosis

nicăieri *adv* nowhere

nichel *subs* nickel

nici *conj* neither

nici un *adj* no

nici unul dintre *pron* none

nicidecum *adv* nothing

niciodata *adv* never

nicotină *subs* nicotine

nicovală *subs* anvil

nimb *subs* nimbus

nimeni *pron* nobody

nimfă *subs* nymph

nimic *subs* nil

nimic *subs* nothing

nimicire *subs* annihilation

nişă *subs* niche

nişă *subs* recess

nisip *subs* sand

nisip mişcător *subs* quicksand

nisipos *adj* sandy

nit *subs* rivet

nivel *subs* level

nivelat *adj* level

noapte *subs* night

noapte a zilei de azi *subs* to-night

nobil *adj* noble

nobil *subs* noble

nobleţe *subs* nobility

nociv *adj* noxious

nocturn *adj* nocturnal

nod *subs* knot

nod *subs* node

nod *subs* tangle

noiembrie *subs* november

nomad *subs* nomad

nomadic *adj* nomadic

nomenclatură *subs* nomenclature

nominal *adj* nominal

nominalizare *subs* nomination

nominalizat *subs* nominee

nonexistenţă *subs* nonentity

nor *subs* cloud

nord *subs* north

nordic *adj* north

nordic *adj* northern

normă *subs* norm

normal *adj* normal

normalitate *subs* normalcy

noroc *subs* luck

noroc neprevăzut *subs* godsend

norocos *adj* fortunate

norocos *adj* lucky

noroi *subs* mud

nostalgie *subs* nostalgia

nostim *subs* funny

nostru *adj* our

notă de plată *subs* bill

notar *subs* notary

notaţie *subs* notation

notificare *subs* notification

notiţă *subs* note

noţiune *subs* notion

noţiune de bază *subs* primer

notorietate *subs* notoriety

notoriu *adj* arrant

notoriu *adj* notorious

nou *adj* new

nouăsprezece nineteen

nouăzeci *subs* ninety

noutăţi *subs* tidings

novice *adj* callow

novice *subs* novice

ntreţinere automobile *subs* service

nu *adv* no

nu *subs* no

nu *adv* not

nu ca *prep* unlike

nu numai *adv* nay

nu prea tare *adj* mild
nuanţă *subs* nuance
nuanţă *subs* tinge
nubil *adj* nubile
nuc *subs* nut
nuc *subs* walnut
nucă de cocos *subs* coconut
nuclear *adj* nuclear
nucleu *subs* nucleus
nud *subs* nude`
nuia de salcie *subs* withe
nul *subs* nought
nul *adj* null
numai *adv* just
numai *conj* only
numai să nu *conj* lest
numaidecât *adv* needs
numaidecât *adv* presently
număr *subs* number
număr de rânduri *subs* lineage
numărător *subs* numerator
numărul nouă *subs* nine
nume *subs* name
nume de familie *subs* surname
nume de fată *subs* maiden
numeral *subs* numeral
numeric *adj* numerical
numeros *adj* numerous
nuntă *subs* wedding
nupţial *adj* nuptial
nupţiale *subs* nuptials
nurcă *subs* mink
nutreţ *subs* fodder
nutriţie *subs* nutrition
nutritiv *adj* nutritive
nuvelă *subs* narrative
nuvelă *subs* novelette

O

o dată *adv* once
o mie *subs* chiliad
o persoană oarecare *pron* one
o personalitate *subs* somebody
oacheş *adj* swarthy
oaie *subs* ewe
oaie *subs* sheep
oală de pământ *subs* pitcher
oameni de rând *subs* people
oarecum *adv* somewhat
oază *subs* oasis
obadă *subs* rim
obezitate *subs* obesity
obicei *subs* custom
obicei *subs* habit
obiect *subs* object
obiectant *adj* objectionable
obiecţie *subs* objection
obiecţie *subs* stricture
obiectiv *subs* objective
obiectiv *adj* objective
obişnuit *adj* customary
obişnuit *adj* ordinary
obişnuit *adj* usual
obişnuit *adj* wonted
obişnuit cu *adj.* accustomed
oblibatoriu *adj* incumbent
oblic *adj* oblique
obligaţie *subs* obligation
obligaţie *subs* onus
obligatoriu *adj* compulsory
obligatoriu *adj* obligatory
oblon *subs* shutter
oboseală *subs* fatigue
obositor *adj* tiresome
obositor *adj* weary
obraz *subs* cheek
obraznic *adj* contemptuous

obscen *adj* nasty
obscen *adj* obscene
obscenitate *subs* obscenity
obscur *adj* obscure
obscuritate *subs* obscurity
observație *subs* observation
observator *subs* observatory
obsesie *subs* obsession
obstacol *subs* drag
obstacol *subs* hindrance
obstacol *subs* hurdle1
obstacol *subs* obstacle
obstrucție *subs* obstruction
obstructiv *adj* obstructive
obtuz *adj* obtuse
ocazie *subs* occasion
ocazional *adj* occasional
ocazional *adv* occasionally
occident *subs* occident
occidental *adj* occidental
occidental *adj* western
ocean *subs* ocean
ochi *subs* eye
ochi de geam *subs* pane
ochiul boului *subs* bull's eye
ocol *subs* bypass
ocrotitor *subs* protector
octagon *subs* octagon
octagonal *adj* octangular
octavă *subs* octave
octombrie *subs* October
ocular *adj* ocular
oculist *subs* oculist
ocult *adj* occult
ocupant *subs* occupant
ocupat *adj* busy
ocupație *subs* occupancy
ocupație *subs* occupation
ocupație *subs* trader
odă *subs* ode
odihnă *subs* rest
odios *adj* odious

odor *subs* odour
ofensă *subs* outrage
ofensă *subs* offensive
ofensiv *adj* offensive
ofertă *subs* offer
oficial *adj* official
oficial *subs* official
oficial *adv* officially
oficiant *subs* ministrant
oficiu poștal *subs* post-office
ofițer *subs* officer
ofradă *subs* oblation
ofrandă *subs* offering
ogar *subs* greyhound
oglindă *subs* mirror
olar *subs* potter
olărie *subs* pottery
olărit *subs* crockery
oligarhie *subs* oligarchy
olimpiadă *subs* olympiad
om cheltuitor *subs* spendthrift
om cu comportare bună *subs* trusty
om de rând *subs* commoner
om de rasă neagră *subs* nigger
om de stat *subs* statesman
om de știință *subs* scientist
om lingușitor *subs* spaniel
om plăpând *subs* weakling
om străin *subs* stranger
omagiu *subs* homage
omagiu *subs* obeisance
omega *subs* omega
omenesc *adj* manlike
omenire *subs* mankind
omidă *subs* caterpillar
omitere *subs* hop
omitere *subs* skip
omletă *subs* omelette
omniprezent *adj* omnipresent
omniprezență *subs* omnipresence
omogen *adj* homogeneous

omolog *subs* counterpart
omonim *subs* namesake
omor *subs* murder
omucidere *subs* homicide
ondulare *subs* undulation
oneros *adj* onerous
onoare *subs* honour
onorabil *adj* honourable
onorariu *subs* honorarium
opac *adj* opaque
opacitate *subs* opacity
opal *subs* opal
operă *subs* opera
operaţie *subs* operation
operativ *adj* operative
operator *subs* operator
opiu *subs* opium
oponent *subs* opponent
oportun *adj* expedient
oportun *adj* opportune
oportunism *subs* opportunism
oportunitate *subs* opportunity
opoziţie *subs* opposition
opresion *subs* oppression
opresiv *adj* oppressive
opresor *subs* oppressor
oprire *subs* stand
oprire *subs* stop
opt *subs* eight
optic *adj* optic
optician *subs* optician
optim *adj* optimum
optimism *subs* optimism
optimism *subs* optimist
optimist *adj* optimistic
opţional *adj* optional
opţiune *subs* option
optsprezece *adj* eighteen
optzeci *subs* eighty
opus *adj* opposite
oră *subs* hour
ora de culcare *adj* bed-time

orăcăit *subs* croak
oracol *subs* oracle
oral *adj* oral
oral *adv* orally
orar *subs* schedule
oraş *subs* city
oraş *subs* town
orator *subs* orator
oratoric *adj* oratorical
orb *adj* blind
orbire *subs* blindness
orbită *subs* orb
orbită *subs* orbit
orchestră *subs* orchestra
orchestral *adj* orchestral
ordin *subs* injunction
ordin *adj* order
ordinar *adv* ordinarily
ordinar *adj* shabby
ordine *subs* tidiness
ordonanţă *subs* orderly
ordonanţă *subs* ruling
ordonat *adj* orderly
ordonat *adj* tidy
oreion *subs* mumps
orez *subs* rice
orez nedecorticat *subs* paddy
orfan *subs* orphan
orfelinat *subs* orphanage
organ *subs* organ
organ rudimentar *subs* rudiment
organic *adj* organic
organism *subs* organism
organizare socială *subs* polity
organizaţie *subs* guild
organizaţie *subs* organization
oribil *adj* horrible
oricând *adv. Conj* whenever
oricare *pron* whichever
oricare *adj* either
orice *adj* any
orice *pron* whatever

oricine *pron* whoever
oricum *adv* anyhow
oricum *adv* however
orient *subs* orient
oriental *adj* oriental
oriental *subs* oriental
orificiu *subs* aperture
original *adj* original
original *subs* original
originalitate *subs* oddity
originalitate *subs* originality
origine *subs* origin
oriunde *adv* wherever
orizont *subs* horizon
ornament *subs* ornament
ornamental *adj* ornamental
ornamentație *subs* ornamentation
oroare *subs* horror
ortodox *adj* orthodox
ortodoxie *subs* orthodoxy
orz *subs* barley
os *subs* bone
os de balenă *subs* baleen
osânză topită *subs* lard
oscilație *subs* oscillation
osie *subs* axle
ospăț *subs* feast
ospătar *subs* waiter
ospătăriț *subs* waitress
ospitalier *adj* hospitable
ospitalitate *subs* hospitality
ostatec *subs* hostage
ostil *adj* hostile
ostilitate *subs* hostility
ostilități *subs* warfare
oțel *subs* steel
oțet *subs* vinegar
oțet din bere *subs* alegar
otravă *subs* poison
otrăvitor *adj* poisonous
ou *subs* egg
oval *adj* oval

oval *subs* oval
ovar *subs* ovary
ovație *subs* ovation
ovăz *subs* oat
oxigen *subs* oxygen

P

păceală *subs* hoax
păcat *subs* pity
păcat *subs* sin
păcătos *adj* sinful
păcătos *subs* sinner
păcătos *adj* sinuous
pace *subs* peace
pachet *subs* pack
pachet *subs* packet
pacient *subs* patient
pacoste *subs* blight
pact *subs* covenant
pact *subs* pact
păcură *subs* pitch
padelă *subs* paddle
păduche *subs* louse
pădurar *subs* forester
pădurar *subs* ranger
pădure *subs* forest
pădure *subs* woods
pagină *subs* page
pagodă *subs* pagoda
pagubă *subs* damage
pagubă *subs* nuisance
pahar *subs* glass
pahar mare *subs* tumbler
pai *subs* straw
păianjen *subs* spider
pâine *subs* bread
pâine întreagă *subs* loaf
pâine prăjită *subs* toast

paisprezece *subs* fourteen
pajişte *subs* lawn
pălărie *subs* hat
palat *subs* palace
palatal *adj* palatal
paletă *subs* palette
palid *adj* ghastly
palid *adj* pale
palid *adj* wan
palmă *subs* palm
palmă *subs* slap
palmă *subs* smack
palpabil *adj* palpable
pâlpâire *subs* flare
palpitaţie *subs* palpitation
palpitaţie *subs* throb
pământ *subs* earth
pământ *subs* land
pământ *subs* soil
pământ afânat *subs* mould
pământ nelucrat *subs* fallow
pământ sterp *subs* barren
pământesc *adj* earthly
pămătuf *subs* whisk
pamflet *subs* lampoon
pamflet *subs* pamphlet
pamflet *subs* tract
pamfletar *subs* pamphleteer
pană *subs* feather
pană *subs* wedge
până acum *adv* hitherto
până când să *conj* till
până când să *conj* until
până la *prep* till
până la *prep* until
până la *prep* pending
panaceu *subs* panacea
pândă *subs* watch
panglică *subs* lace
panică *subs* panic
panică *subs* stampede
panoramă *subs* panorama

panou *subs* panel
pantă *subs* slant
pantă *subs* tilt
pantaloni *subs* trousers
pantaloni bufanţi *subs* breeches
pântece *subs* womb
panteism *subs* pantheism
panteist *subs* pantheist
panteră *subs* panther
pantof *subs* shoe
pantomimă *subs* pantomime
pânză *subs* canvas
pânză de in *subs* linen
pânză de păianjen *subs* cobweb
păpădie *subs* dandelion
papagal *subs* parrot
papal *adj* papal
papetărie *subs* stationery
papuc *subs* slipper
papură *subs* rush
păpuşă *subs* doll
păr *subs* hair
păr des *subs* thatch
para *subs* mite
pară *subs* pear
parabolă *subs* parable
paradă *subs* parade
paradis *subs* paradise
paradox *subs* antinomy
paradox *subs* paradox
paradoxal *adj* paradoxical
parafină *subs* paraffin
parafrază *subs* paraphrase
paragraf *subs* paragraph
paralel *adj* parallel
paralelism *subs* parallelism
paralelogram *subs* parallelogram
paralitic *adj* paralytic
paralizie *subs* palsy
paralizie *subs* paralysis
paranteză *subs* parenthesis
parare *subs* parry

părăsit *adj* forlorn
paraşută *subs* parachute
paraşutist *subs* parachutist
pârâu *subs* creek
parazit *subs* parasite
parazit *subs* pest
parazit *subs* sycophant
paraziţi atmosferici *subs* static
parc *subs* park
parcelă *subs* parcel
parcelă *subs* plot
pardesiu *subs* overcoat
părere *subs* opinion
părere greşită *subs* misbelief
parfum *subs* fragrance
parfum *subs* perfume
parfumat *adj* fragrant
pârghie *subs* lever
pârghie *subs* leverage
părinte *adj* pardonable
părinte *subs* parent
părintesc *adj* parental
pârît *subs* respondent
paritate *subs* par
paritate *subs* parity
pariu *subs* bet
pârîu *subs* brook
pârîu de munte *conj* beck
parlament *subs* parliament
parlamentar *subs* parliamentarian
parlamentar *adj* parliamentary
pârloagă *subs* moor
parodie *subs* parody
paroh *subs* parson
paroh *subs* vicar
parohie *subs* parish
parolă *subs* watchword
părtaş *subs* co-partner
parte *subs* part
parte *subs* share
parte *subs* side

parte interioară *subs* within
parte mai densă *subs* thick
partea cea mai rea *subs* worst
partener *subs* partner
parteneriat *subs* partnership
parţial *adj* partial
părticică *subs* particle
participant *subs* participant
participare *subs* participation
particular *adj* particular
particularitate *subs* particular
particularitate *subs* singularity
părtinire *subs* partiality
partizan *subs* partisan
parvenit *subs* upstart
pas *subs* step
pas mare *subs* stride
pas măsură *subs* pace
pasager *subs* passenger
pasager *subs* voyager
pasaj *subs* passage
pasaj *subs* thoroughfare
paşaport *subs* passport
pasăre *subs* bird
pasăre cântătoare *subs* songster
pasăre de curte *subs* fowl
păsări de curte *subs* poultry
pasionat *adj* passionate
pasiune *subs* hobby
pasiune *subs* passion
pasiv *adj* passive
paşnic *adj* pacific
paşnic *adj* peaceable
pastă *subs* mash
pastă *subs* paste
Paşte *subs* easter
pastel *subs* pastel
păstor *subs* shepherd
păstrare *subs* preservation
păşunat *subs* pasture
păşune *subs* lea
pat *subs* bed

pat de copil *subs* crib
pată *subs* blemish
pată *subs* blot
pată *subs* mottle
pată *subs* spot
pată *subs* stain
pată *v.t* stain
pată *subs* taint
pățanie *subs* mishap
patern *adj* paternal
patetic *adj* pathetic
patina *subs* skate
pătrat *subs* square
pătrat *adj* square
patricid *subs* patricide
patrimoniu *subs* patrimony
patriot *subs* patriot
patriotic *adj* patriotic
patriotism *subs* partiotism
patron *subs* employer
patronaj *subs* patronage
patru *subs* four
patrulă *subs* patrol
patrulater *subs* quadrangle
patrulater *adj/subs* quadrilateral
pătrundere *subs* insight
pătrundere a minții *subs* fathom
patruped *subs* quadruped
patruzeci *subs* forty
pătură *subs* blanket
pătură *subs* wrap
păun *subs* peacock
păuniță *subs* peahen
pauză *subs* pause
pavaj *subs* pavement
pavilion *subs* pavilion
pază *subs* safeguard
pază de corp *subs* bodyguard
păzitor *subs* tender
pe *prep* on
pe *prep* per
pe *prep* upon

pe aici *adv* hereabouts
pe când *adv* as
pe care *pron* that
pe care? *pron* which
pe de-a-ntregul *adv* stark
pe din afară *adv* outwardly
pe ea *subs* her
pe gustul cuiva *adj* palatable
pe jos *adv* afoot
pe jumătate *adj* half
pe lângă *prep* besides
pe lângă aceasta *adv* besides
pe neașteptate *adv* suddenly
pe partea cealaltă *adv* overleaf
pe perete *adj* mural
pe scurt *adv* shortly
pe unde? *adv* whereabout
pe urmă *adv* afterwards
pe vremuri *adv* formerly
pecuniar *adj* pecuniary
pedagog *subs* pedagogue
pedagogie *subs* pedagogy
pedală *subs* pedal
pedant *adj* bookish
pedant *subs* pedant
pedant *subs* pedantic
pedanterie *subs* pedantry
pedeapsă *subs* punishment
pedel la universitate *subs* beadle
peisaj *subs* landscape
pelerin *subs* pilgrim
pelerinaj *subs* pilgrimage
pelin *subs* wormwood
penal *adj* penal
penal *adj* punitive
pendul *subs* pendulum
penetrare *subs* penetration
penibil *adj* awkward
penis *subs* penis
pensie *subs* pension
pensie alimentară *subs* alimony
pensionar *subs* pensioner

pentagon *subs* pentagon
pentru *prep* for
pentru că *conj* because
pentru că *conj* for
pentru ca să *conj* that
pentru toată viaţa *adj* lifelong
pentru un timp *adv* awhile
pepene *subs* melon
pepene *subs* water-melon
percepere *subs* levy
perceptibil *adj* perceptible
percepţie *subs* perception
perceptiv *adj* perceptive
perdea *subs* curtain
pereche *subs* pair
peren *adj* perennial
perete *subs* wall
perfect *subs* perfect
perfecţiune *subs* perfection
perfidie *subs* perfidy
perforator în piatră *subs* miser
performanţă *subs* performance
pericol *subs* danger —
periculos *adj* dangerous
perie *subs* brush
perie cu coadă *subs* mop
periferie *subs* periphery
perimat *adj* obsolete
perioadă *subs* period
periodic *adj* periodical
periodic *adj* recurrent
perlă *subs* pearl
permanent *adj* permanent
permanent *adj* resident
permanenţă *subs* permanence
permis *adj* permissible
permisiune *subs* allowance
permisiune *subs* permission
permutare *subs* permutation
pernă *subs* pillow
pernă de divan *subs* cushion
pernicios *adj* pernicious

perpendicular *adj* perpendicular
perpendiculară *subs*
   perpendicular
perpetuu *adj* perpetual
perplexitate *subs* perplexity
persecuţie *subs* persecution
perseverenţă *subs* perseverance
persistent *adj* persistent
persistenţă *subs* persistence
persoană *subs* person
persoană care aşază *subs* layer
persoană care coase *subs* sewer
persoană ce probează *subs* fitter
persoana cu nărav *subs.* addict
persoană diabolică *subs* fiend
persoană din afară *subs* outsider
persoană la rând *subs* follower
persoană mai în vârstă *subs*
   elder
persoană necioplită *subs* boor
persoană proscrisă *subs* outlaw
personaj *subs* personage
personal *adj* personal
personal *subs* personnel
personal *subs* staff
personalitate *subs* personality
personificare *subs* impersonation
personificare *subs* personification
perspectivă *subs* perspective
perspectivă *subs* prospect
perspectivă *subs* vista
perspicace *adj.* acute
perspicace *adj* sagacious
perspicacitate *subs.* acumen
perspicacitate *subs* sagacity
pertinent *adj* pertinent
perucă *subs* wig
pervers *adj* perverse
perversitate *subs* perversity
perversiune *subs* perversion
pescar *subs* fisherman
pescăruş *subs* gull

pesimism *subs* pessimism
pesimist *subs* pessimist
pesimist *adj* pessimistic
peste *prep.* above
peste *prep.* across
peste *prep* over
peşte *subs* fish
peste bord *adv* overboard
peste graniţă *adv.* abroad
peste noapte *adv* overnight
peşteră *subs* cave
pesticid *subs* pesticide
petală *subs* petal
petic *subs* patch
petiţie *subs* courtship
petiţie *subs* petition
petiţionar *subs* petitioner
petrecere *subs* party
petrol *subs* petroleum
pian *subs* piano
pianist *subs* pianist
piaţă *subs* market
piatră *subs* stone
pică *subs* grudge
pică *subs* spite
picant *adj* piquant
picătură *subs* drop
pichet *subs* picket
pici *subs* youngster
picior *subs* leg
picior de pahar *subs* stalk
picior din faţă *subs* foreleg
picnic *subs* picnic
picoteală *subs* slumber
pictor *subs* painter
pictură *subs* picture
pictura murala *subs* mural
picurare *subs* drip
piedestal *subs* pedestal
piele *subs* leather
piele *subs* skin
piele de animal *subs* hide

piele de bivol *subs* buff
piele de şarpe năpârlită *subs* slough
piept *subs* chest
pieptene *subs* comb
pierdere *subs* loss
pierdut *adj* stray
pieritor *adj* perishable
piersică *subs* peach
pietate *subs* piety
pieton *subs* pedestrian
pietricică *subs* pebble
pigmeu *subs* pygmy
pilă *subs* file
pildă *subs* aphorism
pilot *subs* pilot
pilulă *subs* pill
pin *subs* fir
pin *subs* pine
pingea *subs* sole
pinten *subs* ram
pinten *subs* spur
pionier *subs* pioneer
piper *subs* pepper
piramidă *subs* pyramid
pirat *subs* pirate
piraterie *subs* piracy
piruetă *subs* whirligig
pisc *subs* peak
pisică *subs* cat
pisicuţă *subs* kitten
pistă *subs* track
pistol *subs* gun
pistol *subs* pistol
piston *subs* piston
pitic *subs* dwarf
piton *subs* python
pitoresc *adj* pictorial
pitoresc *adj* picturesque
pitpalac *subs* quail
pitulice *subs* wren
pivniţă *subs* cellar

pivniţă *subs* vault
pivot *subs* pivot
pizmă *subs* malice
plac *subs* liking
plăcere *subs* pleasure
plăcut *adj* congenial
plăcut *adj* pleasant
plajă *subs* beach
plămân *subs* lung
plan *subs* plan
plan *adj* plane
plan *subs* syllabus
plan de studii *subs* curriculum
planetă *subs* planet
planetar *adj* planetary
plângăreţ *adj* lachrymose
plângăreţ *adj* maudlin
plângere *subs* complaint
plângere *subs* grievance
planorist *subs* glider
plânset *subs* cry
plantă *subs* plant
plantă veşnic verde *subs*
    evergreen
plantă vivace *subs* perennial
plantaţie *subs* plantation
plăpând *adj* feeble
plăpând *adj* slight
plapumă *subs* quilt
plasă *subs* mesh
plasator *subs* usher
plasticitate *subs* imagery
plasture *subs* plaster
plată *subs* pay
platformă *subs* platform
platformă *subs* truck
plătibil *adj* payable
plătitor *subs* payee
platonic *adj* platonic
plebiscit *subs* plebiscite
plecare *subs* departure
pled *subs* rug

plesnitoare *subs* cracker
plic *subs* envelope
plicticos *adj* weary
plictiseală *subs* bore
plictiseală *subs* botheration
plictiseală *subs* tedium
plimbare cu barca *subs* row
plimbare scurtă *subs* stroll
plin *adj* full
plin de resurse *adj* resourceful
plin de tinereţe *adj* youthful
plin de viaţă *adj* lively
ploaie *subs* rain
ploaie torenţială *subs* downpour
ploios *adj* rainy
plonjon *subs* dive
plop *subs* poplar
ploscă *subs* flask
plug *subs* plough
plugar *subs* ploughman
plural *adj* plural
pluralitate *subs* plurality
plus *adj* plus
plutind *adv* afloat
pneumonie *subs* pneumonia
poală *subs* lap
poartă *subs* gate
poate *adv* perhaps
pocnet *subs* snap
pocnitură *subs* click
pod *subs* bridge
pod de casă *subs* loft
podea *subs* floor
podoabe *subs pl* paraphernalia
poem *subs* poem
poet *subs* bard
poet *subs* poet
poet mediocru *subs* poetaster
poetă *subs* poetess
poetastru *subs* rhymester
poetic *adj* poetic
poezie *subs* poesy

poezie *subs* poetry
poftă de *subs* appetence
poftă de mâncare *subs* appetite
poftă nestăvilită *subs* longing
pogon *subs.* acre
pojar *subs* measles
pol *subs* pole
polar *subs* polar
polen *subs* pollen
poligam *adj* polygamous
poligamie *subs* polygamy
poliglot *subs* polyglot1
poliglot *adj* polyglot2
poliță *subs* policy
politehnic *adj* polytechnic
politeism *subs* polytheism
politeist *subs* polytheist
politeţe *subs* complaisance
politeţe *subs* pliteness
politic *adj* politic
politic *adj* political
politică *subs* politics
politician *subs* politician
politicos *adj* complaisant
politicos *adj* polite
poliţie *subs* police
poliţist *subs* constable
poliţist *subs* policeman
polo *subs* polo
polonic *subs* ladle
poluare *subs* pollution
pomană *subs* alms
pompă *subs* pomp
pompă *subs* pump
pompos *adj* luscious
pompos *adj* pompous
ponei *subs* pony
poplin *subs* poplin
popular *adj* popular
popularitate *subs* popularity
populat *adj* populous
populaţie *subs* population

por *subs* pore
porc *subs* pig
porc *subs* swine
porc mistreţ *subs* boar
poreclă *subs* alias
poreclă *subs* nickname
pornit *adv* headlong
port *subs* harbour
port *subs* haven
portabil *adj* portable
portal *subs* portal
porţelan *subs* china
porţelan *subs* porcelain
portic *subs* porch
portic *subs* portico
porţie *subs* portion
portiţă de scăpare *subs* loop-hole
portocală *subs* orange
portocaliu *adj* orange
portofel *subs* wallet
portret *subs* portrait
portret *subs* portraiture
porumb *subs* corn
porumb *subs* maize
porumbel *subs* dove
porumbel *subs* pigeon
posac *adj* dumb
posac *adj* moody
posesie *subs* possession
posesiune *subs* tenure
posesor *subs* occupier
posibil *adj* possible
posibilitate *subs* possibility
posomorât *adj* cheerless
posomorât *adj* morose
post *subs* fast
post de radio *subs* station
poştă *subs* mail
poştă *subs* post
poştal *adj* postal
postăvar *subs* draper
postmortem *adj* post-mortem

postmortem *subs* post-mortem
postscriptum *subs* postscript
postum *adj* posthumous
postură *subs* posture
potasă *subs* potash
potasiu *subs* potassium
potecă *subs* path
potecă *subs* trail
potent *subs* potency
potent *adj* potent
potenţial *adj* potential
potenţial *subs* potential
potenţialitate *subs* pontentiality
poticnire *subs* stumble
potofoliu *subs* portfolio
potolit *adj* sedate
potrivire *subs.* adequacy
potrivire *subs* felicity
potrivire *subs* match
potrivire *subs* suitability
potrivit *adj* becoming
potrivit *adv* pat
potrivit *adj* suitable
potrivit pentru *adj* apposite
potrivnic *adj* averse
potrivnic *adj* inimical
povară *subs* burden
povestire *subs* story
povestitor *subs* teller
poziţie *subs* position
poziţie *subs* site
poziţie în picioare *subs* standing
poziţie încovoiată *subs* stoop
pozitiv *adj* positive
poznaş *adj* arch
poznaş *adj* jocular
poznaş *adj* wanton
prăbuşire *subs* downfall
practic *adj* practical
practică *subs* practice
practicabil *adj* practicable
practicabilitate *subs* practicability

pradă *subs* booty
pradă *subs* catch
pradă *subs* loot
pradă *subs* plunder
prădalnic *adj.* accipitral
prădare *subs* sack
prădător *subs* marauder
praf *subs* dust
prag *subs* threshold
pragmatic *adj* pragmatic
pragmatism *subs* pragmatism
prăjeală *subs* fry
prăjină *subs* perch
prăjitură *subs* cake
prânz *subs* lunch
prăpastie *subs* ravine
praştie *subs* sling
prăvălie *subs* repository
praz *subs* leek
prea *adv* too
preambul *subs* preamble
precaut *adj* cautious
precauţie *subs* precaution
precauţie *subs* caution
precauţional *adj* precautionary
precedent *subs* precedent
precedent *adj* previous
precedenţă *subs* precedence
preceptor *subs* preceptor
precis *adj.* accurate
precis *adv* due
precis *subs* precise
precizie *subs.* accuracy
precizie *subs* nicety
precizie *subs* precision
precursor *subs* forerunner
precursor *subs* precursor
predare *subs* surrender
predecesor *subs* predecessor
predestinare *subs* predestination
predică *subs* sermon
predicator *subs* preacher

predicţie *subs* prediction
predominant *adj* predominant
predominant *adj* prevalent
prefăcătorie *subs.* acting
prefăcătorie *subs* sham
prefăcut *adj* hypocritical
prefaţă *subs* foreword
prefaţă *subs* preface
prefect *subs* prefect
preferat *adj* fond
preferinţă *subs* preference
prefix *subs* prefix
pregătit *adj* ready
preistoric *adj* prehistoric
prejudecăţi *subs* jaundice
prejudiciu *subs* prejudice
prelat *subs* prelate
preliminar *adj* preliminary
preludiu *subs* prelude
prematur *adv* abortive
prematur *adj* premature
premeditare *subs* premeditation
premier *subs* premier
premieră *subs* premiere
premiu *subs* award
premiu *subs* prize
premoniţie *subs* premonition
prenatal *adj* antenatal
preocupare *subs* concern
preocupare *subs* preoccupation
preot *subs* reverend
preot *subs* priest
preot ortodox *subs* pope
preoţie *subs* priesthood
preparare *subs* preparation
preparator *adj* preparatory
preponderenţă *subs* preponderance
prepoziţie *subs* preposition
prerogativă *subs* prerogative
presă *subs* press
prescurtare *subs.* abbreviation

prescurtare *subs.* abridgement
preşedinte *subs* chairman
preşedinte *subs* president
presimţire rea *subs* misgiving
presiune *subs* pressure
prestigios *adj* prestigious
prestigiu *subs* prestige
presupunere *subs* conjecture
presupunere *subs* presumption
presupunere *subs* supposition
presupunere *subs* surmise
preţ *subs* price
preţ de transport *subs* portage
preţ excesiv *subs* overcharge
pretendent *subs* suitor
pretenţie *subs* claim
pretenţie *subs* demand
pretenţie *subs* pretence
pretenţios *adj* pretentious
pretext *subs* pretext
pretins *adj* would-be
preţios *subs* precious
pretutindeni *adv* overall
pretutindeni *prep* throughout
prevăzător *adj* provident
prevenire *subs* prevention
preventiv *adj* preventive
prevestire *subs* auspice
previziune *subs* foresight
prezent *adj* present
prezenţă *subs* presence
prezenţă nepotrivită *subs* intrusion
prezentare *subs* presentation
prezidenţial *adj* presidential
prezumţios *adj* immodest
priceput *adj* proficient
prielnic *adj* wholesome
prieten *subs* friend
prieteni *subs* kith
prietenie *subs* amity
prietenos *adj* amicable

prim *adj* prime
primă *subs* premium
primar *subs* mayor
primar *adj* primary
primăvară *subs* sprig
primăvară *subs* spring
primejdie *subs* jeopardy
primejdie *subs* peril
primejdios *adj* breakneck
primejdios *adj* critical
primejdios *adj* perilous
primire călduroasă *subs* welcome
primitiv *adj* primeval
primitiv *adj* primitive
primul *adj* first
primul *pron* former
prin *prep* via
prin împuternicire *adj* vicarious
prin mijlocul *adv* through
prin urmare *adv* therefore
princiar *adj* princely
principal *adj* cardinal
principal *adj* foremost
principal *adj* main
principal *subs* main
principal *adj* principal
principiu *subs* principle
prindere *subs* hold
prinț *subs* prince
prințesă *subs* princess
printre *prep.* among
printre *prep* through
prioriotate *subs* priority
prioritate *subs* lead
pripit *adj* cursory
pripon *subs* lunge
pripon *subs* tether
privat *subs* private
privațiune *subs* privation
priveghi *subs* wake
privighetoare *subs* nightingale

privilegiat *adj* preferential
privilegiu *subs* charter
privilegiu *subs* lien
privilegiu *subs* privilege
privință *subs* regard
privire *subs* look
privire *subs* view
privire de ansamblu *subs* purview
privire fixă *subs* gaze
privire fixă *subs* stare
privire galeşă *subs* ogle
privire posomorâtă *subs* scowl
privire saşie *subs* squint
privitor la maree *adj* tidal
prizonier *subs* prisoner
proastă administrare *subs* misconduct
proastă folosire *subs* misapplication
probă *subs* probation
probabil *adj* likely
probabil *adv* probably
probabilitate *subs* probability
problemă *subs* problem
problemă *subs* issue
problematic *adj* problematic
procedeu *subs* proceeding
procedură *subs* procedure
procentaj *subs* percentage
proces process
procesiune *subs* pageant
proclamaţie *subs* proclamation
procurare *subs.* acquirement
procuror *subs* attorney
producător *subs* grower
producţie *subs* produce
producţie *subs* production
producţie *subs* yield
productiv *adj* productive
productivitate *subs* productivity
produs *subs* product

produs prin topire *adj* molten
produs secundar *subs* by-product
proeminent *adj* pre-eminent
proeminent *adj* prominent
proeminent *adj* salient
proeminenţă *subs* pre-eminence
proeminenţă *subs* prominence
profan *adj* profane
profesie *subs* profession
profesional *adj* professional
profesor *subs* professor
profesor *subs* teacher
profet *subs* prophet
profet *subs* seer
profetic *adj* prophetic
profeţie *subs* prophecy
profil *subs* profile
profit *subs* lucre
profit *subs* profit
profitabil *adj* lucrative
profitabil *adj* profitable
profund *subs* profound
profunzime *subs* profundity
progenitură *subs* progeny
prognoză *subs* forecast
program *subs* programme
programare *subs* appointment
progres *subs* progress
progresiv *adj* progressive
prohibitiv *adj* prohibitive
proiect *subs* draft
proiect *subs* project
proiectare *adj* projectile
proiectare *subs* projection
proiectil *subs* missile
proiectil *subs* projectile
proiector *subs* projector
prolific *adj* prolific
prolix *adj* verbose
prolixitate *subs* verbosity
prolog *subs* prologue
promisiune *subs* promise

promiţător *adj* promising
promovare *subs* promotion
prompt *adj* prompt
prompt *adj* swift
promptitudine *subs* readiness
pronume *subs* pronoun
pronunţare *subs* pronunciation
propagandă *subs* propaganda
propagandist *subs* propagandist
propietate *subs* property
proporţie *subs* proportion
proporţie *subs* ratio
proporţional *adj* proportional
proporţionat *adj* proportionate
propoziţie *subs* sentence
proprietar *subs* owner
proprietar *subs* proprietor
propriu *adj* own
proptea *subs* prop
propunere *subs* proposition
prosop *subs* towel
prospăt *adj* fresh
prospect *subs* prospsectus
prosper *adj* prosperous
prosperitate *subs* prosperity
prost *subs* fool
prost crescut *adj* rude
prostesc *adj* idiotic
prostie *subs* folly
prostituată *subs* prostitute
prostituţie *subs* prostitution
prostuţ *adj* silly
protagonist *subs* protagonist
protecţie *subs* protection
protector *subs* patron
protector *adj* protective
proteină *subs* protein
protest *subs* protest
protestaţie *subs* protestation
prototip *subs* prototype
proverb *subs.* adage
proverb *subs* byword

proverb *subs* proverb
proverbial *adj* proverbial
providență *subs* providence
provincialism *subs* provincialism
provincie *subs* province
provizie *subs* stock
provizie *subs* store
provizorat *subs* interim
provizoriu *subs* provisional
provocare *subs* challenge
provocare *subs* provocation
provocator *adj* provocative
proză *subs* prose
prozaic *adj* prosaic
prozodie *subs* prosody
prpunere *subs* proposal
prudent *adj* prudent
prudență *subs* prudence
prună *subs* plum
prună uscată *v.t* prune
prunc *subs* babe
pruncucidere *subs* infanticide
psalm *subs* psalm
psalmodiere *subs* chant
pseudonim *subs* pseudonym
psihiatrie *subs* psychiatry
psihiatru *subs* psychiatrist
psihic *subs* psychic
psiholog *subs* psychologist
psihologic *adj* psychological
psihologie *subs* psychology
psihopat *subs* psychopath
psihoterapie *subs* psychotherapy
psihoză *subs* psychosis
pubertate *subs* puberty
public *adj* public
public *subs* public
publicație *subs* publication
publicație informativă *subs* digest
publicație periodică *subs* periodical

publicitate *subs* advertisement
publicitate *subs* publicity
pudră *subs* powder
pudră sau fard presat *subs* compact
pueril *subs* puerile
pui *subs* whelp
pui de animal sălbatic *subs* cub
pui de găină *subs* chicken
pulover *subs* sweater
pulpă de fructe *subs* pulp
puls *subs* pulse
pulsație *subs* pulsation
pulverizator *subs* spray
pumn *subs* fist
pumnal *subs* dagger
punct *subs* dot
punct *subs* point
punct culminant *subs* climax
punct de vedere *subs* standpoint
punct mort *subs* standstill
punct sensibil *subs* quick
punct terminus *subs* terminal
punctual *adj* punctual
punctualitate *subs* punctuality
punctuație *subs* punctuation
punere în libertate *subs* release
pungă *subs* pouch
pungă *subs* purse
pungaș *subs* rascal
pungaș *subs* rook
pungășesc *adj* roguish
pungășie *subs* roguery
punte *subs* deck
pupă *subs* stern
pupilă *subs* eyeball
pur *adj* pure
pur și simplu *adj* mere
purgație *subs* purgation
purgativ *subs* purgative
purgative *adj* purgative
purgatoriu *subs* purgatory

purice *subs* flea
purificare *subs* purification
purist *subs* purist
puritate *subs* purity
puroi *subs* pus
purtător de cuvânt *subs* spokesman
puşti *subs* chit
puşti *subs* kid
puşti *subs* urchin
pustietate *subs* desert
pustnic *subs* hermit
pustnic *subs* recluse
pustnicie *subs* hermitage
putere *subs* power
puternic *adj* forceful
puternic *adj* mighty
puternic *adj* powerful
puternic *adj* strong
puţin *adv* little
puţin *adv* something
puţin adânc *adj* shallow
putinei *subs* churn
puzderie *subs* shoal

R

rabat *subs* rabate
răbdare *subs* patience
răbdător *adj* patient
răceală *subs* chill
rachetă *subs* rocket
rachetă de tenis *subs* racket
răcire *subs* refrigeration
răcoros *adj* cool
rădăcină *subs* root
radical *subs* radiation
radical *adj* radical
radio *subs* radio

radiogramă *subs* wireless
radiu *subs* radium
rafală *subs* blast
rafală *subs* gust
rafinament *subs* sophistication
rafinare *subs* refinement
rafinărie *subs* refinery
rafinat *adj* dainty
rafinat *adj* sophisticated
raft *subs* shelf
răgaz *subs* leisure
răget *subs* roar
răguşit *adj* hoarse
rahitic *adj* rickety
rahitism *subs* rickets
rai *subs* heaven
ramă *subs* frame
ramă la încălţăminte *subs* welt
rămas bun *subs.* adieu
rămas bun *subs* farewell
rămas bun *subs* leave
rămăşag *subs* wager
rămăşiţă *subs* remainder
rămăşiţe *subs* wreckage
ramură *subs* bough
ramură de palmier *subs* palm
rană *subs* hurt
rană *subs* injury
rană *subs* sore
rană *subs* wound
ranchiună *subs* rancour
rând *subs* queue
rând *subs* turn
randament *subs* output
rândunică *subs* swallow
rang de lord *subs* lordship
rânjet *subs* sneer
râpă *subs* cliff
rapid *adj* fast
rapid *adj* rapid
rapiditate *subs* rapidity
rapire *subs.* abduction

răpire *subs* rapture
raport *subs* rapport
raport *subs* report
râpos *adj* bumpy
rar *adj* rare
rareori *adv* seldom
râs *subs* laugh
râs *subs* laughter
rasă *subs* breed
rasă de animale *subs* pedigree
răsăritean *adj* east
răscoală *subs* mutiny
răsculat *adj* insurgent
răsculat *subs* insurgent
răsculat *adj* rebellious
răscumpărare *subs* ransom
rasism *subs* racialism
răspândire *subs* spread
răsplată *subs* repayment
răspundere *subs* liability
răspuns *subs* answer
răspuns *subs* response
răspunzător *adj* liable
răspunzător de *adj.* accountable
răspunzător de *adj* answerable
răstimp *subs* lapse
răstimp *subs* while
răsturnare *subs* overthrow
răsucire *subs* twist
răsucire *subs* wriggle
rată *subs* instalment
rată *subs* rate
rață *subs* duck
rație *subs* ration
rațional *subs* rational
raționament *subs* inference
rațiune *subs* rationality
rațiune fundamentală *subs*
   rationale
râu *subs* river
rău *adj* bad
rău *subs* evil

rău *adj* evil
rău *subs* harm
rău *subs* ill
răufăcător *subs* malefactor
râuleț *subs* rivulet
răutăcios *adj* malicious
răutăcios *adj* sardonic
ravagiu *subs* ravage
rază *subs* radius
rază X *subs* x-ray
război *subs* war
războinic *subs* warrior
răzbunare *subs* revenge
răzbunare *subs* vengeance
răzbunător *adj* revengeful
răzeș *subs* yeoman
razie *subs* raid
răzlețit *adj* sparse
razna *adv.* afield
răzvrătire *subs* uprising
răzvrătitor *adj* mutinous
reabilitare *subs* rehabilitation
reacție *subs* reaction
real *adj* real
realism *subs* realism
realist *subs* realist
realist *adj* realistic
realitate *subs* reality
realizabil *adj* feasible
realizare *subs* attainment
realizare *subs* realization
realizat *adj.* accomplished
reînnoire *subs* renewal
reavoință *subs* malignancy
reavoință *subs* malignity
rebel *subs* rebel
rebeliune *subs* rebellion
rebut *subs* refuse
rebut *subs* rejection
rece *adj* cold
recensământ *subs* census
recent *adj* recent

recent *adv* recently
recepție *subs* reception
receptive *adj* receptive
recesiune *subs* recession
rechemare *subs* recall
rechemare *subs* remand
rechin *subs* shark
rechiziție *subs* requisition
recidivă *subs* recurrence
recidivă *subs* relapse
recipient *subs* recipient
recipient gradat *subs* graduate
reciproc *adj* mutual
reciproc *adj* reciprocal
recital *subs* recital
recitare *subs* recitation
reclamant *subs* claimant
reclamant *subs* prosecutor
reclamație *subs* reclamation
recoltă *subs* crop
recoltă *subs* harvest
recomandabil *adj* advisable
recomandabil *adj* commendable
recomandare *subs* commendation
recomandare *subs* recommendation
recompensă *subs* recompense
recompensă *subs* reward
reconciliere *subs* reconciliation
recreație *subs* pastime
recreație *subs* recreation
recrut *subs* recruit
recrutor *subs* crimp
rectificare *subs* rectification
rectificare *subs* rectum
recunoaștere *subs.* admission
recunoaștere *subs* recognition
recunoscător *adj* grateful
recunoscător *subs* thankful
recunoștință *subs* gratitude
recuperare *subs* recovery
recurs *subs* recourse

recviem *subs* requiem
redeșteptare *subs* revival
reducere *subs* discount
reducere *subs* reduction
redus *adv* low
referendum *subs* referendum
referință *subs* reference
reflectare *subs* reflection
reflector *subs* reflector
reflex *subs* reflex
reflex *adj* reflex
reflexiv *adj* reflexive
reflux *subs* ebb
reformă *subs* reform
reformare *subs* reformation
reformator *adj* reformatory
reformator *subs* reformer
refren *subs* refrain
refugiat *subs* refugee
refugiu *subs* refuge
refulă a religiei *subs* observance
refutare *subs* refutation
refuz *subs* refusal
refuz *subs* repulse
regal *adj* regal
regal *adj* royal
regalist *subs* royalist
regalitate *subs* royalty
regat *subs* kingdom
rege *subs* king
regenerare *subs* regeneration
regicid *subs* regicide
regim *subs* regime
regiment *subs* regiment
regină *subs* queen
regional *adj* regional
registrator *subs* registrar
registru *subs* ledger
registru *subs* register
registru *subs* registry
regiune *subs* region
regiune păduroasă *subs* woodland

regret *subs* regret
regrupare de trupe *subs* rally
regulă *subs* norm
regulă *subs* rule
regulament *subs* regulation
regularitate *subs* regularity
regulat *adj* regular
regulator *subs* controller
regulator *subs* regulator
relaţii sexuale *subs* intercourse
relativ *adj* relative
relativ *subs* relative
relaxare *subs* relaxation
relevant *adj* relevant
relevanţă *subs* relevance
religie *subs* religion
religios *adj* religious
reluare *subs* resumption
remarcă *subs* remark
remarcabil *adj* outstanding
remarcabil *adj* remarkable
remediu *subs* remedy
reminiscenţă *subs* reminiscence
remitere de bani *subs* remittance
remorcă *subs* trailer
remuneraţie *subs* emolument
remuneraţie *subs* remuneration
remuneraţie mică *subs* pittance
remuşcare *subs* compunction
remuşcare *subs* remorse
renaştere *subs* renaissance
renaştere *subs* resurgence
renovare *subs* renovation
rentier *subs* annuitant
renume *subs* renown
renumit *adj* renowned
renunţare *subs.* abnegation
renunţare *subs* renunciation
reparabil *adj* raparable
reparare *subs* repair
repartiţie *subs* partition
repartizare *subs* allotment

repatriere *subs* repatriate
repatriere *subs* repatriation
repaus *subs* repose
repede *adv* apace
repede *adv* fast
repede *adj* speedy
repercursiune *subs* repercussion
repetare *subs* reiteration
repetiţie *subs* rehearsal
repetiţie *subs* repetition
repezeală *subs* swoop
repezit *subs* quick
replică *subs* rejoinder
replică *subs* reply
replică negativă *subs* negative
reporter *subs* reporter
reprezentant *subs* representative
reprezentare *subs* representation
reprezentativ *adj* representative
reprimare *subs* repression
reproducere *subs* ditto
reproducere *subs* reproduction
reproductiv *adj* reproductive
reproş *subs* reproach
reptilă *subs* reptile
republică *subs* republic
republican *adj* republican
republican *subs* republican
repudiere *subs* repudiation
repulsie *subs.* abhorrence
repulsie *subs* repulsion
repulsiv *adj* repulsive
reputaţie *subs* reputation
reputaţie *subs* repute
reşedinţă *subs* residence
resentiment *subs* resentment
respect *subs* respect
respectiv *adj* respective
respectuos *adj* respectful
respingator *adj* abominable
respingător *adj* loathsome
respiraţie *subs* breath

respirație *subs* respiration
responsabil *adj* responsible
responsabilitate *subs* responsibility
restabilire *subs* restoration
restabilire *subs* reinstatement
restaurant *subs* restaurant
restituire *subs* refund
restricție *subs* restriction
restrictiv *adj* restrictive
resturi *subs* junk
resursă *subs* resort
resursă *subs* resource
rețea *subs* network
rețetă *subs* prescription
rețetă *subs* recipe
reticent *a* reticent
reticență *subs* reticence
retină *subs* retina
reținere *subs* retention
retipărire *subs* reprint
retoric *subs* rhetoric
retoric *adj* rhetorical
retorică *subs* oratory
retortă *subs* retort
retragere *subs* retirement
retragere *subs* withdrawal
retrospect *subs* retrospection
retrospectiv *subs* retrospective
retrospectivă *subs* retrospect
reumatic *adj* rheumatic
reumatism *subs* rheumatism
reuniune *subs* muster
revanşă *subs* retaliation
revărsare *subs* spate
revelație *subs* revelation
reverență *subs* bow
reverență *subs* reverence
reverie *subs* reverie
revers *subs* reverse
reversibil *adj* reversible
revistă lunară *subs* monthly

revizie *subs* revision
revizuire *subs* review
revocabil *adj* revocable
revocare *subs* repeal
revocare *subs* revocation
revoltă *subs* revolt
revoltă în masă *subs* outbreak
revoluție *subs* revolution
revoluționar *adj* revolutionary
revoluționar *subs* revolutionary
revolver *subs* revolver
rezervare *subs* reservation
rezervor *subs* reservoir
rezervor *subs* tank
rezident *subs* resident
rezidual *adj* residual
reziduu *subs* residue
rezistent *adj* hardy
rezistent *subs* resistant
rezistență *subs* endurance
rezistență *subs* reluctance
rezistență *subs* resistance
rezoluție *subs* resolution
rezonabil *adj* reasonable
rezonant *adj* resonant
rezonanță *subs* resonance
rezultat *subs* result
rezultat *subs* resume
rezumat *subs* precis
rid *subs* wrinkle
ridicare *subs* elevation
ridicare *subs* lift
ridicare *v.t* raise
ridicare a straturilor *subs* upheaval
ridiche *subs* radish
ridicol *adj* ridiculous
rigid *adj* rigid
rigid *adj* stern
rigoare *subs* rigour
rigolă *subs* gutter
riguros *adj* rigorous

rimă *subs* rhyme
rindea *subs* plane
rinichi *subs* kidney
rinocer *subs* rhinoceros
ripostă *subs* repartee
risc *subs* risk
riscant *adj* risky
rişcă *subs* rickshaw
risipă *subs* prodigality
risipă *subs* waste
risipitor *adj* prodigal
risipitor *adj* wasteful
risipitor cu *adj* lavish
ritm *subs* rhythm
ritmic *adj* rhythmic
ritual *subs* rite
ritual *subs* ritual
ritual *adj* ritual
rival *subs* rival
rivalitate *subs* rivalry
roată *subs* wheel
robă *subs* robe
robot *subs* robot
robust *adj* hefty
robust *adj* robust
rochie *subs* dress
rodnic *adj* fruitful
rol *subs* role
rom *subs* rum
roman *subs* novel
romancier *subs* novelist
romanţă *subs* romance
romantic *adj* romantic
rond *subs* round
rosătură *subs* graze
roşeaţa *subs* blush
roşiatic *adj* reddish
roşie *subs* tomato
roşu *adj* red
roşu *subs* red
rotaţie *subs* rotation
rotativ *adj* rotary

rotire *subs* spin
rotire *subs* whirl
rotund *adj* round
rouă *subs* dew
roz *adj* pink
rozător *subs* rodent
roze *adj* pinkish
rubin *subs* ruby
rublă *subs* rouble
rudimentar *adj* rudimentary
rug *subs* bonfire
rug funerar *subs* pyre
rugăciune *subs* prayer
rugăminte *subs* entreaty
rugină *subs* rust
ruginit *adj* rusty
ruină *subs* ruin
rulou *subs* roll
rumegare *subs* rumination
rumegător *adj* ruminant
rumegător *subs* ruminant
rupere *subs* breakage
rupere *subs* rupture
ruptură *subs* break
rural *subs* rural
ruşinat *adj* ashamed
ruşine *subs* shame
ruşinos *adj* shameful
rustic *adj* rustic
rută *subs* route
rutină *subs* routine

s subordona *v.t* subordinate
şa *subs* saddle
sabat *subs* sabbath
sabie *subs* sword
şablon *subs* stencil

sabot de frână *subs* skid
sabotaj *subs* sabotage
şacal *subs* jackal
sacrificiu *subs* sacrifice
sacrilegiu *subs* sacrilege
sacru *adj* sacred
sadism *subs* sadism
sadist *subs* sadist
safir *subs* sapphire
săgeată *subs* arrow
săgeată *subs* dart
şah *subs* chess
şah mat *subs* checkmate
saiba *subs* washer
şaisprezece *subs* sixteen
şaizeci *subs* sixty
şal *subs* shawl
sală *subs* chamber
sală de licitaţie *subs* mart
salahor *subs* labourer
salariu *subs* salary
salariu *subs* wage
salată *subs* salad
sălbatic *subs* savage
sălbatic *adj* wild
sălbăticie *subs* wilderness
salbie *subs* sage
salcie *subs* willow
salin *adj* saline
salinitate *subs* salinity
salivă *subs* saliva
salivă *subs* spittle
salon *subs* drawing-room
salon *subs* saloon
salt *subs* leap
salt *subs* rebound
saltea *subs* mattress
şalupă *subs* barge
salut *subs* salute
salutar *adj* salutary
salutare *subs* salutation
salvare *subs* rescue

salvare *subs* salvage
salvare *subs* salvation
salvator *subs* saviour
sămânţă *subs* seed
sămânţă de in *subs* linseed
sâmbătă *subs* Saturday
şambelan *subs* chamberlain
sâmbure *subs* pit
şampon *subs* shampoo
sân *subs* bosom
sân *subs* breast
sănătate *subs* health
sanatoriu *subs* sanatorium
sănătos *adj* healthy
sănătos *adj* sound
sancţiune *subs* sanction
sanctuar *subs* sanctuary
sandală *subs* sandal
sandviş *subs* sandwich
sânge *subs* blood
sângeros *adj* bloody
sanguin *adj* sanguine
sanie de lansare *subs* cradle
sanitar *adj* sanitary
şansă *subs* chance
şanse de succes *subs* odds
şanţ *subs* ditch
şanţ *subs* trench
şantaj *subs* blackmail
santinelă *subs* sentinel
santinelă *subs* warden
sapă *subs* spade
săpat *subs* dig
şapcă *subs* cap
săptămână *subs* week
săptămânal *adj* weekly
săptămânal *adv* weekly
şapte *subs* seven
şaptesprezece *subs* seventeen
şaptezeci *subs* seventy
săpun *subs* soap
sărac *adj* poor

sărăcie *subs* poverty
saramură *subs* brine
sărat *adj* salty
sărbătoare *subs* holiday
sărbătoare *subs* revel
sărbătorire *subs* celebration
sarcasm *subs* sarcasm
sarcastic *adj* sarcastic
sarcină *subs* pregnancy
sarcină *subs* task
sare *subs* salt
sârguincios *adj* industrious
sârguincios *adj* painstaking
săritură *subs* somersault
săritură *subs* vault
săritură *subs* jump
şarlatanie *subs* quackery
sărman *subs* wretch
şarpe *subs* serpent
şarpe *subs* snake
sărut *subs* kiss
şase *subs* six
sat *subs* village
sătean *subs* rustic
sătean *subs* villager
satelit *subs* satellite
satiră *subs* satire
satiră *subs* skit
satiric *adj* satirical
satisfăcător *adj* satisfactory
satisfacţie *subs* contentment
satisfacţie *subs* satisfaction
sătul de *adj* replete
saturare *subs* satiety
săturare *subs* glut
saturaţie *subs* saturation
saturaţie *subs* surfeit
savoare *subs* savour
savoare *subs* zest
savuros *adj* tasty
scădere *subs* subtraction
scădere a preţurilor *subs* slump

scâlciat *adj* slipshod
scalp *subs* scalp
scamator *subs* wizard
scandal *subs* affray
scandal *subs* brawl
scandal *subs* scandal
scânteie *subs* spark
scânteiere *subs* glitter
scânteiere *subs* scintillation
scânteiere *subs* sparkle
scară *subs* ladder
scară *subs* scale
scară de şa *subs* stirrup
scârţâit *subs* creak
scaun *subs* chair
scaun *subs* seat
scaun de tortură *subs* rack
scăzut *adj* low
scenă *subs* scene
scenă *subs* stage
scenariu *subs* script
sceptic *subs* sceptic
sceptic *adj* sceptical
scepticism *subs* scepticism
sceptru *subs* sceptre
schelă *subs* scaffold
schelet *subs* skeleton
schemă *subs* scheme
schilod *adj* lame
schimb *subs* barter2
schimb *subs* relay
schimb de tură *subs* shift
schimbare *subs* change
schimbare *subs* conversion
schimbător *adj* fickle
schiţă *subs* design
schiţă *subs* sketch
schizmă *subs* schism
sciziune *subs* secession
sclav *subs* slave
sclavie *subs* bondage
sclavie *subs* slavery

sclipire *subs* flash
sclipitor *adj* lustrous
şcoală *subs* school
şcoală politehnică *subs* polytechnic
scoatere *subs* removal
scobit *adj* hollow
scobitură *subs* hollow
scoică *subs* conch
scoică *subs* oyster
şcolar *subs* learner
şcolar *subs* pupil
şcolar *adj* scholastic
scop *subs* scope
scor *subs* score
scorpion *subs* scorpion
scorţişoară *subs* cinnamon
scoţian *subs* Scot
scoţian *adj* scotch
scotocire *subs* rummage
scriitor *subs* writer
scriitor satiric *subs* satirist
scripcă *subs* fiddle
scripete *subs* pulley
scripete *subs* windlass
scriptură *subs* scripture
scriptură *subs* writ
scrisoare *subs* letter
scroafă *subs* sow
scrobeală *subs* starch
scrutin *subs* poll
scuipat *subs* spit
scuipătoare *subs* spittoon
scul *subs* skein
sculptor *subs* sculptor
sculptură *subs* sculpture
scump la preţ *adj* expensive
scurgere de gaz *subs* leakage
scurgere de lichid *subs* leak
scurgere lentă *subs* ooze
scurt *adj* brief
scurt *adj* short

scurt răstimp *subs* span
scutier *subs* squire
scutit de *adj* exempt
scuză *subs* apology
scuză *subs* excuse
seamăn *subs* like
seară *subs* evening
secară *subs* rye
seceră *subs* sickle
secesionist *subs* secessionist
secetă *subs* drought
secol *subs* century
secret *adj* secret
secret *subs* secret
secretară *subs* secretary
secretariat *subs* secretariat (e)
sectă *subs* sect
sectarist *adj* sectarian
secţiune *subs* section
sector *subs* sector
sector de activitate *subs* branch
secundă *subs* second
secundar *adj* secondary
securitate *subs* security
secvenţă *subs* sequence
sedentar *adj* sedentary
şedere *subs* stay
sediment *subs* sediment
sediţios *adj* seditious
seducător *adj* seductive
seducţie *subs* seduction
şef *subs* boss
şef *adj* chief
şef de trib *subs* chieftain
segment *subs* segment
seif *subs* safe
seismic *adj* seismic
selectat *adj* select
selecţie *subs* selection
selectiv *adj* selective
semestru *subs* semester
semeţ *adj* haughty

semeţ *adj* lofty
seminar *subs* seminar
şemineu *subs* chimney
semn *subs* sign
semn *subs* token
semn *subs* vestige
semn de carte *subs* book-mark
semn de întrebare *subs* query
semn distinctiv *subs* cachet
semn distinctiv *subs* cognizance
semnal *subs* signal
semnatar *subs* signatory
semnătură *subs* signature
semnificaţie *subs* meaning
semnificaţie *subs* purport
semnificaţie *subs* significance
semnificaţie *subs* signification
semnificativ *adj* meaningful
semnificativ *adj* significant
semnul adunării *subs* plus
semnul minus *subs* minus
senat *subs* senate
senator *subs* senator
senil *adj* senile
senilitate *subs* senility
senin *adj* serene
seninătate *subs* serenity
senior *adj* senior
senior *subs* senior
sensibil *adj* sensible
sensibil *adj* sensitive
sensibilitate *subs* sensibility
sentiment *subs* feeling
sentiment *subs* sentiment
sentimental *adj* sentimental
sentinţă *subs* doom
senzaţie *subs* sensation
senzaţional *adj* sensational
senzual *adj* sensual
senzualitate *subs* sensuality
separabil *adj* separable
separare *subs* segregation

separare *subs* separation
separat *adv* apart
separat *adv* asunder
separat *adj* separate
septembrie *subs* September
septic *adj* septic
şerb *subs* serf
sergent *subs* sergeant
serial *adj* serial
serial *subs* serial
serie *subs* series
seringă *subs* syringe
serios *adj* serious
serj *subs* serge
serpentină *subs* serpentine
servă *subs* serve
şerveţel *subs* napkin
serviciu *subs* job
servil *adj* slavish
servitor *subs* domestic
servitor *subs* servant
şes *subs* plain
sesiune *subs* session
sesizare *subs* apprehension
sete *subs* thirst
sevă *subs* sap
sever *adj* austere
sever *adj* severe
severitate *subs* severity
severitate *subs* stringency
sex *subs* sex
sexual *adj* sexual
sexualitate *subs* sexuality
sezonier *adj* seasonal
sfânt *adj* holy
sfânt *subs* saint
sfărâmare *subs* smash
sfârc de sân *subs* teat
sfârc de sân *subs* nipple
sfârşit *subs* end
sfârşit *subs* finish
sfat *subs* advice

sfat *subs* counsel
sfat *subs* tip
sfatuire *subs* advisability
sfătuitor *subs* counsellor
sfeclă *subs* beet
sferă *subs* sphere
sferă de cunoştinţe *subs* range
sferic *adj* spherical
sfert *subs* quarter
sfidare *subs* contempt
sfidare *subs* defiance
sfinţire *subs* sacrament
sfios *adj* sheepish
sfoară pentru bici *subs* whipcord
sforăială *subs* snort
sforăit *subs* snore
sfredel *subs* drill
şi *conj* and
şi nici *conj* nor
sicomor *subs* sycamore
sicriu *subs* casket
sicriu *subs* coffin
şifonier *subs* wardrobe
sigiliu *subs* seal
sigur *adj* certain
sigur *adj* sure
siguranţă *subs* certainty
siguranţă *subs* safety
siguranţă *subs* surety
silabă *subs* syllable
silabic *adj* syllabic
silinţă *subs* diligence
silitor *adj* diligent
siluetă *subs* figure
siluetă *subs* silhouette
silvicultură *subs* forestry
simbol *subs* symbol
simbolic *adj* figurative
simbolic *adj* symbolic
simbolism *subs* symbolism
simetric *adj* shapely
simetric *adj* symmetrical

simetrie *subs* symmetry
simfonie *subs* symphony
similar *adj* similar
similaritate *subs* similarity
similitudine *subs* semblance
similitudine *subs* similitude
simpatic *adj* sympathetic
simpatie *subs* sympathy
simplificaţie *subs* simplification
simplitate *subs* simplicity
simplu *adj* plain
simplu *adj* simple
simplu *subs* single
simpozion *subs* symposium
simptom *subs* symptom
simţ *subs* sense
simţitor *adj* sentient
simulat *adj* sham
simultan *adj* simultaneous
şină *subs* rail
sincer *adv* openly
sincer *adj* candid
sincer *adj* frank
sincer *adj* genuine
sincer *adj* honest
sincer *adj* sincere
sincer *adj* truthful
sinceritate *subs* honesty
sinceritate *subs* sincerity
singular *adj* singular
singularitate *subs* oneness
singur *adj* alone
singur *adj* lonely
singur *adj* only
singur *adj* sole
singur *adj* solo
singurătate *adj* loneliness
singurătate *subs* solitude
singuratic *adj* lone
sinistru *adj* sinister
sinonim *subs* synonym
sinonim (cu) *adj* synonymous

sintaxă *subs* syntax
sintetic *adj* synthetic
sintetic *subs* synthetic
sinteză *subs* synthesis
sinucigaş *adj* suicidal
şipcă *subs* lath
şir *subs* row
sirenă *subs* siren
sirenă *subs* mermaid
şiret *adj* sly
şiret *adj* tricky
şiret *adj* wily
şiretenie *subs* cunning
şiretlic *subs* trickery
sirop *subs* syrup
sistem *subs* system
sistem de canalizare *subs* sewerage
sistem monetar *subs* coinage
sistematic *adj* systematic
sită *subs* riddle
situaţie *subs* situation
slăbiciune *subs* weakness
slăbit *adj* slack
slănină *subs* bacon
şlefuire *subs* file
sleit *adj* prostrate
şliţ *subs* slit
slugă *subs* menial
slugarnic *adj* servile
slujitor *subs* attendant
smalţ *subs* enamel
smalţ *subs* varnish
smarald *subs* emerald
şmenar *subs* trickster
smerit *adj* lowly
smerit *adj* reverent
smintit *adj* daft
smirnă *subs* myrrh
smochin *subs* fig
smucire *subs* wrench
smulgere *subs* avulsion

snob *subs* snob
snobism *subs* snobbery
snop *subs* bundle
snop *subs* sheaf
şnur *subs* noose
şnur *subs* string
şoaptă *subs* murmur
şoaptş *subs* whisper
soare *subs* sun
şoarece *subs* mouse
soartă *subs* fate
sobă *subs* stove
şobolan *subs* rat
sobrietate *subs* sobriety
şoc *subs* shock
sociabil *adj* sociable
sociabilitate *subs* sociability
social *subs* social
socialism *subs* socialism
socialist *subs* socialist
societate *subs* society
sociologie *subs* sociology
socoteală *subs* count
şofer *subs* chauffeur
şofer *subs* driver
sofism *subs* sophism
soi *subs* sort
şoim *subs* falcon
şoim *subs* hawk
solar *adj* solar
şold *subs* hip
soldat *subs* soldier
solemn *adj* solemn
solemnitate *subs* solemnity
solicitare *subs* request
solicitare *subs* solicitation
solicitudine *subs* solicitude
solid *adj* solid
solidariate *subs* solidarity
solitar *adj* lonesome
solitar *adj* solitary
solo *subs* solo

solubil *adj* soluble
solubilitate *subs* solubility
soluție *subs* solution
solvabil *adj* solvent
solvabilitate *subs* solvency
somație *subs* precept
somn *subs* sleep
somnambul *subs* somnambulist
somnambulism *subs*
   somnambulism
somnolent *subs* somnolent
somnolență *subs* somnolence
somnoros *adj* sleepy
somptuos *adj* sumptuous
somptuozitate *subs* profusion
sondă *subs* probe
sonet *subs* sonnet
sonoritate *subs* sonority
șopârlă *subs* lizard
șopron *subs* cote
șopron *subs* outhouse
soră *subs* sister
sorbitură *subs* sip
șorț *subs* apron
sorți *subs* lot
sos *subs* sauce
sos picant de roșii *subs* ketchup
șosetă *subs* sock
sosire *subs* arrival
soț *subs* husband
soț înșelat *subs* cuckold
soț, soție *subs* spouse
soția *subs* missis, missus
soție *subs* wife
șovăitor *adj* hesitant
spadă *subs* rapier
spaimă *subs* dread
spaimă *subs* fright
spălare *subs* wash
spălătoreasă *subs* laundress
spanac *subs* spinach
spaniol *subs* Spaniard

spaniolesc *adj* Spanish
spânzurătoare *subs* gallows
spărgător *subs* burglar
spargere *subs* burglary
spărtură *subs* flaw
spasm *subs* spasm
spate *subs* back
spațial *adj* spatial
spațios *adj* spacious
spațiu *subs* space
special *adj* especial
specialist *subs*. adept
specialist *subs* specialist
specialitate *subs* speciality
specializare *subs* specialization
specie *subs* species
specific *adj* peculiar
specific *adj* specific
specificație *subs* specification
speciment *subs* specimen
spectacol *subs* spectacle
spectaculos *adj* spectacular
spectator *subs* spectator
spectru *subs* spectre
speculă la bursă *subs* jobbery
speculant *subs* profiteer
speculație *subs* speculation
speculativ *adj* notional
speranță *subs* hope
speriat *adj* afraid
speriat *subs* scarcity
sperietoare *subs* bogle
sperietură *subs* scare
sperios *adj* timorous
spermă *subs* sperm
spin *subs* thorn
spinal *adj* spinal
spinos *adj* pungent
spion *subs* spy
spirală *subs* spiral
spiriduș *subs* elf
spirit *subs* spirit

spiritele strămoşilor *subs* manes
spiritual *adj* spirited
spiritual *adj* spiritual
spiritual *adj* witty
spiritualism *subs* spiritualism
spiritualitate *subs* spirituality
spiţă de roată *subs* spoke
spital *subs* hospital
splendid *adj* gorgeous
splendid *adj* refulgent
splendid *adj* splendid
splendoare *adj* refulgence
splendoare *subs* splendour
splină *subs* spleen
sponsor *subs* sponsor
spontan *adj* spontaneous
spontaneitate *subs* spontaneity
sporadic *adj* sporadic
sporire *subs.* accession
sporire *subs* boost
sporire *subs* increase
sport *subs* sport
sportiv *subs* sportive
sportiv *subs* sportsman
sprânceană *subs* brow
spre est *adv* east
spre interior *adv* inland
spre sud *adv* south
sprijin *subs* mainstay
sprijin *subs* reliance
sprijin *subs* support
sprinten *adj* nimble
spumă *subs* foam
spumă de săpun *subs* lather
spus clar *adj* outspoken
stabilire *subs* settlement
stabilitate *subs* stability
stabilizare *subs* stabilization
stadion *subs* stadium
stafidă *subs* raisin
stagnant *adj* stagnant
stagnare *subs* stagnation

stâlp *subs* pillar
stâlp *subs* post
stâncă *subs* rock
stâng *adj* left
stânga *subs* left
stângaci *adj* clumsy
stăpân *subs* lord
stăpânire de sine *subs* fortitude
stare *subs* plight
stare de nervozitate *subs* twitter
stare de plutire *subs* buoyancy
stareţ *subs* prior
străuinţă *subs* tenancy
stat *subs* state
statică *subs* statics
staţie finală *subs* terminus
staţionar *adj* stationary
statistic *adj* statistical
statistică *subs* statistics
statornic *adj.* abiding
statuie *subs* statue
statură *subs* stature
stătut *adj* stale
statut legal *subs* status
statutar *adj* statutory
stăvilar *subs* dam
stăvilar *subs* mole
stăvilar *subs* sluice
stea *subs* star
steag *subs* banner
steag *subs* flag
steaua polară *subs* loadstar
stejar *subs* oak
stelar *adj* stellar
stenograf *subs* stenographer
stenografie *subs* stenography
stepă *subs* steppe
stereotip *adj* stereotype
steril *adj* sterile
sterilitate *subs* sterility
sterilizare *subs* sterilization
sterp *adj* arid

ştersătură *subs* obliteration
stetoscop *subs* stethoscope
sticlă *subs* bottle
sticlar *adj* bottler
stigmat *subs* stigma
ştiinţă *subs* knowledge
ştiinţă *subs* science
ştiinţific *adj* scientific
stil *subs* style
stilou *subs* pen
stimul *subs* stimulus
stimulent *subs* incentive
stimulent *subs* stimulant
stins *adj* extinct
stipendiu *subs* stipend
stipulare *subs* stipulation
ştire falsă *subs* canard
ştiri *subs* news
ştiutor de carte *adj* literate
stoc *subs* stock
stofă din păr de cămilă *subs* camlet
stoic *subs* stoic
stomac *subs* stomach
stradă *subs* street
strădanie *subs* endeavour
străduinţă *subs* struggle
străin *adj* foreign
străin *subs* foreigner
străin *adj* outlandish
strajă *subs* sentry
strajă *subs* ward
strălucire *subs* brilliance
strălucire *subs* radiance
strălucire *subs* shine
strălucire orbitoare *subs* glare
strălucitor *adj* bright
strălucitor *adj* brilliant
strălucitor *adj* radiant
strălucitor *adj* resplendent
strălucitor *adj* shiny
strâmb *adj* wry

strămoş *subs* ancestor
strămoş *subs* forefather
strâmt *adj* narrow
strâmt *adj* tight
strâmtoare *subs* strait
strangulare *subs* strangulation
straniu *adj* strange
strânsoare *subs* grasp
strănut *subs* sneeze
strat *subs* coating
strat *subs* stratum
strategic *adj* strategic
strategie *subs* strategist
strategie *subs* strategy
strávechi *adj* immemorial
ştrengăriţă *subs* minx
stres *subs* stress
stricăciune *subs* breakdown
strict *adj* strict
strict *adj* stringent
strident *adj* shrill
strident *adj* strident
strigăt *subs* bawl
strigăt *subs* shout
strigăt de protest *subs* outcry
strivire *subs* squash
strofă *subs* stanza
strop *subs* speck
stropire *subs* splash
structură *subs* fabric
structură *subs* structure
structural *adj* structural
strugure *subs* grape
strung *subs* lathe
strungar *subs* turner
struţ *subs* ostrich
student *subs* undergraduate
studios *adj* studious
studiu *subs* study
stup *subs* beehive
stup *subs* hive
stupid *adj* stupid

stupiditate *subs* stupidity
stupină *subs* apiary
sub *prep* under
sub *adv* under
sub *adj* under
sub rezerva *prep* notwithstanding
subalimentare *subs* malnutrition
subiect *subs* subject
subiect de conversație *subs* topic
subiectiv *adj* subjective
subjugare *subs* subjection
subjugare *subs* subjugation
subjugat *adj* subject
sublim *adj* sublime
sublimitate *subs* sublimity
submarin *subs* submarine
submarin *adj* submarine
subordonare *subs* subordinate
subordonare *subs* subordination
subordonat *adj* subordinate
subsol *subs* basement
substanță *subs* substance
substanțial *adj* substantial
substantiv *subs* noun
substituție *subs* substitution
subteran *adj* subterranean
subtil *subs* subtle
subtilitate *subs* subtlety
subțire *adj* flimsy
subțire *subs* slender
subțire *adj* slim
subțire *adj* thin
suburban *adj* suburban
suburbie *subs* suburb
subvenție *subs* subsidy
suc *subs* juice
succes *subs* success
succesiune *subs* legacy
succesiune *subs* succession
succesiv *adj* successive
succesor *subs* successor
sud *subs* south

sudic *adj* south
sudic *adj* southerly
sudic *adj* southern
sudoare *subs* sweat
sudură *subs* solder
sudură *subs* weld
suferind *adj* unwell
suferință *subs* misery
suferință *subs* tribulation
suferință *subs* smart
suficient *ad* sufficient
suficiență *subs* sufficiency
sufix *subs* suffix
suflare *subs* waft
suflare de vânt, fum *subs* puff
sufler *subs* prompter
suflet *subs* soul
suflu *subs* blow
sufocare *subs* suffocation
sugestie *subs* intimation
sugestie *subs* suggestion
sugestiv *subs* suggestive
sughiț *subs* hiccup
șuierat *subs* zip
șuierat de șarpe *subs* hiss
suită *subs* retinue
suită *subs* suite
sul *subs* scroll
sulf *subs* sulphur
sulfuric *adj* sulphuric
suliță *subs* lance
sumă *subs* amount
sumă *subs* sum
sumă plătită *subs* payment
sumar *adj* sketchy
sumar *adv* summarily
sumar *subs* summary
sumar *adj* summary
sunet *subs* sound
sunstanțial *adv* substantially
sunt *v* am
supă *subs* soup

supărat *adj* angry
supărător *adj* irksome
supărător *adj* troublesome
superb *adj* superb
superficial *adj* superficial
superficialitate *subs* superficiality
superior *adj* superior
superior *adj* upper
superioritate *subs* predominance
superioritate *subs* superiority
superlativ *adj* superlative
superlativ *subs* superlative
supersonic *adj* supersonic
superstiție *subs* superstition
superstițios *adj* superstitious
supliment *subs* supplement
suplimentar *adj.* additional
suplimentar *adj* adscititious
suplimentar *adj* extra
suplimentar *adv* overtime
suplimentar *adj* supplementary
suplu *adj* supple
suplus *subs* superfluity
suportabil *adj* endurable
suportare *subs* bearing
supraâncărcare *subs* overload
supradoză *subs* overdose
suprafață *subs* outside
suprafață *subs* surface
suprafață *subs* top
suprafața de pogon *subs.* acreage
supranatural *adj* supernatural
supraom *subs* superman
supraomenesc *adj* susperhuman
suprataxă *subs* supertax
suprataxă *subs* surtax
supraveghere *subs* oversight
supraveghetor *subs* overseer
supraveghetor *subs*
   superintendent
supraviețuire *subs* survival
suprem *subs* paramount

suprem *subs* paramour
suprem *adj* supreme
supremație *subs* supremacy
suprimare *subs* retrenchment
supt *subs* suck
supunere *subs* allegiance
supunere *subs* obedience
supunere *subs* submission
supus *adj* obedient
supus *adj* submissive
surd *adj* deaf
surdină *subs* silencer
surpătură *subs* hag
surplus *subs* redundance
surplus *adj* redundant
surplus *subs* surcharge
surplus *subs* surplus
surpriză *subs* surprise
sursă *subs* quarry
sursă *subs* source
șurub *subs* screw
sus *adv* up
susceptibil *adj* touchy
susceptibilitate *subs* petulance
suspect *adj* suspect
suspect *subs* suspect
suspendare *subs.* abeyance
suspendare *subs* suspension
suspensie *subs* suspense
suspin *subs* sigh
suspin adânc *subs* gasp
suspus *subs* underdog
susținere *subs* sustenance
sustragere *subs* evasion
sută *subs* hundred
sutană *subs* frock
suveică *subs* shuttle
suvenir *subs* souvenir
suveran *adj* rum
suveran *subs* sovereign
suveran *adj* sovereign
suveranitate *subs* sovereignty

T

tabac *subs* tobacco
tăbăcar *subs* tanner
tabără *subs* camp
tabelar *adj* tabular
tablă *subs* board
tabletă *subs* tablet
tablou *subs* painting
tabu *subs* taboo
taburet *subs* stool
tac de biliard *subs* cue
tăcere *subs* hush
tăcere *subs* silence
tact *subs* tact
tactică *subs* tactics
tactil *adj* tactile
tăcut *adj* mum
tăcut *adj* quiet
tăcut *adj* silent
tăcut *subs* tacit
tăietură *subs* cut
tăietură *subs* slash
taifas *subs* chat1
taifun *subs* typhoon
taină *subs* privacy
taină *subs* secrecy
tăinuire *subs* secretion
tăiş *subs* thread
talaz *subs* billow
talaz *subs* surge
talent *v.t* talent
tâlhar *subs* robber
talie *subs* waist
talisman *subs* talisman
talmeş-balmeş *subs* jumble
talmeş-balmeş *adv* pell-mell
tămâie *subs* incense
tâmplă *subs* temple
tâmplar *subs* carpenter

tâmplar *subs* joiner
tâmplărie *subs* carpentry
tamponare *subs* collision
tânăr *adj.* adolescent
tânăr *adj* young
tânăr *subs* young
tandru *subs* tender
tangent *subs* tangent
tangibil *adj* tangible
ţânţar *subs* mosquito
ţap ispăşitor *subs* scapegoat
tapiserie *subs* tapestry
ţară *subs* country
ţăran *subs* peasant
ţărănime *subs* peasantry
ţarc *subs* pound
tare *adj.* adamant
tare *adv* aloud
tare *adj* tough
târfă *subs* slut
târfă *subs* strumpet
târfă *subs* whore
targă *subs* litter
tarif *subs* fare
tarif *subs* tariff
ţarină *subs* turf
târîre *subs* crawl
ţărm *subs* shore
ţărm *subs* strand
târnăcop *subs* mattock
tărtăcuţă *subs* gourd
târziu *adj* late
ţâşnitură *subs* jet
tată *subs* father
tăticu *subs* dad, daddy
tatuaj *subs* tattoo
tăun *subs* gadfly
tavă *subs* tray
tavan *subs* ceiling
tavernă *subs* tavern
taxă *subs* fee
taxă *subs* tax

taxabil *adj* taxable
taxare *subs* taxation
taxi *subs* cab
taxi *subs* taxi
teacă *subs* husk
teacă *subs* pod
teacă *subs* scabbard
teafăr *adj* scot-free
teamă *subs* awe
teanc *subs* shoal
țeapă *subs* pale
țeapăn *adj* stiff
teatral *adj* theatrical
teatru *subs* theatre
țeavă *subs* pipe
tehnic *subs* technical
tehnică *subs* technique
tehnicalitate *subs* technicality
tehnician *subs* technician
tehnolog *subs* technologist
tehnologic *subs* technological
tehnologie *subs* technology
tejghea *subs* counter
țel *subs* purpose
telecomunicare *subs* telecommunications
telefon *subs* phone
telefon *subs* telephone
telegraf *subs* telegraph
telegrafic *adj* telegraphic
telegrafie *subs* telegraphy
telegrafist *subs* telegraphist
telegramă *subs* telegram
telepatic *adj* telepathic
telepatie *subs* telepathy •
telescop *subs* telescope
telescopic *adj* telescopic
televiziune *subs* television
temă *subs* theme
tematic *adj* thematic
temnicer *subs* jailer
temperament *subs* temper

temperament *subs* temperament
temperamental *adj* temperamental
temperanță *subs* temperance
temperat *adj* temperate
temperatură *subs* temperature
templu *subs* temple
temporal *adj* temporal
temporar *adj* temporary
tenace *adj* tenacious
tenacitate *subs* tenacity
tencuială *subs* daub
tendința *subs* trend
tendință *subs* tendency
tenis *subs* tennis
tensiune *subs* tension
tentă *subs* tint
tentație *subs* temptation
tentativă *adj* tentative
tentator *subs* tempter
teolog *subs* theologian
teologic *adj* theological
teologie *subs* theology
teoremă *subs* theorem
teoretic *adj* theoretical
teorie *subs* theory
țepi din barbă *subs* bristle
țepos *adj* thorny
terapie *subs* therapy
terasă *subs* terrace
terci de ovăz *subs* porridge
terebentină *subs* turpentine
teren *subs* ground
teribil *adj* awful
teribil *adj* terrible
terifiant *adj* terrific
teritorial *adj* territorial
teritoriu *subs* territory
teritoriu rezervat *subs* preserve
termal *adj* thermal
termen *subs* term
terminabil *adj* terminable

terminal *adj* terminal
terminare *subs* termination
terminat *adv* over
terminolocic *adj* terminological
terminologie *subs* terminology
termometru *subs* thermometer
termos *subs* thermos (flask)
teroare *subs* terror
terorism *subs* terrarism
terorist *subs* terrorist
țesător/oare *subs* weaver
țesătorie *subs* loom
țesătură *subs* tissue
test *subs* test
testament *subs* testament
testicul *subs* testicle
text *subs* text
textil *adj* textile
textilă *subs* textile
textual *subs* textual
textual *adj* verbatim
textură *subs* texture
teză *subs* thesis
tezaur public *subs* treasury
tibie *subs* shin
ticălos *subs* cad
ticălos *adj* heinous
ticălos *subs* miscreant
țicneală *subs* craze
tic-tac *subs* tick
tifos exantematic *subs* typhus
țigară *subs* cigarette
țigară de foi *subs* cigar
țiglă *subs* tile
tigroaică *subs* tigress
tigru *subs* tiger
timbrare *subs* postage
timbru *subs* stamp
timid *adj* bashful
timid *subs* shy
timid *adj* timid
timiditate *subs* timidity

timp *subs* tense
timp *subs* time
timp frumos *subs* fine
ținând seama de *prep* considering
tinctură *subs* tincture
tineresc *adj* vernal
tinerețe *subs* youth
țintă *subs* aim
țintă *subs* goal
țintă *subs* target
ținută *subs* port
ținută *subs* trim
ținută a corpului *subs* pose
tip *subs* type
tipar pentru croit *subs* pattern
țipăt *subs* scream
țipăt *subs* yell
țipător *adj* loud
tipic *adj* typical
tir *subs* shoot
tiraj *subs* draw
tiran *subs* tyrant
tiranie *subs* tyranny
titanic *adj* titanic
titirez *subs* spinner
titlu *subs* heading
titlu *subs* title
titular *adj* titular
toaletă *subs* lavatory
toaletă *subs* toilet
toamnă *subs* autumn
toană *subs* vagary
toartă *subs* bail
tobă *subs* drum
tocană *subs* stew
tocit *adj* blunt
tocmeală *subs* bargain
tocsin *subs* curfew
tolbă *subs* satchel
tolerabil *adj* tolerable
tolerant *adj* tolerant

toleranţă *subs* tolerance
toleranţă *subs* toleration
ton *subs* tone
tonă *subs* ton
tonă *subs* tonne
tonic *adj* tonic
tonic *subs* tonic
tonsură *subs* tonsure
tont *adj* dull
top *subs* ream
topaz *subs* topaz
topitorie *subs* foundry
topograf *subs* topographer
topografic *adj* topographical
topografie *subs* topography
topor *subs* axe
torent *subs* flush
torent *subs* torrent
torenţial *adj* torrential
torid *adj* torrid
tornadă *subs* tornado
torpilă *subs* torpedo
tors de pisică *subs* purr
torţă *subs* torch
tortură *subs* torment
tortură *subs* torture
tot *adj* all
total *adj* total
total *subs* total
total *adj* utter
totalitate *subs* totality
toţi *pron* all
totul *subs* all
totuşi *conj* but
totuşi *conj* however
totuşi *adv* nonetheless
totuşi *adv* though
tovarăş *subs* chum
tovarăş *subs* comrade
tovarăş *subs* helpmate
tovarăş *subs* mate
tovarăş *subs* pal

tracţiune *subs* traction
tractor *subs* tractor
trădare *subs* betrayal
trădare *subs* treachery
trădare *subs* treason
trădător *subs* traitor
trădător *adj* treacherous
trădător de ţară *subs* parricide
tradiţie *subs* tradition
tradiţional *adj* traditional
traducere *subs* translation
trafic *subs* traffic
trăgaci *subs* trigger
trăgător de elită *subs* marksman
tragedian *subs* tragedian
tragedie *subs* tragedy
tragere *subs* pull
tragic *adj* tragic
trahee *subs* throttle
trai *subs* livelihood
trai *subs* living
trai *subs* subsistence
tramvai *subs* tram
trăncăneală *subs* clack
trăncăneală *subs* rattle
trandafir *subs* rose
trandafiriu *adj* rosy
trândav *adj* idle
trândăvie *subs* sloth
transă *subs* trance
transcendent *adj* transcendent
transfer *subs* transfer
transferabil *adj* transferable
transfiguraţie *subs* transfiguration
transformare *subs* transformation
transmigraţie *subs* transmigration
transmisiune *subs* broadcast
transmiţător *subs* transmitter
transmitere *subs* conveyance

transparent *adj* lucent
transparent *adj* transparent
transpirație *subs* perspiration
transport *subs* transport
transportare *subs* transportation
trântitor *subs* wrestler
tranzacție *subs* transaction
tranzacții *subs* dealings
tranzit *subs* transit
tranziție *subs* transition
tranzitiv *subs* transitive
trap *subs* trot
trăsătură *subs* feature
trăsătură caracteristică *subs* peculiarity
trăsătură de caracter *subs* trait
trăsături confuze *subs* blur
trasformare *subs* alteration
trasmisie *subs* transmission
trăsură *subs* carriage
tratament *subs* treatment
tratat *subs* treatise
tratat *subs* treaty
tratativ *subs* parley
traversare *subs* crossing
treaptă *subs* rung
treaptă *subs* stair
treaz *adj* awake
treaz *adj* wakeful
trebuie *v* must
trebuincios *adj* requisite
trecătoare *subs* lane
trecătoare *subs* pass
trecător *subs* transitory
trecut *adj* past
trecut *subs* past
trei *subs* three
trei *adj* three
treierător *subs* thresher
treime *subs* third
treisprezece *subs* thirteen
treisprezece *adj* thirteen

treizeci *subs* thirty
treizeci *adj* thirty
tremur *subs* tremor
tremurare *subs* quiver
tremurător *subs* shaky
tren *subs* train
tren expres *subs* express
trepied *subs* tripod
tresărire *subs* thrill
trestie *subs* cane
trezire *subs* wake
trezorier *subs* treasurer
trib *subs* tribe
tribal *adj* tribal
tribună *subs* rostrum
tribunal *subs* court
tribunal *subs* tribunal
tributar *subs* tributary
tributar *adj* tributary
tricicletă *subs* tricycle
tricolor *adj* tricolour
tricolor *subs* tricolour
tril *subs* warble
trimestrial *adj* quarterly
trimitere în direcție falsă *subs* misdirection
trio *subs* trio
triplu *adj* triple
trist *adj* sad
trist *adj* woeful
triton *subs* merman
triumf *subs* triumph
triumfal *adj* triumphal
triumfant *adj* triumphant
triunghi *subs* triangle
triunghiular *adj* triangular
trofeu *subs* trophy
trompetă *subs* trumpet
tron *subs* throne
tropic *subs* tropic
tropical *adj* tropical
trosnitură *subs* smack

trotinetă *subs* scooter
truc *subs* dodge
truc *subs* gag
truc *subs* trick
trudă *subs* labour
trunchi *subs* trunk
trupă *subs* troupe
trupă de actori *subs* troop
trupesc *adj* bodily
tuberculoză *subs* consumption
tufiş *subs* bush
tulburare *subs* commotion
tulburare *subs* trouble
tulbure *adj* blear
tulpină *subs* stem
tumoare *subs* tumour
tumult *subs* tumult
tumultos *adj* tumultuous
tun *subs* cannon
tunel *subs* tunnel
tunet *subs* thunder
tunsori *subs pl* shears
tur *subs* tour
tur de forţă *subs* stunt
turban *subs* turban
turbare *subs* rabies
turbină *subs* turbine
turbulent *adj* turbulent
turbulenţă *subs* turbulence
turculoză *subs* tuberculosis
turism *subs* tourism
turist *subs* tourist
turlă *subs* steeple
turmă *subs* flock
turmenic *subs* turmeric
turmeric *subs* curcuma
turn *subs* tower
turnare *subs* casting
turtă de miere *subs* honeycomb
turtit *adj* flat
ţurţur *subs* icicle
tuse *subs* cough

tutore *subs* custodian
tutun de prizat *subs* snuff
twelve *subs* twelve

ucenic *subs* apprentice
ucigaş *subs* thug
ud *adj* wet
uf! *interj* fie
uger *subs* udder
uimire *subs* amazement
uimitor *adj* marvellous
uimitor *adj* stupendous
uituc *adj* forgetful
uituc *subs* oblivious
uium *subs* toll
ulcer *subs* ulcer
ulceros *adj* ulcerous
ulei *subs* oil
ulei de ricină *subs* castor oil
uleios *adj* oily
uliu *subs* kite
ulterior *adj* after
ulterior *adj* consequent
ulterior *adj* ulterior
ultim *adj* ultimate
ultima clipă *subs* last
ultima dată *adv* last
ultimatum *subs* ultimatum
ultimul *adj* last1
uluire *subs* astonishment
uluire *subs* daze
uman *adj* human
uman *adj* humane
umanitar *adj* humanitarian
umanitate *subs* humanity
umăr *subs* shoulder
umblet ţanţoş *subs* strut

umbră *subs* shade
umbră *subs* shadow
umbrelă *subs* umbrella
umbrit *adj* shadowy
umed *adj* damp
umed *adj* humid
umed *adj* moist
umed şi rece *adj* dank
umezeală *subs* damp
umezeală *subs* wetness
umflătură *subs* swell
umiditate *subs* humidity
umiditate *subs* moisture
umil *adj* humble
umilinţă *subs* humiliation
umor *subs* humour
umorist *subs* humorist
un *art* an
un pumn *subs* handful
unanim *adj* unanimous
unanimitate *subs* unanimity
unchi *subs* uncle
uncie (28,35 g) *subs* ounce
unde *adv* where
unde? *conj* where
undeva *adv* somewhere
undiţă *subs* angle
unealtă *subs* tackle
ungher *subs* nook
unghi *subs* angle
unghiular *adj* angular
unguent *subs* ointment
unic *adj* unique
unificare *subs* unification
unionist *subs* unionist
unitate *subs* unit
unitate *subs* unity
uniune *subs* union
univers *subs* universe
universal *adj* universal
universalitate *subs* universality
universitate *subs* university

unsoare *subs* tallow
unsprezece *subs* eleven
unsuros *adj* greasy
unsuros *adj* sleek
unt *subs* butter
unu/a *adj* one
unul pe altul *pron* each
ură *subs* hate
ura! *interj* hurrah
uragan *subs* hurricane
urât *subs* ugly
urâţenie *subs* ugliness
urban *adj* urban
urban *adj* urbane
urbanitate *subs* urbanity
urcior *subs* jug
urcior la ochi *subs* sty
ureche *subs* ear
urgent *adj* urgent
urgenţă *subs* emergency
urgenţă *subs* urgency
urină *subs* urine
urinal *subs* urinal
urinal *adj* urinary
urinare *subs* urination
urlet *subs* howl
urmă *subs* trace
urmare *subs* pursuance
urmare *subs* sequel
urmărire *subs* chase2
urmărire judiciară *subs* prosecution
urmaş *subs* offspring
următor *adj* next
următorul *adv* next
urnă *subs* urn
urs *subs* bear
ursuz *adj* rugged
urzică *subs* nettle
uşă *subs* door
uscat *adj* dry
uscăţiv *adj* meagre

uşier *subs* bailiff
uşor *adj* easy
uşor *adj* light
uşor de mânuit *adj* manageable
uşor de urmărit *adj* traceable
ustensilă *subs* utensil
usturoi *subs* garlic
uşurare *subs* alleviation
uşurare *subs* relief
uşurinţă *subs* ease
uşurinţă *subs* levity
usurpare *subs* usurpation
uter *subs* uterus
utilitar *adj* utilitarian
utilitate *subs* utility
utilizabil *adj* serviceable
utilizare *subs* utilization
uvertură *subs* overture

V

vacă *subs* cow
vacant *adj* vacant
vacanţă *subs* vacancy
vacanţă *subs* vacation
vaccin *subs* vaccine
vaccinare *subs* vaccination
vaccinator *subs* vaccinator
văduv *subs* widower
vag *adj* remote
vag *adj* vague
vagabond *subs* rover
vagabond *subs* vagabond
vagabond *adj* vagabond
vagin *subs* vagina
vagon de dormit *subs* sleeper
vai! *interj.* alas
val *subs* wave
val de entuziasm *subs* influenza

vâlcea *subs* vale
vale *subs* dale
vale *subs* valley
valid *adj* valid
validitate *subs* validity
valoare *subs* valour
valoare *subs* value
valoros *adj* valuable
valuri *subs* surf
valvă *subs* valve
vâlvătaie *subs* blaze
vânătaie *subs* bruise
vânătoare *subs* hunt
vânător *subs* hunter
vânător *subs* huntsman
vânător de păsări *subs* fowler
vanitate *subs* idleness
vanitate *subs* vainglory
vanitate *subs* vanity
vanitos *adj* vainglorious
vânt *subs* wind
vânt puternic *subs* gale
vântos *adj* windy
vânzare *subs* sale
vânzare angro *subs* wholesale
vânzător *subs* salesman
vânzător *subs* seller
vânzător *subs* vendor
vânzător cu amănuntul *subs* retailer
vânzător de hârtie *subs* stationer
vapor *subs* ship
vapor *subs* steamer
vapor *subs* vapour
vaporos *adj* vaporous
văr *subs* cousin
vară *subs* summer
vârf *subs* top
vârf ascuţit *subs* spike
variabil *adj* variable
variat *adj* manifold
variat *adj* varied

variație *subs* variance
variație *subs* variation
varietate *subs* variety
variolă *subs* smallpox
vârsta *subs* age
vârsta bărbăției *subs* manhood
vârstnic *adj* elderly
vârtej de apă *subs* whirlpool
vârtej de vânt *subs* whirlwind
vârtelniță *subs* winder
văruire *subs* whitewash
varză *subs* cabbage
vas *subs* pot
vas *subs* vessel
vas de escortă *subs* consort
vas mic de lemn *subs* kit
vâsc *subs* mistletoe .
vâscos *adj* slimy
vâscozitate *subs* mucilage
vasectomie *subs* vasectomy
vaselină *subs* vaseline
vâslă *subs* oar
vâslaş *subs* oarsman
vast *adj* vast
vatră *subs* grate
vatră *subs* hearth
vătuire *subs* padding
vecin *subs* neighbour
vedenie *subs* wraith
vedere *subs* sight
vedere generală *subs* survey
vegetarian *subs* vegetarian
vegetarian *adj* vegetarian
vegetație *subs* vegetation
veghe *subs* vigil
vehement *adj* vehement
vehemență *subs* vehemence
vehicul *subs* vehicle
vehicular *adj* vehicular
venă *subs* vein
venerabil *adj* venerable
venerare *subs* veneration

venerație *subs* worship
venerator *subs* worshipper
venin *subs* venom
veninos *adj* venomous
venire *subs* advent
venit *subs* income
venit *subs* revenue
ventilație *subs* ventilation
ventilator *subs* ventilator
veracitate *subs* veracity
verb *subs* verb
verb deponent *subs* deponent
verbal *adj* verbal
verbal *adv* verbally
verbal *adj* wordy
verde *subs* green
verde *adj* green
verdeață *subs* greenery
verdict *subs* verdict
verificare *subs* verification
verificare a scrutinului *subs*
    scrutiny
verigă de lanț *subs* link
verisimilitudine *subs*
    verisimilitude
veritabil *adj* sheer
veritabil *adj* sterling
veritabil *adj* veritable
verosimil *adj* probable
verosimilitate *subs* likelihood
vers *subs* verse
versat *adj* versatile
versat *adj* versed
versatilitate *subs* versatility
versificare *subs* versification
versiune *subs* version
vertical *adj* vertical
verva *subs* verve
vesel *adj* hilarious
vesel *adj* merry
vesel *adj* mirthful
veselă *subs* dish

veselie *subs* fun
veselie *subs* hilarity
veselie *subs* mirth
veselie *subs* gaiety
veselie zgomotoasă *subs* merriment
veşmânt *subs* apparel
veşmânt *subs* garb
veşmânt *subs* guise
veşmânt *subs* vestment
veşnic *adv* forever
veşnic verde *adj* evergreen
vest *subs* west
vestă *subs* vest
vestă *subs* waistcoat
vestic *adj* west
vestitor *subs* herald
veteran *subs* veteran
veteran *adj* veteran
veterinar *adj* veterinary
veto *subs* veto
veveriţă *subs* squirrel
vezică urinară *subs* bladder
viabil *adj* viable
viaţă *subs* life
viaţă conjugală *subs* matrimony
vibraţie *subs* vibration
vicerege *subs* viceroy
vice-versa *adv* vice-versa
vicios *adj* vicious
vicisitudine *subs* vicissitude
viciu *subs* vice
viclean *adj* crafty
viclean *adj* cunning
viclean *adj* shifty
viclenie *subs* guile
viclenie *subs* wile
victimă *subs* casualty
victimă *subs* prey
victimă *subs* victim
victorie *subs* victory
victorie *subs* win

victorios *adj* victorious
vid *subs* vacuum
vidră *subs* otter
vierme *subs* worm
viespe *subs* wasp
vigilent *adj* alert
vigilent *adj* vigilant
vigilenţă *subs* alertness
vigilenţă *subs* outlook
vigilenţă *subs* vigilance
vigoare *subs* stamina
viguros *adj* forcible
viguros *adj* hale
viguros *adj* lusty
viguros *adj* stalwart
viguros *adj* vigorous
viitor *adj* future
viitor *subs* future
vilă *subs* bungalow
vilă *subs* villa
vin *subs* wine
vină *subs* blame
vină *subs* fault
vină *subs* guilt
vindecabil *adj* curable
vindecare *subs* cure
vineri *subs* Friday
vinovat *adj* culpable
vinovat *adj* guilty
viol *subs* rape
violare *subs* violation
violent *adj* fierce
violent *adj* rowdy
violent *adj* tempestuous
violent *adj* violent
violenţă *subs* violence
violină *subs* violin
violonist *subs* violinist
viorea *subs* violet
virgin *subs* virgin
virginitate *subs* virginity
virgulă *subs* comma

viril *adj* virile
virilitate *subs* virility
virtual *adj* virtual
virtuos *adj* virtuous
virtute *subs* virtue
virulenţ virulence
virulenţă *adj* virulent
virus *subs* virus
vis *subs* dream
visător *adj* wistful
viscol *subs* blizzard
viţă de vie *subs* vine
vital *adj* vital
vitalitate *subs* vitality
vitamină *subs* vitamin
vite *subs* cattle
viteaz *adj* valiant
vitejie *subs* bravery
viţel *subs* calf
viteză *subs* gear
viteză *subs* speed
viu *adj* alive
viu *adj* living
vivace *adj* vivacious
vivacitate *subs* vivacity
vizibil *adj* sightly
vizibil *adj* visible
vizibilitate *subs* visibility
vizionar *adj* visionary
vizionar *subs* visionary
vizită *subs* visit
vizitator *subs* caller
vizitator *subs* visitor
vizitiu *subs* coachman
viziune *subs* vision
viziune rapidă *subs* glimpse
vizual *adj* visual
vizuină *subs* burrow
vizuină *subs* den
vizuină *subs* lair
voal *subs* veil
vocabular *subs* lexicon

vocabular *subs* vocabulary
vocal *adj* vocal
vocală *subs* vowel
vocalist *subs* vocalist
vocaţie *subs* relish
vocaţie *subs* vocation
voce *subs* voice
vogă *subs* vogue
voiaj *subs* voyage
voinic *adj* husky
voinţă *subs* volition
voinţă *subs* will
voios *adj* cheerful
volan *subs* frill
volei *subs* volley
volt *subs* volt
voltaj *subs* voltage
volum *subs* bulk
volum *subs* tome
volum *subs* volume
voluminos *adj* bulky
voluminos *adj* voluminous
voluntar *adv* voluntarily
voluntar *adj* voluntary
voluntar *subs* volunteer
voluptos *adj* voluptuous
voluptuos *adj* sensuous
vomitat *subs* vomit
vopsea *subs* dye
vopsea *subs* paint
vorbă *subs* say
vorbăreţ *adj* talkative
vorbitor *subs* parlour
vorbitor *subs* speaker
vot *subs* vote
vrabie *subs* sparrow
vrajă *subs* spell
vrajbă *subs* feud
vrăjitoare *subs* witch
vrăjitor *subs* sorcerer
vrăjitorie *subs* sorcery
vrăjitorie *subs* witchery

vreascuri *subs* lop
vrednic de milă *adj* miserable
vrednic de milă *adj* pitiable
vreme *subs* weather
vreme îndelungată *adv* long
vreodată *adv* ever
vreun *adj* some
vulcan *subs* volcano
vulcanic *adj* volcanic
vulgar *adj* vulgar
vulgaritate *subs* vulgarity
vulnerabil *adj* vulnerable
vulpe *subs* fox
vultur *subs* eagle
vultur *subs* vulture

watt *subs* watt
Wellington *subs* wellignton
whisky *subs* whisky
whisky scoţian *subs* scotch

xerox *subs* xerox
xilofon *subs* xylophone

Yen *subs* Yen

zăbrele *subs* lattice
zădărnicie *subs* futility
zahăr *subs* sugar
zâmbet *subs* smile
zână *subs* fairy
zăpadă *subs* snow
zăpadă fleşcăită *subs* slush
zar de joc *subs* die
zaruri *subs* dice
zarvă *subs* fuss
zarvă *subs* uproar
zăvor *subs* latch
zăvor *subs* bolt
zăvor *subs* lock
zbieret *subs* bellows
zbieret de măgar *subs* bray
zbor *subs* flight
zburdalnic *adj* sprightly
zburdălnicie *subs* spree
zdreanţă *subs* tatter
zdruncinător *adj* jerky
zdruncinătură *subs* shake
zebră *subs* zebra
zece *subs* ten
zecimal *adj* decimal
zeciuială *subs* tithe
zeflemire *subs* raillery
zeiţă *subs* goddess
zeitate *subs* deity
zel *subs* zeal
zelos *adj* earnest
zelos *adj* zealous
zemos *adj* juicy
zer *subs* buttermilk
zero zero
zestre *subs* dowry
zeu *subs* god
zgârcit *subs* niggard

zgârcit *adj* stingy
zgârietură uşoară *subs* scratch
zgomot *subs* din
zgomot *subs* noise
zgomot de paşi *subs* tread
zgomot de uşă trântită *subs* slam
zgomot surd *subs* thud
zgomotos *adj* noisy
zguduitor *adj* poignant
zguduitură *subs* jolt
zi *subs* day
ziar cotidian *subs* daily
zidar *subs* mason
zidărie *subs* masonry
zilnic *adv* daily
zimţ *subs* cog
zinc *subs* zinc

zis şi *adv* alias
ziua următoare *subs* morrow
zodia Leu *subs* Leo
zodiac *subs* zodiac
zonă *subs* area
zonă *subs* zone
zonal *adj* zonal
zoologic *adj* zoological
zoologie *subs* zoology
zoologist *subs* zoologist
zori de zi *subs* dawn
zugrăvire *subs* portrayal
zuluf *subs* forelock
zumzăit *subs* hum
zvon *subs* bruit
zvon *subs* hearsay
zvon *subs* rumour